Co1

British Expeditionary Force

Force

The 1915 Campaign

British Expeditionary Force

Force

The 1915 Campaign

Andrew Rawson

Pen & Sword
MILITARY

First published in Great Britain by
PEN AND SWORD MILITARY
an imprint of
Pen and Sword Books Ltd
47 Church Street
Barnsley
South Yorkshire S70 2AS

ISBN 978 1 47384 615 9

A CIP record for this book is available from the British Library.

Printed and bound in England by
CPI Group (UK) Ltd, Croydon, CR0 4YY

Typeset in Times by CHIC GRAPHICS

Pen & Sword Books Ltd incorporates the imprints of
Pen & Sword Books Ltd incorporates the imprints of Pen & Sword
Archaeology, Atlas, Aviation, Battleground, Discovery,
Family History, History, Maritime, Military, Naval, Politics,
Railways, Select, Social History, Transport, True Crime,
Claymore Press, Frontline Books, Leo Cooper, Praetorian Press,
Remember When, Seaforth Publishing and Wharncliffe.

For a complete list of Pen and Sword titles please contact
Pen and Sword Books Limited
47 Church Street, Barnsley, South Yorkshire, S70 2AS, England
E-mail: enquiries@pen-and-sword.co.uk
Website: www.pen-and-sword.co.uk

Regimental Abbreviations

Regiments in Alphabetical Order	Abbreviations Used
Argyll & Sutherland Highlanders Regiment	Argylls
Bedfordshire Regiment	Bedfords
Black Watch Regiment	Black Watch
Border Regiment	Borders
Buffs (East Kent) Regiment	Buffs
Cambridgeshire Regiment	Cambridgeshire
Cameron Highlanders Regiment	Camerons
Cameronians (Scottish Rifles) Regiment	Scottish Rifles
Cheshire Regiment	Cheshires
Coldstream Guards	Coldstreamers
Connaught Rangers	Connaughts
Devonshire Regiment	Devons
Dorsetshire Regiment	Dorsets
Duke of Cornwall's Light Infantry	DCLI
Duke of Wellington's (West Riding) Regiment	Duke's
Durham Light Infantry	Durhams
East Lancashire Regiment	East Lancashires
East Surrey Regiment	East Surreys
East Yorkshire Regiment	East Yorkshires
Essex Regiment	Essex
Green Howards (Yorkshire) Regiment	Green Howards
Gloucestershire Regiment	Gloucesters
Gordon Highlanders	Gordons
Grenadier Guards	Grenadiers
Hampshire Regiment	Hampshires
Herefordshire Regiment	Herefords
Hertfordshire Regiment	Hertfords
Highland Light Infantry	HLI
Honourable Artillery Company	HAC
Irish Guards	Irish Guards
King's (Liverpool) Regiment	King's
King's Own (Royal Lancaster) Regiment	King's Own
King's Own Scottish Borderers	KOSBs

Regiments in Alphabetical Order	Abbreviations Used
King's (Shropshire Light Infantry) Regiment	KSLIs
King's Own (Yorkshire Light Infantry) Regiment	KOYLIs
King's Royal Rifle Corps	KRRC
Lancashire Fusiliers	Lancashire Fusiliers
Leicestershire Regiment	Leicesters
Lincolnshire Regiment	Lincolns
London Regiment	Londoners
Loyal North Lancashire Regiment	Loyals
Leinster Regiment	Leinsters
Manchester Regiment	Manchesters
Middlesex Regiment	Middlesex
Monmouthshire Regiment	Monmouths
Norfolk Regiment	Norfolks
Northamptonshire Regiment	Northants
North Staffordshire Regiment	North Staffords
Northumberland Fusiliers	Northumberland Fusiliers
Oxford and Buckinghamshire Light Infantry	Ox and Bucks
Rifle Brigade	Rifle Brigade
Royal Berkshire Regiment	Berkshires
Royal Dublin Fusiliers	Dublin Fusiliers
Royal Fusiliers	Royal Fusiliers
Royal Inniskilling Fusiliers	Inniskilling Fusiliers
Royal Irish Fusiliers	Irish Fusiliers
Royal Irish Regiment	Irish Regiment
Royal Irish Rifles	Irish Rifles
Royal Munster Fusiliers	Munsters
Royal Scots Regiment	Royal Scots
Royal Scots Fusiliers	Scots Fusiliers
Royal Sussex Regiment	Sussex
Royal Warwickshire Regiment	Warwicks
Royal Welsh Fusiliers	Welsh Fusiliers
Queen's (Royal West Surrey) Regiment	Queen's
Queen's Own (Royal West Kent) Regiment	Queen's Own
Scots Guards	Scots Guards
Seaforth Highlanders	Seaforths
Sherwood Foresters (Notts and Derbyshire)	Sherwoods

Regiments in Alphabetical Order	Abbreviations Used
Somerset Light Infantry	Somersets
South Lancashire Regiment	South Lancashires
South Staffordshire Regiment	South Staffords
South Wales Borderers	SWBs or Borderers
Suffolk Regiment	Suffolks
Welsh Regiment	Welsh
Welsh Guards	Welsh Guards
West Yorkshire Regiment	West Yorkshires
Wiltshire Regiment	Wiltshires
Worcestershire Regiment	Worcesters
York and Lancaster Regiment	York and Lancasters

Introduction

Surely not another book on the 1915 campaign? What does this one tell me that the others do not? Some concentrate on the generals and the politics, some concentrate on the personal experiences of the men and others cover the whole campaign, of which the British Army was only a part. This one concentrates on the British Expeditionary Force's experiences during eighteen months of warfare.

It starts at the end of 1914, with the close of the fighting around Ypres. It covers the first British offensive at Neuve Chapelle in March and follows with the German gas attack north-east of Ypres Salient in April, and the subsequent fighting to hold the salient. It continues with the battles of Aubers Ridge, Festubert, Givenchy and Hooge. The Loos campaign is then covered over three chapters. The narrative ends by relating ten minor actions between the end of the Loos Battle and the summer of 1916.

The information came from many sources. The backbone of the narrative was created from the *Official History*, the two 1915 volumes and the first 1916 volume, which are part of the 29-volume series compiled by Brigadier General Sir James Edmonds. The first 1915 volume of *Military Operations: France and Belgium* covers the battle of Neuve Chapelle in March and the German attacks on the Ypres Salient in April and May, which began with the first gas attack of the war. The second 1915 volume covers the battles of Aubers Ridge and Festubert in May and the Battle of Loos in September, when the British Army used gas for the first time. Although a great deal of the first 1916 volume covers the build-up to the Somme campaign and the disastrous first day of the offensive, it also covers the earlier actions in the year. The Fromelles battle on 19/20 July 1916 has also been included.

Pen and Sword's *Battleground* series of books are part narrative and part travel guide and there are several volumes dedicated to the 1915 battles, including two of my own. They helped to confirm, or in some cases contradict, the *Official History*. I say contradict because the official version often smoothed over mistakes, problems or instances of pure bad luck – and they are sometimes the most interesting facts of a battle.

The same goes for divisional histories and regimental histories, the majority of which were published on behalf of the units in the 1920s. Their quality varies enormously with some giving the bare details of a unit's accomplishments while others are virtually a copy of the daily unit war diary. Most provided additional interesting detail omitted in the *Official History*. They often give explanations of what went right and what went wrong and they always mention the men that made a difference. But they do have a tendency to blame failures on others, rather than themselves.

Many of the regimental and divisional histories can be accessed for a small fee at www.militaryarchive.co.uk. You can also access medal rolls, army orders and army lists, and get assistance with the location of biographical information, awards and photographs of individuals. Joining the archive gave me prolonged access to all this for the same cost of a day visiting the London archives. If you are interested in researching printed histories and medal rolls on a limited budget, the Military Archive is the website for you.

The WO95 series of war diaries in the National Archives at Kew, London have also been consulted. The detail varies enormously, as does the accuracy. But a study of the diaries of different levels of command, army, corps, division, brigade and battalion gives a comprehensive view of the battles.

The text bucks the Army trend of describing movements and events from right to left. We read text and look at maps from left to right. So I chose to write the narrative from left to right unless the sequence of events dictated otherwise.

The inclusion of many detailed maps, sixty altogether, is to help you understand how the battles developed. The phrase 'a picture is worth a thousand words' applies also to maps. There are many military history books out there with page after page of narrative with only a couple of small scale maps, which usually do little to help the reader's understanding. My inspiration was Noah Trudeau's *A Testing of Courage* about Gettysburg in the American Civil War. I had read several books and watched numerous documentaries on the huge three-day battle but I was still confused. Trudeau's book had a clear large-scale map every few pages, illustrating the day by day actions as they developed. They helped me understand the unfolding battle when I visited Gettysburg. I wanted to do the same for the battles of 1915 and early 1916.

The *Official History* maps are sometimes cited as good examples but the level of detail is often too much. Attempts to include several days of battle on one map serve only to confuse. While the maps in the two extra volumes give a lot of information, those volumes are hard to get hold of. The maps included in the two text books are too small and too detailed.

I chose to create a map for the important day of each battle, occasionally using two to increase the level of detail. Where possible a section of trench map has been used, because those maps are clear and are well-known to anyone with an interest in the First World War. Their grid system is a standard size of 1,000 yards (914 metres) for each large square and 100 yards (91.4 metres) for each minor graduation. One advantage of a trench map is that the terrain is virtually the same today as it was a century ago. Contours, roads, watercourses and woods have barely changed, and villages are only a little larger. Only the trenches and craters are missing. It means the maps can be used to help visitors to the battlefields find the places they are looking for.

As stated earlier this is not a comprehensive study of the campaign. So what has been left out? There is no talk of politics and little on the relationship between the politicians, the War Office and GHQ. The same goes for the relationship between Field Marshal Sir John French and his subordinates, Generals Haig and Smith-Dorrien, apart from a couple of important examples. Details of the meetings between French and Field Marshal Joffre, who had overall control of the Allied campaign, are kept to a minimum too. There is also little information on the German units, but there is information on their offensive and defensive plans and tactics and how they impacted on the British ability to wage war.

You will not find any narratives from personal diaries, letters or printed histories in the narrative either. They usually have a similarly depressing theme of mud, blood and a desire to be somewhere else. And authors usually chose the bleakest ones to set the soberest tone. The few quotes given were chosen for their eloquence in writing, their pride in the men's determination and their dark humour.

There are few mentions of casualties unless they were disproportionately high or low. I felt it served little purpose to keep reeling off the numbers after each action. Also, records are incomplete and I felt it would be inappropriate to mention some units and not others. Casualties were always high: the British, the French and the Germans all suffered badly.

I did consider listing the grave locations of those named in the text but a random survey proved it was impractical. Many men survived to fight another day while equally many survived only to die later, on the Somme, at Arras or Ypres, or during the huge 1918 campaigns. It does make you wonder how any of the men of 1915 survived another three years of fighting.

Many had no known graves because the areas were fought over for another three years and the 1915 cemeteries were often obliterated. Those who died in the Ypres Salient are remembered on the Menin Gate Memorial while the names of those who died south of Armentières are carved on the

Le Touquet Memorial. Dud Corner Memorial remembers those who died during the battle of Loos. There are other smaller memorials such as Ploegsteert Wood and VC Corner near Fromelles.

A large number of those who have known graves are not buried in their original location. Their remains were moved during the post-war clear up in which many small cemeteries were closed and the graves moved to the large concentration cemeteries. Finally, we have those who died of their wounds. They were either buried behind the lines by the dressing stations and casualty clearing stations, near the coast at one of the base hospitals, or in the United Kingdom having been sent home to recover. Ultimately few casualties were buried close to their place of death and most of the graves of those who were have been lost.

So what will you find in the text? There is plenty of information on the reasoning behind each battle, the objectives and the German counter-attacks. The artillery bombardments, tactical innovations and the terrain are all covered, and for each attack there is an attempt to understand the reasons for success or failure. Where possible the men who made a difference are mentioned, the men who charged the German trenches, those who led the desperate defensive battles and those who were awarded the Victoria Cross.

It becomes apparent as you read the narrative that the men of 1915 were tough men who fought for their regimental traditions and their comrades. Some were seasoned regulars who had been out since the beginning, others had recovered from injuries and were seeking revenge. The Territorial Force divisions began to arrive in great numbers in 1915 and the first New Army divisions took part in the 1915 battles. They all shouldered their rifles and fought bitterly to stop their enemy before they got too close, and if necessary they fought them off with bayonet and rifle butt.

The BEF learnt a lot about offensive and defensive warfare during the 1915 campaigns but it cost many casualties before the lessons were put to use. Britain's Regular Army and its Reservists had been decimated in 1914. So the first half of 1915 was when the Territorial Force made its appearance, while the second half of the year saw the first New Army divisions going into action.

In studying the First World War I have now covered the first two years on the Western Front, from August 1914 to November 1916. My first two books were *Battleground* books on the Battle of Loos and they were published over ten years ago by Pen and Sword. They followed several trips to what was then a forgotten battle. Since then I have had a break from writing which has given me the opportunity to learn more about this period of warfare overshadowed by the Somme campaign. This has been a welcome return to the battle. I have enjoyed revisiting the 1915 campaign and I hope you enjoy reading about it.

Finally, I would like to thank those who provided me with accommodation during my visits to the 1915 Western Front. I believe you cannot truly understand a battlefield until you have walked across it. I stayed at the Regina Hotel in Ypres, a fine establishment right opposite the Cloth Hall and its museum. I also stayed at Number 56 in La Boisselle on the Somme. A little far out you may think, but it was a perfect base for my wide ranging travels in France at the time. David and Julie Thompson are great hosts and friends and their place truly is 'an Oasis on the Somme'.

Chapter 1

A Long Winter

By 22 November 1914, the British Expeditionary Force (BEF) was exhausted after five weeks of continuous fighting in the Ypres Salient. It had been reduced to holding a short front, stretching 21 miles from Wytschaete, south of Ypres, to Givenchy, on the La Bassée canal. The wet winter weather made it difficult to do anything more than survive and trench activity was reduced to sniping, shelling and the occasional raid.

On 30 November King George V landed in France for a six day visit. He visited various Army units, he spoke to the President of France, Raymond Poincaré, and the President of the Council of Ministers,[1] René Viviani. He met Generals Joseph Joffre and Ferdinand Foch and the French army and corps commanders cooperating with the BEF. The king also met King Albert I of the Belgians, whose troops were holding the coastal sector.

The king heard how the troops were digging in but there were few tools, a lack of sandbags to shore up the trenches and a shortage of timber to build dug-outs. The engineers were busy supervising the work and mapping the front line while the troops manned, and named, trenches, strong-points, farms and woods.

It was clear that the war was not going to be over by Christmas, as some had suggested when it began in August. It was also obvious that the front was going to be static for some time. So steps were taken to make life easier for the soldiers. Rotation schedules were drawn up so everyone spent a similar time on the front line, in the support trenches and in the rear area. Units were equipped with new weapons, the men received clean uniforms, and warm clothing arrived at the front. Roads were improved and new tracks were added. Billets were built so the men could sleep undercover, and baths and laundries were set up to help them keep clean. Even entertainments and sporting events were organised to keep the men occupied while they were resting.

But the stabilisation of the front brought many problems, not least the shortage of transport needed to move food, water, ammunition and stores.

---

1 The Prime Minister's full title.

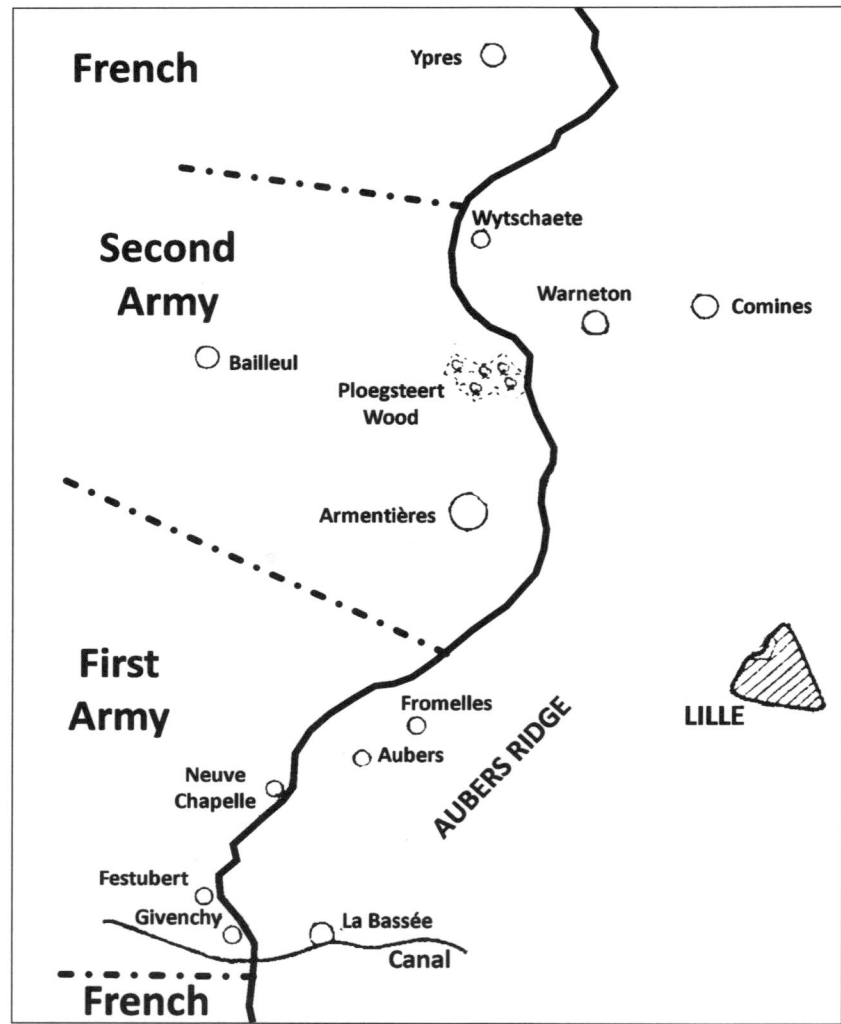

The BEF's sector at the end of 1914

Tens of thousands of sandbags were required to shore up the trenches and miles of communication cables had to be laid. The Royal Engineers took over from the Ordnance Department and set up new parks for stores and workshops to repair equipment. The Army Service Corps also opened depots and workshops for a growing fleet of motor vehicles and horse drawn transport.

Simply getting everything the soldiers needed to live was a big enough problem, let alone providing supplies to defend themselves. Artillery ammunition was always in short supply because quantities had been based on usage in the Boer War. It was soon clear that it was inadequate and it would take months before the munitions factories could match demand.

Inventing New Weapons
The winter of 1914–15 was a time of invention as the soldiers looked for better ways to fight their enemy. While knives and bayonets were supplemented by cudgels and knuckle dusters, the Indian Corps took the lead when it came to experimenting with ranged weapons such as trench mortars and grenades.

Grenades were desirable because they could be thrown along trenches or into dug-outs without exposing the thrower. The weekly supply in November 1914 was only 70 hand grenades and 630 rifle grenades. Trench warfare required more hand grenades so Field Marshal French asked for 1,000 per week, a figure achieved in March 1915. In the meantime, home-made devices were made, though they were sometimes more dangerous to the thrower than the target.

The jam-pot bomb was made by filling a tin with shredded guncotton and nails. A detonator and fuse were added while a plug of clay sealed the container. Captain Battye of the Royal Engineers[2] filled a serrated cast-iron cylinder with ammonal and a wooden plug held the detonator and fuse in place. The hairbrush grenade simply had a slab of guncotton fastened to a bat-shaped piece of wood. Ten different grenades were also sent from England for testing. They were the Hale's Service and Hale's Mexican patterns, the Light and Heavy Royal Laboratory patterns, the Light and Heavy Double Cylinder patterns, the Hairbrush, the Pitcher, the Ball and the Oval grenades.

Matches and cigarettes were used to light the fuse until a French-made friction lighter was introduced; but none worked when it rained. Only Nobel fuse igniters, found in French coal mines, worked in damp conditions. The arrival of the first batch of Mills bombs[3] in March 1915 solved the problem because the spring-loaded trigger worked whatever the weather.

Mortars provided the infantry with short-range indirect fire but the first batch of experimental weapons sent from England were inaccurate and dangerous. A number of designs made from brass and steel tubes in workshops near the front were equally likely to explode unexpectedly. Even catapults were used to project hand grenades further than they could be thrown; they too were unsafe.

---

2 Of the 21st Company Sappers and Miners.
3 Service pattern No. 5 grenade.

The First Offensive

On 30 November 1914 General Joffre reported that the Germans were withdrawing divisions along the French front and he issued orders to take advantage of the situation. A week later he told General Foch and Field Marshal Sir John French that the Tenth and Second French armies should attack at the La Bassée canal and the Oise River while the Fourth French Army advanced across the Champagne region. The BEF and the rest of the French armies would simultaneously probe the Germans lines.

General Joffre specifically wanted the BEF to make a night attack between Messines and Warneton, while the Eighth French Army attacked between Hollebeke and Wytschaete. So Field Marshal French issued instructions to II and III Corps to capture Messines and Warneton on 14 December. The French would capture Wytschaete as 3rd Division pushed on with the 'utmost determination'. Then 5th Division would 'convey the impression that an attack is going to be delivered' towards Spanbroekmolen and Messines. Finally III Corps would 'make demonstrations against the enemy with the object of holding him to his trenches' south of Messines.

The vague orders and the lack of artillery preparation meant the attack was doomed. The French did not take Wytschaete and Brigadier General Bowes' 8 Brigade came under fire when it left the trenches at 7.45am. Lieutenant Colonel Dundas' 2nd Royal Scots captured the first trench only to come under machine gun fire because Major Baird's 1st Gordons had been pinned down in no man's land. A hedge woven with barbed wire blocked the way and Captain the Hon. Bruce was one of many hit, as he led the Royal Scots through the single gate. The survivors found water in the trench beyond and Lieutenant Robson-Scott was mortally wounded trying to find another trench. The 4th Middlesex and the 2nd Suffolk took over the front during the night but further action was cancelled because the French had failed to take Wytschaete.

General Joffre asked Field Marshal French for more help and the BEF's General Headquarters (GHQ) issued Operation Order 1, which called for attacks all along the front on 17 December. Again there was insufficient ammunition and over 1,000 casualties were suffered during the handful of raids.

The Expanding BEF

Many units were brought back up to strength over the winter months but there was always a shortage of trained men. Virtually all the Reservists had been sent to France and Flanders by the end of 1914. Some of the Special Reservists and the older soldiers were unfit or reluctant, causing problems until they could be removed. Meanwhile, the returning convalescents, who had been wounded in early battles, had combat experience and were eager to get back at the Germans.

By Christmas Day 1914 the BEF had grown to eleven divisions and five cavalry divisions[4] so two army headquarters were opened to divide responsibility. General Sir Douglas Haig was promoted to head First Army and General Sir Horace Smith-Dorrien took over Second Army. Meanwhile, Field Marshal French had the British Cavalry Corps and the Indian Cavalry Corps in reserve.

Christmas Day was also a special day for the soldiers because they all received a present from Her Royal Highness Princess Mary. Some had a box of cigarettes while others received tobacco and a pipe. On parts of the front 'the troops came out of their trenches, kicked footballs about, exchanged cigarettes and other small articles and – more curious still – lent one another implements for reinforcing each other's wire entanglements.' After burying their dead, they returned to their trenches to sing carols and for a short time they forgot they were at war.

On 25 January, Lieutenant General Sir William Robertson replaced Lieutenant General Sir Arthur Murray as Chief of the General Staff while Major General Edward Perceval replaced Major General Henry Wilson as his sub-chief. Robertson and Wilson faced many challenges concerning how to manage the expanding Expeditionary Force.

At the end of December, 27th Division arrived in France and 28th Division[5] followed a couple of weeks later. Twenty-two Territorial Force infantry battalions and six Yeomanry cavalry regiments had also been attached to the Regular Army divisions in France. The Canadian Division[6] landed in France on 15 February 1915 and the North Midland Division[7] arrived at the end of the same month, it was the first of many Territorial Force Divisions to join the BEF.[8]

But the men still fought the weather rather than each other, as rain and thawing snow turned the battlefield into a quagmire and filled the trenches with water. The men spent too long standing in cold water and many suffered from trench foot, a painful condition which led to blisters, gangrene and amputations if left untreated.

Early Engagements
The German artillery began shelling the Indian Corps' trenches at dawn on 20 December 1914 and ten small mines detonated around Givenchy at 9am. German infantry captured the trenches either side of the 1st Manchesters and some advanced 300 metres towards Festubert.

---

4 Over one third of them were Indian troops; two infantry and four cavalry divisions.
5 It too was formed from units recalled from overseas garrisons.
6 The first of four Canadian Divisions to serve on the Western Front.
7 Later numbered the 46th (North Midland) Division.
8 Around one third of the units serving in France and Flanders by the end of February 1915 were Territorial Force units.

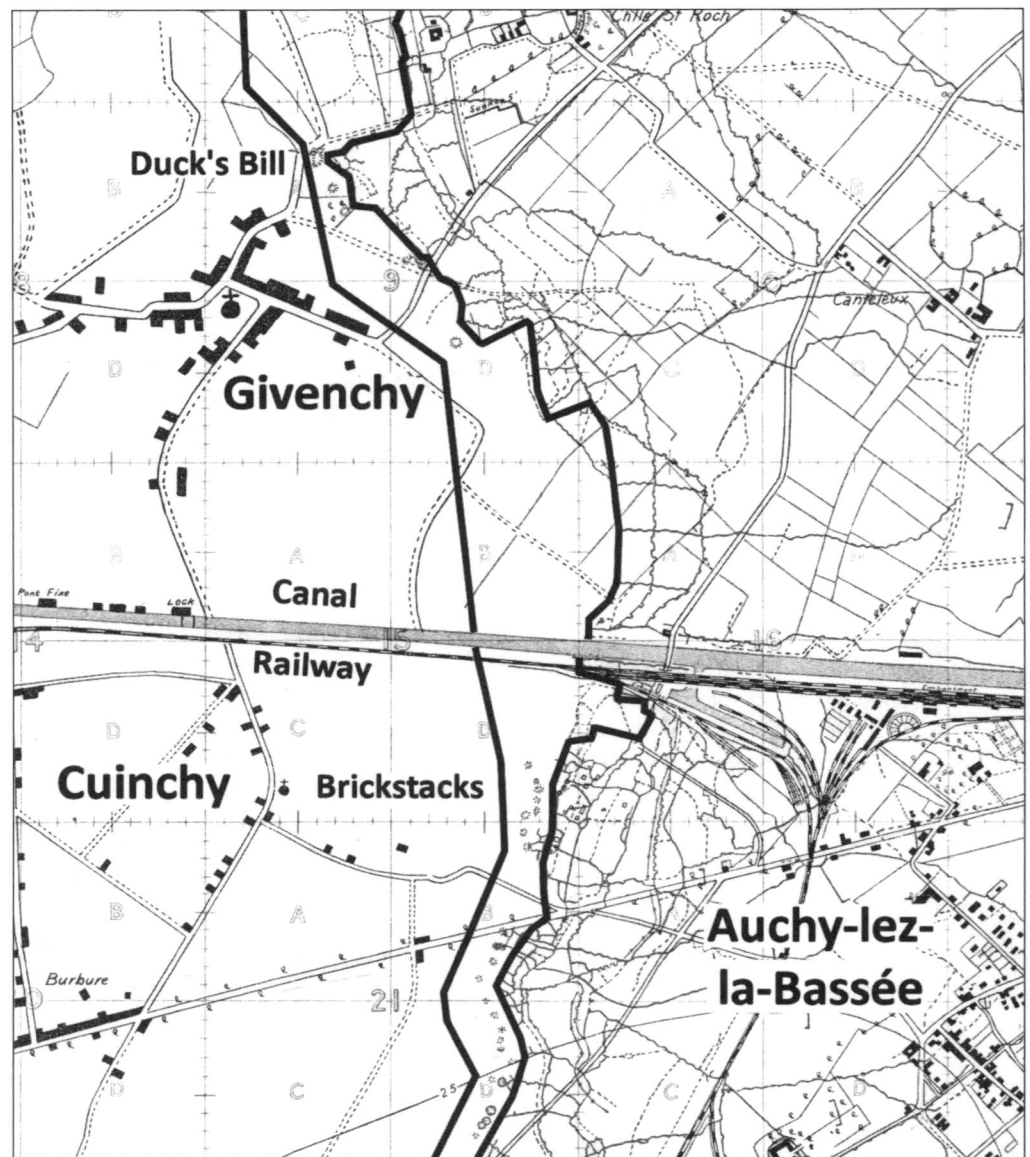

Cuinchy and Givenchy in January 1915

GHQ ordered Major General Richard Haking to send two of 1st Division's infantry brigades to the area to make a counter-attack and they were ready to advance by noon. 3 Brigade were pinned down by machine gun fire as they squelched through the deep mud towards the pocket near Festubert. 1 (Guards) Brigade experienced similar difficulties as the 1st Manchesters evacuated Givenchy; the village was later retaken. A fleet of London buses carried 2 Brigade to the area but it was dark before they were ready to counter-attack.

The Germans began the New Year by capturing a machine gun post along the railway line, on the south bank of the La Bassée canal on 1 January. The 2nd KRRC failed to seize the post later that evening, as did the 1st Scots Guards the following morning. The position was retaken on 10 January but it was only held for forty hours.

On 25 January a deserter warned of an imminent attack around Givenchy and a mine exploded under the 1st Coldstream Guards[9] only thirty minutes later. Captain Campbell's trench was overrun but the railway embankment position held, as did Lieutenant Viscount Acheson's garrison in the Keep strongpoint, east of Cuinchy. The 1st Scots Guards also refused to budge in the Brickstacks but reinforcements were unable to retake the lost trenches. *Minenwerfers*[10] bombarded the Keep on the morning of 29 January but Captain Villiers' men held on until the 1st Northants arrived.

Early on 1 February, the Germans captured a 2nd Coldstream Guards outpost on the railway line.[11] The Irish Guards bombers were unable to move along the trenches while the same trenches funnelled Lieutenant Blacker-Douglass' men into a death trap as they moved over the top. Blacker-Douglass was killed and Captain Long-Innes was injured but Company Quarter Master Sergeant Carton refused to withdraw his men until dawn.

Lieutenant Colonel Pereira of the Coldstreamers argued against attacking until a short barrage by siege guns had been organised. Captain Leigh-Bennett dropped his handkerchief at 10.15am and Private White ran forward hurling rocket grenades at the head of the Coldstreamers. Lieutenants Graham and Innes led the 1st Irish Guards and Lance-Corporal Michael O'Leary shot five Germans at the first barricade. He then moved forward 'intent upon killing another German to whom he had taken a dislike' at a second barricade; he was awarded the Victoria Cross.

The Brickstacks, 6 February
The 2nd Division took over the Brickstacks sector and Brigadier General

---

9 3 Brigade.
10 *Minenwerfers* were German trench mortars.
11 2 Brigade.

Lord Cavan was instructed to prepare for an attack with 4 (Guards) Brigade. The guns opened fire at 2.15pm on 6 February and the bombers left their trenches fifteen minutes later. No man's land was pitted with clay pits but Second Lieutenant Cottrell-Dormer's 3rd Coldstream Guards captured some of the brick stacks. Lieutenant Musgrave was killed as the 1st Irish Guards charged forward but the first line of brick stacks were seized in a record four minutes.

The Irish Guards continued beyond the brickfield, to a trench with a better view, and the Coldstreamers moved alongside; Major Foulkes's engineers then fortified the brick stacks. A German counter-attack the following day failed and one large party approached the British line shouting 'Don't shoot, we are engineers'; the Guards were not fooled.

The line had held; but there was evidence the Germans were digging more tunnels through the clay and packing explosives into underground chambers so they could blow up trenches. A call was put out to gather together professional miners and tunnellers who could be organised into tunnelling companies. The first group arrived at the end of February and were immediately put to work digging under the German lines.

Plans for a Combined Offensive

Spring was approaching and it was time to consider how to attack with the limited resources available, while the Germans were heavily committed to the Eastern Front. General Joffre wanted to attack as soon as the weather permitted but he knew his guns were short of ammunition, particularly high explosive shells.

The War Councils in London and Paris were discussing Gallipoli, a new theatre of operations in the Eastern Mediterranean but General Joffre and Field Marshal French did not want troops and ammunition sent elsewhere. Joffre was particularly anxious to get rid of the salient north-east of Paris and wanted to continue operations in the Champagne while preparing attacks across the Artois plateau and east of Verdun.

Generals Haig and Smith-Dorrien were informed of the plans on 8 February and while Second Army's seizure of the Messines Ridge was the best tactical option, First Army's capture of the Aubers Ridge was the strategic favourite. It could be co-ordinated with the French operation on the Artois plateau and together they could threaten the important railhead at Lille.

General Haig was asked to prepare an attack on 15 February, but a letter from Joffre dictating what the French wanted arrived at GHQ the following day. Tenth French Army was planning to capture Vimy Ridge and he wanted the British to advance towards La Bassée. His long term plan was to cut the railways supplying the German salient between Arras and Rheims.

Although Field Marshal French had agreed to take over the rest of the Ypres Salient, he was unable to do so because 29th Division was heading for Gallipoli. Instead he chose to attack with First Army. But after visiting General Louis de Maud'huy of Tenth French Army, General Haig reported that 'our proposed offensive action must be considered an entirely independent operation'.

Chapter 2

Carry Them Off Their Legs
Neuve Chapelle Begins
10 March 1915

General Haig announced First Army would attack the Neuve Chapelle salient on 12 February 1915. The first objective was Smith-Dorrien Trench, east of the village, and then the attack could fan out, widening the gap. First Army would finally advance towards Illies and Herlies on the Aubers Ridge.

Three days later Field Marshal French approved Haig's plan and agreed the offensive would begin on 9 March, or as soon as the weather allowed. Neuve Chapelle would be the BEF's first corps-sized offensive and there was a lot to consider; so commanders aired their views at conferences while feasibility studies were made. First Army would attack with IV Corps and the Indian Corps and it had the Cavalry Corps, the Indian Cavalry Corps and 46th (North Midland) Division in reserve. Second Army would simultaneously attack to the north, to make it look like there was an offensive east of Ypres.

The assumption was that First Army's six divisions faced two German divisions. GHQ's intelligence section estimated 4,000 soldiers would be able to reinforce the front in the first twelve hours but the number would rise to 20,000 after thirty-six hours. So Haig wanted a heavy preliminary bombardment followed by a rapid advance 'to surprise the Germans, carry them right off their legs, and push forward at once to the Haute Pommereau–Aubers Ridge.' But as First Army began its preparations, General Haig's valued Chief of the Staff, Brigadier General John Edmond Gough VC, was killed by a sniper while visiting 2nd Rifle Brigade on 22 February.[12]

The Artillery Preparations
Experiments had shown that high-explosive created tangled bunches of wire

---

12 He was succeeded by Brigadier General Richard Butler.

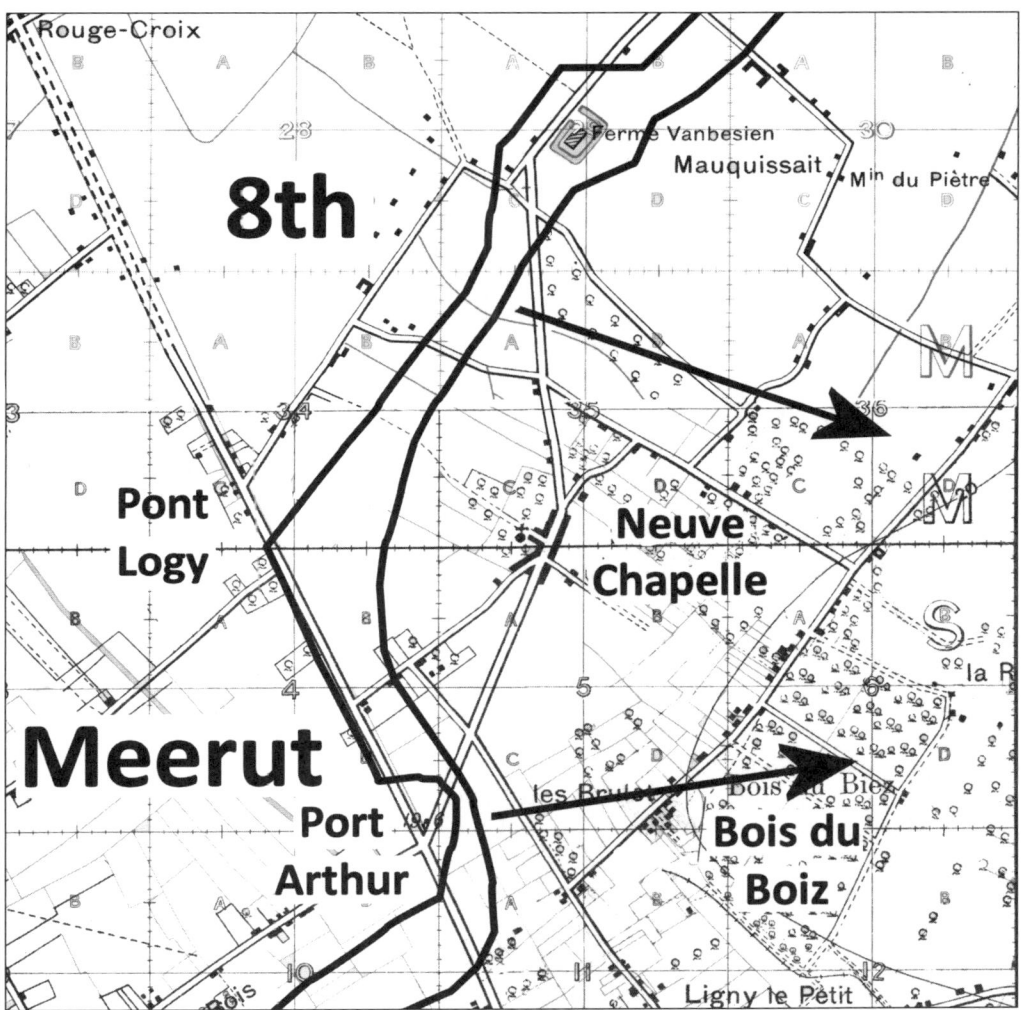

First Army's Plan to capture Neuve Chapelle

whereas shrapnel shredded entanglements into small pieces. The tests also proved 18-pounder guns took around thirty minutes to blast gaps in the wire, and on 3 March the artillery commanders were told they had thirty-five minutes to destroy the German parapets.

An infantry timetable was proposed at First Army's conference on 5

March and the deployment of the assault troops into no man's land and through the British wire was also discussed. Plans for consolidating the captured trenches and for moving the support troops forward were also tabled.

First Army's artillery commander wanted all his batteries in place ten days before the battle, to give the crews time to settle in. The field guns and trench mortars were moved into camouflaged positions, a few at a time, and registration of targets was carefully planned so it did not alert the enemy. But many were late and some guns only arrived the afternoon before the battle, leaving them no time to register their targets.

GHQ's Heavy Artillery Reserve had too few large calibre guns: only two 6-inch howitzer batteries, one 6-inch gun battery and three 9.2-inch howitzers. Two 15-inch howitzers were promised but only one reached First Army, and 'its ammunition was faulty and there was not much of it'. An armoured train called the *Churchill*[13] also steamed into position behind the line. It brought the number of guns supporting First Army's offensive to 233.

The engineers had struggled to make artillery platforms of bricks, planks and bundles of tree branches on the muddy ground and they had to build camouflaged shelters. The field battery crews found it difficult to anchor their guns in the mud and they used logs and sandbags to limit their recoil. The ground observers also found it difficult to find good observation posts; some made use of ruined houses, others were inside hay stacks and a few were perched inside false trees.[14]

The Royal Flying Corps flew observation missions over enemy territory. The squadrons had been given two tasks: they would help the guns register targets, so they would fire accurately on the day; and they would also photograph the enemy trenches with special aerial cameras, so they could be plotted on maps. Unfortunately, the damp and misty weather made it difficult to see anything, either from the ground or the air.

Each field battery had a specific target to destroy before zero hour, whether it was to cut the wire or to hit the enemy parapet. The guns would then extend their ranges according to a timetable; this was the first time an artillery barrage had set the pace for the infantry advance. The infantry were also issued with maps with coloured objective lines which were linked to the Germans' defensive positions.

The bombardment would start at 7.30am, an hour after sunrise, giving the observers time to complete registration of their targets. The 18-pounders would fire on the German wire, the howitzer batteries would target the German trenches and the heavy howitzers would target billets in the village.

---

13 Named after Lord of the Admiralty, Winston Churchill.
14 Around thirty observers shared one ruined building at Pont Logy.

Other field batteries would shell the trenches to the flanks, to disguise the extent of the attack.

The gunners would extend their range at 8.05am, as the three assault brigades crossed the 200 metres of no man's land. The field guns would lift to the far side of Neuve Chapelle while all the howitzers concentrated on the village and strongpoints to the north and south. The infantry had thirty minutes to reach to the German support trenches, 200 metres beyond the front parapet. The artillery would lift from Neuve Chapelle at 8.35am, as the infantry moved through the ruins, heading for Smith-Dorrien Trench.

The rest of IV Corps and the Indian Corps could join the advance towards Aubers Ridge once a new line had been established between the Moated Grange and Port Arthur. It was also hoped the attack could expand to the flanks, outflanking the Germans facing the Canadian Division to the north and I Corps to the south. The Cavalry Corps and Indian Cavalry Corps could then advance through the gap created by First Army and then wheel south along the ridge behind the German line.

But First Army only had enough ammunition for three or four days, meaning that the attack had to succeed in the first few hours. Even then the advance would have to stop on the top of Aubers Ridge if the French could not cooperate to the south.

The Infantry Preparations

The preparations for the offensive began with an adjustment of frontages at the end of February. The Canadian Division took over 7th Division's front north of Bois Grenier, Indian Corps took over 800 metres of IV Corps front and I Corps took over the Indian Corps' right.

First Army had to organise the digging of assembly trenches, moving troops into position and advancing according to a timetable; they were all new concepts. To begin with the three assault brigades were withdrawn into reserve on 2 March to rehearse. Every officer was given an objective and they visited the front trenches to see the ground they would have to advance across. They then returned to their men to explain the task ahead.

Roads had to be improved, tracks built and tramways laid to carry everything forward. Dummy breastworks and screens were erected to mislead the enemy as advanced depots[15] were built and filled with ammunition, rations, tools and stores. The high water table made it impossible to dig deep trenches, so breastworks had to be built using thousands of sandbags. Once everything was ready, the three assault brigades moved forward under cover of darkness.

Each man picked up 150 rounds, two empty sandbags, an emergency

---

15 Known as dumps.

ration and the rest of his day's ration as he marched forward. Each battalion had two machine guns and each infantry brigade had a grenade company.[16] Each battalion also had twenty bombers, carrying around ten bombs each.

Battalions were issued with coloured flags[17] to fly above captured trenches or buildings so they could report progress. The artillery observers would then convey developments to the infantry and artillery. The only other way to communicate with the front was by using runners who carried messages by hand.

Rain turned the soil into sticky mud, but the night before the battle the weather turned cold and a little snow filled the dark sky. Around midnight the assault troops began the difficult move into the breastworks and while 23 and 25 Brigades lined out north-west east of Neuve Chapelle, the Garhwal Brigade did the same to the south-west of the village. All the assault troops reported they were in position by 4.30am. If anyone was unsure whether the Germans knew anything, the 2nd Leicesters near Port Arthur were not. A placard with the words 'Come on, we are waiting for you' had been spotted on the enemy parapet.

The Attack on Neuve Chapelle

Everything was done to make sure the assault troops could deploy and move forward quickly. Footbridges were placed over ditches, steps were cut in the breastworks and ladders were placed against the parapet. Wire fences were replaced by moveable sections known as 'knife-edges'[18] and gaps were cut in hedges.

Sunrise was at 6.30am and General Haig gave permission to start the attack as the clouds and mist started to clear, giving the artillery observers a clear view over the battlefield. It allowed the planes to take to the air, but a German machine was first to fly low over the British trenches and the crew would have seen that the trenches were packed with troops.

The 15-inch howitzer nicknamed Granny fired its first shot towards Aubers church at 7.30am and the huge boom was the signal to start the bombardment. Five minutes later the *Churchill* railway gun began shooting at Aubers. The ninety 18-pounders each had fifty rounds to fire at the German wire entanglement protecting the German breastwork while another ninety 18-pounders and sixty 4.5-inch howitzers hit the German parapet. There was a support trench 100 metres behind but the British observers had not noticed it; it had been abandoned due to flooding.

The barrage smashed the rows of knife edge entanglements and destroyed large parts of the German breastwork, killing or burying many of the garrison beneath piles of sandbags. At 7.40am all the field artillery

---

16 Later called a bombing company. They were formed by taking thirty men from each battalion.
17 The Indian Corps brigades gave pink flags to the flank battalions and light or dark blue to the centre battalions.
18 Wire was wrapped around pre-made wooden frames and carried into no man's land at night. It meant an entanglement could be erected in silence.

lengthened their range to sweep the area east of the village, hitting the garrison as they ran.[19] Simultaneously, the heavy artillery fired at the German batteries which had exposed their positions to the aerial observers. Eight aeroplanes fitted with wirelesses circled overhead, organising counter-battery fire, the first time the technique had been tried on such a large scale. At the same time, the assault troops doubled across no man's land, as fast as the mud allowed.

<u>8th Division's Assault</u>
Brigadier General Pinney's 23 Brigade held 8th Division's left, facing the enemy line south of the Moated Grange. The 2nd Middlesex faced a problem on the extreme because the two siege batteries detailed to hit the German trenches had been delayed en route from England. They reached their positions at midday on 9 March but the poor weather stopped them registering their targets, so they missed the trenches. The Germans shot down the first three Middlesex waves, including the adjutant and three company commanders, and pinned the survivors down. Lieutenant Colonel Hayes' officers tried in vain to get their men to go forward, but their three attempts failed.

The 2nd Scottish Rifles overran the smashed German breastwork but they soon came under enfilade fire from where the Middlesex should have been moving forward. Ten officers were killed en route to the support trench but the rest of Lieutenant Colonel Bliss's officers organised the survivors.

General Pinney made plans for a new bombardment when he heard of the Middlesex failure. Meanwhile, Bliss collected as many of the Scottish Rifles as he could find and took Lieutenant Bristowe's platoon forward to reinforce the front line. Both Bliss and Bristowe were hit but their men made sure the line was safe.

General Pinney visited Lieutenant Colonels Hayes and Travers when the second bombardment at 8.30am failed to shake the Germans in front of the Middlesex. He instructed Travers to take the 2nd Devons forward but Lieutenant Bates was killed leading the left company across no man's land. The right company moved along Signpost Lane while Second Lieutenant Wright's bombers tackled the Germans facing the Middlesex.

The 2nd West Yorkshires had occupied the Middlesex front trench and Lieutenant Colonel Drew could only watch as they were cut down each time they tried to complete the murderous journey across no man's land. At 9.40am a wounded officer reached the West Yorkshires with news that the Scottish Rifles had taken their objective to the right, so Drew sent Captain Francis with two companies along Signpost Lane to reinforce them.

---

19 The first time a box barrage had been used.

General Pinney asked Major General Franics Davies for another bombardment of the trench opposite the Middlesex and the rest of the Devons were ready alongside the Scottish Rifles when it started at 10am. The Devons' bombers cleared 400 metres of trench but Wright was shot in the back by a wounded German officer as the last group surrendered; Lance Corporal Woods killed the officer. Around 11.15am everyone was pleased to hear the 'Germans in the front trench [had] chucked it in and one officer and sixty-four Jägers' hands upped and came over.' It had been a costly assault; 23 Brigade had suffered over 1,240 casualties, most of them from the Middlesex and Scottish Rifles.

But the advance could continue and 23 Brigade encountered no opposition as they crossed the Moated Grange road around 1pm. The West Yorkshires on the left had gone even further, clearing the orchard beyond the road. Captain Ingpen wanted to take the West Yorkshires forward but neither they nor the Devons could advance any further because the British artillery continued to shell the abandoned trench to their front. All communications to the rear had been cut and German troops had entered the trench before the gunners got the message to stop firing.

Brigadier General Lowry-Cole's 25 Brigade was deployed between Signpost Lane and the Neuve Chapelle road on 8th Division's right. The Indian Corps was 700 metres to the south and 25 Brigade's advance was directed to contact it in Neuve Chapelle.

The 2nd Lincolns 'dashed forward gallantly' and while Captain Eagar was wounded, Captain Bastard was first into the trench. Captains Harris and Fraser were wounded leading the 2nd Berkshires forward and Lieutenant Colonel McAndrew of the 2nd Lincolns was mortally injured. His last words as he watched his men advance were 'Have they taken the trenches?' They had.

Captain Peake organised blocks on the left flank and he raised a flag so observers could see their progress. He was killed soon afterwards while rounding up prisoners. Lieutenant Graham was severely injured by a surrendering German as he blocked the trenches to the right but his men waved another flag so Lieutenant Colonel Feetham could see how far his men had gone.

Some British guns were firing short but the Lincolns pushed on to a water-filled ditch which they had to cross by a single plank bridge. The Germans could be seen sheltering from the barrage up ahead but Lieutenants Wylie and Billiant had to withdraw the Lincolns behind the ditch when the British shells started falling short. A German sniper wearing a British uniform came out of hiding to shoot Wylie as he organised the withdrawal.

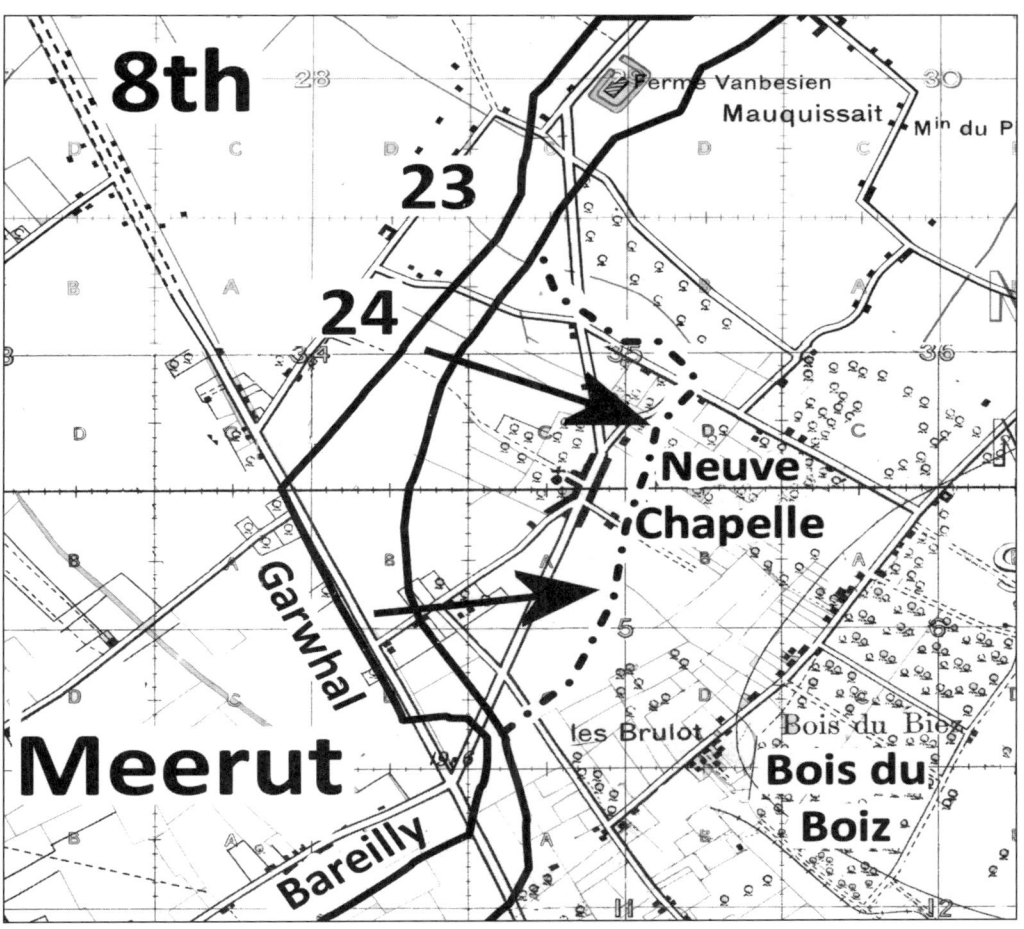

IV Corps attack at Neuve Chapelle on 10 March 1915

The artillery barrage lifted east of the village at 8.35am and the 1st Irish Rifles and the 2nd Rifle Brigade moved forward in artillery formation[20] to take over the advance. The Lincolns cheered as the Irish Rifles passed through, with Captain Graham's horn 'giving a View Hulloa occasionally, just as a master collects his pack' to encourage his men. Major Cox and some Lincolns went forward with the Irish while the rest dug in.

The Irish Rifles and Rifle Brigade encountered little opposition en route to the Armentières road but 23 Brigade was lagging behind to the left. Machine gun teams fired into the Irish Rifles' flank, killing Lieutenant

---

20 Four lines of small columns each of half a platoon.

Colonel Laurie and Captain Burgess and injuring Captain Biscoe and Lieutenant Graham. The survivors wheeled through the orchards and the chateau north of the village and while Captain Galwey pulled the Irish Rifles' left flank back, Major Baker echeloned the right flank back to the 2nd Rifle Brigade. They stopped a counter-attack and then the Germans withdrew to regroup.

The 2nd Rifle Brigade cleared Neuve Chapelle's ruined houses and then moved across the fields beyond, making contact with the Indians of the Garhwal Brigade. They could have continued into Bois du Biez but the British guns were firing short and it was impossible to tell them to stop. Lieutenant Colonel Stephens asked if the Rifle Brigade should continue to advance but General Lowry-Cole told him to dig in because 23 Brigade was held up.

7th (Meerut) Division's Assault
General Charles Anderson had deployed the Garhwal Brigade in line south-west of Neuve Chapelle. Brigadier General Blackader had four battalions in the trenches parallel with the road connecting Pont Logy and Port Arthur, while the 3rd London was in brigade reserve. Step ladders helped the Indians climb the parapet and they then used small bridges to cross the dyke in front of their trench.

It is believed that German patrols had spotted a lot of movement in the Indian trenches before zero hour but their requests for artillery support had been refused by higher command. Instead they waited for a reconnaissance plane to fly low overhead and the guns began firing as soon as it confirmed the reports.

Lieutenant Colonel Drake-Brockman made sure the 2/39th Garhwal Rifles had deployed in no man's land before it was light and they moved forward as soon as the artillery lifted. An injured Subadar-Major, Nain Sing Chinwarh, and Rifleman Gobar Sing Negi led the Garhwalis into the battered trench where Jemadars Sangram Sing Negi and Pancham Sing Mahar each captured a machine gun. The second and the third trenches were then taken before the guns extended the range. Rifleman Gobar Sing Negi's bombers chased the Germans down the communication trenches until he was killed; he was posthumously awarded the Victoria Cross.

The Garhwalis suffered many casualties advancing into Neuve Chapelle. Naik Jaman Sing Bisht eventually forced many Germans to retire and they were captured by the right company. Another party of Germans beckoned the approaching Indians to come forward and take them prisoner. They refused and then discovered a hidden machine gun would have shot them down if they had taken the bait.

The Garhwalis were soon clearing houses in Neuve Chapelle and a store of German supplies was used to fortify them. Captain Grigg led the 2/3rd Gurkhas through the south corner of the village before coming up on the Garhwali's right flank; they had taken 200 prisoners and five machine guns by 9am. Lieutenant Colonel Ormsby then wheeled the Gurkhas east to Smith-Dorrien Trench. But the trench was full of water, so they dug a new trench behind it.

Captains Weir and Morgan led the 2nd Leicesters across no man's land and into the first trench; Morgan fell after his sixth wound. Major Tillard's company of Gurkhas helped the Leicesters capture the village brewery while Captain Romilly and Lieutenant Buxton cleared Germans from the nearby ruined houses. Romilly thought the bombers were moving too slow along a trench so he jumped out, followed by his runner carrying bags of bombs. They ran along the top, tossing grenades into the trench below, forcing eighty Germans to surrender. The Leicesters commanding officer, Major Gordon, said of Romilly, 'he was the keenest man I had ever met in a battle and bombs were a hobby to him.'

Gordon would eventually deploy the Leicesters alongside the Garhwalis as Private Hill kept him up to date by running back and forth with messages. Private William Buckingham was one of many who braved the shrapnel and bullets to carry wounded men to safety.[21]

The 1/39th Garhwalis were on the right flank and their trench was at an angle to the German front line. Smoke obscured the tree which marked the direction of the advance, causing Captains Clarke and Owen to veer to the right into uncut wire. It left Captain Kenny and Lieutenant Welchman facing a trench untouched by the bombardment. Colonel Swiney could see the advance was faltering so he ordered Captains Murray and Sparrow to move their companies forward.

Lieutenant Cammell was the artillery observer accompanying the infantry but took command when the rest of the officers fell. He urged the survivors to cut through the wire and clear the trench beyond before he too was hit. Lance Corporal Thompson of the 2nd Black Watch dashed into no man's land and dragged the injured Cammell back to safety.

The three battalions on the left had formed a continuous line but they all failed to send out scouts to locate the German line.[22] There was, however, a gap on the right east of Port Arthur, where the 1/39th Garhwalis had deviated, leaving the Leicesters' right exposed. Subadar Kedar Sing Rawat made sure none of the Garhwalis retired while an

---

21 Private Buckingham would do the same two days later and was awarded the Victoria Cross.
22 An oversight due to the lack of surviving officers.

injured Colonel Swiney called brigade headquarters for help at 8.45am.

Lieutenant Colonel Ritchie of the 1st Seaforths[23] received an order to reinforce the Garhwali Brigade at 11.45am but he decided to visit Colonel Swiney at Port Arthur first. It was 1pm before Captains Baillie-Hamilton and Wicks led their companies into no man's land. They were to pivot behind the Leicesters and bomb along the German trench while the 3rd London made a frontal attack from Port Arthur.

But the Seaforths struggled to cross the ditches and then came under British artillery fire as they moved into position. Wicks' men were then hit by mortar fire at 2.15pm, the specified zero hour, and the attack never started. German troops began to threaten the Leicesters rear during the delay, so Colonel Gordon had to order Captain Romilly to drive them back. Captain Hobart brought his men forward to build a barricade but British artillery fire forced him to fall back.

Colonel Ritchie sent the rest of the Seaforths forward and Lieutenant the Hon. Bruce and Captain Murray bombed along the German held trench. Murray was mortally wounded before 120 Germans surrendered to his men but the rest opened fire as the two London companies climbed over the parapet. Many of Captains Moore's and Livingstone's men were hit crossing no man's land but the survivors cleared the troublesome trench.

Major MacTier of the 2/39th Garhwalis relieved the wounded Swiney and he organised parties to clear the south side of Neuve Chapelle where Germans were still hiding in houses. Snipers and hidden machine guns continued to shoot at the Indian and British troops right through the night and while most were silenced, it took several days to round them all up.

The Second Wave

First Army's centre had made a gap around 1,600 metres wide but the Germans were still holding the flanks. On 8th Division's front 23 Brigade's delay exposed 25 Brigade's left flank about the road triangle, so General Davies ordered 24 Brigade to send a battalion forward to cover it. Brigadier General Carter instructed the 2nd East Lancashires to move at 10.20am but Major Maclear had to take over when Lieutenant Colonel Nicholson was wounded.

General Pinney moved his troops along the north side of Neuve Chapelle and gathered the Yorkshire and Devonshire bombers as a new bombardment hit the German held trench in front of 23 Brigade. The bombers then advanced north from Signpost Lane, and sixty-five Germans eventually surrendered to the 2nd Middlesex. After nearly four hours delay, General Pinney could report his first objective had been taken.

---

23 From Brigadier General Jacob's Dera Dun Brigade.

The rest of the West Yorkshires reinforced the Middlesex while Pinney called up the 1st Worcesters[24] as a reserve. The Middlesex and half the West Yorkshires cleared the orchard after the short barrage ended and the rest of the West Yorkshires then bombed north, heading for the Moated Grange. Meanwhile, the Devons and the Scottish Rifles had been busy digging in behind Smith-Dorrien Trench, alongside 25 Brigade. Only then was Pinney ready for the reserves and General Davies issued instructions to advance at 1.30pm.

General Haig's advanced headquarters was based at Merville and he messaged Field Marshal French at 9am asking for a cavalry brigade to be ready to move through any gaps. French responded by sending 5th Cavalry Brigade[25] to Estaires. But General Rawlinson was cautious after hearing the Middlesex had been stopped south of the Moated Grange, threatening his left flank. He delayed 7th Division's move forward until he heard the rest of 23 Brigade had cleared the Orchard at 1.15pm. Nearly six hours after zero hour, Major General Sir Thompson Capper was ordered to move forward. Brigadier General Watts was in turn told to move 21 Brigade towards the Moated Grange, ready to advance alongside 24 Brigade.

The Indian Corps also had a dilemma, caused by the problem around Port Arthur, on its right flank. General Rawlinson told Lieutenant General James Willcocks about IV Corps' situation around 1.30pm and asked if the Meerut Division would be able to continue its advance towards Bois du Biez at 2pm. It would not, because it was still waiting for the 1st Seaforths to clear the German trenches. General Rawlinson in turn told First Army headquarters about the postponement, much to General Haig's annoyance.

As the hours ticked by, General Willcocks realised the Meerut Division's situation was better than first imagined and told General Anderson to advance towards Bois du Biez. He also told the Jullundur Brigade[26] to support the advance. On hearing the news, General Haig moved the 5th Cavalry Brigade close behind 8th Division's front.

The attack on Neuve Chapelle had virtually obliterated six German companies or around 1,400 men. Many had been killed or injured by the bombardment while most of the survivors had been taken prisoner. The break-in had been made and only a few stragglers stood between First Army and a major breakthrough. Only Generals Rawlinson and Willcocks did not know the scale of the success and they were focusing on problems on the flanks.

As the British generals dithered, German reinforcements were rushing forward to man their second line of trenches and strongpoints. By 9.30am two companies reached the trench facing the break-in on the centre and right

---

24 Lieutenant Colonel Wodehouse was killed. Major Grogan replaced him.
25 2nd Cavalry Division.
26 Lahore Division.

flank and two more were close by. As the hours ticked by, the Germans had ample time to prepare for the next onslaught. The biggest missed opportunity was opposite the Indian Corps where Bois du Biez was unoccupied all morning and afternoon. Two German battalions had entered the wood by the time the Indian troops were ready to move.

The Afternoon Situation
General Rawlinson's orders to advance on Aubers were issued to his reserves at 2.55pm. On the left, 21 Brigade[27] was to advance north of Mauquissart, heading east towards Rue d'Enfer. On the right, 24 Brigade[28] had to move through the cottages next to High Trees Junction and then

IV Corps' afternoon advance on 10 March

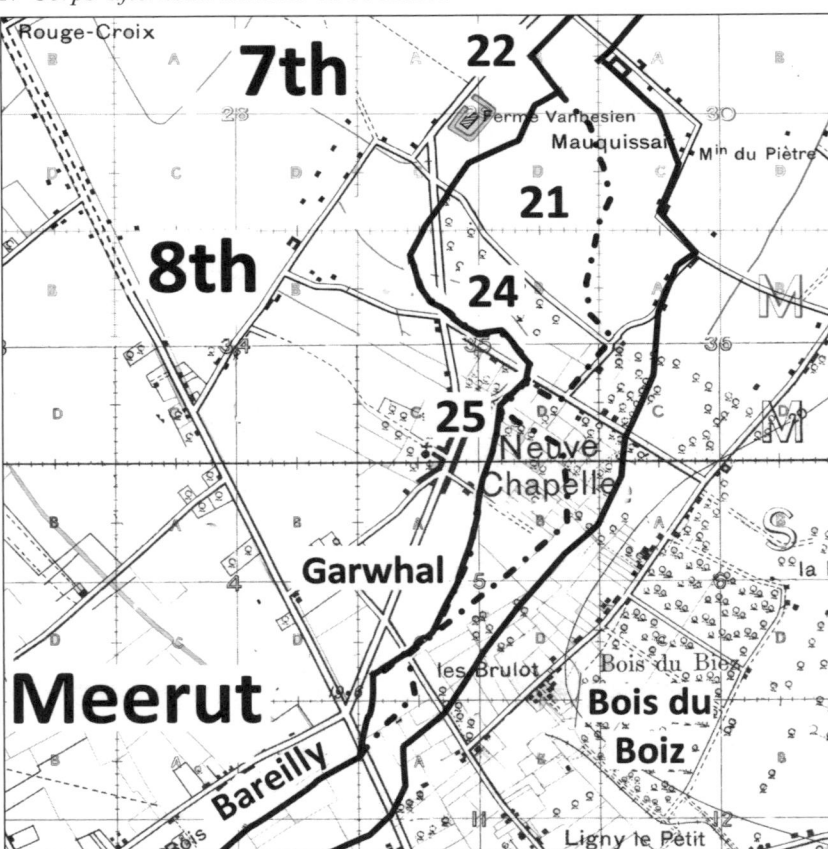

27 7th Division.
28 8th Division.

between Mauquissart and the Layes bridge, heading for Pietre. The Indian Corps would advance into Bois du Biez at the same time.

Rawlinson expected the infantry to advance at 3.30pm following a short artillery barrage. But the batteries had no time to register their guns on the trenches and strongpoints being reported by their observers. Communications had been cut and runners had to negotiate trenches and flooded ditches to get messages to the front, leaving the infantry no time to organise ready to advance.

<u>7th Division's Advance</u>
General Capper ordered Brigadier General Watts to assemble 21 Brigade between the Moated Grange and the Orchard while Brigadier General Heyworth was instructed to be ready to follow with 20 Brigade. The plan was to advance north-east to outflank the trenches north of the Moated Grange, widening the breach in the German line.[29]

The 2nd Green Howards and 2nd Royal Scots Fusiliers moved off at 2pm and both Lieutenant Colonel and Major Pollard-Alexander[30] reported there was no opposition. Unfortunately, they were heading east towards Mauquissart rather than north-east towards the Moated Grange. They had crossed the Armentières road and passed through 23 Brigade's left when a message from General Capper told General Watts to wait for 24 Brigade to come up on his left. They stopped but the British guns started firing on them and there was no way of telling them to lengthen their range. They had to endure the shelling until 24 Brigade came alongside at 6pm, as the sky was darkening.

The Green Howards and Scots Fusiliers were soon stopped by fire from the front and left and Major Onslow halted his 2nd Bedfords behind the Scots. The two 2nd Wiltshires companies ordered to bomb towards the Moated Grange were delayed and Captain Gillison was wounded investigating the problem. Captain Matkin took over and his men took one hundred prisoners before they were stopped by a water-filled ditch. Captain Hoare and Lieutenant Spencer crossed the obstacle and took another eighty prisoners, only to be killed close to the Moated Grange. The Wiltshires were to deploy in the open so they could contact the Green Howards and they had to spend a difficult night under shell fire.

General Capper sent a staff officer forward because he wanted the advance to continue but Brigadier General Watts reported his battalions had already lost many officers and the survivors were struggling to coordinate their movements in the dark. Capper accepted the situation and Watts was ordered to dig in along the Mauquissart road, ready to advance the following

---

29 The garrison facing Brigadier General Lawford's 22 Brigade.
30 Later Major Forbes.

morning. While it was a wise move, the delay gave the Germans plenty of time to re-man the trenches in front of 7th Division.

8th Division Pushes Forward

General Davies ordered 24 Brigade to assemble astride Signpost Lane, ready to advance between 23 and 25 Brigades. But it took Brigadier General Carter a long time to recall the 2nd Northants and 1st Sherwood Foresters from 23 Brigade. It was nearly dark by the time they were ready to move, by which time 7th Division's advance had ground to a halt. The officers struggled to maintain control as they moved across the network of ditches and two 1st Worcesters' companies had to be sent forward to fill the gap opening between them.

Colonel Prichard eventually reported that machine gun from the cottages around High Trees Corner had stopped the Northants. Major Mortimore also sent back a message stating the Sherwoods had been pinned down by the Layes Bridge redoubt. Carter had to tell Davies that 25 Brigade was digging in east of Neuve Chapelle, having suffered over 775 casualties.

The Meerut Division Tries Again

The order to advance reached the Dehra Dun Brigade at 3.30pm, exactly at zero hour. It took thirty minutes to pass the message to the front line and the artillery had lifted long before the Indians moved. Brigadier General Jacob had three battalions on the left, the 1st Seaforths[31], the 47th Sikhs[32] and the 1st Manchesters. They moved north astride the Edgware Road before wheeling east to avoid the Germans facing Port Arthur.

Although the Bois de Biez had been empty for most of the day, the 1/9th Gurkhas came under cross-fire as they negotiated the plank bridges across the Layes stream in the fading light. Lieutenant Colonel Widdicombe's men reached the wood, guided by a burning cottage, while under fire from the Layes Bridge redoubt. Meanwhile, Lieutenant Murray's machine guns stopped the Germans threatening the open right flank.

The 2nd Gurkhas' two left companies veered north, to keep in touch with the 1/9th Gurkhas, meaning Major Nicolay and Lieutenant Clifford became separated from Major Watts and Captain Dallas-Smith. Nicolay was killed as he tried to connect the two halves of the battalion while Major Boileau heard that scouts had taken a prisoner who reported there were many Germans inside Bois de Biez.

The news eventually reached General Jacob and it was the final straw in what was turning into a nightmare situation for the Meerut Division. There was no sign of 8th Division on the left and there was a strong German

---

31 Garhwal Brigade.
32 Jullundur Brigade.

presence in Bois de Biez on the right. General Jacob had no option but to tell the Gurkhas to retire across the Layes brook, a difficult manoeuvre in the dark. The 4th Seaforths reinforced the new line while the 47th Sikhs and 1st Manchesters were returned to the reserve.

As the Dehra Dun Brigade moved on Bois de Biez Colonel Swiney organised an attack on the Port Arthur salient. The 1st Seaforths moved south in open order as Lieutenant Colonel Howell sent two 3rd London companies to reinforce a company of the 1/39th Garhwal Rifles. The frontal assault suffered heavy casualties but the flanking movement convinced the eighty-strong garrison to surrender. By nightfall the Garhwal and Dehra Dun Brigades had secured Port Arthur.

First Army had broken through the German line on a 4,000 yard front between the Moated Grange and Port Arthur; it had advanced up to 1,200 metres and had taken nearly 750 prisoners. Its reserves were on hand, but so were the Germans and they knew the ground well while the British and Indian troops were moving into unknown territory.

The Subsidiary Attacks
Subsidiary attacks, designed to pin reserves down, were limited to a few infantry attacks and artillery bombardments. The III Corps and Canadian Division's artillery shelled the German lines north of IV Corps at zero hour. From time to time the infantry would open fire and cheer, to make it look as though an attack was underway.[33] It made little difference.

To the south, 1st Division[34] was holding a swampy area where an attack was impossible so Major General Richard Haking's artillery supported attacks on its flanks. Major General Henry Horne's 2nd Division attacked at Givenchy and Brigadier General Fanshawe's 6 Brigade advanced from three points north of the canal. The artillery began firing at 7.30am, as the infantry assault started at Neuve Chapelle, and three columns of infantry clambered out of their trenches forty minutes later. No man's land varied in width but a low crest meant the observers could not see the wire and the gunners struggled to cut it.

The 1st KRRC advanced 'at the double' from the White House, coming under heavy fire as they crossed the crest in no man's land. Captain Grazewood's men crawled through the wire on the left so they could bomb along the enemy trench but only three uninjured men returned. No one could get through the wire on the right, so Major Shakerley cancelled further attacks. Captain Feneran and Lieutenant Snatt led the 1st King's advance from the Shrine but no one reached the enemy wire, forcing Lieutenant Colonel Carter to call off the attack.

---

33 These dummy attacks were known as Chinese Attacks. They became more sophisticated in later battles.
34 On I Corps' left flank.

The 2nd South Staffords came under heavy crossfire from the Duck's Bill and few made it to the wire. Second Lieutenant Hewat and a group of fifteen men reached an enemy machine gun post but no one returned. Second Lieutenant Wood also entered the trench but his small group had to retire and Lieutenant Colonel Routledge called off the attack after Second Lieutenant Richardson's final attempt failed.

General Horne wanted to try again and there was another short bombardment followed by a second assault at 2.15pm. The Germans stopped the 1st King's and 2nd South Staffords in no man's land. Horne's plan to make a third attack after dusk was stopped by I Corps commander, General Sir Charles Monro.

Despite the subsidiary attacks, the Germans knew exactly where First Army's attack was by midday and reserves were rushing to the Neuve Chapelle area.

Chapter 3

A Mere Waste of Life
Neuve Chapelle Continues
11–13 March

As German reserves marched through the night towards the battlefield, the survivors of the first day's fighting built new breastworks, erected wire fences and improved strongpoints. They even built a new line 200 metres from the west edge of Bois du Biez, covering the Layes stream. Meanwhile, Haig issued an order at 11.30pm to continue the attack the following morning. He believed that 'from information received, it appears the enemy before us is in no great strength' and no new divisions had moved to the area.

First Army's main attack would be made by IV Corps on the left flank while the Indian Corps advanced through the Bois du Biez. Rawlinson in turn told 7th and 8th Divisions to advance at 7am, following a fifteen minute bombardment. The plan was for 21 Brigade[35] to advance north-east and for 24 Brigade[36] to advance east as 20 Brigade[37] filled the gap between them. The battalion commanders had asked for a large scale artillery preparation but any bombardment would be limited by the very low levels of ammunition.[38] Meanwhile, the German guns had plenty of shells and the assault troops endured a three-hour bombardment as they trudged across the battlefield.

The British guns opened fire at 6.45am but morning mist prevented the aerial observers from flying while the ground observers could not see the targets. No one knew the Germans had built a new breastwork so it was not shelled. The infantry moved off fifteen minutes later as some guns, particularly the worn out 4.7-inch howitzers, continued to fire short.

7th Division Attack the Moated Grange and the Orchard
On 7th Division's left, the 2nd Gordons and 1st Grenadier Guards[39] came

---

35 7th Division.
36 8th Division.
37 7th Division.
38 The siege guns were only allocated five rounds, the howitzers seven and the field guns fifteen.
39 Both 20 Brigade.

under fire as they moved towards the Moated Grange and the Orchard. Major Duberly's company of Guardsmen came under enfilade fire and the rest of the battalion took cover in ditches and trenches. Lieutenant Colonel Fisher-Rowe mistakenly reported he had reached the Layes stream, giving the impression the Guardsmen were further forward then they were.[40] It is also thought that an artillery observer saw British prisoners being sent to the rear and thought they were advancing troops; his report added to the confusion.

The battle of Neuve Chapelle continues on 11 March

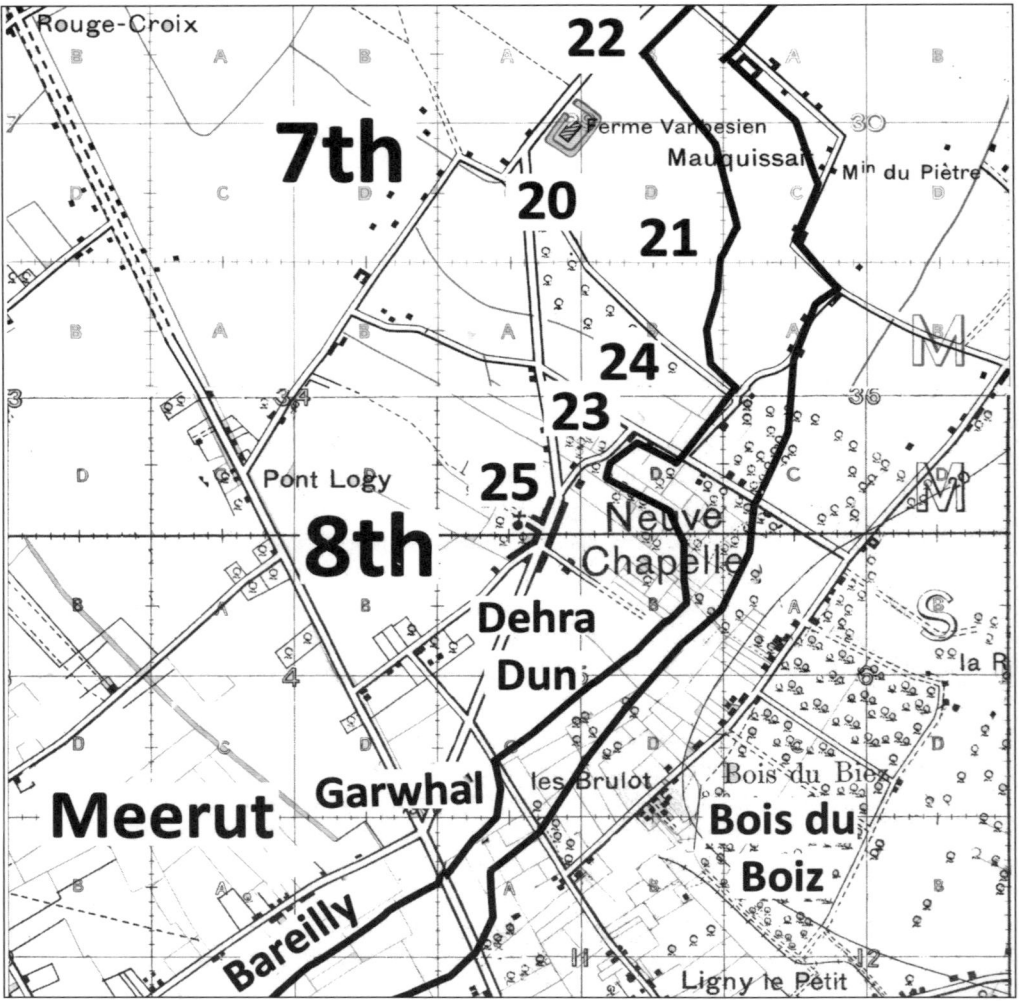

---

40 He had been stopped by an unnamed wide ditch.

On hearing the news, Brigadier General Heyworth thought the Guardsmen had captured the German position, and instructed Fisher-Rowe to dig in while the Gordons cleared the orchard on their left. But they were unable to, so Heyworth ordered the 2nd Border Regiment forward to cover the Gordons' open flank.

General Capper instructed the field artillery to lengthen their range when he heard of the false breakthrough and it was several hours before the true situation was known. General Heyworth was ordered to dig in at dusk but it was impossible to do so because the water table was high and the troops had no sandbags to build a parapet. Heyworth's brigade had suffered 500 casualties crossing ground which had already been cleared.

The 2nd Scots Guards[41] were instructed to secure the division's right flank but the only safe way forward was along a water-filled communication trench. It was nigh on impossible to walk through the deep mud in the dark, never mind deploy to threaten the enemy.

8th Division Attack towards Mauquissart

The 24 Brigade also had a difficult time moving up from reserve and at 3.10am Brigadier General Oxley was told to capture the houses lining the road half a mile east of the Orchard. The advance was interrupted by numerous ditches and it was soon clear the Germans had machine guns in the houses. Lieutenant Colonel Pritchard was wounded supervising the 2nd Northants' advance and Major Morley could not get closer than 300 metres. Major Mortimer was injured as the 1st Sherwoods advanced with their right on Sign Post Lane but they reached the road junction on the objective.

General Davies ordered a second bombardment to start at 8.45am but the battalions never received the message to renew the advance; 'Owing to the weather conditions, which did not permit of aerial observation, and the fact that nearly all the telephonic communications between the artillery observers and their batteries had been cut, it was impossible to direct the artillery fire with accuracy.' The messengers were shot down as they ran across the open fields and waded through ditches. Dark rain clouds added to the men's misery.

During the early hours the 2nd West Yorkshires[42] started relieving 25 Brigade. Most of the troops had left the trenches by dawn but the 2nd Rifle Brigade waited after hearing the Indian Corps had seen infantry assembling in the north end of Bois du Biez. The report proved to be inaccurate and it was late morning before the relief was complete.

---

41 21 Brigade.
42 23 Brigade.

The Meerut Division

General Anderson issued orders to Brigadier General Jacob during the early hours of 11 March. The Dehra Dun Brigade would cross the Layes stream and clear Bois du Biez while the 2/39th Garhwal Rifles[43] covered its south flank. The rest of the Garhwal Brigade would dig in south of Neuve Chapelle while the Jullundur Brigade[44] waited in support.

The plan was for the Dehra Dun Brigade to move as soon as 8th Division advanced past its left flank but no one had told Brigadier General Jacob, so he could not tell his battalions. Jacob assumed he had to wait for 25 Brigade to move up behind his left flank but it had been directed to support 24 Brigade. The Indians could see nothing through the morning mist so General Jacob waited in vain for 25 Brigade to arrive. Brigadier General Jacob had sent his brigade-major, Major Walker, to speak to 2nd Rifle Brigade[45] on his left, and eventually learnt it had orders to hold its position.

The bombardment hit Bois du Biez but it did not touch the new trench in front of the trees, so General Jacob called off the attack. As usual there were no telephone communications with the artillery and it took several hours to get messages to the gunners. The mist persisted and the guns continued shelling Bois de Biez rather than the trench.

Afternoon Advances

The Germans did not counter-attack so Rawlinson issued orders to advance in the afternoon: 'It is most important that the buildings at the Moulin du Pietre and at the Mauquissart–Pietre cross roads should be captured without further delay. Lose no time in getting the guns onto them and assault the buildings with infantry.'

General Capper told General Heyworth that a one-hour bombardment would start at 2pm and that his 21 Brigade would be supported by the rest of the division. The late decision to attack meant it was impossible to get orders to all the companies in time and each one advanced as soon as they heard. No one knew the Germans had dug a new trench and the bombardment missed it, allowing the German machine gunners to target each company as they moved forward.

8th Division, East of Neuve Chapelle

General Davies was doubtful an afternoon attack would succeed but General Rawlinson told him to proceed. General Willcocks agreed the Dehra Dun Brigade would move forward when 21 Brigade advanced past. Again insufficient time was allowed to get the instructions to the battalions. Brigadier General Carter received the attack order at 1.42pm and three

---

43 Garhwal Brigade.
44 Lahore Division.
45 25 Brigade, 8th Division.

minutes later the guns opened fire. He also ordered the Worcesters to send two companies to the front, in the hope that they would carry the rest of the brigade forward.

General Carter's messengers had thirty minutes to cross 1,200 metres of ground which was cut by ditches and trenches and swept by fire. Only two of the Northants companies received the attack order, only five minutes after the bombardment finished. Enfilade machine gunfire stopped anyone going further than a few metres.

Colonel Prichard later related how he '…received a note from the Worcesters. "We have got to advance. Will you give the order?" I answered "no, it is a mere waste of life, impossible to go 20 metres much less 200 metres. The trenches have not been touched by the artillery. If the artillery cannot touch them the only way is to advance from right flank. A frontal attack will not get near them."' The two Worcester companies were also shot down. The Sherwoods made three attempts to reach the enemy trench but they could only reach a farm on the Mauquissart road.

General Davies issued the order for 25 Brigade to advance towards the Layes Bridge redoubt at 2.50pm. General Lowry-Cole received the message thirty minutes later and he went to the 2nd Rifle Brigade to make arrangements to coordinate the advance. One version of the misunderstanding is that Lieutenant Colonel Stephens reported the Dehra Dun's brigade-major had just left, believing there was no plan to advance. Lowry-Cole had no way of contacting the Dehra Dun Brigade in time, so he decided against advancing alone.

The Meerut Division, Attack towards Bois du Biez
General Willcocks' order to advance reached the Dehra Dun Brigade headquarters only five minutes before zero hour and the waiting messengers had to race to their battalion headquarters. Lieutenant Colonel Mason MacFarlane was wounded as the two 1/4th Seaforth companies ran forward under machine gun fire and crowded into the Gurkha trenches. Major Cuthbert was also suffering from a head wound as he did his best to organise his men.

The 1/9th and 2/2nd Gurkhas would advance as soon as the 2nd Rifle Brigade[46] moved past their left flank and while some of the 1/4th Seaforths kept moving forward at the appointed time, they were soon shot down. The Gurkhas waited and waited until Brigadier General Jacob eventually sent his brigade major to ask why 2nd Rifle Brigade was not moving. A second version of the misunderstanding is that Lieutenant Colonel Stephens had no knowledge of the attack. Brigadier General Jacob reported it would be

---

46 25 Brigade, 8th Division.

suicidal to advance alone and he was given permission to withdraw from the trench along the Layes stream and behind the Garhwal Brigade as soon as it was dark.

The inability to spot the new trenches and the late issuing of the orders doomed the attack to failure. If the infantry knew of the trenches, the message had not been passed back to be acted on. Cut telephone cables between the observing officers and the batteries meant they were unable to respond to information quickly, so the guns kept firing at their original targets. The heavy guns were in an even worse situation because they were relying on map fire, using mathematics to shoot blindly at their targets, not knowing if they were hitting them.

General Haig visited the battle front in the evening and gave instructions to move the guns forward, to improve communications and registration. He planned to attack again at 10.30am the following morning, giving time for the mist to disappear and let the observers do their work.

The German Counter-Attack, 12 March
Six German infantry battalions were marching towards the battlefield at dusk, with orders to recapture Neuve Chapelle. Zero hour was set for 5am but units found it difficult to find their assembly positions in the dark and some were still deploying when the bombardment started. There were ten battalions deployed along the front line with another four in support and six in reserve; altogether 16,000 men were poised to strike at First Army's trenches.

The rumble of gunfire began at 4.30am. The Germans' guns had not had time to register, so many overshot and hit the British rear areas. The Jullundur Brigade alone had 300 casualties because it was laid in the open behind the Meerut Division's front. Thirty minutes later thousands of German infantry clambered over their parapet and advanced through the dawn mist. Most British lookouts did not spot them until they were close and the firing began as the final charge began. There were four separate attacks.

7th Division, West of Mauquissart
The northern attack hit 21 Brigade between Moated Grange and Signpost Lane. German bombers used some old trenches to get close and then rushed the 2nd Wiltshires' left company as the rations were being distributed. The next company fell back across no man's land but the third one stopped the Germans crossing a ditch. Second Lieutenant Hunter organised a counter-attack with the help of Lieutenant Morrison and the 2nd Green Howards'

bombers. Morrison was killed but Corporal Anderson drove them back using his own and captured German bombs to capture sixty men and a lot of lost ground.[47] Captain Makin and the 1st Grenadier Guards bombers recovered the rest of the Wiltshires trenches in time to stop a second, larger attack. Dozens of prisoners had been taken by the time the fighting was over.

Counterattacks at Neuve Chapelle on 12 March

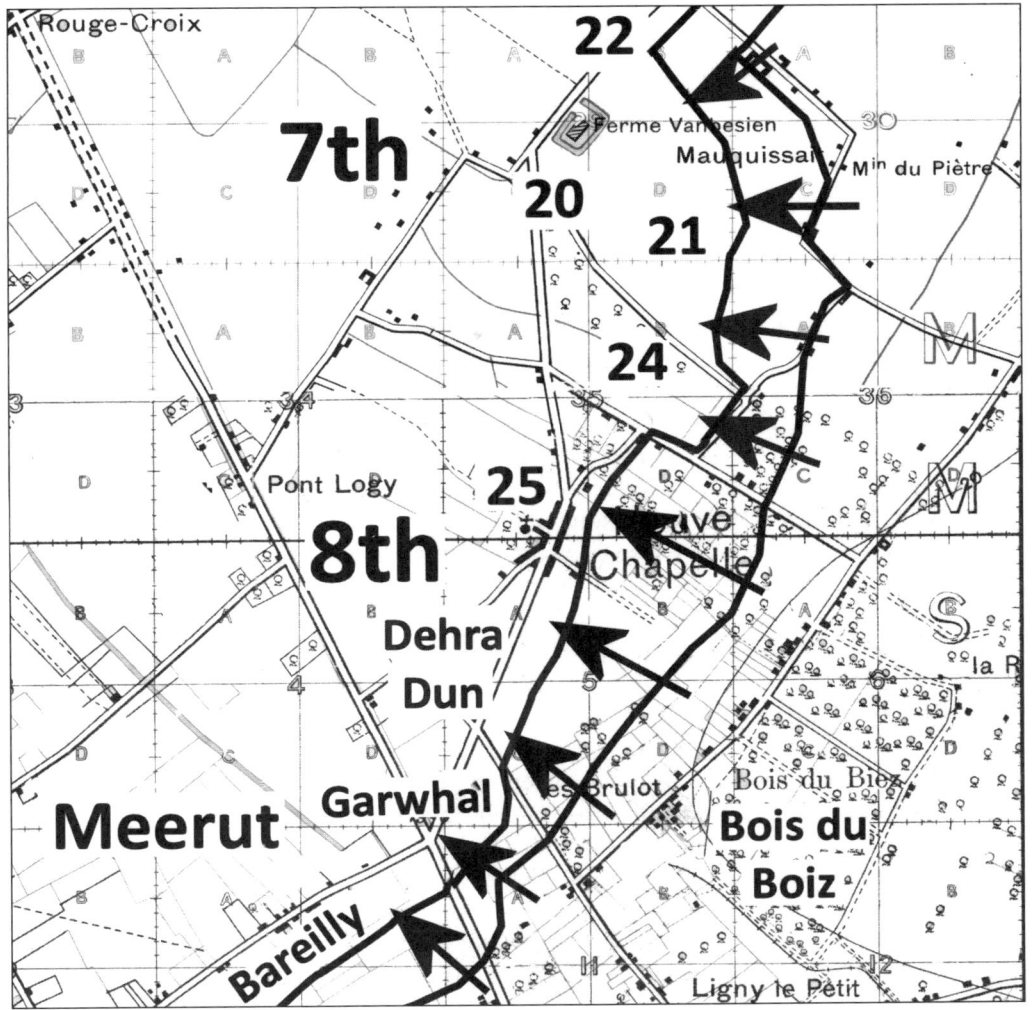

---

47 Morrison was killed the following day but he was posthumously awarded the Victoria Cross.

In the centre, the 2nd Green Howards stopped the Germans in no man's land with rapid fire and around 450 had been hit by the time the rest fell back. The 2nd Royal Scots Fusiliers right company was driven from its advanced position because it had no officers to organise the defence. Private Reid used his machine gun to stop the Germans going any further while Major Denne was seriously injured organising a counter-attack by the 2nd Bedfords. Captains Baird and Cumberbatch were also hit as they tried to drive the Germans back. The Scots Fusiliers also managed to stop a second attack.

The Bedfords adjutant, Captain Foss, led eight bombers along the Northants trench, taking the Germans in the flank and forcing fifty to surrender. Another sixty who had been hiding in craters then stood up with their hands up as their comrades made a run for it. Major Onslow's Bedfords were then able to reoccupy the lost ground.

8th Division, West of Neuve Chapelle

Both the 2nd Northants and the 1st Worcesters[48] stopped the German attack with their rifles and machine guns. The 1st Sherwoods[49] were in an exposed position, holding two farm buildings on the Mauquissart road, in front of the main position. The sentries on the north side of the salient mistook the German infantry for British soldiers returning from a listening post. The Sherwoods were rushed before the alarm could be raised and they were soon forced back. The Germans moved through the gap as the Worcesters and the 2nd West Yorkshires pulled back their flanks and began shooting into the Germans' flanks. The Worcesters then charged, driving them back, and they left over 400 dead and injured behind. Two more attacks against the West Yorkshires were also stopped. The 2nd Rifle Brigade[50] had also prevented the Germans gaining any ground, north of Brewery road.

Meerut Division, South of Neuve Chapelle

The Sirhind Brigade had relieved the Dehra Dunn Brigade during the early hours. Meanwhile, the Germans had assembled in Bois du Biez and they crossed the Layes stream and the old Dehra Dun trench in the early morning mist. The 2/3rd Gurkha Rifles listening posts withdrew from the Layes stream to alert their comrades but elsewhere German infantry could be seen 'jog-trotting' across no man's land. To begin with their greatcoats made them look like the kilted Seaforth Highlanders but the Indians opened fire when they noticed the 'Scots' had spikes on their helmets.

Captain Lodwick positioned all twenty of the division's machine guns so they had interlocking fields of fire. The 2/3rd Gurkhas and the 2nd

---

48 24 Brigade.
49 24 Brigade.
50 25 Brigade.

Leicesters were close to the Layes brook and they opened rapid fire at the last minute, leaving the area in front of their trench covered with 'piles of wriggling, heaving bodies' as 'the air resounded with shrieks, groans and curses'. Many crawled to the Indians' trench for help but over 600 dead and an equal number of wounded were later counted. Some Germans sought cover in an empty trench opposite the Leicesters but Captain McIntyre's machine guns stopped them advancing any further. The survivors eventually withdrew to Bois du Biez and those left behind waved a white flag around 9am. The 1/4th Gurkhas took some prisoners but others opened fire when Second Lieutenant McIntyre's men went forward to round them up.

The final attack was against Port Arthur. The listening posts raised the alarm by lighting up the lines of advancing German infantry with flare pistols.[51] The 1st Seaforths[52] and 1/39th Garhwal Rifles stopped the attack with rapid fire and the survivors withdrew through the mist, leaving 200 dead and wounded in front of the breastwork.

Those on the left headed past the Garhwalis' right flank until the 2nd Black Watch[53] forced them to take cover in an old trench. The trench mortars opened fire on the stranded Germans as soon as it was light and then the Black Watch bombers closed in. Nearly one hundred surrendered and around forty were shot down as they ran for it. The Garhwalis then cleared the old German front trench as far as the La Bassée road and incorporated it into their own front line.

First Army's Attacks
First Army headquarters was in the dark about the German attacks and how they had been defeated, so General Haig's operation orders still stood. A high level haze forced the pilots to fly below 300 feet, making it difficult for the aerial observers to get their bearings as they swooped low over the trenches. Haig called for a two hour postponement and the late change in the zero hour again caused problems. The haze did not clear, so the artillery had to fire blind but the attack still went ahead.

7th Division, the Quadrilateral
The German attacks had exhausted the 2nd Scots Fusiliers and the 2nd Green Howards[54] so General Capper wanted the 2nd Border Regiment and the 2nd Scots Guards[55] to advance through them towards the Quadrilateral, west of Mauquissart. Unfortunately the two runners carrying the postponement orders were killed en route and the two battalions advanced at 10.30am. Colonel Wood stopped the Borders' attack when he realised there was no artillery support and Major Paynter did the same with the 2nd

---

51 Firing flares called Very lights.
52 Dehra Dun Brigade.
53 Bareilly Brigade.
54 Both 21 Brigade.
55 Both 20 Brigade.

Scots Guards. Twenty minutes later the battalions to the flanks enquired why they had advanced so early; only then did the two commanders realise the attack had been postponed.

The Borders and Scots Guards chose to remain in no man's land and they began creeping forward as the artillery hit the German trench. One German officer later complained that the bombardment 'wasn't war, it was carnage'; the two battalions rushed the Quadrilateral and the neighbouring trench as soon as it ceased. Around 400 prisoners were taken and the Green Howards and Scots Fusiliers shot at anyone who ran.

The 1st Grenadier Guards[56] joined in and Captain Nicol took the battalion bombers along a disused communication trench. Private Edward Barber's bag of bombs was hit by a bullet so he threw them away before they exploded. He took another bag off a dead comrade and went onto capture forty metres of trench and one hundred Germans before he was killed.[57] Lance Corporal Fuller then ran after another group of fifty Germans, forcing them to surrender.[58] Around 200 prisoners were taken altogether with the help of a company of 2nd Wiltshires. Simultaneously on the opposite flank, two Wiltshire companies followed the 20 Brigade bombers through the trenches but they were unable to get far.

It was fortunate the two Guardsmen did so well because the rest of the 1st Grenadier Guards had a difficult time moving east of the Orchard. They had to swim ditches under fire and then became lost because smoke obscured all the landmarks. Lieutenant Colonel Fisher-Rowe was killed but Captain Lygon eventually got the battalion into a support position.

8th Division, Layes Bridge Redoubt
The plan was for 8th Division to capture the Layes Bridge redoubt first, so the Meerut Division's left could advance. The thirty minute bombardment on 8th Division's front would start at 10am and the Indian Corps barrage would start as soon as it lifted. But IV Corps' heavy guns fired short, hitting 2nd East Lancashires and parts of the 2nd Northants and the 1st Worcesters[59] along the Mauquissart road. General Carter reported the impending disaster but the Germans opened fire as his men abandoned their trench around 10am.[60] The guns continued shelling the trench for another two hours and the Germans reoccupied it as soon as they fell silent.

The battalion commanders along 25 Brigade's front thought their companies were too weak to recapture the German trenches either side of Layes Bridge redoubt, and they refused to advance when the bombardment stopped. But General Davies insisted General-Lowry Cole make another attempt. The 1st Irish Rifles and 2nd Rifle Brigade climbed out of their

---

56 20 Brigade.
57 Barber was posthumously awarded the Victoria Cross.
58 Fuller was also awarded the Victoria Cross.
59 24 Brigade.
60 The 1st Worcesters commanding officer, Lieutenant Colonel Wodehouse, and his adjutant, were killed.

trench at 5.15pm, following a short and ineffective bombardment and they were soon pinned down. Observers counted at least fifteen machine guns firing from the Layes Bridge redoubt.

The Indian Corps, Opposite Bois du Biez

The senior brigadier, Brigadier General Walker, was preparing for the Jullundur and Sirhind Brigades to pass through the Garhwal Brigade at 11am, following a thirty minute bombardment of Bois du Biez. But the message postponing the attack by two hours only reached Walker's headquarters ten minutes before zero hour and messengers had to run to stop the assault troops going over the top.

The Germans opposite 1/4th Gurkhas were showing signs of surrender around midday but Captain Collins thought they were trying to trick him. He decided not to go forward and attacked as planned at 1pm, capturing 150 metres of trench along the Layes stream with the help of a company of the 2nd Leicesters. The Gurkhas then cleared the trench to the left where 100 Germans, who had been hiding since the morning, surrendered; another fifty were shot as they ran away.

The Jullundur Brigade came under fire from the Layes bridge machine guns, as they were aimed at the gaps where roads and ditches cut the trenches. The 1st Manchesters could see that 25 Brigade had stopped moving to its left and then their commanding officer Captain Browne was wounded, so they halted in the Garhwal trenches astride Brewery Road. The rest of the brigade had spent a miserable two hours laid in the open waiting for the new zero hour. The 1/4th Suffolks only had 140 men still standing while the 59th Rifles only had 125; none of them made it beyond the British front line.

The 1st HLI also came under fire from the Layes bridge redoubt as it moved in short rushes, but Captains Knight and Halswelle captured the trench along the stream, taking 200 prisoners. Halswelle also took some men across the stream but they returned from the exposed position after dark. Major Young led the rest of the 1/4th Gurkhas to their company, holding the trench along the stream. Later in the afternoon Young was mortally wounded trying to help a casualty; Captains Hogg and McGann were both injured trying to rescue him.

A Further Attack Ordered

News of the early German attack soon filtered up to First Army headquarters, as did reports of large numbers surrendering. Around 1pm General Rawlinson reported 8th Division had troops at High Trees Corner and along the road to the south. While the news was promising, the German trench had been evacuated three hours earlier because the British artillery was shooting short. An hour later First Army headquarters heard 7th Division had reached Moulin du Pietre, 400 metres east of Mauquissart. Again the news was incorrect.

The combined reports gave General Haig the impression that IV Corps had broken the German line around Mauquissart. He asked for 2nd Cavalry Division to be released and Field Marshal French instructed it to prepare to move. The 5th Cavalry Brigade and two armoured motor cars were also ordered to move along Rue du Bacquerot ready to help 7th Division's anticipated advance beyond Moulin du Pietre.

Everything was looking good. The counter-attack had been defeated, the German line was broken and reinforcements were on their way. So Haig sent the following message to all his commanders just after 3pm: 'Information indicates that enemy on our front are much demoralized. IV Corps and Indian Corps will push through the barrage of fire regardless of loss, using reserves if required.' General Rawlinson received General Haig's instructions to keep advancing at 3.20pm and he visited Generals Capper and Davies to urge them to do the same. The artillery began firing at 4.40pm and would continue to do so until dusk. The problem was they thought British troops were holding the Mauquissart road rather than the Germans and fired at targets to the north and east instead. It meant the enemy front line was left untouched.

First Army headquarters was ignorant of the true situation until evening because of the usual communication problems between the battalions and the brigades. Even as late as 6.20pm Haig told French, 'in view of the promising situation, the 46th (North Midland) Division from the General Reserve might relieve the two left brigades of the Canadian Division, so these two Canadian brigades could be massed in rear of the right Canadian brigade, with a view to breaking through opposite Rouges Bancs and co-operating with the advance of the 7th Division.'

First Army headquarters was also preparing to include I Corps in the imaginary breakthrough. Haig had told General Monro to warn 1st Division so it could cooperate with the Indian Corps. That was, of course, if IV Corps and the Indian Corps continued to advance.

7th Division, the Mauquissart Road

As usual it was difficult to get any news back to divisional headquarters and General Capper had to rely on the artillery observers for information. The first real news reached him just after 1pm when he heard the Scots

Fusiliers were approaching Mauquissart while other troops had crossed the Mauquissart road; he was also told large numbers of Germans were surrendering. The news was incorrect but Capper ordered 20 and 21 Brigades to advance, regardless of loss, at 3.25pm. But the instruction bore no relation to the reality at the front line and the battalions were told to stay put. The real situation was that the Germans were working hard to turn a communication trench into a fire trench ready to stop the next attack.

On hearing reports that the Germans held the Mauquissart road in strength, Capper sent a staff officer forward to check, but it was dark before he returned with the bad news. Only the Quadrilateral had been captured and the front line battalions were in a bad way. All General Capper could do was to explain the sad state of affairs to General Rawlinson. His men had been fighting continuously for thirty-six hours and they needed a rest. His division had suffered considerable losses and was incapable of further offensive action so it was agreed to relieve it.

8th Division, East of Neuve Chapelle
General Lowry Cole reported that 25 Brigade's new attack, north of Neuve Chapelle, had failed around 5.45pm. So General Davies told General Pinney to move his 23 Brigade through 24 Brigade when it was dark and get to the road ahead, regardless of loss. But it was dark by the time the battalion commanders had gathered to hear their instructions, leaving them no time to reconnoitre the ground. Not that it would have helped because the night was misty and they would have seen nothing.

It was 9.30pm before the 2nd Devons were in position and they could not find the 2nd Scottish Rifles on their right. The 4th Camerons lost their way and came up behind the centre of the brigade around midnight, rather than on the right. The officer who had been sent to brigade headquarters to get instructions had not returned by zero hour, but the battalion commanders would eventually learn there had been a two hour delay. The gunners fired blind into the dark and did little damage to a thorn hedge which the Germans had laced with barbed wire. Many exhausted men fell asleep during the long wait and the officers had difficulty keeping them awake, sometimes mistaking the dead for the sleeping.

Zero hour was set for 1.30am and the Devons and the Scottish Rifles had advanced 200 metres astride the Sunken Road when a message calling off the attack arrived; it had taken over three hours to reach them. The Devons' left company was isolated from the rest of the battalion by a dyke, and Captain Imbert-Terry was close to the enemy lines when he heard he had to fall back; he lost thirty men withdrawing his company. Another message twenty minutes later told Brigadier General Pinney to use his 23 Brigade to consolidate the front line and he used the 2nd Middlesex, the 2nd Devons and 2nd Scottish Rifles to accomplish the task.

The Lahore Division, Facing Bois du Biez

Just after 3pm General Willcocks instructed Major General Henry Keary to advance towards the Bois du Biez at all costs. The fifteen minute barrage started at 5.50pm but it again missed the trench in front of the wood and the Jullundur and Sirhind Brigades were hit by heavy fire as they climbed out of Dehra Dun trench. No one advanced more than a few metres but Keary had already ordered the Ferozepore Brigade forward to reinforce the attack and Brigadier General Egerton would have to be told to take command of all three brigades. General Haig was visiting General Willcocks when news of the failure reached the Indian Corps headquarters. It was obvious that the Layes Bridge redoubt was a major problem, so Willcocks was told to push his right flank towards Bois du Biez and down the La Bassée road to avoid it.

A staff officer gave General Egerton instructions to attack again but he asked for time to assess the state of the three brigades first. The news was bad because both the Jullundur and Sirhind Brigades were pinned down, having lost many men. Egerton said it would be impossible to advance at the suggested time of 8.30pm and asked for a two hour delay, even though he was not confident it would succeed even then. General Keary wanted to attack again but Willcocks vetoed any more attempts, believing it was foolish to advance over unknown ground in the dark.

The Battle Draws to a Close, 13 March

Hopes for a breakthrough at Neuve Chapelle had ended on 12 March but General Capper organised one final attack on 7th Division's front at 9.30am the following morning. It was a shambles. Major Duberly found his allocated trench full of Scots Fusiliers, so the 1st Grenadier Guards spent the night laid in the open behind it. The German artillery and machine guns found their mark when it was light and Duberly was killed before zero hour. Captain Lygon was then forced to crawl along the line of shell scrapes under fire as he tried to get the message to his men.

Colonel MacLean was hit bringing the 6th Gordons forward across the battlefield, a process which took all night; his men only went 200 metres beyond the front line. The Warwicks had been unable to relieve the Wiltshires because their guides got lost, so only one company was in a position to move forward at zero hour.

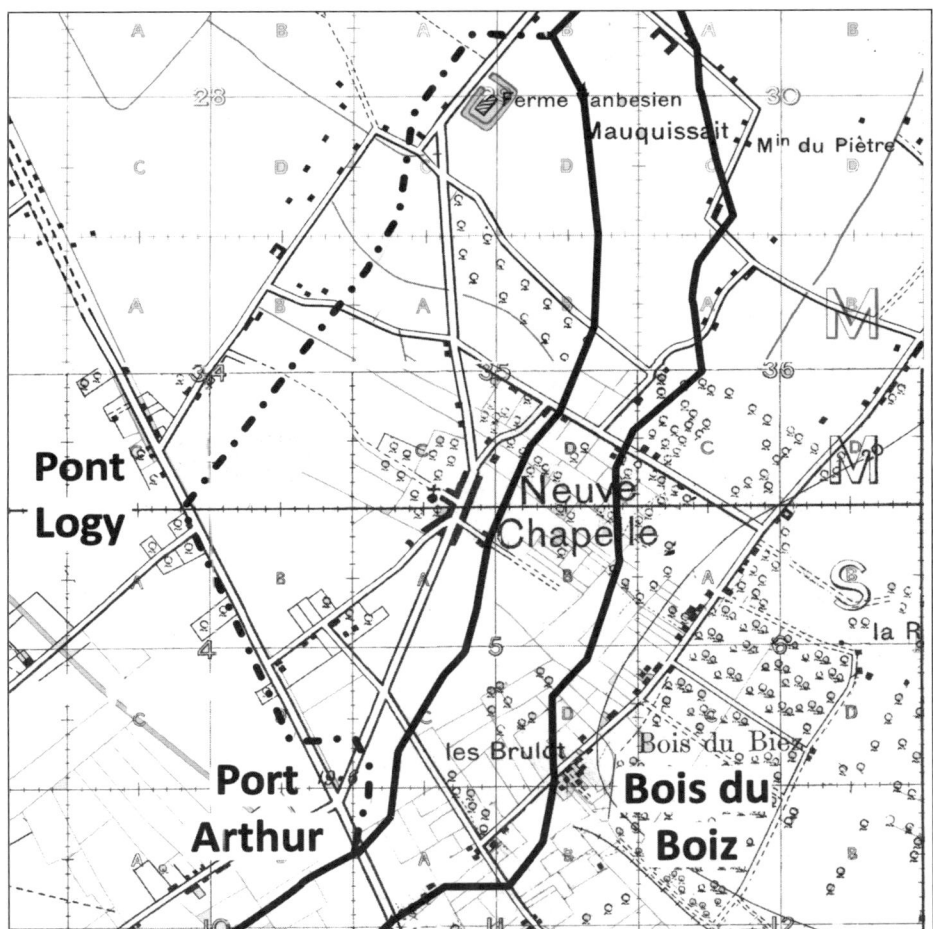

The battle of Neuve Chapelle comes to an end

The thirty minute barrage started at 9am and it hit the 2nd Gordons on the left, because the artillery observers had mistaken them for Germans. They withdrew to their support trench after Colonel Uniacke was killed and his adjutant, Major Stansfeld, was wounded. There was so much machine gun and artillery fire by the time Captain Lygon had crawled across to coordinate an advance that the decision was taken not to move. All the survivors could do was lie in the open and wait for the order to withdraw at dusk.

Postponement of Further Attacks
During the evening General Haig again learned that First Army had been unable to break the new German line east of Neuve Chapelle. On the left 7th Division had made little progress while the trenches around Layes bridge redoubt barred the way to 8th Division. The Indian Corps was also unable to advance on the right.

At 10.40pm that night, Haig issued new instructions calling for the preparation of a new defensive line. He planned to attack elsewhere instead and suggested 22 March as the date to aim for. Field Marshal French agreed and sent a message to Kitchener the following morning: 'Cessation of the forward movement is necessitated today by the fatigue of the troops and, above all, by the want of ammunition. The First Army is consolidating and strengthening its new line. Further plans are being matured for a vigorous offensive.'

Although it would be possible to move divisions to anywhere on the front, ammunition stocks were far lower than estimated. To put it bluntly, the BEF did not have enough shells to launch another offensive. French had to follow up his message to Kitchener, explaining why he had to stop all offensive action: 'The supply of gun ammunition, especially the 18-pounder and 4.5-inch howitzer, has fallen short of what I was led to expect and I am therefore compelled to abandon further offensive operations until sufficient reserves are accumulated.'

First Army brought the battle of Neuve Chapelle to a close after four days. The losses in the four attacking divisions had been high, considering only some battalions had been engaged. General Capper's 7th Division had suffered nearly 2,800 casualties on the north flank and General Davies' 8th Division had suffered over 4,800 in the centre. The Indian Corps had suffered over 4,300 casualties with the Meerut Division suffering more than half of them.[61]

Resumption of the Plan for a Combined Franco-British Offensive
Joffre was asking for another larger offensive as soon as the battle ended. The French needed until the end of April to gather their resources and the British were asked to do the same. On 1 April Field Marshal French said he hoped to be ready by 20 April but reminded Joffre that the British Government dictated his resources and he needed their answer before he could make plans. Two Territorial Army divisions had arrived but he had no information about the New Army divisions. He also noted that the new Dardanelles offensive would take up some of the resources he had been expecting.

---

61 The split was around 50 per cent British and 50 per cent Indian.

Chapter 4

A Cloud of Green Vapour
The German Gas Attack

The BEF took over the east and south-east sectors of the Ypres Salient during the first weeks of April, leaving two French divisions holding the north-east part, next to the Belgian Army. It extended Field Marshal French's front to thirty miles and he had sixteen divisions to hold it. The front line was a mixture of dry trenches and water-logged sandbagged breastworks, and while some areas had well-built defensive systems, others were little more than disconnected stretches of shallow trenches. But there were insufficient men to dig enough communication trenches and the few trenches connecting the front line to the rear were too shallow and narrow.

The French had dug a second line of trenches, complete with strongpoints, and a third line, called the GHQ Line, was planned to take advantage of the terrain. Although the French had left a reasonable defensive position, they took away their anti-aircraft guns. The number of German planes over the salient increased because the British had no guns to replace them.

Second Army received a report from General Putz on 12 April and General Smith-Dorrien forwarded it to GHQ. It said: 'An attack on the Ypres Salient has been arranged for the night 15th/16th April...' A German prisoner believed the attack 'had been prepared for noon 13th'. He was also carrying a small bag filled with cotton waste.[62] All the Germans needed was a strong wind to carry the gas across no man's land. Other prisoners reported seeing large numbers of gas cylinders along the Zillebeke front, on the south-east side of the salient. Although a raid could have settled the matter, there was insufficient heavy artillery ammunition to support one. Instead the field artillery shelled the enemy trenches to try and stir up a reaction.

---

62 The cotton waste would have been dipped into a chemical solution to counteract chlorine gas.

The Struggle for Hill 60

The Roulers railway ran through a cutting near Zillebeke, south-east of Ypres. There were two mounds of spoil, called the Dump and the Caterpillar, on the south-west side, and a higher one called Hill 60 on the north-east side. The Germans had expansive views across Ypres from the hill and the Second Army wanted it.

Major General Thomas Morland's 5th Division held the sector and 13 Brigade took over the Hill 60 sector on the night of 16/17 April. Brigadier General Wanless O'Gowan had the 1st Queen's Own and 2nd KOSBs in

The battle for Hill 60 in April 1915

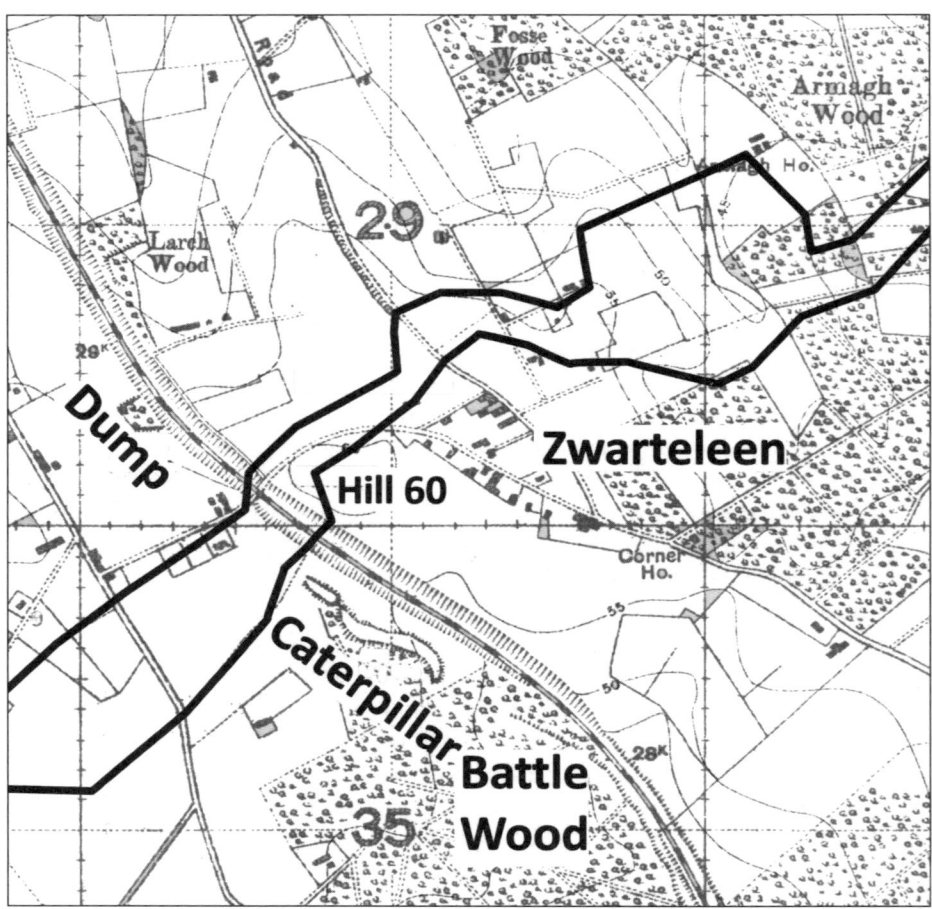

line[63] with the 2nd Duke of Wellington's in support. Starting at 7.05pm, three mines exploded at fifteen second intervals, wiping out the enemy garrison. The guns then opened fire and any Germans who showed their heads to see what was happening were hit by shrapnel and machine gun fire. Surprise was complete and Major Joslin's company of the Queen's Own took the hill with few casualties, including some hit by falling debris thrown up by the mines; Joslin was one of the men killed in the attack.

All the Germans could do was to fire their artillery at pre-registered targets, affecting Lieutenant Colonel Sladen's Queen's Own, because they had nothing with which to protect themselves. Even tear gas shells[64] had been fired at the British batteries' positions. The KOSBs took over Hill 60 as soon as it was dark and Major Robinson reported the crest was secure after midnight. But at 4am enemy infantry were spotted approaching through the darkness and Robinson's men ran at the Germans armed only with picks and shovels. The German machine guns on the Caterpillar fired across the railway while artillery fire destroyed the KOSBs' flimsy parapets. Colonel Sladen sent two Queen's Own companies to help but they were all forced back to the crest, so General Wanless O'Gowan prepared a counter-attack.

Lieutenant Colonel Turner's 2nd Duke of Wellington's took over the hill early the following morning and they re-captured the crest at 6pm with the help of Lieutenant Colonel Withycombe's 2nd KOYLIs. The Germans again retaliated and one shell hit the brigade headquarters at Transport Farm, killing the staff captain and injuring others. The 1st Bedfords[65] and 1st East Surrey[66] took over the front line, only for the fighting to start again on the 20th.

Captain George Roupell of the 1st East Surrey was wounded several times but he remained in command of his company, even returning after having his wounds dressed during a lull in the fighting. When the situation became precarious he went back to ask Major Paterson for reinforcements and then led them forward under heavy fire to make sure they reached the right spot as quickly as possible. Roupell held his position and was one of only a handful of his company to survive; he was awarded the Victoria Cross.

Corporal Edward Dwyer had crawled into no man's land to administer first aid during the early stages of the attack. When a bombing attack threatened to drive his comrades back, he climbed into the open and ran along a trench, hurling bombs at the Germans below. Dwyer's actions were rewarded with the Victoria Cross. By nightfall the only officer still standing was Lieutenant Geoffrey Woolley; he and a few men held on, hurling bombs

---

63 The Queen Victoria's Rifles supplied a machine gun section.
64 The first time gas of any sort had been used in the Great War.
65 15 Brigade.
66 14 Brigade attached to 15 Brigade.

at anyone who came near. Woolley would be the first Territorial Force officer to be awarded the Victoria Cross.

The 1st Devons[67] would take over the sector on 21 April and the fighting ended soon after, because the Germans launched the threatened gas attack north-east of Ypres the following afternoon. The struggle for Hill 60 had cost 5th Division over 100 officers and 3,000 men; it was only the size of a football field.

The First Gas Attack, 22 April
The Belgians held the canal line north of Ypres and two French Territorial Divisions held a five-mile sector between Steenstraat and the Poelcappelle road, north of Langemarck. The recently arrived Canadian Division was on V Corps' left, north-east of St Julien and Lieutenant General Sir Edwin Alderson had 3 and 2 Canadian Brigades in line, each with two battalions in the front line. Next came 28th Division, and Major General Edward Bulfin had 85 and 84 Brigades, each with all four battalions in line, covering Zonnebeke and Polygon Wood.

The 22nd was a bright spring day and there was the usual morning bombardment of Ypres while German planes circled in the distance noting the fall of shot. Once the guns had registered their targets, they fell quiet. The bombardment of Ypres and villages behind the British line resumed at 5pm but this time the observers spotted something unusual. Two clouds formed in front of the enemy trench either side of Langemarck and they joined up creating 'a cloud of green vapour several hundred metres in length'. The Germans had released over 160 tons of chlorine gas from dozens of cylinders in around seven minutes.

A gentle wind pushed the gas slowly[68] across no man's land while German infantry walked behind it. Everyone smelt an acrid smell, then their eyes watered and their throats and noses tingled as the chlorine started irritating their lungs and mucous membranes. Some men ran and inhaled more gas, due to their laboured breathing. Some lay down in their trenches where the gas settled; the wounded would suffer the most. Those who stood still on the fire-step suffered the least because the gas drifted past them.

Most of the French Territorials ran rather than wait to see what horrors came next. The men of the 87th (Territorial) Division crossed the canal around Boesinghe, north of Ypres, or headed south through Pilckem. The African troops of the 45th (Algerian) Division fell back from the Canadians left flank and across V Corps' back areas.

Many British observers could see the phenomenon, including General Alderson of the Canadian Division and Major General Horace Smith-

---

67 14 Brigade.
68 Around five miles an hour.

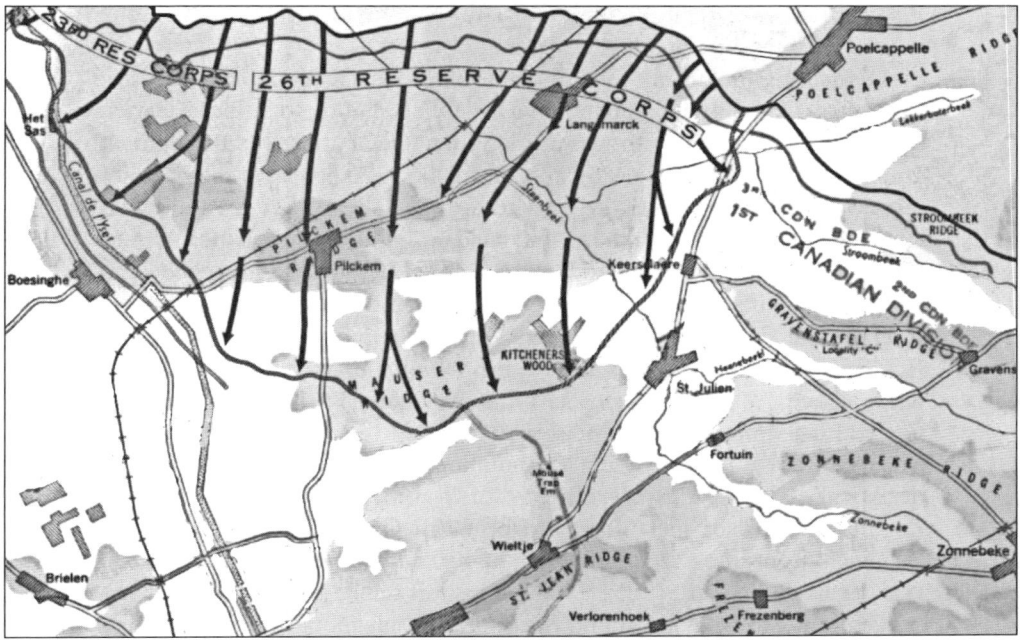

The extent of the gas attack on 22 April 1915

Dorrien of the 27th Division. They saw the French troops streaming back in panic, gasping and clutching at their throats. They also watched the French field guns being hauled back one by one, until they all fell silent.

The Belgians held onto the canal north of Steenstraat, forming a defensive flank along a communication trench. A few Germans crossed the canal at Steenstraat but they were unable to cross anywhere else. The main thrust of the German advance was towards Boesinghe on their right, Pilckem in their centre and through Langemarck, behind the Canadian flank.

The 3 Canadian Brigade had 13th and 15th Battalions, in line south of Poelcappelle. The gas missed a few of the 1st Tirailleurs and 1/2nd Zouaves and they remained on Lieutenant Colonel Loomis' left flank. The Germans moved parallel with the St Julien road, annihilating two platoons of the 13th Canadian Battalion, north of Keerselaere crossroads. They ran into sixty men of 14th and 15th Battalions and they protected two of 10th Canadian Battery's guns near Keerselaere, while they could fire, until the last moment. Lance-Corporal Frederick Fisher's detachment of the 13th Battalion kept firing their Colt machine guns while the limbers hauled the guns to safety.

Fisher was awarded the Victoria Cross for helping to save the guns but he was killed the following day.

On hearing the news of the disaster, Brigadier General Turner ordered Lieutenant Colonel Meighan to move his 14th Battalion to his headquarters at Mouse Trap Farm, south-west of St Julien. One company was deployed around Hampshire Farm, north-west of the farm, as the rest of the battalion moved north-east to cover the roads out of St Julien. They then did what General Alderson asked of them: they held on. Time after time the Germans tried to capture Mouse Trap Farm and St Julien but they never reached them.

General Turner received the 16th Canadian Battalion from divisional reserve. The 10th Canadians were also sent to help but Lieutenant Colonel Boyle deployed in the GHQ Line covering Wieltje because the road forward was blocked. As the situation deteriorated, General Turner asked Brigadier General Currie for more help around 7pm and Lieutenant Colonel Hart-McHarg was told to move his 7th Battalion behind Turner's front; so half deployed at Spree Farm, south-east of St Julien, as the rest moved to Locality C, east of the village. At nightfall General Turner reported 3 Brigade's front line was holding and he had companies deployed between Hampshire Farm and St Julien, behind his left flank.

General Smith-Dorrien and Second Army headquarters did not hear about the gas attack until around 6.45pm. General Putz reported his right was at Pilckem and there were no organised units covering the 3,000 metre gap to the Canadian left. The question was, could Second Army's reserves reach the Canadian Division before the Germans exploited the breakthrough? Brigadier General Mercer was ordered to move 1 Canadian Brigade to the Vlamertinghe area, west of Ypres, and report to V Corps. Lieutenant General Herbert Plumer in turn gave the 2nd and 3rd Battalions to General Alderson and they were sent to help 3 Canadian Brigade.

Generals Snow and Bulfin moved parts of 27th and 28th Divisions' reserves forward without waiting for orders and while some gathered around St Jean and Potijze, others secured Brielen Bridge over the canal north of Ypres. They all sent patrols forward to locate the extent of the German breakthrough. Four battalions were grouped together under Colonel Geddes of the 2nd Buffs[69] and they were placed under the Canadian Division. General Bulfin had also sent the 2nd Cheshires and 1st Monmouths forwards and they had deployed as a local reserve on the Frezenberg ridge.

By 9pm there was a three-mile gap in the Allied line between Brielen Bridge and the left of the Canadian Division. There were a few Zouaves and 3 Canadian Brigade's reserves around Mouse Trap Farm and Lieutenant Colonel Loomis had two companies covering St Julien. The 13th

---

69 Called the Geddes Detachment.

Canadians' left company had fallen back east of the St Julien–Poelcappelle road but Captain Tomlinson led two platoons back to the front line.

The attack had struck while many of the Canadian field batteries[70] were being relieved and they had been unable to give covering fire. The 2nd London Battery had abandoned their guns in Kitchener's Wood while many of the French batteries had stood silent since the gas enveloped their positions. The rest of the Allied artillery brigades had to withdraw to the outskirts of Ypres, where they had to re-establish communications before they could start firing at targets.

The Germans had achieved a breakthrough but they could have done much more with better planning. General Balck would later report that the effects of the gas had been underestimated and he did not have enough reserves to continue the advance. The infantry had no masks and they were wary of advancing into the gas cloud, so they had started digging in as early as 7.30pm. After the initial shock of the attack, the battlefield was soon quiet.

General Plumer received the first report from the French around 8.45pm. It stated that the first formed unit west of the Canadian line was at Steenstraat. Second Army had a gap of 8,000 metres on its left and the Germans were only two miles from Ypres, with nothing to stop them reaching the town. The nearest reserves were the Cavalry Corps and the Northumbrian Division[71] and they were fifteen miles to the west. To make matters worse, every road was being shelled, making it difficult to move troops to the front.

At midnight General Smith-Dorrien told GHQ that Lieutenant General Alderson had formed a new flank facing north. Field Marshal French also heard that the French were preparing to attack at 4.30am. Meanwhile, the French had told General Alderson they intended to make an immediate counter-attack towards Pilckem and 3 Canadian Brigade was expected to capture Kitchener's Wood. But it was nearly midnight before Lieutenant Colonel Boyle ordered his 10th Battalion to advance with Lieutenant Colonel Leckie's 16th Battalion in support. The Canadians advanced in lines thirty metres apart and while they were unable to see that the French had not moved to their left, they could see the wood silhouetted up ahead. They broke into a jog when the Germans opened fire from the perimeter and while Colonel Boyle was mortally wounded, his men cleared the wood and dug in north-east of the trees.

Artillery fire reduced the two Canadian battalions to around 400 men but Lieutenant Colonel Watson sent some of the 2nd Battalion forward to reinforce the position during the early hours. But as soon as it was light the

---

70 They would not be reunited with their infantry brigades until after 4 May.
71 50th (Northumbrian) Division.

Canadians discovered there were parties of Germans all around the wood and the only sensible option was to fall back to the German trench on the south edge of the wood. Only 500 men made it back, abandoning the London heavy guns in the wood for a second time. While 2nd Battalion reinforced the Canadian left, 3rd Battalion prolonged the right towards St Julien. Colonel Geddes had also been instructed to contact General Turner's battalions while three 7th Battalion companies moved through St Julien and stopped the German advance from Keerselaere. While the situation had been stabilised for the time being, there was still a mile wide gap between Keerselaere and the Canadian's original front line, near Poelcappelle.

Exploiting the Breach, 23 April
Confusion still reigned at dawn on 23 April but aerial reconnaissance soon confirmed the disastrous situation. The French had lost all their artillery and they had no reinforcements close by. Only a few small groups of men could be seen and there was little if no organised defensive line.

Two ad hoc groups were given orders to deploy north of Ypres and close the two-mile gap between the canal and Kitchener's Wood. Both Brigadier General Mercer who had two Canadian battalions[72] and Colonel Geddes who had three and a half battalions[73] were instructed to cooperate with a French advance, taking any troops they found forward with them. The idea was to seize Mauser Ridge, depriving the Germans of the views across the Ypres Salient, before they had time to dig in.

Brigadier General Mercer[74] had orders to cooperate with a French counter-attack at 5.25am and Lieutenant Colonel Birchall led his 4th Battalion from the Brielen Bridge astride the Pilckem Road while the 1st Battalion followed. There was little artillery support and the Canadians came under fire from Mauser Ridge and Turco Farm. Birchall's men took cover behind a bank over 600 metres from the enemy and Lieutenant Colonel Hill deployed his 1st Canadian Battalion to the left.

Hill's Canadians could not see the French on their flank and for a time thought they were hidden by hedges. They were wrong, the French had not advanced. All manner of shrapnel, high-explosive and gas shells hit the Canadians, making it difficult to dig in. Eventually the Zouaves were spotted advancing to the north-west around 7am but they too could get nowhere near the enemy line on Mauser Ridge.

Geddes' Detachment had to cover the approaches to Ypres but Colonel Geddes had few staff and it took time to find all the battalions, meaning it was daylight before they were ready to advance towards Mauser Ridge. Two 3rd Middlesex companies found the French flank near the canal, so

---

72 1 Canadian Brigade.
73 28th Division.
74 1 Canadian Brigade.

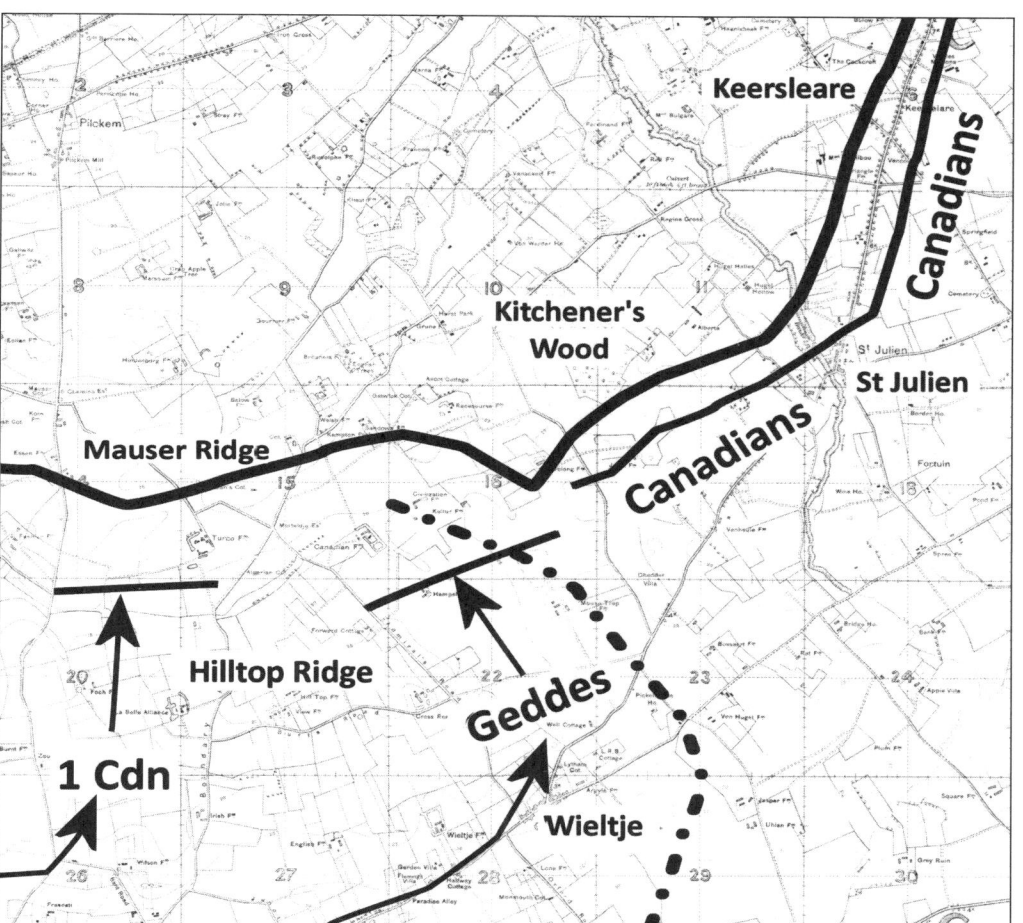

13 Brigade and Geddes Detachment attack Mauser Ridge on 23 April 1915

Lieutenant Colonel Stephenson could deploy his men to the east. The 2nd
Buffs found 3 Canadian Brigade near Kitchener's Wood and Major Power
deployed his men towards Mouse Trap Farm, using old French trenches.
Power's men covered the GHQ Line, freeing the 14th Canadian Battalion
to dig a new support trench behind 3 Canadian Brigade's line in Kitchener's
Wood. The 5th King's Own then moved forward in the centre, with the 1st
York and Lancaster following. Although they were supposed to find the
flanks of the other two battalions, Lieutenant Colonel Lord Cavendish

stopped the advance behind the crest of Hill Top Ridge, because of the volume of fire coming from Mauser Ridge.

A lull now took place as the thin line of British and Canadian battalions waited for the next German attack and watched for reinforcements. Although seven battalions were heading to the area, they came from different units and there were no staff officers available to coordinate their movements. The Northumbrian Division[75] was also moving forward, some on foot and others on buses. Two brigades of the 4th Division and the Lahore Division had also been warned to be ready to march to the area and Second Army still had the Cavalry Corps in reserve.

Although reinforcements were moving to Ypres, they could not hold the town if the French fell back again. Field Marshal French visited Foch and was assured he too had reinforcements heading to the area to regain the ground. French agreed the British would participate in any counter-attacks but he also made it clear that Second Army would have to withdraw from the salient if its flank was endangered.

Geddes's Detachment and 13 Brigade
Generals Mercer and Geddes had been digging in and waiting for the next French attack, but it failed to materialise. Their men had formed a continuous line by mid-morning but Smith-Dorrien and Plumer wanted to drive the Germans off Mauser Ridge. So they planned an advance with 13 Brigade on the left of the Pilckem road and Geddes' detachment to the right. Unfortunately, no one told Geddes he was acting under Brigadier General Wanless O'Gowan and he continued to act independently.

General Putz was also planning to advance alongside the British and his French troops interfered with 13 Brigade's deployment, so zero hour had to be postponed. Mercer's battalions then drifted into the French zone and arrived late. Wanless O'Gowan went forward only to find there was a gap between the French and British troops but he did not have time to make a full reconnaissance of the area.

Zero hour was eventually set at 4.25pm but no one told the artillery it had changed and the guns opened fire at 2.45pm, putting the Germans on the alert. The artillery then had insufficient shells to fire a second preliminary bombardment when the infantry eventually advanced. The Zouaves moved at the same time, crowding in on Captain Moulton-Barrett's 1st Queen's Own near the canal, so only one platoon could advance at a time. Captains Anderson and Bland led the 2nd KOSBs but they were pinned down in an old trench some 300 metres from the German line. Captain Bland took one party forward until they were all killed. While the

---

75 Later the 50th (Northumbrian) Division.

KOSBs suffered 240 casualties, Colonel Robinson would have realised the Zouave interference in his deployment had saved many of his battalion. The 2nd KOYLIs were able to move up on his left when the Zouaves fell back.

Lieutenant Colonel Tuson, of the 2nd DCLI, had been placed in charge of the composite brigade on the right of the attack. Each battalion advanced in five or six lines, thirty minutes after the troops to their flanks moved off. They soon disappeared into a cloud of dust and smoke. Heavy officer casualties meant there was no news for some time.

Captains Dene and Tatton were wounded leading the DCLI to Turco Farm on Mauser Ridge, where an artillery observer was shot with a phone receiver in his hand. Major Cameron led two 9th Royal Scots companies on their right up to a hedge threaded with barbed wire. Lieutenant Lyon cut gaps so Captain Green and Captain Moncreiff could advance towards Hampshire Farm where they were reinforced by Lieutenant Colonel Blair and the rest of the battalion.

Although they had driven the Germans off Mauser Ridge, Brigadier Wanless O'Gowan and Colonel Geddes had to withdraw their men under cover of darkness due to the volume of fire. They started digging in some 600 metres from the enemy, only to find water close to the surface, leaving them standing in deep mud. There were few officers left to supervise the men but still they dug, and in some cases 'daylight found them digging in facing the wrong way'. It had also been difficult to find the new line in the darkness and little food and ammunition came forward. But the line was safe for the time being and the two Canadian battalions[76] and the twenty survivors of the two Middlesex companies could be withdrawn.

The Belgians and French still held the canal line, but the Germans captured Lizerne, leaving seven bridges in their hands. Nightfall found 13Brigade holding a line from Fusilier Farm to Glimpse Cottage to South Zwaanhof Farm, improving the situation on V Corps' left. A thankful General Alderson wrote: 'Words cannot express what the Canadians owe the 13th for their splendid attack and the way they restored confidence.' Although Field Marshal French had fulfilled his promise to Foch, every available battalion had been committed and most of them had suffered heavy casualties. The tragedy was the ground in front of Mauser Ridge could have been occupied during the night without any casualties.

3 Canadian Brigade under Attack, 23 April
North of St Julien, 7th Battalion stopped the Germans advancing from Keerselaere into St Julien, but Lieutenant Colonel McHarg was mortally wounded as he reconnoitred the ground in front of his battalion. There was

---

76 The 1st Canadian Battalion suffered over 400 casualties and 4th Canadian Battalion lost over 500.

then a gap of 1,500 metres to where the 13th Canadians and Captain Tomlinson's company of 2nd Buffs were holding the original trenches facing Poelcappelle. Lieutenant Colonel Loomis' men were subjected to bombing attacks while heavy fire stopped supplies getting through. General Alderson suggested abandoning the exposed apex and they withdrew to a shorter line at nightfall without interference. The German bombers entered the deserted trenches during the night.

Another Gas Attack against 3 and 2 Canadian Brigades, 24 April

The loss of Lizerne along the canal during the night increased the threat to Second Army's left. So much so that Chief of the General Staff, Lieutenant General Sir William Robertson, reminded General Smith-Dorrien he had to fight east of the canal to stop the Germans driving the French back any further. But the next attack hit the apex where the 13th Canadian Battalion and the 2nd Buffs company had withdrawn to a safer line between 7th and 15th Canadian Battalion. A short bombardment hit the apex at 4am while wind pushed a cloud of gas across the north-east side of the salient. It engulfed Lieutenant Colonel Currie's 15th Battalion[77] and Lieutenant Colonel Lipsett's 8th Battalion[78] before it drifted south-west towards Locality C.

The Canadians manned the parapet with damp handkerchiefs, towels and bandoliers tied around their faces. Many fell into the trench, writhing in agony as they breathed the gas but the rest shot at the approaching German infantry the best they could. Their Ross rifles kept jamming due to the mud and the men had to kick the bolts open with their boot heel or hammer them with their entrenching tools, reducing the rate of fire to a feeble level. To make matters worse, the artillery batteries behind 15th Battalion had been withdrawn to the GHQ Line and they were out of effective range. All 15th Battalion could do was retire over 1,200 metres to an old trench along the road between Keerselaere and Locality C. A few men of the 15th Battalion remained behind on the left and 7th Battalion's machine gun officer, Lieutenant Edward Bellew, kept firing until he ran out of ammunition. He then destroyed the weapon and fought on with rifle butt and bayonet until he was taken prisoner; he was awarded the Victoria Cross.[79]

The Germans failed to drive 8th Battalion out of its trenches and its reserves covered the open flank. After seeing Corporal Payne and Private Robertson injured trying to rescue an injured man, Company Sergeant Major Frederick Hall went to him only to be mortally wounded as he lifted him up; he was posthumously awarded the Victoria Cross.

---

77 3 Canadian Brigade.
78 2 Canadian Brigade.
79 Lieutenant Bellew did not learn of the award until he was released in 1919.

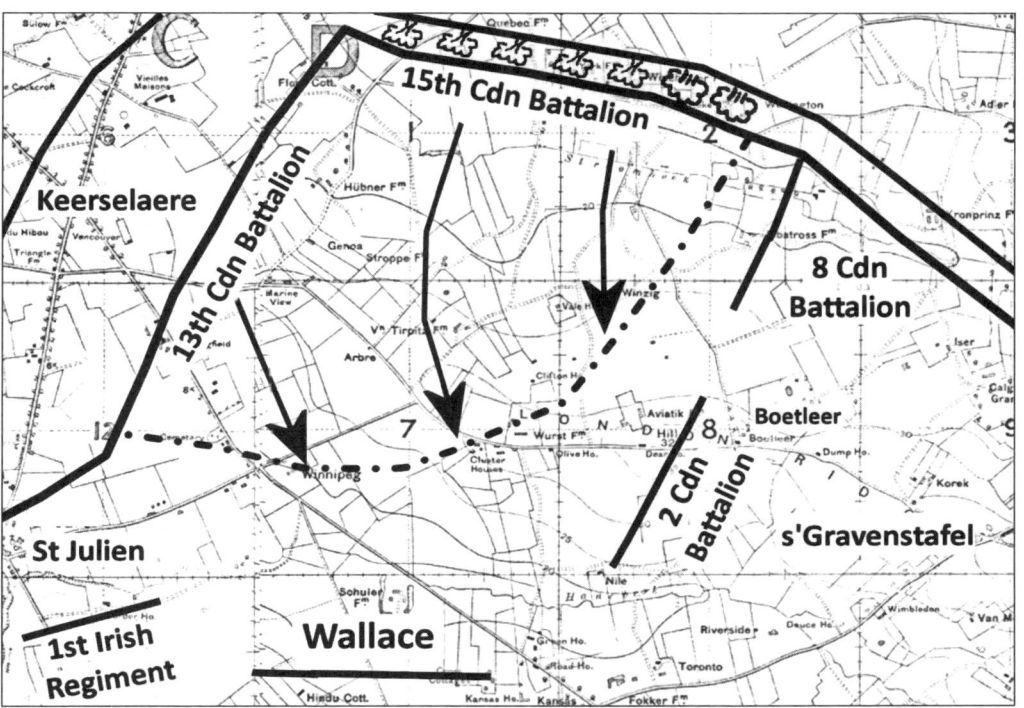

A gas attack against the Canadian Apex position on 24 April 1915

On hearing news of the breakthrough, Brigadier General Turner told 2nd Battalion[80] to take over Kitchener's Wood so the 10th and 16th Battalions,[81] both of them very weak, could form a rally line behind the breakthrough. The Canadian Division headquarters heard that the flanks of the gap, where 15th Battalion should have been, were safe, but the situation was about to get worse.

The Germans attacked 13th Battalion around Keerselaere from the front and the rear as soon as it was light. Major Buchanan's men held them at bay to begin with but the observers in Poelcappelle's houses directed their guns onto the Canadians as soon as they saw them moving. The Canadian guns did not reply and 13th Battalion had lost over half its number before Buchanan ordered a retirement parallel with the Gravenstafel road. Two platoons and Captain Tomlinson's company of Buffs did not get the order so they fought on until captured, increasing the gap in the Canadian line to around a mile.

---

80 1 Canadian Brigade.
81 Both 3 Canadian Brigade.

General Alderson responded to the bad news by ordering the 4th East Yorkshires and 4th Green Howards[82] to the GHQ Line covering Wieltje. The other two battalions of the Yorkshire Brigade[83] re-joined their headquarters soon after. General Plumer heard the first rumour about the break-in around 7.40am but it was another four hours before the news was confirmed. He placed the Durham Brigade[84] under the Cavalry Corps so it could help man the defences along the canal.

The Attack on St Julien and Left Flank
The Germans had achieved their first objective and after regrouping they attacked the new Canadian line, starting with a pincer movement on St Julien around 11am. General Turner was out of touch with the front line so Lieutenant Colonel Burland of 14th Battalion, Major Odlum of 7th Battalion and Lieutenant Colonel Currie of 15th Battalion met at the crossroads between St Julien and Locality C. They agreed to withdraw their men from the forward slope of Gravenstafel ridge, to get them out of sight of the German artillery observers, and the move would begin on the left. The men north of St Julien made a fighting withdrawal across the fields east of the village but it was soon clear observers could see them because they were under heavy artillery fire.

General Alderson had wanted to hold onto Keerselaere until 10 Brigade arrived but the Germans had other ideas. They struck 3rd Canadian Brigade's right, near Locality C, and then its left, north-east of St Julien. The three Canadian battalion commanders met again and agreed to withdraw for a second time before they were overrun. Their men fell back in small groups, but they again came under heavy fire on the new line, so the withdrawal continued as far as the road between Wieltje and Gravenstafel. Only Captain Warden's company of the 7th Battalion remained behind around Locality C, stopping the enemy from widening the gap in the Canadian line.

The Germans were crossing the Canadian trenches covering St Julien by 1pm. General Turner wanted to withdraw to the GHQ Line, where stragglers were gathering, because he thought his men would be cut to pieces withdrawing across the low-lying ground if the village fell. He told General Alderson's chief general staff officer, Colonel Romer, his dilemma and the divisional headquarters told him to use the East Yorkshires and Green Howards 'to strengthen your line and hold on'. But Turner misunderstood the instruction and issued orders to fall back to the GHQ Line. Only it was not as simple as that.

Part of the 2nd Battalion withdrew from Kitchener's Wood on the left

---

82 Both of the Yorkshire Brigade.
83 Later renumbered 150 Brigade.
84 Later renumbered 151 Brigade.

while the 7th and 10th Battalions eventually rallied south-east of Fortuin on the right. But 2nd Battalion's right and 3rd Battalion faced a dangerous move across flat, open ground between the wood and St Julien. So Major Kirkpatrick decided it was better to stand and fight the Germans advancing astride the Steenbeek stream towards the village.

Turner's plan to rally his troops in the GHQ Line had made the situation worse, especially when the Germans moved into St Julien after overrunning Major Kirkpatrick's group.[85] On hearing the news, General Snow told General Turner to move every available unit forward to stop them advancing any further. Captain Balders was instructed to hold Fortuin with the 1st Suffolks[86] while Turner organised a counter-attack with six battalions. He already had the 1st Irish Regiment,[87] and the 4th Canadian Battalion[88] was on its way forward. But the 2nd KOYLIs and 1/9th London[89] had to dig in behind the crowded GHQ Line, as the 4th Green Howards and 4th East Yorkshires assembled near Potijze.

The Green Howards and East Yorkshires were immediately told to deploy in front of the GHQ Line when the news that St Julien had fallen was heard. They moved north-east to Fortuin in artillery formation where they had to lie in the open because the few trenches were full of men. After receiving confusing orders about supporting a Canadian attack, they came under heavy howitzer fire as they advanced towards St Julien. Nearby Canadian guns fired over open sights at the Germans, leaving the village as the Yorkshiremen advanced past the Irish Regiment. The Irishmen were so impressed by Lieutenant Colonel Bell's Green Howards, they nicknamed them the 'Yorkshire Gurkhas'. The German attack collapsed in the face of the Yorkshiremen's advance, but the cost had been high. Lieutenant Colonel Shaw was shot by a sniper at the head of the East Yorkshires while Major Matthews and Captains Eykyn and Nancarrow were killed leading the Green Howards.

Meanwhile, the 1/9th London and 1st Suffolks advanced north-east to find Germans dug in along the road between Keerselaere to Zonnebeke while British artillery continued to shell the area. Lieutenant Colonel Wallace's Suffolks lost 280 casualties while Lieutenant Colonel Bayliffe and sixty men of the 1/9th London were wounded. While Wallace was away, a staff officer ordered Captain Balders to move forward but he first used a stray artillery horse to ride back to get permission from his commanding officer. Balders returned to be met by a wounded Canadian officer who pleaded with him to send troops forward before the line broke. He sent two companies and Lieutenant Bradley found the 200 survivors of 7th and 10th Canadian Battalions fighting for their lives at Boetleer's Farm.

---

85 Only 43 wounded survivors returned.
86 84 Brigade, 28th Division.
87 The 1st Irish Regiment was down to around 350 men.
88 1st Canadian Brigade.
89 13 Brigade.

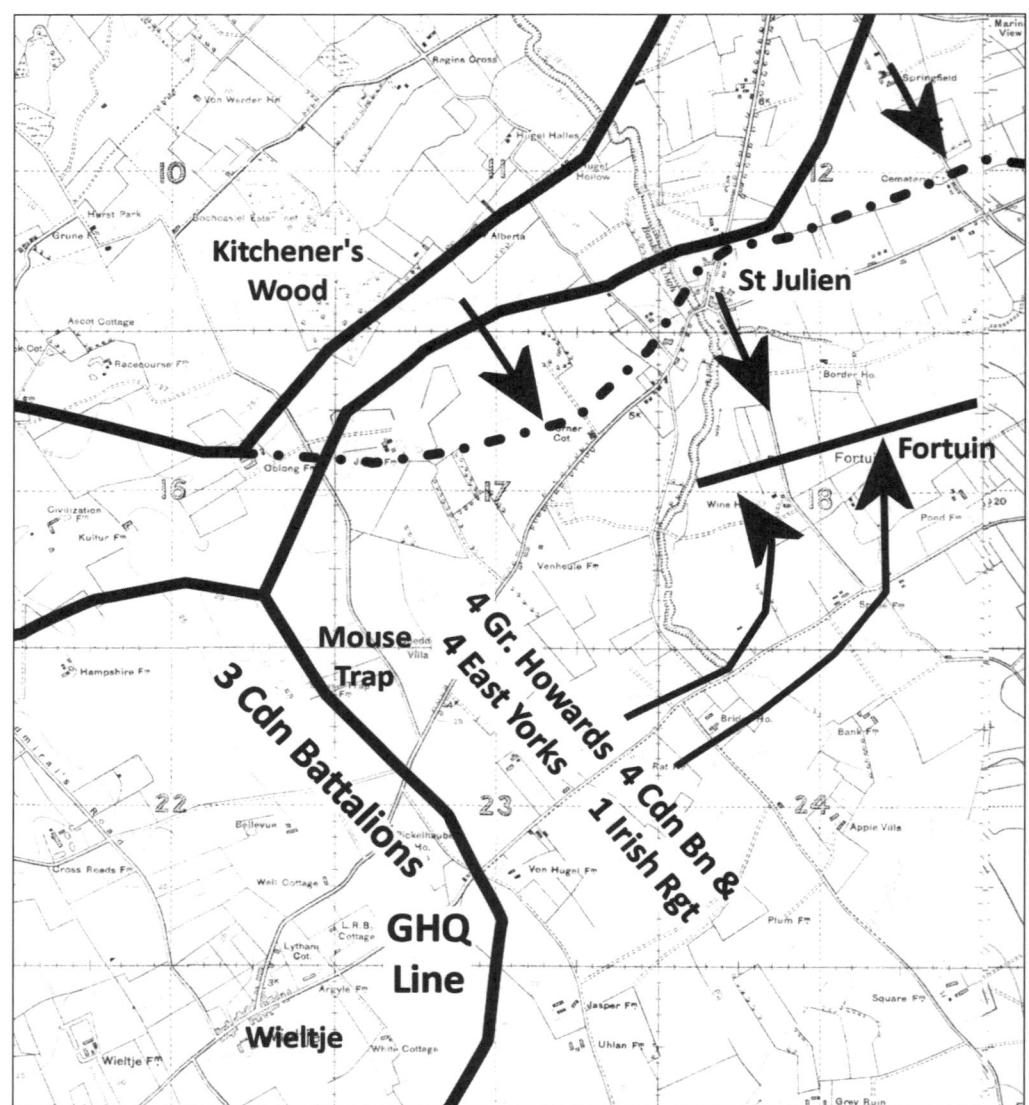

The Yorkshiremen counter-attack towards St Julien on 24 April 1915

The two Yorkshire battalions and the Irish Regiment were eventually withdrawn into reserve while Major Odlum's Canadians covered the gap south of St Julien. The group of Londoners and Suffolks were pulled back from their exposed position behind the Keerselaere to Gravenstafel road while Major Moulton-Barrett gathered a mixed group of the 2nd Northumberland Fusiliers, the 2nd Cheshires and the 1st Monmouths south-west of Gravenstafel. After dusk Lieutenant Colonel Lipsett asked Moulton-Barrett to reinforce the Canadian left, by joining Lieutenant Bradley's Suffolks south-west of Boetleer's Farm. Major Johnson also sent a company of the 8th Middlesex to the farm while 28th Division sent reinforcements to the Canadian's right flank, north of Gravenstafel.

Reinforcements and Plans
General Plumer had sent the Northumbrian Brigade's[90] four battalions to Potijze during the afternoon '…for the purpose of repelling any advance on the part of the enemy from the north and north-east. I place it under your orders as it will be close to you, and if communication is cut and you cannot refer to me, you will use the brigade at your discretion.' It would be dark before they reached their destination, soon to be followed by the Northumbrian Division's final brigade, the Durham Brigade. Plumer had also told General Snow 'to make every effort to restore the situation where the Germans are reported to have broken through,' and he had done.

But Second Army had to hold on until the French had secured the left flank, otherwise it would have to evacuate the salient. General Robertson wrote to Smith-Dorrien to make Field Marshal French's views clear: 'He does not wish you to give up any ground if it can be helped, but if pressure from the north becomes such that the 28th Division ought to fall back from its line, then of course it must fall back, for such distance as circumstances necessitate. But we hope the necessity will not arise. The Germans must be a bit tired by now, and they are numerically inferior to us as far as we can judge. In fact, there seems no doubt about it.' Robertson was also calling for offensive action in cooperation with the French.

Smith-Dorrien in turn told Plumer that Lieutenant General Edmund Allenby's Cavalry Corps would support the French along the canal while he attacked with all his available reserves. Plumer instructed General Alderson to counter-attack but daylight was fading by the time General Hull[91] was given the order. While he had fifteen battalions[92] they were from different divisions and he had to organise everything in the dark ready to attack Kitchener's Wood and St Julien at 3.30am. He had no staff officers and no signal company to coordinate them all; and then the rain began, soaking everyone and everything.

General Hull did not know the ground and he could not check it in the dark. He called a briefing but only Brigadier General Burstall of the Canadian Divisional Artillery attended, while General Riddell of the

---

90 Later renumbered 149 Brigade.
91 10th Brigade.
92 The 10 Brigade, the 150 Brigade, the 2nd KOYLIs and Queen Victoria's Rifles of 13 Brigade, the 1st Suffolk and the Rangers, the 4th Canadian Battalion and the 1st Irish Regiment.

Northumbrian Brigade turned up by accident. When Hull eventually reached Wieltje he found his troops queuing up to pass through the two narrow gaps in the GHQ Line wire. There was no way everyone would be deployed south of St Julien in time, so he postponed the attack until 5.30am, knowing it would be getting light by the time they advanced.

By midnight Plumer knew V Corps' situation so he ordered the Yorkshire Brigade and Alderson's Force to fill the gap between what was left of 3 Canadian Brigade and 2 Canadian Brigade. But they first had to locate the flanks of the gap and close it before the Germans attacked again and time was running out.

Protecting the Men from Gas

There was the problem of what to do about the danger from another gas attack. The first instructions told everyone to wet a handkerchief or cloth with water or urine and then tie it across their mouth and nose. Next came the recommendation that each division collect materials so everyone could have some protection. Lieutenant Colonel Ferguson, 28th Division's medical officer, had suggested making lint masks which could be tied around the face with tape. The lint could be dipped in a bicarbonate of soda solution whenever there was a whiff of gas in the air. The problem was where to get the materials from so officers were sent to Paris to buy them. The next problem was how to distribute the masks and solution to the thousands of men at the front.

GHQ would open an experimental laboratory to study gas on 26 April and Professors Watson, Haldane and Baker arrived over the next few days. They came up with a design for a respirator which included gauze to protect the eyes, nose and mouth. The *Daily Mail* newspaper even put out a plea calling on the women of England to make a million gas masks for the soldiers at the front. Early in May Major Cluny McPherson of the Newfoundland Medical Corps and Professor Watson proposed a design for the gas helmet. Then there was the problem of how to warn everyone. The wind direction had to be watched, observers had to keep a look out and an alarm system had to be put in place. But Second Army first had to secure its open flank around St Julien.

Chapter 5

Hang On at all Costs

An Attack on St Julien, 25 April

Brigadier General Hull had been expecting a great deal of artillery support for his morning attack on 25 April but 28th and 27th Divisions' batteries did not hear about the change in zero hour. The guns fired at the original time and they had few shells left when the infantry advanced at 5.30am. Meanwhile, the Canadian batteries struggled to hit their targets at long range because their observers could not see far in the overcast weather.

The lack of staff to give out orders meant that few of the fifteen battalions allocated to General Hull were ready, even for the postponed hour. Some battalions were unaware of the orders to clear Kitchener's Wood and St Julien until it was too late. It was misty when the four battalions[93] moved through the troops holding the GHQ Line, Second Army's last line of defence.

Only the 5th Durhams and 5th Green Howards[94] advanced at the original hour, 3.30am, towards Fortuin on the right flank. They came under shell fire as they moved forward and saw no one else advancing, only Germans coming towards them. So they fell back, went prone and took aim having been told 'the position must be held at any cost as there is no support or second line upon which we might fall back.' Captain Barber occupied a farm between the lines during the stalemate that followed but his men fell back after he was killed. The rest of the Durhams and Howards fell back as far as Verlorenhoek, over a mile to the south, having lost nearly 300 men.

The rest of General Hull's battalions discovered snipers hiding in the crops. The officers encouraged their men to advance by rushes, running and firing platoon by platoon, and the snipers shot at them as they did so. Lieutenant Colonel Poole's 1st Warwicks came under fire from Oblong Farm and Lieutenant Colonel Vandeleur's 2nd Seaforths were shot at from Juliet Farm. Machine guns in Kitchener's Wood opened fire as they drew closer and the advance stopped 400 metres from the trees. General Hull instructed Lieutenant Colonel Carden to try and go further but his 7th

---

93 All from 10 Brigade, 4th Division.
94 Both 150 Brigade, 50th Division.

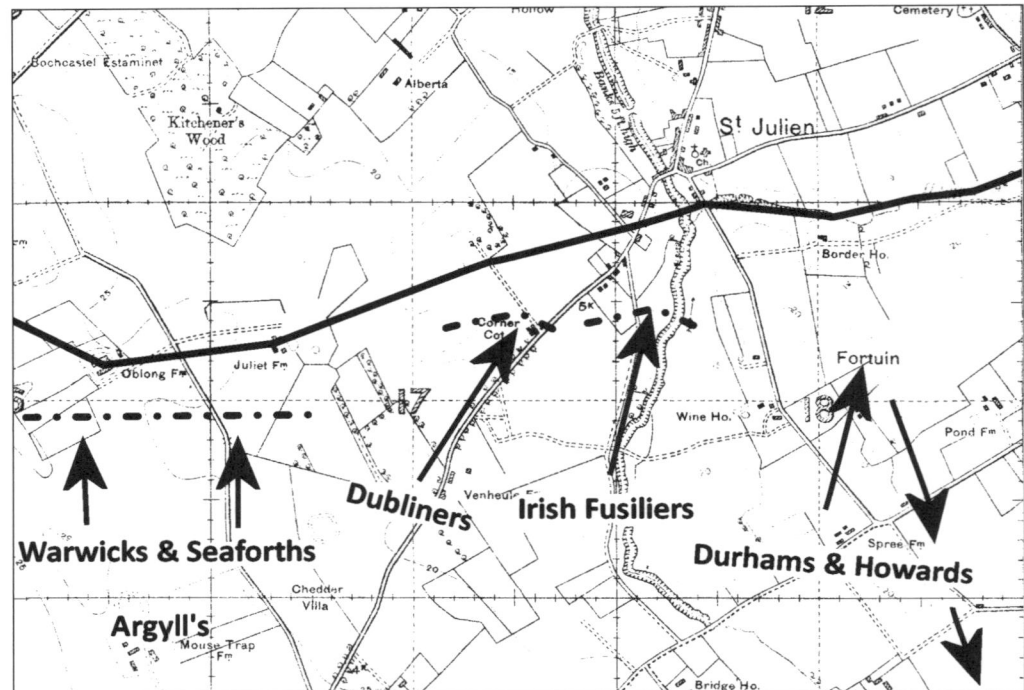

The Indian attack on Kitchener's Wood and St Julien on 25 April 1915

Argylls were soon pinned down as well. The attack ended with the British guns firing short on the three pinned-down battalions.

The right of Hull's attack was directed towards St Julien but Lieutenant Colonel Loveband's 2nd Dublin Fusiliers came under machine gun fire as they advanced astride the Wieltje road. It was the same for Lieutenant Colonel Burrowes' 1st Irish Fusiliers astride the Haanebeek stream. Lieutenant MacMullen had gone ahead of the Irish Fusiliers and he could see the machine gun teams firing at his comrades from the upper story windows of the houses. Captains Penrose and Jeudwine reported the impossible situation on the flanks to Burrowes while Captain Eklan's company stopped a counter-attack in the centre. The leading companies of the two battalions were pinned down close to the outskirts of the village and only a few brave souls managed to crawl back to safety; the rest were dead or seriously injured. Many from the support companies made a run for it but a few stopped behind to help the wounded.

The attack had cost 10 Brigade nearly 2,400 casualties but it had stopped a counter-attack from St Julien. It was fortunate the Germans did not choose not to follow up their successful defence because they only faced a thin line of men. When the mist cleared General Hull noticed the 5th Green Howards and 5th Durhams were missing from Fortuin, so he instructed the 4th and 7th Northumberland Fusiliers[95] to cover his right flank. They filled the gap, more by luck than by design, but they could not find the 5th Green Howards or the 5th Durhams. General Hull eventually heard they had assembled at Verlorenhoek and he would order them to reinforce the Northumberland battalions. They would fill the gap between them and Colonel Wallace's group, on the Canadian's left.

Major Odlum still had 300 men of the 7th and 10th Canadian Battalions between the Haanebeek and Boetleer's farm. Major Moulton-Barrett also had his mixed group of Suffolks, Northumberland Fusiliers and Cheshires around the farm with a few 1st Monmouths and 8th Middlesex were in support.

The Germans Attack Gravenstafel

General Hull reported the attack had failed and he believed it was too dangerous to try again. Then came news of an attack against the Canadians covering Gravenstafel. Captain Harvey's and Bradford's companies of the 8th Durhams were on 2 Canadian Brigade's left along the Stroombeek stream, alongside the 8th and 5th Canadian Battalions. Lieutenant Colonels Lipsett and Tuxford had both placed a company on the left flank, covering Boetleer's Farm and Locality C. The trenches were shallow and full of bodies, while the dug-outs were full of gassed and injured men waiting to be evacuated.

All the battalions were low on numbers and the men still holding the Stroombeek position were tired and short of food. The Canadian Ross rifle was still jamming in the muddy conditions and it was not always possible to get the special ammunition to the front. Although Lee-Enfield ammunition was supposed to be same calibre, it often jammed the rifle.[96]

The German bombardment began at 5am and the guns switched to firing gas shell and high explosive four hours later. The shelling died down around noon but it restarted at 2pm as the German infantry crept forward. Then at 3.30pm the gunners lengthened their range and waves of infantry advanced against the Stroombeek position. The Durhams and Canadians held on but ammunition was running short and the Ross rifles continued to jam.

General Currie had gone back to ask for reinforcements believing 'that they might move for me when unlikely to move for officers of lesser rank' but he had been unsuccessful. All that was available were the few 8th

---

95 Northumberland Fusiliers Brigade, Northumbrian Division (later 149 Brigade, 50 Division).
96 The Ross rifle was officially replaced by the Lee-Enfield in June 1915.

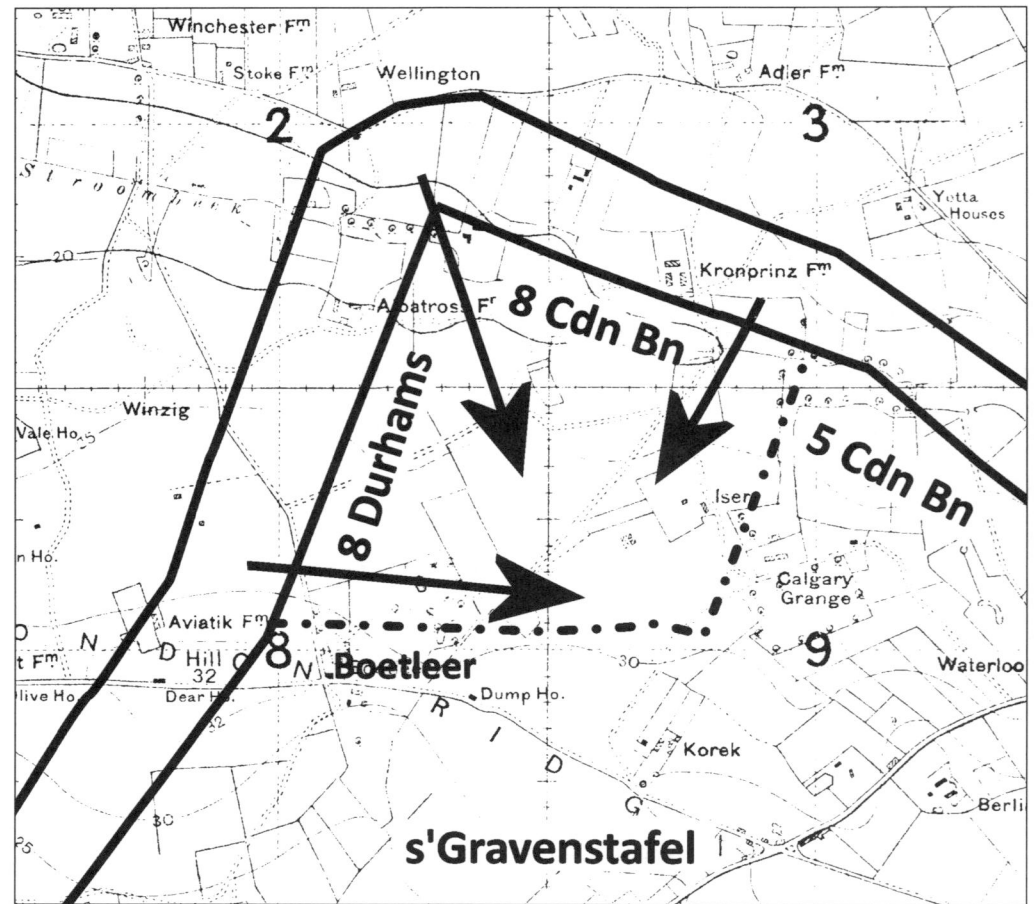

The loss of the Canadian Apex on 25 April 1915

Middlesex and 1st Monmouths at Locality C and they could not move forward because machine gun fire was sweeping the Stroombeek stream. Currie was planning to evacuate the line, but the front line commanders were already sending their men back from the exposed position.

The 5th Canadians retired on the right, only to discover that the 3rd Royal Fusiliers were staying put, so Lieutenant Colonels Tuxford and Lipsett sent their men back. But it was a different story on the Canadians' left flank. The mixed group around Boetleer's Farm held on but artillery fire stopped Major Ritson and Captain Veitch reinforcing the Durhams. The machine gun covering the Durhams' left flank then jammed, allowing the Germans to infiltrate behind them.

Captain Harvey had been told 'You <u>must</u> hang on at all costs' and the Durhams did hang on until it grew dark. Harvey then withdrew as many men as possible while those who stayed behind to cover their withdrawal were overrun. Lieutenant Colonel Turnbull was unsure what to do next because he could not find Currie, so he held on around Boetleer's farm. Only two platoons of the 8th Canadians had pulled out before the rest of the battalion were overrun; only forty-two men escaped. The rest of 2 Canadian Brigade would eventually withdraw into reserve.

There had also been an attack against 85 Brigade's line, on the Canadian's right, and the Germans had captured two parts of the 2nd East Surreys line. Lieutenant Colonel Ashton's men were unable to evict them but a counter-attack by the 8th Middlesex recaptured one section. No man's land was much wider on the 3rd Royal Fusiliers' front and Major Johnson's men had time to man the parapet and stop the attack.

V Corps Reorganises

That evening the decision was taken to divide the front into two areas of command. General Alderson took over the left while General Bulfin became responsible for the right. They both had to sort out their line and send any spare troops to join V Corps' reserve at Potijze. The artillery would begin reorganising the following day.

Brigadier General Hasler was instructed to move his 11 Brigade forward during the night and then take command of the 2 Canadian Brigade and all the detachments he found in the sector. The 1st Hampshires found the 3rd Royal Fusiliers[97] headquarters during the early hours but the guides could not find the battalion. Lieutenant Colonel Hicks sensibly gave the order to dig in between Gravenstafel and Berlin Wood before dawn, some distance behind the Fusiliers.

General Hasler had taken the rest of his brigade as far forward as Fortuin when he was warned there were few troops up ahead and German patrols were believed to be covering the road. So he headed south-east and deployed before dawn, unaware that Wallace's detachment was covering the Gravenstafel road, some 700 metres to the north.

General Alderson instructed General Wanless O'Gowan's 13 Brigade to take over from Geddes' Detachment and General Hull to take over the sector between Mouse Trap Farm and Fortuin. The weary battalions assembled between Potijze and St Jean with 149 Brigade in reserve, south of Wieltje. The Canadian Division had assembled astride the canal when Field Marshal

---

97 85 Brigade.

French telegraphed Alderson with the following congratulatory message: 'With less gallant and determined troops, the disaster which occurred outside the line they were holding might have been converted into a serious defeat for our troops.'

The situation in the salient was still confused after three days of fighting and the poor weather had prevented aerial reconnaissance. But what was clear was that the Canadian Division had made a huge sacrifice to hold its position for three days and nights, under the most difficult circumstances. It had suffered over 5,000 casualties in its first battle.[98] Captain Francis Scrimger had spent the past 72 hours working with the wounded of the 14th Canadian Battalion and on 25 April he supervised the evacuation of his dressing station under shell fire. He was awarded the Victoria Cross for saving many lives and for devotion to duty.

All was quiet in the French sector, north of Ypres, because both sides were exhausted and waiting for fresh reinforcements. General Smith-Dorrien visited GHQ where Field Marshal French told him he had to hold on, knowing that Second Army would have to evacuate the salient unless the French could secure its left flank. There was a worry that the Ypres situation would interfere with the planned Allied offensive. There was also the belief that the French had put Second Army in the difficult situation, so they should help it to get out of it. General Putz planned to attack until the following afternoon and Smith-Dorrien agreed the Lahore Division would advance alongside. He protested when zero hour was moved forward from 5pm to 2pm but GHQ told him to proceed.

The Lahore Division's Attack, 26 April
Major General Henry Keary was ordered to deploy his Lahore Division between St Jean and Wieltje ready to advance north, alongside the French, at 2pm.[99] General Alderson also wanted Brigadier General Riddell to move his Northumbrian Brigade towards St Julien on the right flank. Again most of the batteries supporting the attack were firing from the west bank of the canal, too far away to be accurate, and there was also a general shortage of heavy guns.

Meanwhile, the Indian battalions[100] deployed under accurate shell-fire because German observers watched their every movement from Mauser Ridge. German planes also flew low overhead, locating batteries for the heavy guns to shoot at. Five batteries had been put on call, ready to open fire when the German line was located, but it was doubtful if the observers could see anything on Mauser Ridge.

The bombardment started at 1.20pm and the Lahore Division moved off

---

98 It suffered over 5,675 casualties between 22 April and 4 May but most occurred in the first three days.
99 General Keary deployed the two British Army battalions on the flanks, to set the example to the Indians.
100 All battalions were weak due to sickness and a no reinforcements.

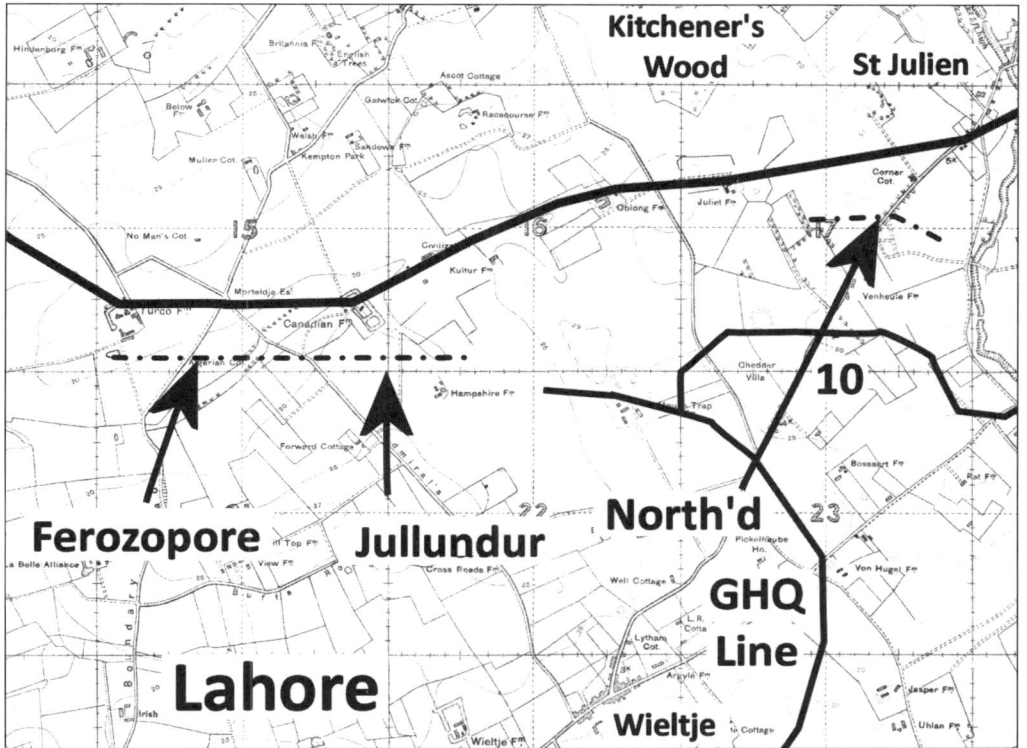

The Lahore Division's advance towards Mauser Ridge on 26 April 1915

after twenty minutes, with the French infantry moving five minutes later.

The Ferozepore Brigade was on the left, in contact with the French, and Brigadier General Egerton had the Connaughts on his left. Lieutenant Colonel Murray's men were delayed crossing a number of hedges and the barrage had finished before they got close to the German trench; over 360 were hit. Major Williams was wounded leading the 57th Rifles but they kept going until they were close to the German trench. Then Major Duhan, Captains Mackie and Banks were killed in quick succession and six Indian officers were hit, leaving only a wounded Captain Mahon and Lieutenant Deedes still standing; around 270 Riflemen had been hit. The 129th Baluchis were on the right but the 47th Sikhs drifted into its area, delaying Major Hannyngton's battalion. Over 230 were hit as they came into sight of the German trench and Sepoy Ghulam Hussain had to rescue an injured Major Holbrooke.

Brigadier General Strickland had the 47th Sikhs on the Jullundur Brigade's left but they drifted to the west to avoid machine gun fire from Oblong Farm. They came under fire as soon as they crossed the ridge and Major Talbot and Captains Cook and Scott were all killed, while 'the men were falling in swathes'. Lieutenant Brunskill saw some Germans running so he led a group of Sikhs forward, hoping to enter their trench. Unfortunately, German reinforcements reached it first and shot them all down. Lance-Corporal Reilly of the Connaughts would drag the injured Brunskill back to safety.[101] Eventually only Lieutenant Drysdale was still standing and he led the survivors in the final charge, but no one could reach the German trench.[102] Not one of the yellow flags carried forward were hoisted up to show a trench had been captured.

Major Perkins led the 40th Pathans at the run, so it suffered fewer casualties to begin with, but Lieutenant Colonel Rennick was still mortally wounded. Then as soon as they breasted the ridge, the machine gun fire from Juliet Farm was like 'a scythe being drawn across the legs of the troops as they advanced. At one moment they were moving forward as if nothing would stop them; the next they simply collapsed.' Thereafter they advanced by rushes but Major Perkins, Captains Dalmahoy, Christopher and Waters were shot down one by one leaving Jemadar Lehna Singh and Subadar Jahandad Khan to rally the survivors. The Pathans suffered over 300 casualties.

Lieutenant Colonel Hitchins' 1st Manchesters also came under deadly fire as they crossed the ridge line on the right, and the four lieutenants with the leading company were hit in quick succession. Hitchins was an early casualty but a gassed Captain Buchan kept staggering forward. Captain Paulson and Lieutenant Roberts were the next to fall wounded but Corporals Issy and Mervin and Private Richardson kept the men going. Sergeant Bates would rally the men on the left of the attack while Issy rescued many wounded men, carrying one over 250 metres to safety.

Before long the Lahore Division's attack had come to a halt, with its troops in a scattered line close to the German trench. Then around 2.20pm a gas cloud was seen creeping forward and the men had nothing with which to protect themselves apart from their hands or handkerchiefs. The French suffered the worst and they fell back, taking many British and Indians troops with them. A group of around sixty Connaughts, under Major Deacon and Captain Ingham, around fifty Manchesters, under Lieutenant Henderson, and a few other scattered groups stayed put until the Germans forced them to retire. Jemadar Mir Dast had gathered as many men as he could find in

---

101 The Sikhs suffered over 280 casualties.
102 Less than one hundred Sikhs out of 444 marched back that night.

an old trench; he returned at dusk, bringing many others back with him. Dast then rescued eight wounded officers from no man's land; he was awarded the Victoria Cross.

A new advance was ordered, in the hope it would carry the survivors forward, but it was too dangerous for the Ferozepore Brigade to move because of the French withdrawal. The 1/1st Gurkhas and the 2nd HLI were supposed to carry the Jullundur Brigade forward to Major Deacon; they eventually found Deacon's little band of men surrounded by their dead comrades. Brigadier General Walker had also sent forward the 1/4th Gurkhas and Sikhs from his Sirhind Brigade but Lieutenant Colonel Hill had been unable to find the Jullundur Brigade, so another advance was called off.

The First Territorial Brigade Attacks
Brigadier General Riddell did not receive General Alderson's orders to participate in the attack but he knew he had to cooperate with the Lahore Division. The three Northumberland Fusilier battalions[103] moved off only ten minutes before zero hour, even though they had not been given any extra ammunition. Riddell had no idea what he faced and was surprised to find the GHQ Line blocking his way. It took time for his men to file through the gaps in the wire and the three battalions deployed beyond as the German guns found their range.

The objective was Kitchener's Wood and Lieutenant Colonel Spain's 6th Northumberland Fusiliers and Lieutenant Colonel Foster's 4th Northumberland Fusiliers led while Lieutenant Colonel Scott Jackson's 7th Northumberland Fusiliers followed the 4th Battalion. No one else was advancing because the Indians had been pushed west by the machine guns in Juliet and Oblong Farms and there was no artillery support because they were nearly an hour late. So every German artillery piece and machine gun in range could fire on General Riddell's men, cutting them down in great swathes as they passed through 10 Brigade's line.

Brigadier General Riddell was killed so Colonel Foster ordered everyone to take cover and while some sought shelter in old trenches others tried to dig in. Foster knew his men were short of ammunition and he was relieved to get the order to withdraw behind 10 Brigade's line as soon as it was dark. The Northumberland Brigade had suffered nearly 1,950 casualties, over two-thirds of its strength, and it had achieved nothing.

Night Attacks towards Gravenstafel
The Germans probed the new line between Boetleer's Farm and Berlin

---

103 The Northumberland Fusilier Brigade would later be numbered 149 Brigade.

Wood during the night, looking to capture Gravenstafel. Around 2am a group of Germans captured a 1st Hampshires[104] patrol in no man's land. They then shouted 'we are the Royal Fusiliers', but the company commander detected a foreign accent and gave the order to fire. Later on men dressed in British uniforms approached the 8th Durhams through the mist shouting they were from the Suffolks. Some moved through a gap where the Monmouths should have been on the left while others forced the Middlesex to retire on the right, forcing Colonel Turnbull to abandon Boetleer's Farm.

The German guns began shelling Gravenstafel as soon as the mist lifted and then the infantry forced Auld's detachment back to Otto Farm[105] and overran the company of 8th Middlesex between the Hampshires and Royal Fusiliers. Meanwhile, the officers with Wallace's detachment destroyed all their maps and paperwork and prepared to make a last stand. The new line would be along the Haanebeek stream and 11 Brigade sent reinforcements forward to help hold it. The 8th Durhams were later withdrawn having suffered nearly 600 casualties in their first action.

The General Situation at Evening
As night fell across the Ypres Salient; the sound of digging could be heard across no man's land because the Germans were again installing gas cylinders. But General Smith-Dorrien's main concern was Second Army's artillery situation. The batteries west of the canal were too far away to give effective support and the artillery crews to the east were in exposed positions. Random shelling made it dangerous to move anything on the roads but there was also a concern that a few lucky shots could knock out the bridges over the canal, cutting off the north part of the salient.

The Lahore Division, 27 April
Captains Kisch and Nosworthy reconnoitred the German trench in front of the Lahore Division on the night of 26–27 April, as flares lit up the sky. Kisch was wounded but they were able to sketch out the line, so a plan could be made. The bombardment would begin at 12.30pm with the French Moroccans moving at 1.30pm. The Ferozepore Brigade had to move first, to bring itself into line with the Sirhind Brigade, so they could both move together at 1.15pm.

The French were pinned down, but the Sirhind Brigade moved as soon as the barrage started. Most of Lieutenant Colonel Anderson's 1/1st Gurkhas were stopped 400 metres from the German line but Second Lieutenant Fry went as far as Canadian Farm. Major Brodhurst was killed early on leading

104 11 Brigade.
105 Previously Moulton-Barrett's detachment.

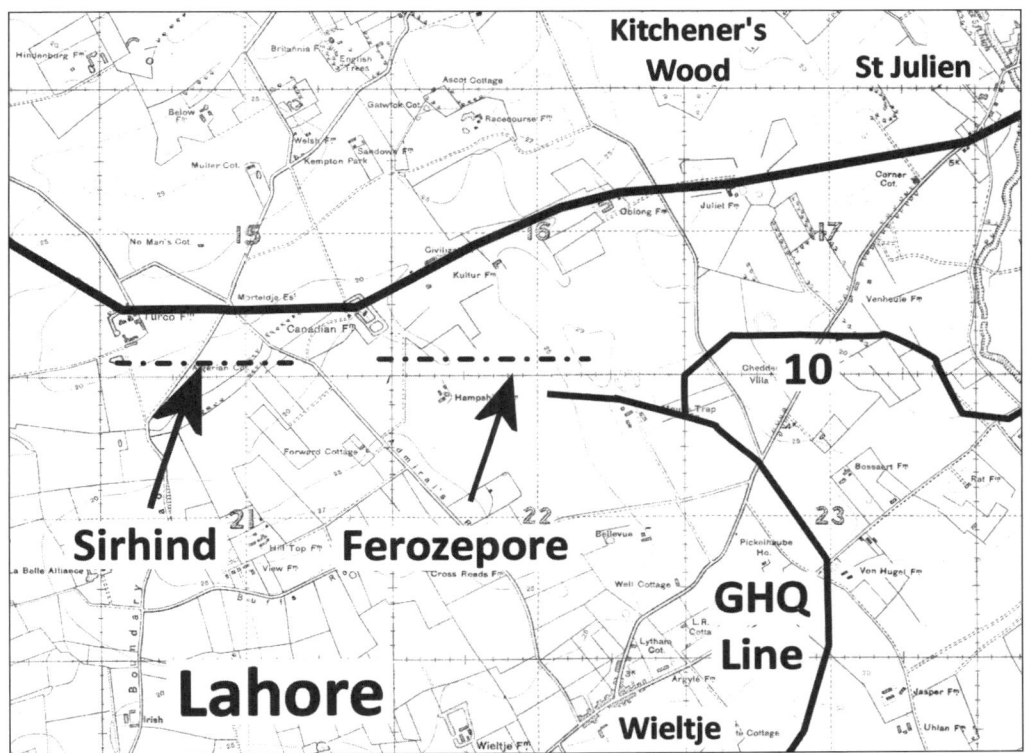

The Lahore Division's second attack against Mauser Ridge on 27 April 1915

the 1/4th Gurkhas and his men could go no further than the bottom of the slope. At 4pm Lieutenant Colonel Allen moved his 4th King's forward but Major Beall found barbed wire blocking his way. The only advantage of the short advance was that some French limbers were able to rescue some abandoned guns.

On the Ferozepore Brigade's front, the 15th Sikhs and 9th Bhopals negotiated hedges, followed by Connaughts, until they were pinned down near Mouse Trap Farm, some 300 metres from the German trench. Captain Tarrant's company of the Highland Light Infantry reached a trench near the Germans, but the rest were pinned down behind. The 4th Londons kept going forward until the last officer, Lieutenant Coates, fell and Captain Saunders died cheering the support companies on.

General Smith-Dorrien was anxious to help the Indians so he formed a composite brigade, numbering around 1,300 men,[106] to reinforce the Sirhind

---

106 From the Duke's, the DCLI, the York and Lancasters and the 5th King's Own.

Brigade. Lieutenant Colonel Tuson of the DCLI was warned to be ready, with the artillery opening fire at 5.30pm. The French Moroccans recaptured Lizerne, driving the Germans from an important foothold across the canal with 250 prisoners. The 15th Sikhs assembled behind an embankment only to be shot down as soon as they crossed it at 6.30pm. Lieutenant Colonel Vivian was killed and Major Carden was mortally wounded. The 1st HLI also struggled to advance and Colonel Hill could see the French Moroccans were falling back, having smelt chlorine caused by a few gas shells. Captain Tarrant's brave group held on even after Tarrant was killed but they could go no further.

The Reorganization of the Ypres Command

General Smith-Dorrien had written to General Robertson, asking to withdraw to a shorter line of defence so he could send the surplus men and guns west of Ypres reducing the unnecessary casualties. He also made it clear that a 'big offensive elsewhere would do more to relieve the situation than anything else.' Second Army's commander became even more convinced a withdrawal was the best option when he heard the French had no intention of deploying extra troops along the Ypres canal.

But Field Marshal French thought the situation was not as serious as described and he wanted Second Army to continue cooperating with the French. Although the tactical situation might have looked bad, the French high command was planning a large offensive in the Artois region and First Army was preparing to cooperate. The Ypres Salient had to be held, to stop the Germans moving troops south, so once again orders were issued to recover the line north-east of Ypres.

During the afternoon, General Smith-Dorrien was given an hour's notice to hand over command to General Plumer at 5.30pm. His staff would be attached to the new staff, so they could explain the situation. General Plumer then became General Officer Commanding of both Plumer's Force and V Corps.

Plumer's instructions were to prepare a new defensive line east of Ypres; exactly what Smith-Dorrien had been proposing. He was also told to coordinate and attack with the French the following day. But first he had to reorganise the salient. Colonel Geddes' detachment was disbanded and the battalions were returned to their brigades. General Alderson was left with the 10th, 13th and 149th Brigades; 28th Division was given the 11th, 150th and 151st Brigades; 27th Division welcomed his battalions back.

Colonel Geddes closed his headquarters and then stayed the night with 13 Brigade in St Jean. He was asking General Wanless O'Gowan for a replacement map the following morning when a shell exploded in the room; Geddes was killed and several of his staff officers were injured.

Plumer's Force Formed, 28 April

After a frantic week, 28 April marked the start of a lull in the fighting. During the morning GHQ issued an instruction grouping all the units under General Plumer as 'Plumer's Force'. Then the Chief of the General Staff, General Robertson, confirmed that Field Marshal French thought it would 'in all probability be necessary tonight to commence measures for the withdrawal from the Salient to a more westerly line.' General Plumer was asked to submit a report on the line he proposed to pull back to and had to 'take such preliminary measures for commencing retirement tonight, if in the C-in-C's opinion it proves necessary.'

The withdrawal from the cramped and exposed salient made tactical sense but it was going to be difficult. Getting everyone away without the Germans noticing was a dangerous challenge. The troops were tired and it was going to be a struggle to keep them supplied. The Germans had artillery on three sides of the salient and they all had good observation over large parts of it.

General Foch protested when he heard about Field Marshal French's plans to withdraw because he believed the planned Arras offensive was more important that the Ypres battle. Evacuating the salient would give the Germans the incentive to attack again, bringing them even closer to Ypres. Foch asked the British to postpone the move until they had seen the results of the French attacks planned for the following day. French agreed but Robertson still issued instructions to evacuate all surplus troops and material from the salient and then clear all the roads ready to withdraw. When General Foch sent a written protest to GHQ, the reply was that Second Army was preparing for the worst; it had to be ready to pullback if the French attack failed.

The main problem was that Plumer's left was in an exposed position until the French regained the Pilckem ridge. His centre was also on the forward slope of the Frezenberg ridge and it was difficult to supply the troops. General Plumer wanted to fall back 2½ miles from Frezenberg and 1 mile near Hooge. He believed it would take four nights to execute the withdrawal if they began immediately but it would take longer, and be costlier, the longer they waited.

The French attack Foch had been waiting for yielded *'peu de resultats'* – little results. But the British engineers discovered that the valley bottom between Mauser Ridge and Hill Top Ridge was dead ground.[107] So Major

---

107 The German observers on Mauser Ridge could not see the bottom of the valley.

Boileau pegged out a line running east from Turco Farm, past Canadian Farm to Mouse Trap Farm and then supervised the digging of a new trench. For once ground had been secured without a huge loss of life, but the line was still vulnerable because the Germans could see the slope behind the new trench, making it difficult to supply.

A Postponement of the Withdrawal, 29 and 30 April
Foch was still calling for 'simultaneous, not successive, efforts of the British and French troops' east of Ypres. He delayed General Putz's attack by twenty-four hours but asked for Plumer's Force 'to attack with the greatest energy and the most complete co-operation' when it did begin. All Field Marshal French could do was to be diplomatic and promise to delay the withdrawal while General Plumer arranged it with his divisional commanders.

Second Army's artillery was already lined out along the west bank of the canal north of Ypres, where it could fire from safe positions without the fear of getting trapped east of the waterway. The front line would be taken over by 4th, 28th and 27th Divisions. Meanwhile, the Lahore, Northumbrian, and 2nd Cavalry Divisions had to be withdrawn without alerting the enemy.

Brigadier General Petrie, V Corps' Chief Engineer, was given the job of preparing the new defensive line and his engineers supervised the men of the 28th and Northumbrian Divisions as they dug trenches and erected wire entanglements. They also built extra bridges across the canal to ease the bottleneck caused by the waterway.

The early morning French attack on 30 April was postponed until 11.15am, due to a thick mist cloaking the salient. The Sirhind Brigade was supposed to join in but the French were unable to advance. While General Putz agreed to scale his attacks down, he still wanted the Sirhind Brigade to cooperate in one last attack the following day. Again Field Marshal French warned Foch he intended to withdraw that night but later agreed to another postponement.

The Withdrawal Begins, 1 May
The Sirhind Brigade moved into 12 Brigade's trenches ready to cooperate with the French one last time, but this time their infantry stayed in their trenches. Foch visited French to let him know that General Joffre had overruled him. As far as the French were concerned, the Ypres sector was now a defensive sector, so the British and French armies could begin preparing for an offensive between Neuve Chapelle and Arras.

Joffre now wanted the British to withdraw troops from the Ypres front so they could reinforce the attack to the south. French agreed and later that afternoon Plumer received an order to 'begin to-night to carry out the withdrawal of your troops on the eastern part of the Salient' starting as soon as it was dark. The Lahore Division left the salient, leaving the 4th, 28th and 27th Divisions to hold the line, while the Northumbrian and Canadian Divisions joined the 2nd Cavalry Division east of the canal. The artillery also continued redeploying, with some guns crossing the canal while the rest moved closer to it.

Major General Keary left the Lahore Division's headquarters at Potijze the following morning, just before a large calibre shell demolished his dugout. General Plumer also relocated his headquarters to Abeele because a 15-inch gun was targeting Poperinghe. Otherwise everything went to plan and the Germans had not noticed anything unusual. Plans and instructions were therefore issued for the next stage of the withdrawal to start thirty-six hours later.[108]

A Gas Attack at Hill 60
While the salient was busy with troops preparing to withdraw, the Germans attacked Hill 60 on 1 May. The 1st Dorsets[109] were hit by a heavy bombardment around dusk and then gas was released. No man's land was so narrow that Major Cowie's men had little time to put on their respirators. Second Lieutenant Kestell-Cornish directed the fire of the few men still standing. Bombing parties attacked the Dorsets' flanks while the artillery shifted to the approaches to the hill, to hit the reinforcements. The 1st Bedfords[110] and 1st Devons[111] ignored the bursting shells and kept moving through the gas cloud until they reached the Dorsets' trench. Lieutenant Colonel Williams[112] then organised all the bombers he could find to drive the Germans back.

The 1st Bedfords were also gassed to the north and Private Edward Warner fought on alone after the rest of his platoon had been overcome. He fetched up reinforcements during a lull in the fighting but died soon afterwards from the effects of gas. Private Warner was posthumously awarded the Victoria Cross. The attack had been a complete surprise and it showed how dangerous gas could be when the situation was right. Around ninety Dorsets died from gas poisoning while over two hundred had to be evacuated.

Resumption of the Enemy Offensive, 2 May
The morning was quiet so General Plumer issued orders to continue the

---

108 On the night of the 3/4 May.
109 15 Brigade, 5th Division.
110 15 Brigade.
111 14 Brigade.
112 The Bedfords' commanding officer.

withdrawal the following night. Then artillery fire hit 4th Division's line between Turco Farm and Berlin Wood, north-east of Ypres, at noon. After four hours of hammering the area with high explosive and shrapnel, the guns started firing gas shells to incapacitate the gun batteries. Thirty minutes later clouds of gas were seen in front of the enemy trenches along Mauser Ridge and in front of St Julien.

The gas alarms rang out and men pulled on their gas hoods as fast as they could. But no man's land was narrow. The gas reached the British parapet in only a couple of minutes, smothering 12 Brigade and 10 Brigade's right. But the cloud was only waist high in many places, making it safer to walk in the open than take cover in the trenches.

The 1st King's Own held their own around Turco Farm on 12 Brigade's left. When Lieutenant Colonel Griffin reported some of his 2nd Lancashire Fusiliers had been driven back, Lieutenant Colonel Jackson occupied a farm in no man's land, to cover the gap. Brigadier General Anley then ordered Lieutenant Colonel Carden to take his 7th Argylls[113] and a company of 5th South Lancashires[114] forward to reinforce the line. The 4th Hussars and 5th Lancers[115] also helped the Lancashire Fusiliers recapture their line. Captain Jones' company of the 2nd Essex was forced back near Fortuin, but the support company recovered the trenches before Lieutenant Colonel Cuthbertson and two 2nd Monmouth companies arrived.

Nearly 450 officers and men were admitted to hospital with gas poisoning but the line had not been breached. The Germans were left puzzled by the failure to capture any trenches and came to the conclusion that the gas had been too weak, so they planned another attack with more cylinders than before.

By dusk all was quiet so General Plumer felt confident enough to resume the retirement at 9.45pm. Again everything went to plan, despite the shelling of the roads and the thick mist covering the salient. But while Plumer's Force now occupied a better geographical position, the new defensive line left a lot to be desired because it had been prepared at short notice. The trenches were narrow and shallow and protected by a flimsy barbed wire fence. Plumer just had to hope they could be improved before the Germans arrived.

An early morning attack against 12 Brigade was stopped and fresh German reinforcements had been seen marching up the front. The time to withdraw had arrived and Plumer issued orders to 4th, 28th and 27th Divisions at 11.45am. All movements would be regulated by 28th Division in the centre and the artillery would start moving at 8.30pm with half the infantry following 30 minutes later. More infantry would move off at

---

113 10 Brigade.
114 12 Brigade.
115 2nd Cavalry Division.

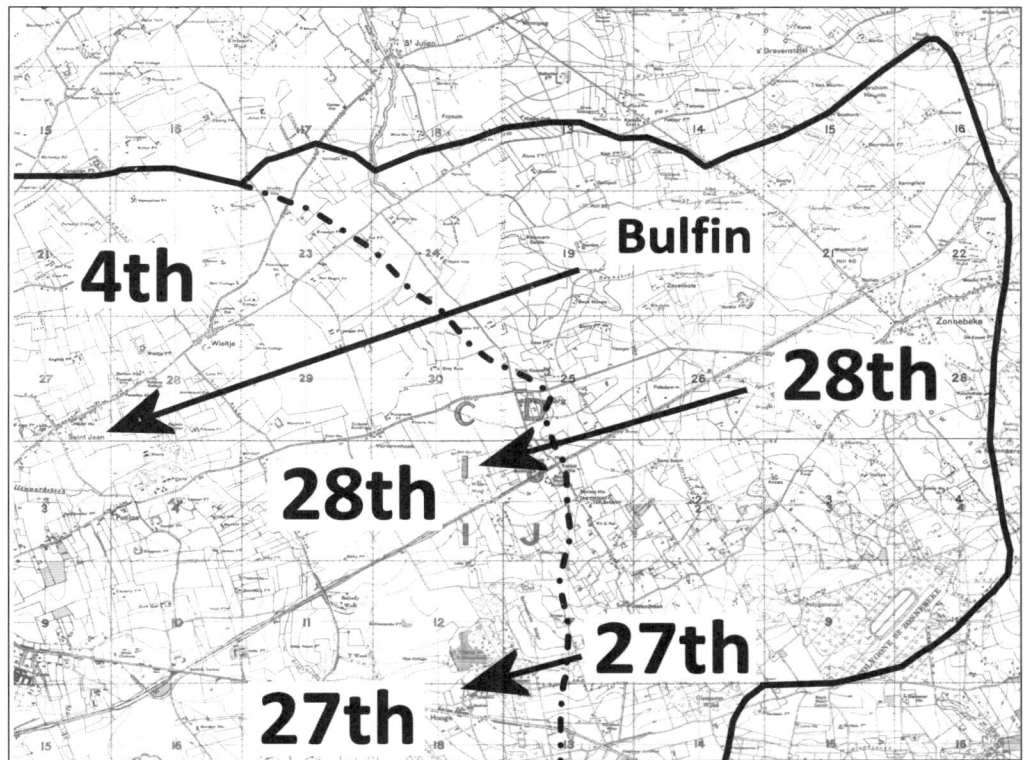

Second Army's withdrawal to the Frezenberg Ridge 1915

10.30pm with the last groups leaving at midnight. On average, units had to withdraw 4,000 metres and those with furthest to go would stop half way to reorganise.

But first the Germans made one final attack at Berlin Wood. The 2nd Buffs front line was overrun but Major Power's support line held on. Lieutenant Colonel Seymour's 1st Rifle Brigade also repelled the attack with help from companies of the 1st York and Lancaster and 5th King's Own. The fighting had died down by evening and the first groups withdrew through the mist, even though the Germans were close by. Everyone was accounted for as more and more headed off until there were only a few brave officers and scouts left behind to fire rifles and Very lights to make it look like the line was still occupied. They eventually left in the early hours, leaving behind a few medics, who had volunteered to look after the seriously wounded.

Chapter 6

The Whole Countryside
is Yellow

A Pause, 4 to 7 May

The German artillery continued to shell the abandoned trenches as Plumer's Force settled into its new line, a semi-circle of trenches roughly three miles from Ypres. The 4th Division, under its new commander, Major General Henry Wilson, now held a short sector from Turco Farm to Mouse Trap Farm, north-east of the town. Next came 28th Division to the east and 27th Division to the south-east. The trenches were on the reverse slope of the low Flanders ridges but there was a lot of work to be done before the reduced salient was safe. General Plumer wanted a second trench line backed by strongpoints to be built and a final line of defence along the canal and the town ramparts.

It did not take long for the Germans to realise Plumer's Force had withdrawn. Their infantry moved forward across no man's land and the British trenches to discover 'the whole countryside is yellow... the battlefield is fearful. A curious sour, heavy, penetrating smell of dead bodies strikes one... Bodies of cows and pigs lie, half decayed; splintered trees, the stumps of avenues; shell crater after shell crater on the roads and in the fields.' The artillery batteries followed close behind and registration of new targets began as soon as they were dug in. Plumer's Force would only have three days to prepare for the next onslaught.

The Germans started probing the new line on 4 May and their first attempt hit Mouse Trap Farm, a key point on 12 Brigade's right flank. The following day the 5th King's Own and the 2nd East Yorkshires[116] stopped an attack down the Frezenberg road with the help of two 3rd Monmouth companies. But the big German effort on 2 May was against Hill 60 which was held by the 2nd Duke of Wellington's.[117] Around 8.40am gas was released from two points but only one sentry spotted it, creeping across no

---

116 Both 83 Brigade.
117 13 Brigade, 5th Division.

man's land. The gas hung over the British front and support trench, so they could not withdraw to avoid it; instead they had to fight on using only their rudimentary masks for protection.[118] Fifteen minutes later the German infantry rushed Captain Barton's men and captured most of the front line. Captain Robins[119] was the last man to leave the trench, gasping for breath; he would die of gas poisoning the following night. A company of the 1st Dorsets ran forward along the railway cutting and they used a trench to bomb their way onto the hill. Brigadier General Northey also ordered Lieutenant Colonel Scott[120] to reinforce the line with the 1st Cheshire and 6th King's.

Around 11am another release of gas hit the 1st Bedfords to the north-east and Captain Gledstanes rallied his men after the Zwarteleen salient was abandoned. The mixture of battalions regained some of the lost trenches and while a new attack at dusk was stopped, the Germans still held the summit of the low hill.

Brigadier General Wanless O'Gowan arrived after nightfall with orders to retake Hill 60 with his 13 Brigade. The twenty minute bombardment failed to suppress the Germans and the 2nd KOYLIs advanced late because they mistakenly started from their support trench. Two companies disappeared into the gloom and were never seen again; they were all taken prisoner or killed. Meanwhile, some of the 2nd KOSBs reached the summit of Hill 60 only to come under cross-fire from Zwarteleen hamlet and the Caterpillar, a spoil heap across the railway.[121]

At dawn on 7 May the Cheshires were unable to recapture the Zwarteleen salient while the KOYLIs failed to take the crest of Hill 60. And so it remained. The battle for Hill 60 had cost 5th Division over 3,100 casualties; 15 Brigade alone had lost nearly 1,600 in a week and 13 Brigade suffered 300 casualties making its counter-attack.

During the lull there were confrontations of a different kind in the British high command. Relations between General Smith-Dorrien and the commander-in-chief had been strained for some time. He had been unhappy about the order which had reduced his command to Plumer's Forces, no more than a single corps. On 6 May he said that Field Marshal French's apparent lack of trust in him was the weak link in the chain of command and suggested it would be better for everyone if he served elsewhere. French ignored his offer to resign, accused him of being pessimistic and told him to hand over command of Second Army to General Plumer and return to England. Plumer's Force ended when V Corps reverted to Second Army.

---

118 The piece of gauze had to be regularly dipped in a solution as the man held his breath.
119 Attached from the East Yorkshires.
120 Colonel Scott was killed in the fighting.
121 The *Official History of the Great War* states it was the 1st Queen's Own which attacked Hill 60.

The Frezenberg Ridge, 8 May

The Germans had spent four days moving and registering their heavy artillery forward opposite 28th and 27th Division. The British trenches on Frezenberg Ridge were shallow and the dugouts were too shallow to stand a prolonged bombardment. There was the GHQ Line to the rear but it could not withstand a major attack. General Plumer's Chief Engineer, Major General Frederick Glubb, was also preparing a line of defence along the canal and strongpoints at Brandhoek, covering the main road into Ypres.

Second Army's order for 8 May was to hold because there were no more reinforcements to spare; they were all with First Army and about to join a new offensive to capture the Aubers Ridge. German patrols probed the Mouse Trap Farm area during the night of 7/8 May but the 2nd Northumberland Fusiliers[122] had kept them at bay. Then the German artillery began battering 83 Brigade's trenches on the forward slopes of Frezenberg ridge at dawn. The guns later spread their fire across everywhere north of the Menin Road and then lifted to the support trenches. A private of the Cheshires later wrote: 'for two hours we crouched at the bottom of the trench, pressed against the side. Hot metal flew at all angles. Dug-outs went sailing in the air. The ground trembled. Trenches tumbled in.'

The German artillery was stopping reinforcements reaching the front line and Lieutenant Colonel Enderby's 2nd Northumberland Fusiliers could not reach Mousetrap Farm.[123] Just after 11am General Bols sent the 12th London Regiment forward to reinforce the 1st Monmouths, even though Major Challen only had 200 men. Many were hit by artillery fire as they passed through the wire covering the GHQ Line and more fell as they crossed Frezenberg ridge; only fifty-three Londoners reached the Monmouths.

The breakthrough on 83 Brigade's front exposed the 2nd Cheshire's[124] right flank, north of Frezenberg, and Major Stone was one of the many casualties when they were overrun around 1pm.[125] Lieutenant Colonel Robinson warned Lieutenant Colonel Enderby he intended to pull the Monmouths' flank back to contain the breakthrough but it was too late. The Germans were behind their flank and the Monmouths were soon wiped out, allowing the German artillery to concentrate on the Northumberlands' battered trench.

Brigadier General Bols told Enderby to hold on because a counter-attack was being prepared, only it was going to be made at the opposite end of the breakthrough, nearly two miles away. As dusk approached he had decided to withdraw his men, but a rocket was fired into the evening sky before they could leave. The German guns stopped firing and the infantry charged. They

---

122 84 Brigade.
123 Originally called Shell Trap Farm; the name was changed because it was deemed unlucky.
124 84 Brigade.
125 Only one hundred Cheshires answered the roll call that night.

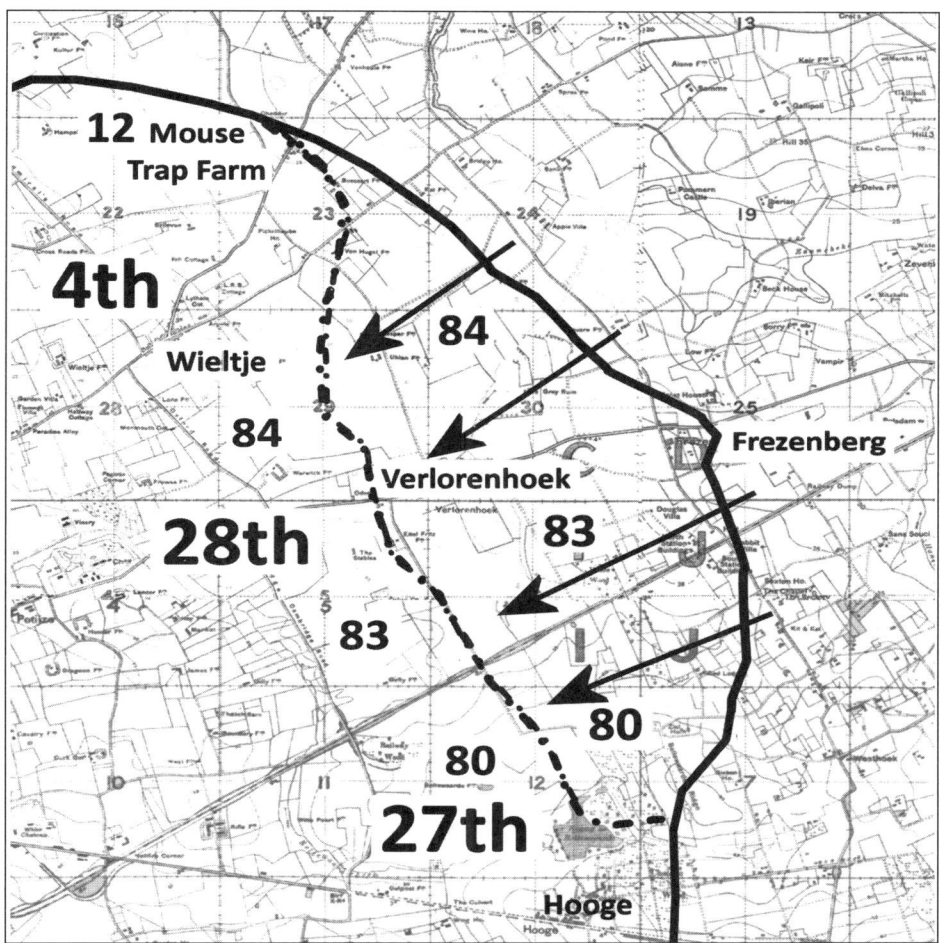

The loss of the Frezenberg Ridge on 8 May 1915

wiped out three Northumberland companies, capturing Enderby and his adjutant, Captain Aud. Captain Hart fought on with survivors, shooting the German officer calling for his surrender, before he was killed. A wounded Second Lieutenant Lord took his place and drove the Germans back, with the help of Sergeants Lane and Halliday.[126] The 1st Monmouths, the 2nd Cheshires and 1st Suffolk had all been overrun and no one recorded the fate of the men who had been captured or killed.

Meanwhile, the 2nd King's Own were fighting to stop the Germans

---

126 Only 118 2nd Northumberland Fusiliers rallied that night.

getting across Frezenberg ridge at the opposite end of the gap. Brigadier General Boyle had issued the order to withdraw, but it arrived too late to save many of the 2nd King's Own. Major Clough's men were overwhelmed in the front trench and Lieutenant Colonel Martin was killed defending the support trench. Lieutenant Colonel Worsley-Gough organised a counter-attack by the 3rd Monmouths and then gave the order to retire to the support trenches behind the ridge.

The Germans moved to the crest but bombed the flanks of the gap rather than go any further forward. General Boyle gave orders for a withdrawal and instructed Major Powell to take his 2nd East Yorkshires forward to help the 3rd Monmouths. Major General Bulfin also sent two 85 Brigade battalions to defend the gap. But it was too late to help the 1st KOYLIs, on the right of the 3rd Monmouths. An injured Major Brooke stumbled into General Boyle's headquarters in St Jean to report the Germans were pushing past his left flank and his men had being forced back. Despite the breakthrough, Captains Mallinson and Gattie refused to abandon their trenches and their two companies of the 3rd Monmouths held on until nightfall.

On hearing that 80 Brigade's left was retiring, General Boyle sent an order to Major Powell[127] to form a rally line with his 2nd East Yorkshire at the GHQ Line. The battalion was less than 230 strong but it was already well on the way to the front. Unfortunately, Boyle's message was interpreted as a general retirement order for the 3rd Monmouths and the 2nd King's Own to join the East Yorkshires in the GHQ Line. In the confusion that followed, some groups retired but most fought on because it was too dangerous to abandon their positions with the Germans so close.

When General Boyle heard of the misunderstanding, he immediately ordered the 2nd East Yorkshires forward to plug the gap, telling Lieutenant Colonel Lord Cavendish to support him with the 5th King's Own. The problem was that the combined total of men in the two battalions was no more than 500 men and the gap was over 800 yard wide. Still they advanced, as the exploding shells thinned their ranks, but they could go no further than the crest of the Bellewaarde Ridge. The Monmouths and 2nd King's Own were still 1,000 metres ahead on the Frezenberg ridge and they fought on until they were killed or captured.[128]

Brigadier General Smith had Major Gault's Princess Patricia's Canadian Light Infantry on the Bellewaarde ridge and Major Majendie's 4th KRRC in the Hooge woods. The bombardment had forced the evacuation of the front trench but they held onto the support trench and both battalions sent every available man forward. Gault even sent the Princess Pat's signallers,

---

127 Major Powell was wounded, as was his replacement Major Pike.
128 Only thirty 3rd Monmouths and forty 2nd King's Own escaped.

pioneers, orderlies and batmen to help, while General Smith sent a company of the 4th Rifle Brigade to shore up the line.

But the Germans captured a mound in the centre of the brigade front, enabling them to enfilade the two battalions. When the Princess Pat's left lost touch with the KOYLIs of 83 Brigade, Lieutenant Colonel Bridgford was ordered to take the rest of the 2nd Shropshires forward to form a flank. The situation soon stabilised as the Germans refused to advance beyond the crest of the Frezenberg ridge, giving reinforcements the chance to shore up 84 Brigade's line.

At the same time the 1st Suffolk's endured the bombardment on 83rd Brigade's right: 'the din was terrific... High explosive shells crashed in all directions, scattering bricks and timber like chaff before the wind. Huge guns and howitzers roared incessantly, shaking the earth...' Then a cloud of gas floated across no man's land and the German infantry who followed it surrounded Lieutenant Colonel Wallace's choking men. Only thirty escaped to safety.

Yet another battalion had succumbed, leaving a gap of over two miles between Mouse Trap Farm and the Zonnebeke railway. There were only a few isolated groups holding on and General Bulfin had few reserves to help them. Brigadier General Chapman was told to send the 3rd Middlesex and 1st York and Lancaster forward, using the Zonnebeke railway as their guide, and Lieutenant Colonel Isherwood had instructions to counter-attack south of Frezenberg. The 2nd East Surrey and 3rd Royal Fusiliers[129] were soon heading off to reinforce the attack.[130]

General Chapman's reinforcements found the Germans had dug in across the gap in 28th Division's line and they were waiting for them. The Middlesex were reduced to less than 300 men while the York and Lancasters were cut to pieces; Isherwood was killed and only eighty-nine of his men would draw their rations the following morning. Lieutenant Colonel Ashton had moved his 2nd East Surrey behind the York and Lancaster's left and Major Johnson brought the 3rd Royal Fusiliers on its right. They too suffered many casualties restoring the line.[131]

10 Brigade's Night Advance
By nightfall 28th Division was shattered and its front line was broken. The old front line on Frezenberg ridge had been overrun and there were only a few hundred men on Bellewaarde ridge. Around 200 men of the 1st Welch were preparing to make a last stand in the GHQ Line. General Bulfin had no more troops left and so he asked 4th Division for help to plug the gap.

Major General Wilson handed over part of his local reserve, a measly

---

129 Both 85 Brigade.
130 They took stragglers who had gathered in the GHQ Line with them.
131 The 2nd East Yorkshire was reduced to 200 men and the 5th King's Own reported only ninety-one rifles.

few hundred men of the 1st Irish Fusiliers[132] and 5th South Lancashire,[133] and they were sent to hold the GHQ Line. They were soon followed by the 2nd Dublin Fusiliers, the 1st Warwicks[134] and the rest of the Irish Fusiliers. General Bols planned to recapture Mouse Trap Farm but it was dark by the time they had assembled. Lieutenant Colonels Loveband and Poole were ordered to deploy in front of the GHQ Line and their appearance caused the Germans digging in east of Wieltje to withdraw beyond the crest of the low ridge.

General Bulfin later received a misleading report concerning the loss of Wieltje and he instructed the 7th Argylls and 1st East Lancashires[135] to retake it. Colonels Carden and Lawrence protested it was too dangerous to advance into the unknown at night so the order was cancelled, averting a potential disaster. Instead the night was spent digging trenches opposite the breakthrough, making use of the GHQ Line east of Wieltje. The new line was behind the crest of the Verlorenhoek ridge and only two miles from the gates of Ypres. General Bulfin's battalions had also lost a lot of men, making his thin line even thinner. Brigades were the size of battalions, battalions were the size of companies and companies the size of platoons. For example the 1st York and Lancasters had 150 men, the 1st KOYLIs 120, the 3rd Monmouths only thirty and the 5th King's Own only twenty-four.

Another Lull in the Fighting, 9 to 12 May

First Army launched the battle of Aubers Ridge attack on 9 May while the French began the battle of Artois further to the south. Between them they drew the Germans' attention away from Ypres, even if only for a few days. The few efforts to reach 4th Division's trenches around Mousetrap Farm were stopped by the infantry. On 9 May German infantry, many dressed in British uniforms and shouting not to fire, advanced. Neither the 2nd Shropshires[136] nor the 3rd Royal Fusiliers[137] were fooled. After the hours of shelling, the British infantry looked forward to getting their own back and they waited until they had targets in their sights before opening fire. An attempt to retake lost ground on 28th Division's front on the night of 12/13 May also failed. Instead the Germans focused on probing 27th Division's positions astride the Menin road.

Most of the attacks on the afternoon of 9 May were stopped but a platoon of the 2nd Gloucesters was wiped out near Stirling Castle. Lieutenant Colonel Tulloh was unable to recover the lost trench and Captain Farquharson was killed leading a counter-attack by the 1st Royal Scots, so Brigadier General Croker called off further attempts to retake the exposed trench.

---

132 10 Brigade.
133 12 Brigade.
134 Both of 10 Brigade.
135 Argylls 10th Brigade and East Lancashires 11 Brigade.
136 80 Brigade, 27th Division.
137 85 Brigade, 28th Division.

The following day the German artillery pounded the trenches astride the Menin Road until the 4th Rifle Brigade, the 4th KRRC and the 2nd Camerons were forced to withdraw to their support trench. But the infantry attack which followed was stopped by rifle fire. The next attack on 11 May was supposed to hit the 1st Argylls and 2nd Camerons south of the Menin road but a change in the wind direction blew the gas back over the German trenches. Again the German artillery levelled several trenches and the Camerons were forced to withdraw to their support line.

Finally the salient was quiet on 12 May and the troopers of the 1st and 3rd Cavalry Divisions relieved 28th Division's infantry later that night. Major General de Lisle took command of what was called the 'Cavalry Force' while 28th Division went into Army reserve. Major General Bulfin's division had suffered a staggering 15,000 casualties in three weeks.

Verlorenhoek Ridge, 13 May

The 4th Division and the Cavalry Force[138] held an arc from Mouse Trap Farm around to Bellewaarde Lake but there was little barbed wire, the trenches were shallow and there were no communication trenches. German reports say the planned attack was cancelled due to an ammunition shortage but the men holding the front line would have disagreed because the shelling never stopped.

The heaviest barrage of the battle started in the early hours. By 1pm many of 4th Division's trenches had been flattened and their garrisons had been buried, killed or were falling back. But wire stopped the Germans west of Mouse Trap Farm and the 1st Somersets and 1st Hampshires stood up and dared them to come on when the artillery fire died down. The 1st Rifle Brigade were holding the line west of Mouse Trap Farm and they repeatedly counted over a hundred shells a minute hitting their area until the two platoons holding the farm were wiped out.

South of the farm the 1st East Lancashires and 5th London Regiment[139] had to abandon their battered trenches north-east of Wieltje. But Lance-Sergeant Douglas Belcher refused to leave and opened fire every time the enemy came near, stopping the Germans reaching the village. Attempts were made to reinforce the line, but they had to run the gauntlet of shells hitting all the roads behind the British front. Captain Jones led the 2nd Essex and part of the 11th Hussars forward to support the faltering line, as the 1st Rifle Brigade stood up and cheered their brave attempt to reinforce the line; over 180 men were hit crossing the open fields. A squadron of the 18th Hussars[140] and the 5th Dragoon Guards[141] were also shelled out of their front line on the Bellewaarde Ridge.

---

138 Typically a cavalry brigade fielded around fifty officers and 850 men.
139 Both 11 Brigade, 4th Division.
140 2 Cavalry Brigade, 1st Cavalry Division.
141 1 Cavalry Brigade, 1st Cavalry Division.

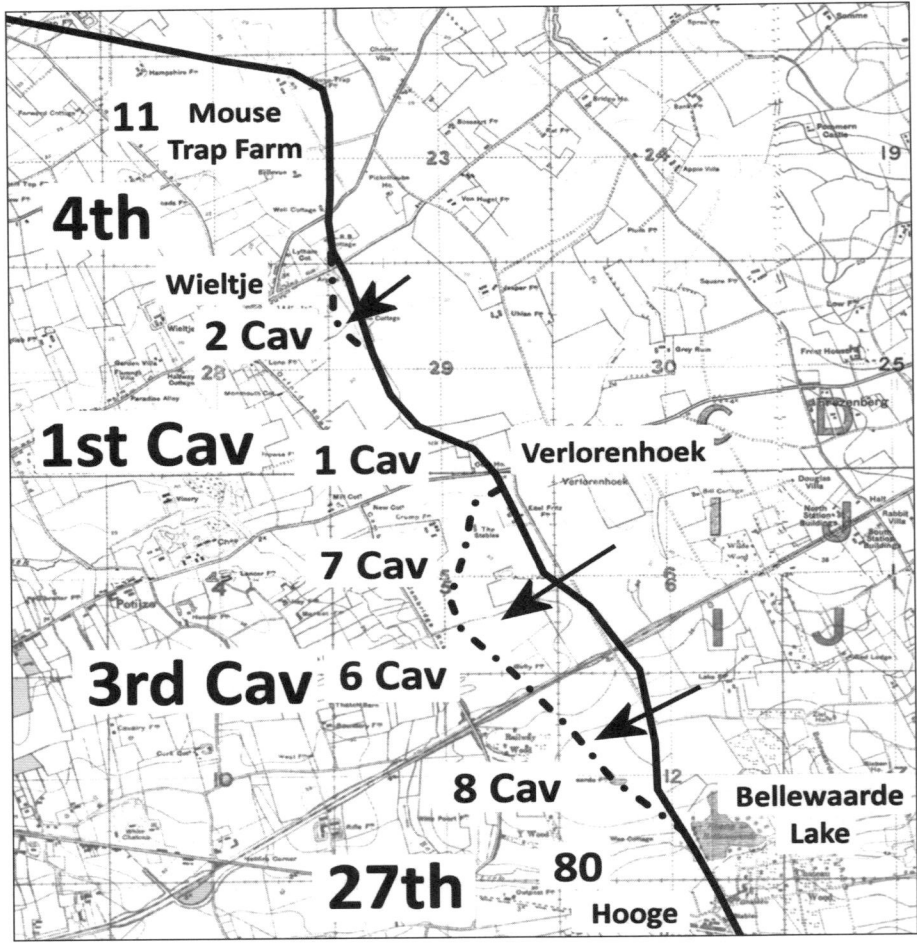

The German attack against Verlorenhoek Ridge on 13 May 1915

The German artillery hammered the Cavalry Force trenches on the forward slope of the Verlorenhoek Ridge and then the infantry attacked 7 Cavalry Brigade around 8am. Two squadrons of the Leicestershire Yeomanry[142] were driven out of their trench after they ran out of grenades but the squadron in the support trench contained the attack while the 2nd Dragoon Guards[143] and North Somerset Yeomanry[144] refused to budge either side. The Essex Yeomanry, 10th Hussars and Royal Horse Guards[145] had

---

142 The Leicestershire Yeomanry were only about 300 strong.
143 1 Cavalry Brigade.
144 6 Cavalry Brigade.
145 8 Cavalry Brigade.

soon deployed behind the threatened sector and Major General Charles Briggs wanted to counter-attack to retake the lost ground.

Brigadier General Bulkeley-Johnson was reinforced by part of 9 Cavalry Brigade while the Leicester Yeomanry recaptured the lost trenches. But the troopers had to fall back behind the crest of the Verlorenhoek Ridge as soon as the German artillery resumed shelling the area. The Cavalry Force had suffered heavy casualties containing the breakthrough and 151 Brigade moved into the GHQ Line to support it later that evening. The 4th Division relieved 2 Cavalry Brigade opposite Verlorenhoek while 27th Division took over the sector north of Bellewaarde Lake. In six days V Corps had suffered nearly 9,400 casualties, the majority on 8 and 13 May.

Another Pause, 14 to 23 May

On 14 May artillery fire dispersed German troops seen assembling opposite Bellewaarde and Hooge. The same day the Germans drove the 1st East Lancashire from Mouse Trap Farm but the 5th South Lancashire recovered the key position. This minor action brought the fighting to an end in the salient for the time being and there was good news the following day because the French captured the Steenstraat road bridge. The lull in the fighting lasted for nine days and General Plumer took the opportunity to reorganise his line. The 27th Division was relieved after twenty-four days in battle; it had suffered over 6,200 casualties. He also disbanded the Cavalry Force so the Cavalry Corps could reform and take responsibility for the east side of the salient.

Meanwhile, work on protecting the troops against chlorine gas continued apace. The first gas helmet was a flannel sack impregnated with a solution which neutralised the chlorine. It pulled over the head and a small celluloid eye-piece allowed the soldier to see; or at least that was the plan – in practise it steamed up with condensation from the man's breath. Each battalion was given only sixteen helmets to give to the machine gunners, so they would stay at their post during a gas attack. Equipping the entire BEF was a monumental task but everyone had what became known as the 'smoke helmet' by early July.

It was known that chlorine gas settled in low-lying places, particularly in dug-outs where air could not circulate, and the chemists had looked at ways of dispersing it. They came up with the Vermorel sprayer, composed of a back pack filled with a chemical and a gardening type spray powered by a small hand pump. Designated men would tour the trenches following a gas attack and neutralise pockets of gas before the troops returned.

The Gas Attack on V Corps, 24-25 May

At 2.45am on the morning of 24 May four red flares were fired above the German lines and then they were followed by two more. They told the artillery crews to start firing their guns and the engineers to start opening their cylinders. Gas spread across no man's land from Turco Farm[146] around to Hooge, covering the whole of V Corps' front, a distance of around five miles. It was the largest gas attack so far.

The British sentries heard the hissing of the gas and sounded the alarm but there was insufficient time to warn everyone because no man's land was so narrow. The men scrambled to put on their gas helmets and although some were overcome by the fumes, the rest manned the parapet and fired as fast as they could at the waves of German infantry.

The Break in 4th Division's Line

Major General Wilson's 4th Division line was north-east of Ypres and 12 Brigade was west of Mouse Trap Farm while 10 Brigade was to the east. Gas discipline was good all along the line and while the first wave of infantry was stopped with rifle and machine gun fire, it was not the last. Captain Jones' 2nd Essex and Lieutenant Colonel Jackson's 1st King's Own[147] stopped all attacks but the 2nd Royal Irish were in an unfortunate position north-west of Mouse Trap Farm. The angle of their trench meant the gas took a long time to drift over it and many men were gassed. The Germans drove the two 2nd Dublin Fusiliers[148] platoons from Mouse Trap Farm and they then took Lieutenant Colonel Moriarty's 1st Irish Regiment in the flank. Brigadier General Anley asked Lieutenant Colonel Griffin to send first one company and then the rest of the 2nd Lancashire Fusiliers to help the Royal Irish. The battle for the trenches north-west of the farm ended in the afternoon when the 2nd Royal Irish and a company of Lancashire Fusiliers were annihilated.

The rest of the Dublin Fusiliers were pushed back to the support trenches south of Mouse Trap Farm and Brigadier General Hull told Major Christie to help Lieutenant Colonel Loveband, so he led his two companies of the 9th Argylls forward through the gas. But they were too little, too late and the Dublin Fusiliers were overwhelmed. The 7th Argylls' left was pushed back but the rest of Lieutenant Colonel Carden's men contained the German bombers with the help of two 2nd Seaforth companies. Lieutenant Colonel Burrowes' 1st Irish Fusiliers also held 10 Brigade's right flank, due to good gas discipline. General Hull eventually sent the 1st Warwicks forward and Lieutenant Colonel Poole's counter-attack restored the brigade line.

General Wilson placed General Anley in command of all of 4th Division

---

146 South of Pilckem.
147 Both 12 Brigade.
148 10 Brigade.

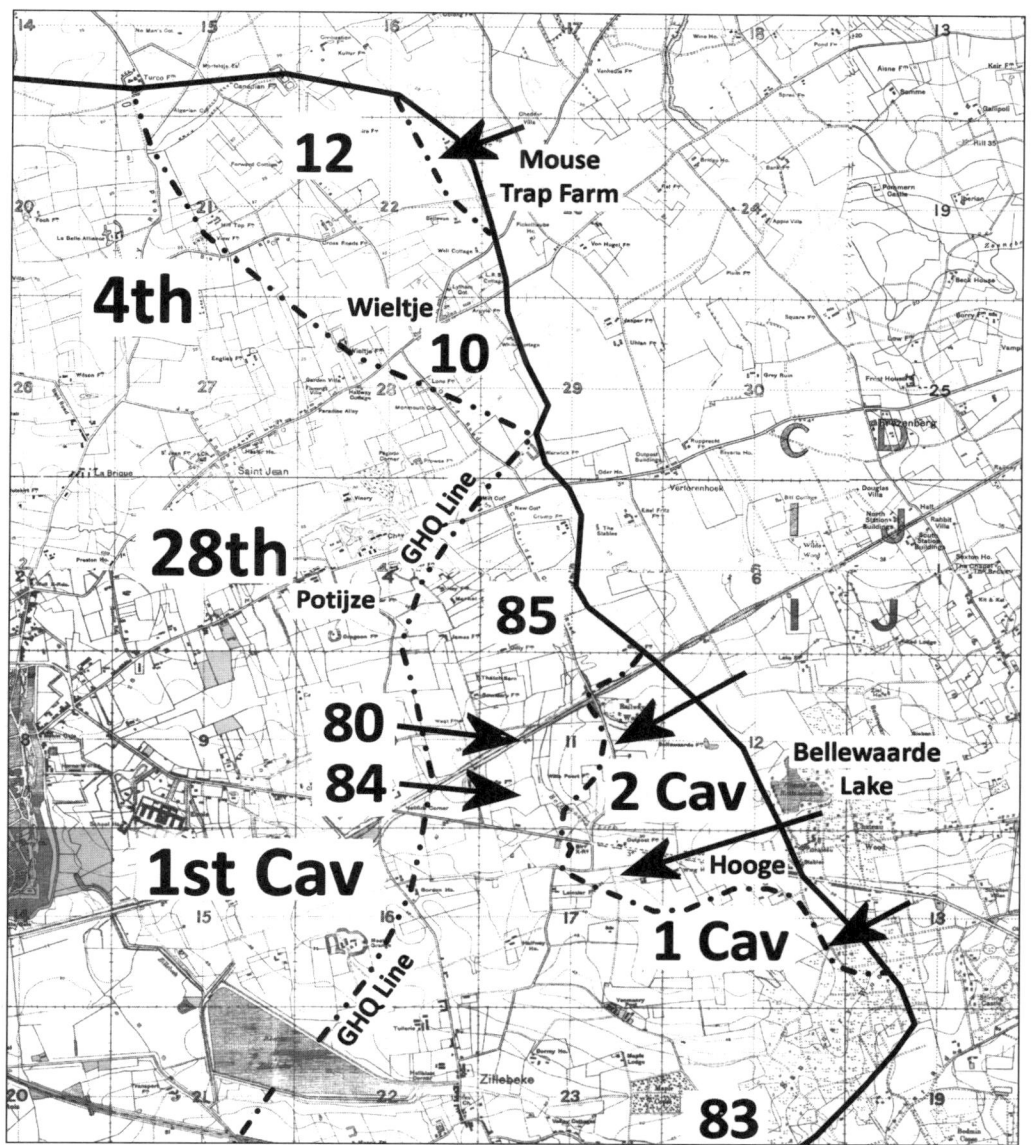

The attack on Mouse Trap Farm and Bellewaarde Ridge on 24 May 1915

troops east of the canal and he sent three Northumberland Fusilier battalions forward to form a reserve. Wilson believed he had insufficient forces to counter-attack Mouse Trap Farm, so the new line followed the support line, 1,000 metres to the west. It meant that a long section of the GHQ Line covering Wieltje had to be abandoned, leaving the Germans little more than one mile from Ypres.

The Break in the Line North and South of Bellewaarde Lake

The men of Brigadier General Pereira's 85 Brigade were in shallow trenches on the forward slope of the Verlorenhoek Ridge in the centre of V Corps' line. Part of the 2nd East Surrey and all the 8th Middlesex, north of the railway line, were overcome by gas but Lieutenant Colonel Henderson's 9th Durhams held on next to the Zonnebeke road. An attempt to cover the left flank of the breakthrough resulted in Major Johnson's 3rd Royal Fusiliers and Lieutenant Hammond's 2nd Buffs being overrun, but some held on along the railway line, with the help of Lieutenant Colonel Turnbull's 8th Durham's. Meanwhile, Second Lieutenant Mantle's group of Buffs were pounded by artillery fire around the level crossing.

The Germans moved through the gap on the left and then overran the 18th Hussars between Bellewaarde and Hooge. Captain Court reported the 9th Lancers were 'on their knees', while Brigadier General Mullens men were incapacitated near the Menin Road. Captain Barnard and Lieutenant Swayne took two companies of the 2nd Buffs forward to help hold the line and they fought on in trenches knee-deep in water.

A mixed group of 1st York and Lancasters, 4th East Yorkshire and a15th Hussars squadron in Zouave Wood fought back so the Germans left them alone. At dusk Brigadier General Greenly[149] directed Major Bayley to send a company of the 1st York and Lancaster towards the Menin road. So they advanced from Zouave Wood and the Germans shot their retiring comrades, believing they were advancing British troops.

84 and 80 Brigades Counter-Attack

The gap around Bellewaarde was growing because 2 Cavalry Brigade's left had been broken and 85 Brigade's right had been forced back to Railway Wood. Major General Bulfin had 84 Brigade available but its battalions were weak and short of officers. At noon General Bols was told to move forward. His men marched around Ypres, passed through the GHQ Line and headed for the Bellewaarde Ridge. They eventually counter-attacked between the railway and Bellewaarde Lake around 5pm and captured Witte Poort Farm.

The plan was for 80 Brigade[150] to advance at the same time but Brigadier General Smith did not receive the order until it was too late and his troops reached the GHQ Line at dusk. General Smith eventually found General Bols and they decided to make a night attack but it was 11pm before 80 Brigade was ready. A bright moon meant the Germans spotted the advancing troops and they were forced to withdraw.

---

149 Brigadier General Mullen's replacement.
150 27th Division.

4th Division Withdraws

Around 5pm a staff officer told General Anley that he had three French battalions at his disposal, but he soon learnt they would not counter-attack because they were only supposed to act in support. Lieutenant Colonel Montgomery, the chief staff officer of 4th Division,[151] was present when the message came in but he had no way of telling General Wilson. All that was left were two weak 11th Brigade battalions and two Lancashire Fusiliers companies so they withdrew from the Mouse Trap Farm area, followed by the Essex, the King's Own and the 7th Argylls. Later that evening the German Fourth Army issued orders stopping all offensive operations after a month of trying to break Second Army's line in the Ypres Salient.

The Close of the Battle

The 25 May was a quiet day and it can be considered to be the end of the Second Battle of Ypres. The combined casualties from the defensive battle at Ypres and the offensives at Aubers Ridge and Festubert had been heavy. Between 22 April and 31 May 1915, 2,150 officers and 57,125 other ranks of the BEF had been killed, injured or gassed. But the digging continued and exhausted units looked forward to being replaced by fresh ones. The only change in the front line came at the end of the month when the Cavalry Corps recaptured Hooge and the stables of the nearby chateau.

The British Army was also running low on ammunition and on 27 May Field Marshal French told the War Office he was unable to make any more attacks until his ammunition reserve had been restocked. Once again the front would settle down to a comparatively peaceful period in which the troops concentrated on improving their situation.

---

151 The GSO 1, or General Staff Officer 1.

Chapter 7

Anything for an Inch of Cover
The Battle for Aubers Ridge

General Haig's First Army headquarters was sure it could capture the German trenches after the success at Neuve Chapelle on 10 March. A memorandum issued on 4 April summarised GHQ's confident attitude: 'By means of careful preparation as regards details and thorough previous registration of the enemy's trenches by our artillery, it appears that a sector of the enemy's front line defence can be captured with comparatively little loss.' But what they did not account for was the German reaction to the attack, because they too had learnt many lessons. They had strengthened existing trenches and dug new ones, and erected more wire and building strongpoints. They had also increased the number of troops holding the front line.

The Germans had started work on a second line of breastworks earlier in the year and efforts were stepped up to complete them, where they could be built without enemy interference. The garrison lived in new dug-outs and used communication trenches while sentries and machine gun teams manned the fire trench. Parts of the communication trenches were turned into fire trenches, ready to use if there was a breakthrough. A line of strongpoints was also built to the rear, to serve as defensive positions and rallying points.[152]

The battle had also illustrated that defences needed to be beefed up to survive a properly coordinated bombardment. Breastworks were quadrupled in width and embrasures and pits were built into the foot of the breastworks for machine guns teams. The wire entanglements were also widened and thickened.

The Preparations
The German attacks at Ypres would not delay the planned Franco-British

---

152 The British had been building and using strongpoints to break up attacks and rally troops since the First Battle of Ypres in November 1914.

offensive on 9 May because the Allies knew the Germans were looking to take advantage of the spring weather to breakthrough on the Eastern front. Divisions were being moved from the Western Front to the east and it was a good time to attack while the German reserves were still far away.

Discussions over the attack had started as soon as Neuve Chapelle had ended. General Joffre had written to Field Marshal French on 24 March to ask if the British could attack at the end of April, when the ground was drier. French replied a week later, stating he hoped his army would be ready. On 6 April Joffre sent details of a plan to capture the Aubers ridge and the Douai plain. It was just one part of the French plan to attack German communications at three points. 'In the last days of April the French Tenth Army, acting in concert with the British First Army, will undertake an important attack north of Arras with a view to piercing the enemy's line.'

The French Tenth Army would advance on a twenty mile front on the British right, moving from the foothills of the Artois plateau onto and beyond the Notre Dame de Lorette Ridge. The centre of the attack would cross the plateau, then descend Vimy Ridge and advance to a line between Douai and Cambrai. The main attack would be supported by three subsidiary attacks. The first would capture the east spur of Notre Dame de Lorette Ridge the day before the main attack. The next would be launched simultaneously with the main attack, to divide the Germans attention. The final attack would widen the breach created by the main attack. Joffre wanted the British First Army to advance towards Aubers Ridge and La Bassée, a day after the main attack, extending the gap in the German line and engaging their reinforcements.

On 9 April Field Marshal French told Foch he could have ten infantry divisions available to attack, backed up by five cavalry divisions in reserve. He promised to support them with 100 heavy artillery pieces and 500 field guns. But French wanted to start on the same day as the main French offensive. He also planned the main attack between Neuve Chapelle and Festubert and the secondary attack towards Aubers and Fromelles.

While the Allies had agreed on where the offensives would be, the Germans would prompt them into deciding when to launch them. A massive Austro-German offensive began in the Gorlice-Tarnow region on 1 May. The following day Foch told French the main assault would be made on 7 May and he wanted the British to attack the following day. French agreed and he issued his orders on 4 May.

The offensive was going to be carried out by Indian Corps and I Corps and there were several re-adjustments to be made to get the assault troops into line. The Indian Corps took over the 1,500 metres of the north sector, and the Lahore and Meerut Divisions settled in between Neuve Chapelle and Orchard Redoubt. In I Corps' new sector, 1st Division was concentrated on a front of 1,300 metres with the 2nd Division in reserve. On the flanks, IV Corps held the 5,000 yard front between Picantin and Neuve Chapelle to the north. A subsidiary attack was going to be made by 8th Division astride the Sailly-Fromelles road.

But there were delays to the deployments due to the German attack on the Ypres Salient. The Lahore Division had to be sent to help Second Army on 24 April and part of 7th Division was moved into GHQ reserve four days

First Army's plan for a pincer movement on Aubers Ridge on 9 May 1915

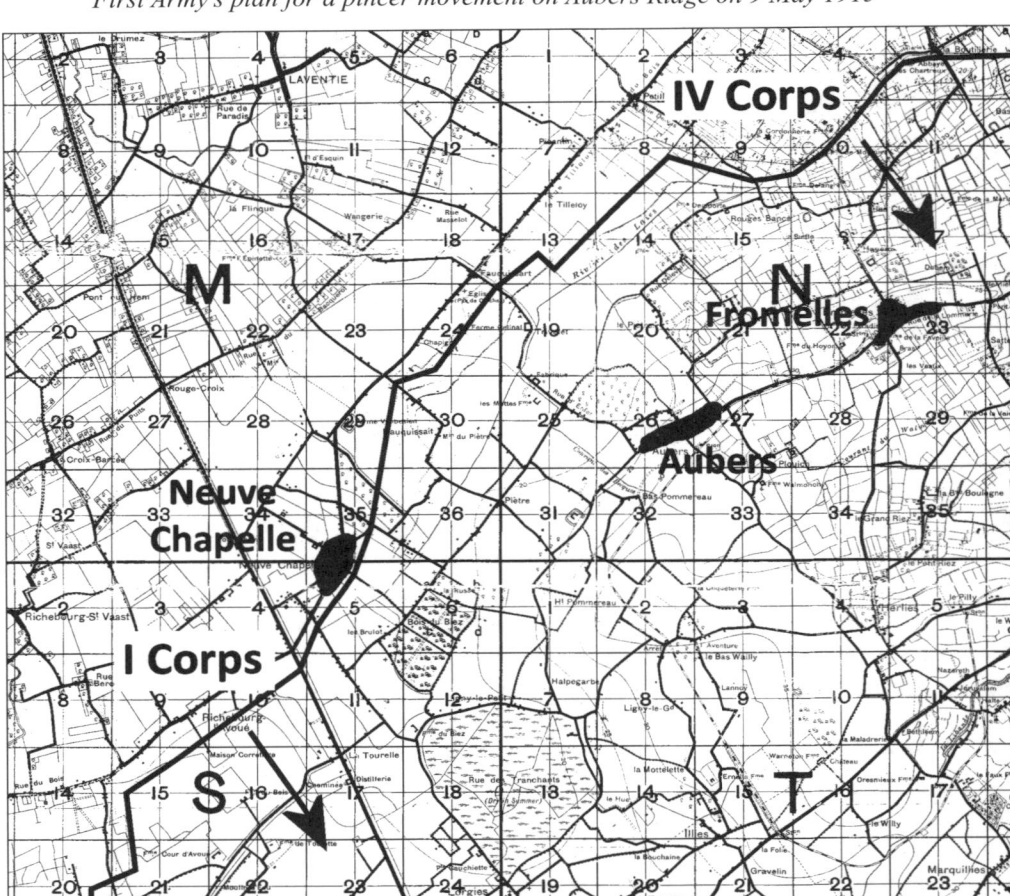

later. Despite the problems to the north, First Army had all its units in position by early May.

General Haig spoke to his corps and divisional commanders at a conference in Bethune on 27 April and again on 6 May. He explained how IV Corps, the Indian Corps and I Corps would meet east of Neuve Chapelle, cutting off six or seven German battalions, before advancing across Aubers Ridge.

The French Tenth Army planned to shell the German trenches for four days with heavy artillery. The bombardment would be 'slow, methodical and prolonged, with the object of destroying the enemy's morale, disorganising his defensive measures and breaking up his obstacles and strong points.' But First Army only had 516 field and light guns and howitzers and 121 heavies.[153] It was also short of ammunition so its artillery officers could only plan for a short bombardment of forty minutes.

The preliminary bombardment of forty minutes would end with a ten minute intense barrage and the Heavy Artillery Reserve (HAR) Group commanders and the divisional artillery commanders worked together to prepare the artillery timetable. The 18-pounders would cut the wire while the field howitzers demolished the German parapet and strongpoints. The two HAR Groups would cooperate with the ground and aerial observers to hit the German batteries and other long-range targets.

The field artillery would create belts of fire beyond the German front position after zero hour. For the first time 'infantry artillery' groups were formed and attached to infantry brigades. These mortar groups would move behind the infantry, ready to deal with strongpoints.

The Royal Flying Corps' 1st Wing began flying over the battlefield four days before the attack. Planes made defensive patrols to stop enemy reconnaissance planes looking to spot the batteries and infantry units moving into position. The planes were equipped with wireless telegraphy so they could keep in touch with the artillery and adjust their shots.

Three machines would take it in turn to fly over the battlefield and look out for large white linen strips the infantry would lay on the ground to report progress. They would also watch for enemy reinforcements and new defensive positions. While 1st Wing bombed the German headquarters, villages and bridges in the area, the Headquarters Wing would fly deeper and attack railway junctions.

The infantry were kept busy in the days before zero hour. They carried everything from ammunition and rations to tools and stores up to the dumps. Some dug new trenches to assemble in, widened the communication trenches and built dugouts. Despite the mass of activity behind the front,

---

153 The French Tenth Army had 220 heavy guns and over 720 field guns and howitzers.

the Germans failed to notice anything unusual until the day before the attack, by which time it was too late to make a difference.

General Haig issued First Army's operation orders on 6 May. Unfortunately, heavy rain fell all day and night, followed by mist in the morning. The French artillery had started its four day bombardment on 3 May but the bad weather meant Tenth Army's attack was postponed first to 8 May and then to the morning of the 9th because the mist continued into the afternoon.

News of the postponement reached First Army Advanced Headquarters at Merville at 5pm on 7 May, so Haig stopped the assault brigades moving into the trenches. Field Marshal French asked if First Army could attack at the same time as the Tenth Army and his request was granted. The skies over the battlefield cleared during the night so the French bombardment could continue on the 8th. After a frustrating day of waiting, the assault troops began moving forward at dusk and they were all in position by midnight.

IV Corps Attack at Fromelles

The left hand assault was to be made between Bois Grenier and Neuve Chapelle by IV Corps. General Rawlinson planned to use Major General Francis Davies' 8th Division to break through the German line and it would advance south-east towards Rouges Bancs, spreading out to take the Germans in the flank. Major General Hubert Gough's 7th Division would then move through the gap and advance onto Aubers Ridge, looking to link up with the Indian Corps. The pincer movement would tear a five mile wide gap in the German line for the minimum of effort. But the front was waterlogged, making it impossible to dig deep so huge breastworks had been built to protect the infantry. It was also criss-crossed by water-filled ditches which the infantry would have to negotiate while under fire.

The assault brigades moved into the trenches the night before the battle and as 25 Brigade settled down on the left, 24 Brigade took up their positions on the right while 23 Brigade was in divisional reserve. The reserves were close with most of 7th Division only one mile behind. All the troops were in their assigned trenches or at their assembly points by the early hours and the bombardment began at 5am.

The field artillery of 7th and 8th Divisions were supported by Brigadier General Uniacke's No. 2 Group Heavy Artillery Reserve with the VII Siege Brigade attached. But the flat ground had made it difficult to deploy the guns in secret, so the majority had been camouflaged at least a mile from the front line. This made registration difficult and the timing of the attack made it impossible to observe the fall of shot. This was unfortunate because the worn out guns were firing short and the observers would have also seen that many of the faulty shells were failing to explode.

The guns were also too far back to carry out wire-cutting so Captain the Hon Russell had supervised the building of two emplacements in the front breastwork. Field guns were secretly moved into the positions and they opened fire on the wire at zero hour. They only had a short time to accomplish their important task but as one blasted gaps in the wire, the other punched a hole in the floor of its emplacement, rendering it useless.

The leading companies climbed out of their trenches and deployed as the artillery carried out the final ten minutes of intense fire. But the bombardment seemed to be making little difference because machine gun fire was already hitting the assault troops and bayonets were appearing

I Corps attack towards Fromelles on 9 May

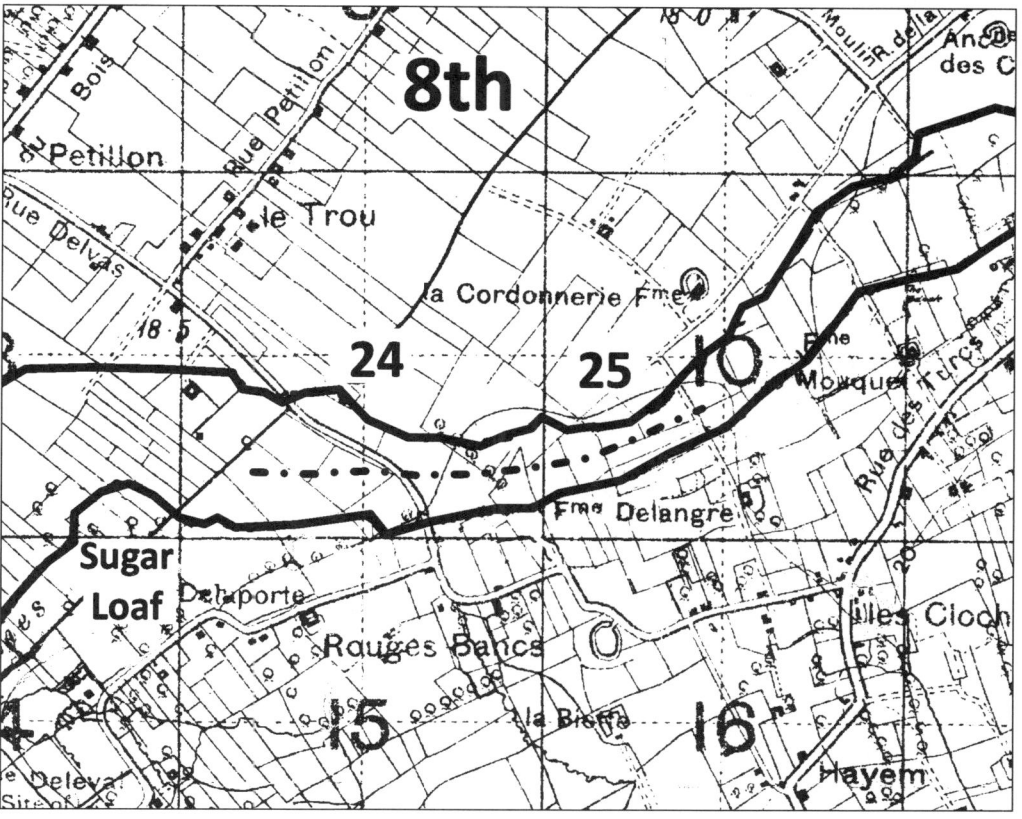

above the parapet. It appeared the Germans were ready and waiting for the attack to begin.

On the left attack, 25 Brigade was deployed to attack the German line at two points. The 1/13th London formed the left column and then there was a 400 yard gap to the right column, which had the 1st Irish Rifles and 2nd Rifle Brigade advancing side by side.

Major Williams and the men of 173rd Tunnelling Company RE had set two mines under the left sector. They were detonated at 5.40pm and the Londoners leading companies ran out to occupy the craters. Lieutenant Colonel Lewis' support companies passed through them, advanced past Delangre Farm, and reached the third German trench. They then occupied a German communication trench and turned it into a firing trench, to cover the division's flank.

The wire facing Major Baker's 1st Irish Rifles and Lieutenant Colonel Stephens' 2nd Rifle Brigade had been cut and wave after wave of platoons doubled across no man's land. They clambered over the German breastwork, cleared the trench and then pushed on another 200 metres. Major Baker took his two platoons of Irish Rifles to his left to clear a trench the Londoners had been unable to take, securing his flank.

The volume of fire increased from the trench to the east, which had not been attacked, as Captains French and Griffin led two 2nd Lincoln companies across. Corporal Charles Sharpe had cleared 50 metres of trench by the time all of his group had fallen, so he got Privates Bills, Donderdale and Leeman to join him and they cleared another 250 metres of trenches.

Having taken their objective, the 2nd Rifle Brigade bombed the trenches to its flanks, but Colonel Stephens' men were still in a cramped position. Two 2nd Berkshire companies had followed the Rifle Brigade across no man's land, only to find the trenches full of men while others laid in the open waiting to advance. The 2nd Berkshires' senior officer decided to keep moving forward but they were only halfway to the next trench when they suddenly began falling back. No reason was given for the retirement but some say some Germans could have been shouting 'retire' and the men had responded. Captain Hunt stopped them falling back across no man's land and Captain MacGregor led his company forward to try to renew the advance. Although 25 Brigade had broken into the German trenches, misunderstandings had led to gridlock and delay.

General Lowry-Cole went to the front trench when he heard the news, arriving about forty minutes after zero. He found the trenches full of men and no one daring to go forward because no man's land was under heavy fire. Lowry-Cole wanted to exploit the limited success they had had so far and he was telling Major Cox to send the rest of the Lincolns forward when disaster struck. The Rifle Brigade and Irish Rifles began running back from the German trench, taking the Lincolns lying behind the breastwork with them. A number of German prisoners seen running for cover behind the British front line were mistaken for a counter-attack, causing even more confusion.

The rest of the brigade front was a shambles. The support battalions were waiting to advance while the assault battalions were running back across no man's land for no apparent reason. The brigade staff tried to restore order but it was impossible to move in the congested trenches. Lowry-Cole was standing on the parapet shouting and waving at everyone to go back when he fell mortally wounded. Major Cox had to take control of the chaos because the senior brigade officer, Colonel Stephens, was across in the German trenches.

On the right, Brigadier General Oxley had left a 300 yard gap between 24 Brigade's two assault battalions so they could attack the flanks of a salient in the German trenches. No man's land was over 300 metres wide in the 2nd East Lancashires' sector because the water-logged ground had prevented them digging any closer. The Germans opened fire as soon as Major Maclear's men began to deploy and everyone was pinned before they had gone far.

The 2nd Northants started ten minutes later and they had 200 metres to go. The left company was stopped by wire but Lieutenant Parker's men headed for a gap and around thirty men entered the enemy trench. Machine gunfire stopped the support companies so Private Lapham ran back to report Parker's desperate situation to Major Mowatt, and General Oxley sent the 1st Sherwood Foresters forward when he heard.

Unfortunately, the Sherwoods were directed to help the East Lancashires, rather than to exploit the Northants' success. Major Morley's men were cut down as they crowded through the single gap in the entanglement and they then ran into a wire-filled ditch. By the time a message had been sent back, the reserves were crowding into the trenches and were under German artillery fire.

Brigadier General Pinney of 23 Brigade was sent forward to take command of all 8th Division's battalions north of the Sailly-Fromelles road. Major General Davies wanted to find out what the situation was, so his senior staff officer, Colonel Anderson, went forward to find out what was happening. By 8.30am Anderson knew the awful truth. There were only three isolated lodgements in the German trench; a few of the 13th London were on the division's left flank; some of the Rifle Brigade and the Irish

Rifles were holding out in the centre, and the Northants had a foothold on the right. The final attempt in the centre was made around noon by Lieutenant Gray and around fifty men of the Rifle Brigade. Only half reached an abandoned trench in the middle of no man's land.

The only place showing any promise was on the left, around Delangre Farm. The Londoners were soon out of bombs so the 2nd Scottish Rifles crawled forward in single file along a battered trench, taking fresh supplies and a machine gun with them. Captain Thruston also took the rest of the Lincoln's forward, using the mine craters as cover to cross no man's land. They reached the trench west of the Londoners but Thruston could not contact them, so he set about improving his own position.

Thruston sent the Scottish Rifles bombers to clear one trench while Second Lieutenant Black and the Lincoln bombers cleared 300 metres of trench and silenced two German machine guns in the other direction. As his men set about creating a defensive position, Thruston sent back a message around 10.30am reporting his situation.

Soon afterwards, Major Harvey[154] sent Captain Nugent and 200 2nd Berkshires crawling forward along the crater sap. Around 12.30pm, the rest of the battalion were working their way along the sap when the London and Lincolns started running back. The Berkshires also fell back when they learnt the 2nd Scottish Rifles had withdrawn from the untenable position.

The advance was at a standstill but the supports were still moving forward, meeting wounded and leaderless men coming back. The divisional artillery could not help because they had no idea where the British troops were. So they continued shelling distant targets or stayed silent until requests for support came in. All the telephone lines were cut and the runners either had to push through the congested trenches, or take a chance and run out in the open.

General Rawlinson reported the chaos to General Haig and was simply told to 'press the attack vigorously and without delay on Rouges Bancs.' Rawlinson told the artillery to fire at the Sugar Loaf salient, next to the Northants on the right (west) flank of the attack. He also instructed a new attack by 25 and 24 Brigades, starting at 1.30pm. The Germans suspected something was happening and stepped up their artillery fire on the British trenches, catching the troops as they assembled. The attack was a complete disaster; few men made it as far as the British front line and no one crossed no-man's land.

General Haig again urged Rawlinson to make another attempt, even giving him 21 Brigade[155] to support the decimated brigades. But IV Corps still had the same problem, too many men to put in the trenches. But

154 Lieutenant Colonel Finch had been killed.
155 7th Division.

Rawlinson convinced General Gough it was useless to do more until the front had been reorganised, so the next attempt was timed for dusk. But could the three footholds hold on long enough?

Colonel Stephens handed over command of his Londoners to Lieutenant Nieuport of the 1st Irish Rifles so he could fetch reinforcements from the British trenches. He returned with seventy men, two machine guns and the Berkshires' bombers. Meanwhile, Sergeant Clarke risked his life cutting new gaps in the wire so it was less of an obstacle. Major Betty also spent the afternoon supervising the digging of a trench across no man's land, so men and supplies could be moved forward and casualties could be evacuated.

But the plan to launch another attack was interrupted when the Germans counter-attacked and Captain Thruston and Lieutenants Black and Parker led their men back to safety. During the night General Pinney's 23 Brigade and the 1st Worcesters[156] took over the line but they too were in a precarious position. The Germans started attacking Lieutenant Newport's barricades in the early hours and they overwhelmed his group after they ran out of bombs.

The Indian Corps, Rue du Bois

The bombardment began at 5am. The field artillery targeted the wire and the front trench as the heavy artillery hit the strongpoints behind. Thirty minutes later the rate of fire intensified and the guns firing at the wire in no man's land switched from shrapnel to high explosive ammunition.[157]

Steps had been cut into the parapet and ladders had been set up so the men could climb quickly over the breastwork. Gaps had been made in the British wire and bridges had been laid across dykes so they could deploy. Everything was ready, but the Germans' sentries had been watching and reporting every movement.

Although the Flying Corps observers had spotted many of the German emplacements, the forward observers working with the batteries could not see because hedges and trees hid most things on the flat ground. Instead aeroplanes fitted with wireless had been allocated to the two Heavy Artillery Reserve (HAR) Groups to control counter-battery fire.[158] It was also hoped the infantry would be able to pinpoint strongpoints for the artillery.

Lieutenant General Sir Charles Anderson's Meerut Division was on the left of the attack, around the road junction south of Neuve Chapelle called Port Arthur.[159] Brigadier General Jacob's Dehra Dun Brigade was astride the Estaires to the La Bassée road but Lieutenant Colonel Ritchie's 1st Seaforths stayed in their trench, west of the road.

---

156 Attached from 24 Brigade.
157 It was hoped the shrapnel had cut the wire into many pieces and the high-explosive would then smash the timber frames and posts holding it all together, creating large gaps.
158 Three planes were allocated to No 1 Group and four planes were allocated to No 2 Group.
159 Major General Henry Keary's Lahore Division was holding the Neuve Chapelle sector to the north.

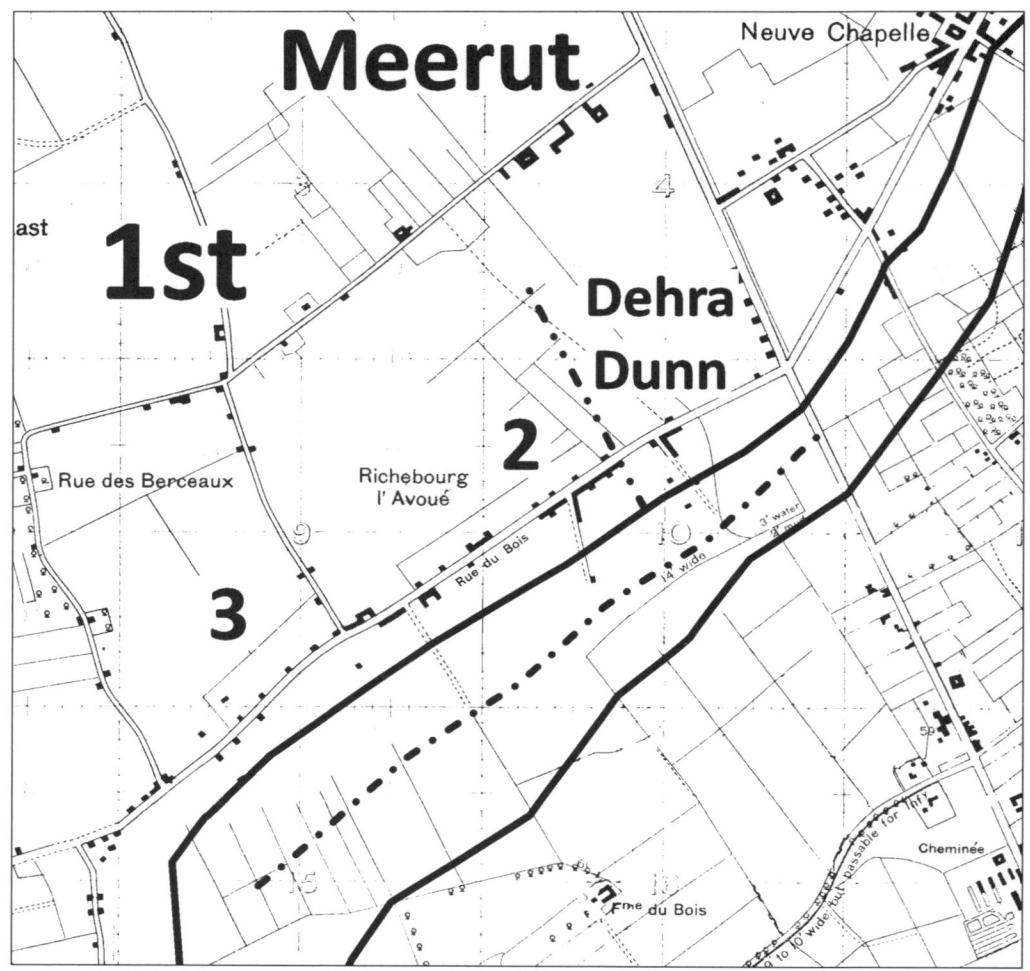

IV Corps attack south of Neuve Chapelle on 9 May

Lieutenant Colonel Cuthbert's 1/4th Seaforths and Major Boileau's 2/2nd Gurkhas set off side by side, walking straight into a hail of machine gun fire. 'Up we get: machine guns sweep the parapet up and down, backwards and forwards, and many fall back into the trench mortally wounded. Once on the level again, down we go flat. The number of dead and wounded lying around is awful, and the shells!'

Over 400 1st Seaforths fell as 'officers and men were cut down as if by an invisible reaping machine.' The 1/4th Seaforths suffered the same fate and the survivors were pinned down in a ditch. Captain Dudley and Subadar Lekh Ram were killed and Lieutenant Hebbert was severely wounded as two platoons of Jats were cut down. Captains Mullaly and Park were wounded and Lieutenant Collins was killed leading the 2/2nd Gurkhas; the survivors also found cover in a ditch.

It was estimated that over twenty machine guns put down a deadly cross-fire which no one standing up could survive. Each wave in turn was shot down, on or in front of the breastwork, and few went more than a few metres. The British guns were firing short, hitting those pinned in no man's land, while the German artillery shelled the trenches. Orders were issued for the survivors to withdraw to the trench but few returned and a second bombardment made no difference.

Both Cuthbert and Boileau took the wise decision not to send any more men over the top and as one anonymous participant noted, 'I was one of the last to leave the trenches. One got a dim, hazy vision of the leading platoon doubling forward and of seeing them simply fade under the terrific machine gun and rifle fire which opened on us as soon as we got over.'

Brigadier General Blackader was worried the Germans might counter-attack, so he ordered the 1/9th Gurkhas to occupy the front trench. Only 200 men could squeeze into the smashed trench and they could do little because the trench was full of dazed and wounded men crawling around.

But for those already in no man's land, it was just the start of a dangerous day laid out in the open and under fire. 'Inch by inch, foot by foot, yard by yard, we work ourselves forward, through grass in many places even then soaking with blood. No talk or thought of revenge now – everything, anything for an inch of cover. Thank God, a slight depression, scarcely four inches below the surrounding level, but it is cover! The place is an inferno – a red hell – and oh those frightful lyddites;[160] blow the place to bits and rip and slash and tear to pieces those puny things lying in the grass so still.'

Some men crawled back to the parapet and hauled themselves over as hands reached out to pull them to safety; a few took the risk and ran back. Others went to the aid of injured friends, either tending to their wounds or dragging them back.[161] The rest just lay where they were and scraped at the soil with their bayonets, trying to create an earth shelter.[162]

The attack had been a complete disaster. General Anderson ordered a repeat barrage as soon as he heard the news, starting at 6.30am, and this time the 1st Seaforths would join in. Thirty minutes later the infantry went over the top again and while Cuthbert refused to let the 1/4th Seaforths' left

---

160 Lyddite (or picric acid) was the explosive used in shells.
161 The 1st Seaforths suffered over 500 casualties while the 1/4th Seaforths suffered 175 casualties.
162 Known as digging head cover, a mound of earth large enough to protect the head and shoulders.

company leave the trenches, the waves of the 1st Seaforths went forward one after another. They advanced in short rushes but the casualties were horrendous and fewer and fewer men responded each time the officers waved them forward. Lieutenant Tennant was the last officer standing but he and his men were all shot down at the wire.

For a second time no man's land was littered with bodies, some crawling back, some digging in and the rest motionless. Men left behind in the front trench tunnelled under the parapet in several places so men could get back in without having to expose themselves climbing over the breastwork. Several men went out to rescue injured friends and Sergeant Mackenzie alone brought in five wounded men.

The Cinder Track, I Corps

Lieutenant General Charles Monro had Major General Richard Haking's 1st Division deployed astride the Cinder Track. Major General Charles Barter's 2nd London Division[163] was holding the line to the south while Major General Henry Horne's 2nd Division was in reserve, ready to take over any captured territory. Water-filled ditches crossed no man's land and while 3 Brigade only had on average 200 metres to cross, 2 Brigade had twice that distance to go.

Again the German machine guns were in fortified dugouts under their parapet or in camouflaged emplacements in no man's land. The deadly weapons had survived the artillery barrage and they opened fire as soon as the first wave of assault troops went over the top.

Lieutenant Colonel Prothero's 2nd Welch[164] were shot down as they weaved their way through the few gaps in the wire and no one reached the enemy trench. A German machine gun team dragged their weapon down a shallow tunnel[165] to a camouflaged position in no man's land facing the 2nd Munsters[166] flank as Captain Hewitt led his men over the top. They fired into Lieutenant Price's company, hitting many as they doubled forward. Those who reached the enemy parapet kept moving, because the support company had been detailed to clear out the dugouts. Observers spotted one of the Munsters standing on the German parapet waving a green flag, indicating it had been reached, but it still had to be cleared.

The Germans emerged from their dug-outs before Captain Campbell-Dick's company arrived and they fell back, literally chasing the few dozen Munsters who were pressing on towards the objective. Hewitt and Price made their men take cover in a stream bed to engage them. Lieutenant Stewart was taking the last wave across no man's land when Lieutenant Colonel Rickard was killed.

---

163 Later numbered 47th Division.
164 3 Brigade.
165 Known as a Russian sap.
166 3 Brigade.

The British artillery then started firing short and a shell killed Campbell-Dick and Stewart as they were conferring. An injured Second Lieutenant Wainwright crawled back across no man's land to ask the guns to lengthen their range but it took a long time to pass the message on. Captain Hewitt's company was left isolated and under fire from the front and behind; only two men, Privates Meehan and Scanlon, returned. Many risked their lives to rescue the wounded; Private Barry dragged Captain Hawkes back and Sergeant Gannon went out five times to rescue injured comrades.[167]

Lieutenant Colonel Green's 2nd Sussex[168] were shot to pieces as they bunched up to get through the German wire. Lieutenant Colonel Dobbin's[169] 1st Northants came under enfilade fire as they made the longest journey to the German trench, around 500 metres. Captain Ward-Hunt's company was virtually wiped out but Lieutenant Parker reached the German trench with about thirty men. Lieutenant Middleton's company was unable to reach them and Lieutenant Lawrence's company was shot down when they tried at 6.30am. Parker and a few men eventually returned after dusk, followed by Sergeant Brightham and a few more.[170]

There is little to tell of the support battalions. The 1/4th Welsh Fusiliers never reached 3 Brigade's front line.[171] The 1/5th Sussex and 2nd KRRC[172] came under fire the moment they entered no man's land and many were cut down just in front of the parapet.

Both Generals Davies and Thesiger quickly realised something was wrong. They were both asking for another short bombardment not long after zero hour and General Haking gave instructions to begin a forty-five minute bombardment at 6.15am. General Anderson agreed the Meerut Division would join in but there was no time to deploy the assault troops in the congested trenches. Only a few men were in position by the time the guns lifted and their gallant attempt to cross no man's land was futile.

At 7.20am General Haking reported the catastrophe to I Corps headquarters and General Monro told him to send the 1 (Guards) Brigade forward. Haking replied he could not break into the German position even if he used all of the 2nd Division. General Anderson ordered a further bombardment at 7.45am on the Indian Corps front but it just encouraged the German guns to return fire. He called it off after an hour, after hearing 1st Division needed two hours to reorganise. All that could be done was to shell the German trenches to help the stranded men escape no man's land, but most did not come back until dusk.

The Second Assault at Rue de Bois
By 8am General Haig had received reports on the I Corps and Indian Corps

---

167 The Welch suffered around 225 casualties but the Munsters suffered nearly 400.
168 2 Brigade.
169 2 Brigade.
170 The 2nd Sussex and 1st Northants both suffered around 560 casualties.
171 Lieutenant Colonel France-Hayhurst was killed.
172 2 Brigade.

attack. While they said there been little progress, it was not made clear that the attack had been a total failure with heavy casualties. So Haig wanted to try again because the French were advancing to the south.

General Richard Haking said 1st Division could attack at midday, as long as the artillery could cut more of the wire and destroy some of the machine guns. But Haig postponed zero hour to 2.40pm after General Willcocks said the Bareilly Brigade needed time to replace the Dehra Dun Brigade. His next stop was I Corps headquarters near Essars, where General Monro was told the new time.

At 11.20am Brigadier General Southey reported the Bareilly Brigade would not be ready, so First Army postponed zero hour to 4pm. Then Brigadier General Thesiger reported 2 Brigade was in no condition to go over the top again, so Brigadier General Lowther was instructed to move his 1 (Guards) Brigade into position.

The late decision to change the assault troops on the Meerut Division front meant the reliefs were rushed and the German guns continued to shell the trenches, hitting over 200 men. The British heavy artillery did their best to silence the German guns while the field artillery targeted the trenches and wire. Observers could see better in the afternoon light and they reported the gaps in the wire were growing while the breastworks were being demolished a few sandbags at a time. Brigadier General Southey thought the artillery bombardment had made no difference and asked for the attack to be postponed. General Willcocks told him to press the attack home and to keep trying until he succeeded.

A hail of machine gun fire swept back and forth as the Bareilly Brigade scrambled over the parapet; only a few reached the dyke a few metres in front of the Indian trench. The Germans were so confident that they could be seen standing up on the parapet to get a better shot at the prone men in no man's land. Southey allowed two further attempts and then called an end to the massacre.[173]

Meanwhile, 1st Division's trenches were very crowded and at 3.45pm Major Brown told General Lowther that his 1st Camerons would not be ready to join 1 (Guards) Brigade's attack. So Lowther told Lieutenant Colonel Stewart to send his 1st Black Watch forward at zero hour and told Brown to follow as soon as he could.

German lookouts could be seen peering over the parapet opposite 3 Brigade's front, meaning the barrage was not doing its job. They shouted warnings the moment the 1st South Wales Borderers and 1st Gloucesters clambered over the parapet. No one went further than 100 metres. The Black Watch doubled forward on the brigade right as the pipers played *Highland*

---

173 The Bareilly Brigade lost over 1,000 men in a few minutes.

Laddie and the first wave charged into the enemy trench. The Germans put up a tough fight and many of the Highlanders were hit including Major Robertson and Second Lieutenants Gray, Wanliss and Wallace.

Corporal Ripley had been the first to enter the German trench through a gap in the sandbag parapet and he continued onto the second line. Lieutenant Scott went the furthest on the left while Second Lieutenant Lyle led fifty men into the support trench on the right. German reinforcements ran into the escaping garrison so the Highlanders dispersed the crowd. They used the communication trenches to surround the Scots while machine gun fire stopped the rest of Colonel Stewart's men getting forward. Ripley, Scott and Lyle were never seen again and neither were their men.[174]

At 4.35pm General Haking issued orders for a repeat attack following a ten minute bombardment. It had no chance of succeeding and the experience of the Black Watch and the Camerons sums up the futility of this final attempt. Thirty bridges had been put across the dyke in front of the 2nd Black Watch but most had been destroyed by German shelling by the time Lieutenant Sutherland and Captain McLeod led the first wave into no man's land.

Colonel Harvey and Major Wauchope could only watch as a few Black Watch crossed the dyke. All but two of Lance Corporal David Finlay's bombing party were hit so he ordered them to crawl back. He then half carried, half dragged one of his wounded men over 100 metres to safety; he was awarded the Victoria Cross. Two companies of the Camerons suffered the same fate but the rest were saved because the attack was called off.

Both brigadiers reported the failure and said their battalions could do no more. A withdrawal from no man's land was ordered but most men returned when it was dark. General Haig heard the news around 5pm and decided to wait for 2nd Division to replace 1st Division.

Breaking off the Battle
It was late afternoon before everything was ready and everyone was in place. Even then many of the trenches were filled with men and it was too dangerous to move bodies of men about in the open. The roads were jammed with traffic, and artillery fire added to the difficulties of preparing for the new attack. So Haig took the decision to cancel the 8pm attack and he visited the Indian Corps headquarters in Lestrem to talk to his corps commanders.

While they all wanted to continue the offensive, the dilemma was should they attack at night without artillery support or attack after a bombardment?

---

174 The Black Watch suffered 475 casualties.

Either way, the attack needed fresh units and they would not know the ground, making a night attack a dangerous prospect. First Army had to attack in daylight and the decision was confirmed by telephone to the corps commanders at 11.30pm.

The problem was the new attack would come too late to save 8th Division's footholds in the German trenches. No man's land was swept by machine gunfire, making it impossible to get to them. The group on the right was the first to evacuate their position. Sixteen Northants returned at nightfall, carrying ten wounded men with them. On the left, Major Finch crawled forward with a mixed group of the 2nd Berkshires and the 2nd Lincolns[175] to the Londoners. They were too few and they all withdrew after Finch was killed. It was impossible to reach the 1st Irish Rifles and the Rifle Brigade in the centre until a trench had been dug across no man's land. Only then could reinforcements, bombs and ammunition be sent across, but again it was too little too late. Around 200 survivors used the trench to escape soon afterwards, ending the battle on 8th Division's front.

The combined losses of the three divisions was over 9,500 officers and men.[176] General Haig called his corps commanders to I Corps headquarters the following morning and told them there was an ammunition shortage.[177] He cancelled the 4pm attack, called off IV Corps' operations north of Neuve Chapelle and announced that all First Army resources should be concentrated on I Corps front at Festubert. French agreed with Haig's decision and 7th Division left IV Corps area and headed to I Corps as soon as it was dark.

---

175 In 25 Brigade's sector.
176 The 2nd Rifle Brigade suffered over 650; the 1st Royal Irish Rifles over 475; 1/13th London 435.
177 Defective 4.7-inch shells had been delivered to IV Corps so the howitzers could not fire at the enemy batteries.

Chapter 8

We Are Ready For You
The Battle of Festubert

As Second Army was struggling to hold its own at Ypres, First Army started planning for its next offensive on 10 May, only a day after the Aubers Ridge failure. General Haig wasted no time in transferring 7th Division from IV Corps to I Corps and 21 Brigade and 2nd Division took over the line between Neuve Chapelle and Festubert over the next three nights. Two 1st Division brigades moved into line between Givenchy and Cuinchy at the same time.

Joffre and Foch kept on at Field Marshal French to continue First Army's offensive, even though Second Army was fighting to hold the salient. The French kept promising to restore the lost ground on the north side of the salient but they did not. British divisions had to be sent north to help hold the area around Ypres and a frustrated Joffre said the movements were upsetting his plans for a new offensive across the Artois plateau.

But French and Haig had more problems than the Ypres situation. The BEF was short of artillery ammunition. The invasion of Gallipoli had begun on 25 April and large amounts of munitions were being sent to the Dardanelles, leaving the industry struggling to supply both fronts. It was a frustrating state of affairs because the plans for cooperation with the French had been based on the reinforcements promised by the Secretary of State. Time was slipping away because the Austro-Germans had broken the Galician front and German divisions could soon be returning from the east. But the lack of ammunition meant that the New Army divisions could not be sent overseas, leaving French in the dark about how many divisions he would have for the foreseeable future.

French met Joffre and Foch on 12 May and they made it clear they were unhappy with First Army's delays. They wanted it to attack immediately or relieve a French division south of the La Bassée canal. They agreed on the second option and 47th Division took over the line north of the canal so 1st Division could take over the French sector south of Cuinchy. The two divisions were grouped under Major General Charles Barter, 47th Division and they were collectively referred to as Barter's Force.

The reason Haig did not want to attack immediately was that the failure on 9 May had led him to believe that a short bombardment was useless. The next offensive had to be preceded by a bombardment lasting two or three days, to reduce the Germans' morale. He also wanted plenty of heavy artillery to destroy their wire and machine gun emplacements. Haig made his thoughts clear to French and they agreed to delay the offensive until 15 May.

The Plan of Operations

Haig met his corps and divisional commanders and their senior staff at I Corps advanced headquarters on 12 May. First Army issued its orders on 13 May and I Corps circulated its version to the divisions the following day. There would be a two pronged attack with a 600 yard gap between 2nd Division and 7th Division. Major General Henry Horne wanted his 2nd Division to make a night attack because his troops knew the ground and they could establish a footing in the German trenches before dawn, before moving into unknown territory in daylight.

Major General Thompson Capper's 7th Division had just taken over the area so it would attack at daylight, as the 2nd Division advanced from the German support trench. The troops would reform along the La Quinque Rue while another bombardment prepared the ground, ready for the next stage of the advance. The Meerut Division would establish a flank south of Neuve Chapelle on the left while 47th Division would secure the right flank.

The Royal Flying Corps' 1st Wing would observe for the artillery and infantry, the same as it had during the Battle of Aubers Ridge. Pilots would also bomb rest billets and observation posts while long range flights would target headquarters and trains.

The Preliminary Bombardment

The two-day artillery bombardment began on the morning of 13 May and the divisional batteries were supported by Heavy Artillery Group 1 and eighteen French guns. The Indian Cavalry Corps, 47th Division and 51st (Highland) Division had also sent help, increasing the number of guns and howitzers to 433.

Lieutenant General Charles Monro had attached artillery advisers to each division and the guns shelled the German defences for two hours, three

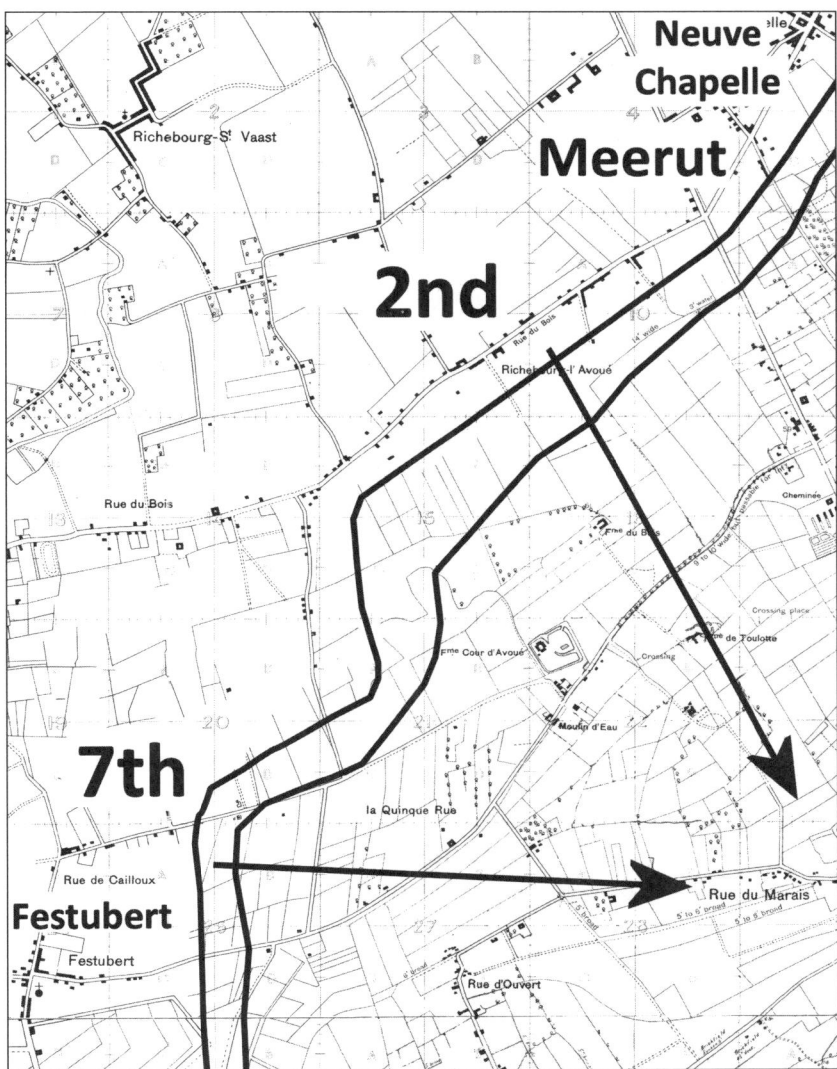

The plan for I Corps two pronged attack east of Festubert on 15–16 May 1915

times a day. Some of the field guns shelled the wire entanglements while the rest hit the communication trenches. The 4.5-inch howitzers bombarded the support and communication trenches as the 6-inch siege howitzer batteries blasted the parapet apart. Three French 155mm batteries dealt with the German batteries south of Violaines.

Special attention was paid to observe the fall of shot, with observers and battery commanders staying in close contact to register the guns. They could then continue shelling the targets at night, stopping repair work and hitting troop movements. Gaps were cut in the wire but many shells had failed to explode. The munitions factories had been forced to lower their standards to keep the front supplied. It would be the start of the problem of dud shells which would bother the BEF for months to come.

Again the weather would have a part to play in the run up to the attack. It was fine on 10 and 11 May but it started raining on the evening of the 12th. It continued through the following day and night, brightening up on the morning of the 14th. General Haig asked about the ground conditions and while General Capper said he had no problems, General Horne thought the wet ground would slow the men down. General Anderson's report was the most worrying because the batteries designated to cut the wire in front of the Meerut Division were still not in position.

Haig was forced to postpone the assault for twenty-four hours, stretching the limited amount of ammunition much further than he wanted. There was only enough to shell the fronts which were going to be attacked. It meant the Germans could easily work out the limits of the offensive.

Attempts were made to fool the Germans into thinking the assault would start earlier. On 14 May a three minute bombardment was followed by a two minute break, to encourage the Germans to man the parapets; another two minute field artillery barrage followed as the British infantry cheered. The ruse was repeated twice more. The following day the same short artillery bombardment was tried twice again, only this time the intense bombardment lasted for five minutes. Then 15 May dawned sunny, drying the muddy ground, and the assault troops filed into the trenches at nightfall and lined out along the four lines of breastworks.

The Night Assault of the Meerut and 2nd Divisions
The Meerut Division was on the left and General Anderson had the Garhwal Brigade in the line, the Sirhind Brigade in support and the Bareilly Brigade in reserve. The 2nd Division was on the right and Major General Henry Horne had 5 Brigade on its left, 6 Brigade on its right and 4 (Guards) Brigade in support.

The cloudy sky hid the moon and the first wave quietly left the front trench, crossed the water-filled dyke and lay down in line before 11.30pm. Some of the British shells were landing behind the front line and the observers could not see to tell the gunners. The enemy line was 300 metres away and the plan had been for the Indians to creep forward before the barrage lifted, but it was impossible to edge forward with so many British shells landing in no man's land.

Another worry was would the troops walk in the right direction if they could not see their officers? In places it had been noted that the furrows in the soil headed towards the enemy trenches and the men had been told to follow them. Every man had a white patch stitched to his chest and back for identification but many men must have thought it was nothing more than a target.

The Corps order instructed the Lahore Division on the north flank of the attack to 'assist with rifle and machine gunfire throughout the bombardment.' That involved the Jullundur Brigade firing for five minutes

2nd Division's night attack towards Ferme de Bois

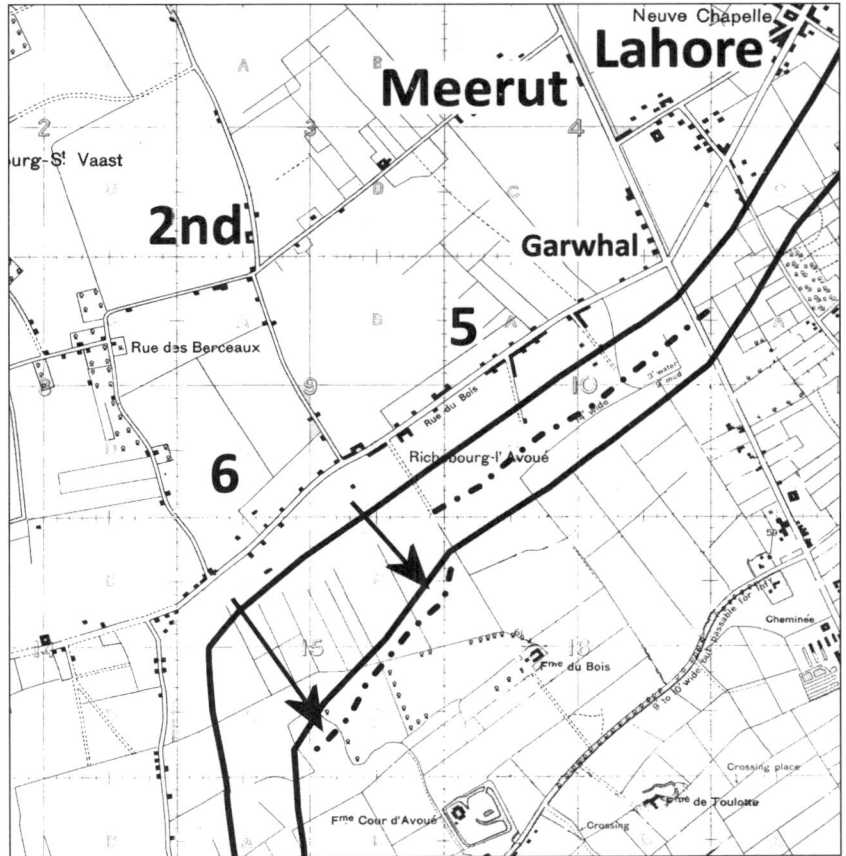

at random intervals during the three hours before zero. All it did was alert the Germans; they lit up no man's land and spotted the men putting the bridges over the dyke. The moment the British field guns extended their range, the Germans fired into no man's land expecting to hit something; and they did.

The 1/39th Garhwalis and the 2nd Leicesters had made sixty bridges to cross the ditch in front of their trench but shell-fire destroyed many. The first wave of the Garhwalis and the 2nd Leicesters filed across the remaining bridges and lined out while the next two waves waited in the trenches and the final wave lay in the open behind. The Germans used flares and a searchlight and began shouting 'Come on we are ready for you' at the figures in the distance. After shooting the first wave down the machine gunners trained on the bridges, blocking them with the dead and injured. The Garhwalis suffered over 150 casualties while the Leicesters suffered over 220.

The Germans opposite 5 Brigade suspected something was afoot and they used a searchlight to sweep no man's land. They used flares and light-ball grenades when they spotted movement and opened fire on the 2nd Worcesters and 2nd Inniskillings as they deployed. They also fire SOS rockets,[178] alerting the German artillery to shell the British trenches.

Captain Crawford and Captain Smythe reached the German trench on the Inniskillings left but their companies suffered severe casualties and they fell back. Captain Hewitt's men captured the first two trenches on the right but Second Lieutenant Wingate was killed as he stood on the parapet directing the bombers. Lieutenant Duffin consolidated the position but Hewitt soon had to fall back to the first line. Brigadier General Chichester sent the two companies of the 2nd Ox and Bucks to help the Inniskillings make a flank for the 1st KRRC, but they were too few to make a difference and everyone was soon back in their own trenches.[179]

On 6 Brigade's front the plan had been to make tunnels under the parapet so the assault troops did not have to climb over the parapet, but they were not ready in time. The first wave moved out into no man's land and they were in place in time. After waiting for a tense fifteen minutes, the Germans had still not spotted them and there were no flares in the sky. At 11.30pm the first wave walked forward at quick time, moving in silence, bayonets fixed, increasing to the double after 100 metres. Then they were spotted and the alarm was raised; they still had 150 metres to go.

The 1st KRRC ran through the bullets, leapt into the German front trench and then advanced to the support trench. They then set up two head-lamps on the German parapet; the lights indicated the trench had been reached.

---

178 SOS rockets were fired in pre-arranged patterns and colours to tell the artillery to fire pre-set barrages.
179 The Inniskillings suffered 671 casualties.

The Germans ran along the communication trench, parallel with the Cinder Track and past Ferme du Bois. The 1st KRRC followed but stopped to turn it into a fire trench[180]while under crossfire from the front and to the left. The objective had been taken and casualties had been low but Major Shakerley had been mortally wounded after asking Brigadier General Fanshawe for reinforcements. Captain Gunner's company of the 2nd Staffords was sent forward and it helped consolidate the captured position.

German snipers started shooting at the 1st Berkshires as they deployed in no man's land and the machine gunners opened fire as they doubled forward. Captain Radford's men led the charge over the enemy parapet 'and in many cases they caught hold of the Germans' rifles and shot the firer.' Captain Allfrey was wounded as his men bombed their way along the first trench and Captain Frizell's company continued to the support trench. Captain Belcher was killed at the head of the third company and his men were delayed en route to consolidate the support trench. Lieutenant Cox was killed early on so Major Hill led his company forward to consolidate the first trench and then asked for reinforcements. Two 1st Kings' companies were sent forward but they became scattered en route and did little to help. This form of deployment was designed to capture, clear and consolidate the trenches. It was an early form of what would become known as leap-frogging.

The 1/7th King's split into groups as it made its way through the few gaps in the wire. Some merged with the Berkshires on the left, leaving a section of Germans in the centre of the battalion and they continued to fire on the support waves crossing no man's land. Lieutenant Colonel Stott's men kept going forward and a flashing torch around midnight indicated the second line had been taken. The rest of the King's had surrounded the group of Germans in the front trench; they closed in at first light, killing all those who fought or refused to surrender; around 200 were taken prisoner.

Reports reached the Indian Corps and I Corps headquarters an hour after zero hour and Generals Willcocks and Monro knew about the mixture of failure and success by 12.45pm. Both were eager to try again to exploit 6 Brigade's achievements and they organised a thirty minute bombardment with zero hour at 3.15am.

But the Germans were ready and the first wave of the 1/3rd London and the 2/3rd Gurkha Rifles were shot down close to their own parapet, so Lieutenant Colonels Howell and Ormsby stopped any more men going over the top. Meanwhile, the 9th HLI had been unable to get through the congested trenches to relieve the 2nd Worcesters in 5 Brigade's sector. The German machine guns easily covered no man's land behind 6 Brigade's

---

180 Which involved rearranging the sandbags to form a fire-step, so the men could shoot over the parapet.

foothold and Lieutenant Colonel Routledge decided against sending any of the 2nd South Staffords forward.[181] But two 1st King's platoons went over the top fifteen minutes later only to be cut down. Lieutenant Colonel Steavenson wanted to stop any more men going forward but his men across no man's land needed ammunition. Captain Hutchinson volunteered to take some men and they crawled across, each carrying four bandoliers and bombs.

The dawn attack by the Meerut Division and 2nd Division had failed and precious reserves had been wasted but First Army's line had not moved any further forward. All Haig could do was to call off further attacks where they had failed before and move the left boundary of the offensive to the Cinder Track. He also moved the Sirhind Brigade behind 2nd Division to act as a reserve.

The Northern Breastwork, 7th Division

The bombardment increased on 7th Division's front at 2.45am and this time lessons had been learned from the Aubers Ridge fiasco a week earlier. Six field guns had been fitted with rubber tyres so they made no noise as they were wheeled into special emplacements in the front breastwork. The crews targeted the German parapet with high explosive shells, reducing the amount of ammunition required and it gave the Germans no time to repair the damage. The guns also hit the parapets to the flanks, to disguise the limits of the attack.

The plan was to take two rocket guns across no man's land so coded flares could be fired when the front trench had been captured. It was an early attempt to solve the problem of communicating progress to the artillery and higher commands when it was dark. Unfortunately, the artillery plan stopped the bombardment of the trenches to the flanks at zero. This was not an oversight on Major General Hubert Gough's part; it was due to the shortage of guns and ammunition to cover the attack front. It meant the Germans immediately knew the limits of the attack.

After thirty minutes of intense shelling the assault troops moved towards the German trench. The 2nd Borders and 2nd Scots Guards[182] came under fire as they waited astride Princes Road for zero hour so they ran through their own barrage to avoid it. The Borders suffered many casualties, including Lieutenant Colonel Wood, but they captured the first trench. They crossed Rue des Cailloux but a deep dyke stopped them reaching the North Breastwork. Machine guns in the Quadrilateral strongpoint fired into the Borders left flank and the bombers were unable to progress along the communication trenches.

---

181 Both Garhwal Brigades.
182 Both 20 Brigade.

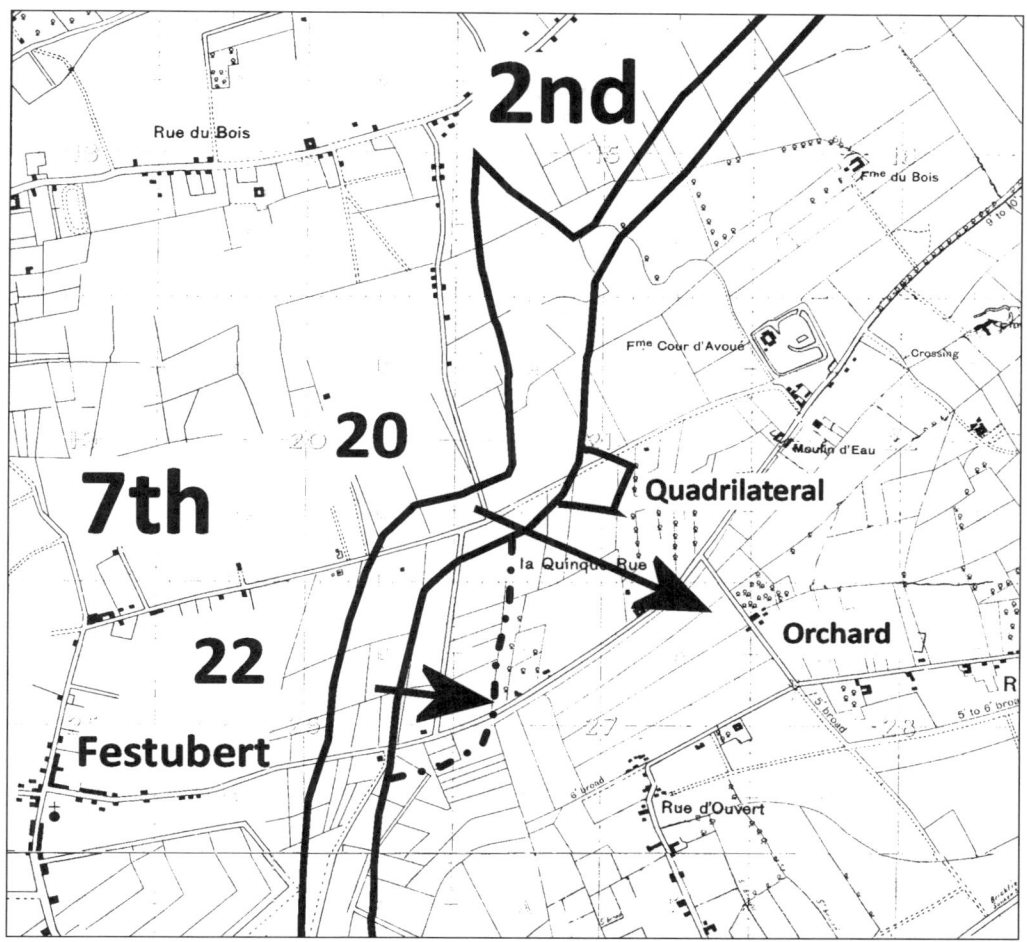

7th Division's dawn attack towards the Quadrilateral

The Scots Guards pressed on beyond La Quinque Rue while Captain Stockwell's group of 1st Welch Fusiliers[183] covered their right flank. Lieutenant Colonel Cator was pleased to hear the two leading Guards companies had reached their objective but they were under enfilade fire from Adalbert Alley[184] on the left and the Orchard to their front; Captain Fitzwygram even reached the small wood with around eighty men. To make matters worse, the British artillery starting firing short, forcing the right company and the Welch Fusiliers to fall back across La Quinque Rue.

---

183 22 Brigade.
184 The communication trench linking the Quadrilateral to the rear.

A counter-attack overwhelmed the Scots left, leaving Fitzwygram's group cut off. Only four were captured alive and the bodies of the rest were found together. A counter-attack then threatened the Scots Guards' support company so it pulled back its flank into an old, shallow trench. Two machine gun teams stopped the onslaught and the Germans fell back to Adalbert Alley. Colonel Cator gave the order to withdraw and the Guardsmen had to wade chest deep in water along a ditch to escape.

The 1st Welch Fusiliers and 2nd Queen's[185] both suffered severe casualties crossing no man's land.[186] The Welch Fusiliers rushed the German front trench and Captain Stockwell then overcame opposition in the support line before advancing towards the Orchard alongside the Scots Guards. The Queen's leading companies were raked by machine guns as they advanced parallel to North Breastwork and they were soon pinned down. Major Bottomley asked for another fifteen minutes bombardment and led the support companies forward as the shells exploded. The whole battalion then rushed forward but Bottomley was mortally wounded as his men clambered over the German parapet. The 1st South Staffords bombers entered the Northern Breastwork at Stafford Corner and then cleared 300 metres of trench on the division's flank.

Lieutenant Hassel and the South Staffords bombers cleared another 400 metres of trench and took over 100 prisoners astride La Quinque Rue, moving behind the German position facing Festubert. Company Sergeant-Major Frederick Barter organised volunteers to occupy the cleared trench and then discovered the trench from the front line to Stafford Corner had been booby-trapped. Barter was awarded the Victoria Cross for cutting all twenty mine leads which had been set to demolish the parapet. Two Stafford companies then occupied the area.

By 7am 22 Brigade had advanced 600 metres and taken an equal distance of its objective, the Northern Breastwork. There were few Germans in front of General Lawford's men but the Queen's and the Welch Fusiliers had both suffered too many casualties to continue. The right flank was secure but the left was exposed because 20 Brigade was falling back from the Orchard.

The Indian Corps Tries Again

A new bombardment was planned for another attack at 7.45am but it had to be postponed because 1st Division still faced uncut wire. General Anderson initially set zero for 2pm but the Bareilly Brigade could not relieve the Garhwalis in time so it was postponed for another two hours. The delay gave the Germans time to reinforce their trench and General Southey

185 Both 22 Brigade.
186 Lieutenant Colonel Gabbett of the Welsh Fusiliers was killed and his second-in-command was severely wounded.

reported that the volume of fire across no man's land was increasing rather than decreasing. The German guns were also hammering the congested assembly trenches.

Despite the problems, General Willcocks wanted the attack to go ahead. The 58th Rifles and 2nd Black Watch had a difficult time getting into position but the whistles blew and the men mounted the parapet on time. Many were shot down before they stepped on the ground and no one went further than the ditch just in front of the trench. The British guns were also falling short, adding to the mayhem. Some of the survivors ran or crawled back and used holes dug under the parapet to escape. The only inspiring event of the disastrous attack was the sight of Lance Corporal David Finlay of the Black Watch carrying a wounded man 100 metres to safety.

16 May between 9 and 9.30am
General Monro had heard about the partial success from 2nd and 7th Divisions' headquarters by 9.30am. Unfortunately, there was a large gap of over 1,000 metres between them so he ordered a pincer movement to close it, starting at 10am. As 6 Brigade[187] moved towards Ferme Cour d'Avoué from the north, 20 Brigade would attack the Quadrilateral from the south. But the plan was too ambitious. All of 6 Brigade was pinned down and it had been impossible to get men or ammunition to it. Meanwhile, the German reinforcements were using three communication trenches. The 1/5th King's had sent two companies across no man's land but their captains, both called Grindley, had been wounded and the leaderless men were unable to organise themselves. Lieutenant Colonel McMaster reported the 1/7th King's had already suffered 250 casualties but Fanshawe told him to attack again, so Captain Evans led two platoons into no man's land where they were shot down. Major Cohen and Captain Fairclough were both wounded organising the rescue of the wounded. By now General Fanshawe's men were more concerned about surviving and Lance-Corporal Joseph Tombs was one of many who had been busy rescuing injured comrades. Tombs rescued four 1st King's men under fire and was awarded the Victoria Cross for his bravery.

The 1st Grenadier Guards[188] had crawled across no man's land via a half-dug trench full of wounded but Lieutenant Colonel Cator made it clear that a frontal attack would be suicidal when Lieutenant Colonel Corkran reached the front. So Captains Maitland and Hughes reinforced the Scots while Captains Moss and Swaine extended their left flank, where several Scots Guards platoons had gone beyond the German lines. The two battalion commanders agreed to try and contact the lost men but Captain Moss's

---

187 2nd Division.
188 20 Brigade, 7th Division.

company was shot down as it tried to advance over the top. Captain Hughes had more luck, clearing 300 metres of trench, while Captain Nichols' bombers cleared more.

Corkran reported his progress and General Heyworth told him to make another attempt at 2.30pm with help from the 1/8th Royal Scots[189] and around one hundred men of the 1/7th London Regiment.[190] Unfortunately, the artillery stopped before the infantry were ready to move and they could not capture the Orchard or the adjacent moated farm.

Major Walshe was also pleased to report that the 1st South Staffords bombers had cleared another 400 metres of German front line, south from Stafford Corner to Willow Corner, opposite 47th Division. Captain Bonner had 'led the men through hell and kept them cheery'; they had captured nearly 200 prisoners. The British bombers were, at last, getting the upper hand.

Meanwhile the situation in 7th Division's centre[191] was deteriorating as the German batteries zeroed in on the North Breastwork. Great lengths of the parapet had been demolished by dusk and Captain Stockwell had to withdraw his 1st Welch Fusiliers behind La Quinque Rue. Unfortunately, only the 2nd Queen's left flank followed the instructions, leaving the rest of the battalion holding on alongside the successful 1st South Staffords.

Closing the Gap, 17 and 18 May
On the afternoon of 16 May, General Haig learnt that 2nd Division would struggle to approach Ferme Cour d'Avoué from the north because its trenches were at an awkward angle. But 7th Division could advance north so Haig modified his plan and instructed I Corps to close the gap. The orders were circulated before nightfall and the artillery bombardment started immediately while observers were warned to report as soon as it was light. The divisions had to be ready to advance as soon as the results came in, which left them little time to prepare.

The bombardment began at 2.45am and it was so heavy the Germans between Ferme du Bois and Southern Breastwork withdrew up to 1,000 metres without the British noticing. The observers started reporting the trenches had been devastated so General Monro asked his generals if their infantry would be ready to advance at 8am. Horne said 2nd Division would be, but Capper was doubtful if 7th Division could. Zero hour was initially postponed to 9pm and then to 10.30pm.

At around 8am dozens of unarmed Germans ran across no man's land towards the 1/7th King's east of Chocolat Menier Corner waving white flags, but most were killed by German artillery fire. The 1/6th Gordons had

189 22 Brigade, 7th Division.
190 47th Division.
191 Held by 22 Brigade.

been working their way forward towards the Quadrilateral when another group of Germans ran towards them. Initially the Scots thought they were under attack, but stopped fire in time to take 200 prisoners. Another 450 surrendering men ran towards the British line at various times.

On hearing the news, General Horne wanted to take advantage of the situation and obtained I Corps' permission to attack at 9.30am. Unfortunately, it took time to get the message out to the battalions and their advance into the unknown would be staggered. There had also been an important oversight which would compromise the attack. No 16 Squadron had found it difficult to see anything as it flew through the cloudy skies but it sent back a single message reporting two new German trenches. The report was ignored and the planes returned to their airfield when it started raining at around 8am.

Closing the gap between I Corps and IV Corps

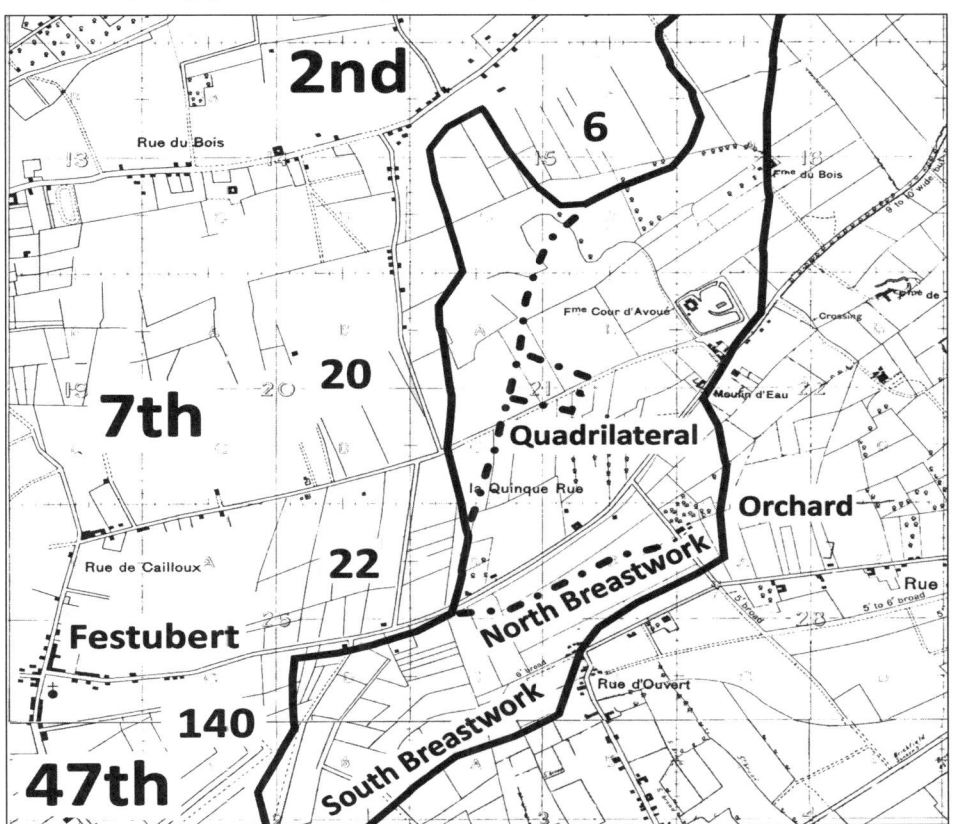

The 2nd Division had chosen 6 Brigade to close the north side of the gap but the advance started thirty minutes late due to the changed timings. Many of the 2nd HLI were hit by cross-fire, including Captain Gaussen, and they fell back. The 2nd South Staffords and the 1st King's advanced close to Ferme Cour d'Avoué but the HLI's failure left the Staffords exposed to enfilade fire and it caused many casualties including Lieutenant Colonel Routledge. Some of the King's bombers may have reached the German trench but none returned.

South of the gap, the 2nd Scots Fusiliers[192] advanced astride and north of the Rue des Cailloux with 2nd Green Howards[193] following, and they found few Germans to stop them. The Scots Fusiliers took their objective, only to be hit by British 4.7-inch howitzers which were firing short. The obsolete guns were also hitting the support companies and Lieutenant Colonel Pollard had to withdraw the Scots instead of pushing forward. He planned a second advance when Captain Fish's company of Green Howards arrived but the moment had passed. Second Lieutenant Cleaver's platoon would eventually contact the 1st King's, closing the gap between 2nd Division and 7th Division.

On the right, Captain Makin led the 2nd Wiltshires forward along a communication trench towards the Orchard later than hoped. The bombers cleared the Quadrilateral but the Germans had knocked down the final section of parapet and the machine gun teams were trained on the gap. There was no way of reaching the Orchard and while the Germans often waved white flags, they had no intention of surrendering. Lieutenant Monson's bombers failed to silence the machine gunners and many were killed crawling back through the long grass. The Wiltshires did their best to turn the communication trench into a fire trench but the German barrage stopped the supports getting forward and they had to fall back later in the afternoon.

To begin with both Generals Horne and Capper were told the attacks had been a success. When Haig heard the same news at 11.30pm, he messaged I Corps headquarters to keep advancing. He also put Brigadier General Turner's 3 Canadian Brigade at General Monro's disposal and instructed the Indian Corps to take over 2nd Division's line as far as the Cinder Track, so 5th Brigade could reinforce the attack. Haig visited I Corps to tell Monro that First Army's new objective was La Bassée village and the Railway Triangle[194] and he wanted I Corps operations to advance towards Chapelle St Roch and Violaines. He also visited Generals Capper and Horne to tell them to attack at 3pm.

Overnight First Army issued instructions to renew the advance on La Quinque Rue. The artillery began shelling Ferme Cour d'Avoué and the

---

192 21 Brigade.
193 Lieutenant Colonel Alexander was an early casualty.
194 A large railway junction where three lines met in a triangle of curves.

Orchard as soon as it was light but rain stopped the observers registering the guns. The 9am infantry attack was postponed with only thirty minutes to go while everyone was put on standby until the mist cleared. Haig had to wait all morning and eventually issued orders at 1.55pm for a new two-hour bombardment to start at 2.30pm. Again insufficient time was given to get the instructions to the trenches and the battalions received them only minutes before zero hour.

Neither division would be ready in time so zero hour was postponed to 7pm. The barrage was adjusted accordingly but the guns only shelled the strongpoints because no one knew where the trenches were. Meanwhile a subsidiary attack by the 1st HLI and 4th King's[195] failed to capture Ferme du Bois.

The 1st Irish Guards and 2nd Grenadier Guards[196] had a difficult journey across the muddy battlefield and they advanced towards the Ferme Cour d'Avoué area an hour late. Lieutenant Colonels Smith and Trefusis both reported little resistance, and they established contact around the Princes Road and Rue des Cailloux crossroads. The Grenadiers established contact with 20 Brigade during the night, securing contact with 7th Division.

Neither the 1/4th Camerons nor the 2nd Bedfords were in place on 7th Division's front and they advanced thirty-five minutes late, having had no time to make a reconnaissance. The Camerons had to wade and swim across ditches and they lost all their bombs. Lieutenant Colonel Fraser was one of the many men killed but around two hundred Camerons reached reach South Breastwork. Two 2nd Green Howards companies were preparing to reinforce the Camerons' left but they had to withdraw along the ditches instead. Major Mackenzie was killed as machine guns enfiladed the Bedfords when they waded across a deep water-filled ditch. Lieutenants Stonier and Brewer bombed along a communication trench and cleared two strongpoints but the trench was blocked in front of a third sand bagged position which had six machine guns inside. Lieutenant Colonel Onslow had no option but to order his men to consolidate their position.

On 3 Canadian Brigade's front, Brigadier General Turner's men advanced at 5.25 pm, knowing the Guards had already been stopped. Artillery fire stopped the two 14th Battalion companies in their tracks and they were unable to reach North Breastwork. Two 16th Battalion companies eventually assembled in a communication trench on La Quinque Rue but the shelling was so effective that 'the attack collapsed after a few minutes', with one salvo alone causing nearly fifty casualties.

---

195 Sirhind Brigade.
196 4 (Guards) Brigade.

Alderson's Force

General Haig placed 51st and 1st Canadian Divisions and the 2nd and 7th Divisional Artilleries under General Alderson of the Indian Corps to tackle the German position. Unfortunately, the temporary arrangement did not work because he had to use his own chief staff officer to coordinate the divisions and his own organisation suffered. As 51st Division's relief of the 2nd Division was delayed, Alderson ordered the two Canadian brigades in line to attack; the Indian Corps would again try to take Ferme du Bois.

The end of the battle of Festubert

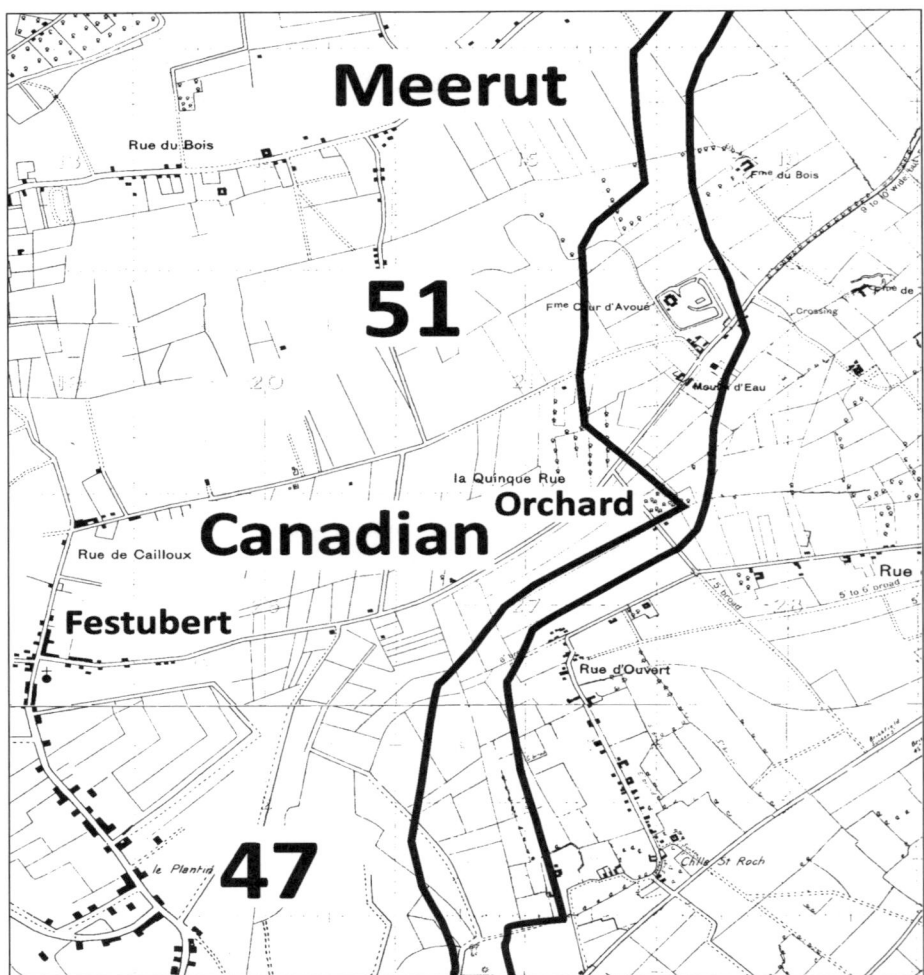

The bombardment started at 4.00pm and the Canadians went over the top at 7.45pm. Two 16th Battalion companies cleared what became known as the Canadian Orchard but they could not capture the fortified house known as M10. At the same time the 15th Battalion crossed the North Breastwork only to be stopped soon afterwards.

Two 10th Battalion companies were supposed to advance at the same time but their assembly trenches had been so badly damaged that Brigadier General Currie had asked for a postponement; permission was denied. The two 9.2-inch howitzers detailed to support the advance were also cancelled because the withdrawal of the Canadian infantry from the front trench during the shelling would alert the Germans. Although the brigade bombers cleared a communication trench they were shot down as they emerged in single file, and the company commanders called off the attack.

The attack planned for the morning of 21 May was postponed until nightfall. But the three-and-a-half hour long barrage lacked heavy guns and there were ammunition shortages. The plan was to advance out of two holes cut in the parapet at 8.30pm but the left group was shot down in front of K5. The right group, however, captured 400 metres of trench only to face repeated counter-attacks during the night. As soon as it was light the German guns battered the trench until the Canadians were forced to abandon most of it, having suffered nearly 270 casualties. General Haig later visited General Alderson's headquarters to express his dissatisfaction at the lack of progress. He dissolved Alderson's Force before leaving; it had lasted four days.

At the First Army conference the following morning, Haig ordered a reconnaissance of the German salient which ran from the Canadian Orchard to K5 and then opposite Givenchy. The Canadians were to capture K5 as the 47th (London) Division advanced towards Chapelle St Roch. A preliminary attack was made astride the South Breastwork and for once the troops had time to prepare their trenches and reconnoitre the enemy's.

Following a prolonged, continuous barrage the infantry left their trenches at 2.30am on 24 May. Two 5th Battalion companies charged shouting 'Lusitania'[197] and while they suffered 250 casualties they seized K5 and 130 metres of trench to the north-west. On the right, 47th Division's advance started thirty minutes late and the Londoners failed to capture any trenches. Later that same night a company of the 3rd Battalion failed to capture the trench north of M10.

The last attack in the battle of Festubert took place on the evening of 25 May. Two 142 Brigade battalions attacked north of the Givenchy–Chapelle St Roch road at 6.30pm and they captured the forward and support trenches.

---

197 The British liner had been sunk by a German submarine on 7 May 1915 with the loss of nearly 1,200 lives.

Two-and-a-half hours later the Lord Strathcona's Horse started bombing north from K5 using gas bombs.[198] Seely's Detachment[199] had no experience of trench warfare but it was still deployed and it soon reported it had taken South Breastwork. Unfortunately, it was lost in the maze of old trenches and ditches, partly due to inexperience, partly due to inaccurate maps and partly because the maps had been printed upside down.[200]

Eventually 3 Canadian Brigade would link up with 47th Division on 27 May, bringing the fighting east of Festubert to an end.

The Battle of Festubert Ends
On 18 May General Haig had hoped that 2nd and 7th Divisions would have enough strength left to establish a line along La Quinque Rue, so the 51st (Highland) and Canadian Divisions would then be able to take over and continue to push south-east. But he was to be disappointed. The Canadian Division relieved 7th Division later that night and the 51st Division had relieved 2nd Division by late on 20 May. The two divisions were grouped together as a temporary corps and called 'Alderson's Force', after the senior commander, the Canadian Division's Lieutenant General Edwin Alderson.

On the night of 22 May Private William Mariner left the 2nd KRRC trenches near Cambrin in a thunderstorm and crossed no man's land to bomb a machine gun emplacement. He returned ninety minutes later and was awarded the Victoria Cross for his exploits.

General Haig visited General Alderson on 22 May and made it clear he was disappointed by the failures, so he dissolved Alderson's Force. He placed 51st (Highland) Division under Indian Corps' command while the 1st Canadian Division reported to First Army. The following day he held a conference to discuss a new combined attack by the Canadian and 47th Divisions. This time he wanted a thorough reconnaissance of the enemy's positions so that the Canadians could take K5 strongpoint as 47th Division advanced towards Chapelle St Roch.

But two preliminary operations had to be carried out first. After a slow but deliberate bombardment, 3rd Canadian Battalion[201] entered the trench in front of Canadian Orchard at 2.30am on 24 May. But the Germans soon located Lieutenant Colonel Rennie's men and they had to withdraw before it was light. Bombers led two companies of the 5th Battalion[202] across a water-filled ditch opposite South Breastwork. They then seized K5 and bombed along the trench to the north-west as 7th Battalion sent three companies forward to reinforce them. To the right the 1/8th London Regiment[203] made repeated attacks along the trench south of South

---

198 The first authorized use of gas in the BEF.
199 Composed of the dismounted Canadian Cavalry Brigade which had left its horses in England.
200 The Canadian Division suffered nearly 2,500 casualties at Festubert.
201 1 Canadian Brigade.
202 2 Canadian Brigade.
203 140 Brigade.

Breastwork. Although the trench was finally cleared, Lieutenant Colonel Harvey's men could not take J3 strongpoint at the end. One of the main problems was the lack of artillery ammunition and the Canadian soldiers were also at a disadvantage because they were still armed with the Ross rifle, which jammed in muddy conditions.

At 6.30pm on 25 May, 142 Brigade advanced to the trench called the 'S-Bend', with its right on the Givenchy–Chapelle St Roch road. Brigadier General Willoughby had a lot to consider because it was the London Division's first big attack. But the 1/23rd and 1/24th Battalions remembered their training and 'swept across the open ground just like a field-day attack at St Albans.' They overran the front and support trenches, an advance of 400 metres, and while Lord Montagu-Douglas-Scott's men were able to consolidate their position on the left, Lieutenant Colonel Simpson's men came under fire from Auchy-les-la-Bassée across the canal.

Lance-Corporal Leonard Keyworth repeatedly climbed on the parapet to throw around 150 jam-pot bombs at the approaching Germans; he would be awarded the Victoria Cross. The 1/20th London tried to reinforce the position but German artillery systematically destroyed the trenches until they had to withdraw to the first line. It was later discovered that the Germans were listening into the Londoners trench telephones, so the guns knew exactly when to fire to get maximum effect.

The Close of Operations
The battle of Festubert came to an end on 25 May although local counter-attacks continued for another forty-eight hours. First Army had advanced over 1,000 metres in places but it had not moved at other points. The plan to tear a large hole in the German line by making two converging attacks had failed at the first hurdle because they had been unable to make contact. Instead the gap had to be closed yard by yard in repeated costly attacks. First Army had suffered about 16,650 casualties and while valuable lessons had been learnt, they had come at high price.

Chapter 9

We Must Do Our Utmost

Third Army Forms

From the end of May 1915 until the final days of September there was little or no change on the British sector of the Western Front, just a daily grind of around 300 casualties from shell-fire, sniping and raids. But there was plenty of action on other fronts. General Joffre moved troops to operations in Champagne at the beginning of July while the Germans pushed the Russians back on the Eastern Front. The Italians gained ground in the First and Second Battles of the Isonzo between 29 June and 10 August while a renewed offensive on the Gallipoli peninsula took place at Suvla Bay on 6 August. The advance through Mesopotamia was going well and German South-West Africa surrendered to General Louis Botha on 9 July.

Field Marshal Joffre wanted the BEF to take a greater share of the front. He also wanted to evacuate the Ypres Salient so the troops could relieve General de Castelnau's army on the Somme. Field Marshal French objected, arguing that the withdrawal would also shorten the German line and they could increase their reserve. He also did not want to put British divisions in the middle of the French sector.

Field Marshal French wrote to the War Office 23 June, explaining how he could capture German trenches if only he had enough artillery and infantry. He asked for more divisions to break through before they could dig in any more. Another thirteen would be sent over the summer but they were used to extend the British sector, rather than build up a reserve. First Army took over the Loos sector at the end of May and the new Third Army took over the Somme sector in August.

The First Inter-Allied Military Conference

Italy had just entered the war in June 1915 and Joffre was looking for a combined Allied offensive to defeat the Central Powers. He made his thoughts known to President René Viviani and Minister of War, Alexandre Millerand, at the Chantilly conference on the 23rd. The French Armies would be organised into three Groups commanded by Ferdinand Foch, Noel de Castelnau and Auguste Dubail. They also agreed to hold the first Inter-Allied Military Conference at Chantilly on 7 July.

Millerand was in the chair, supported by General Joffre and his Chief of Staff, Major General Maurice Pellé. The British were represented by Field Marshal Sir John French and his Chief of General Staff, General Sir William Robertson. Major General Wielemans spoke on behalf of the Belgians while the Italian, Russian and Serbian military attachés, Lieutenant Colonel di Breganze, Colonel Igniatiev and Colonel Stephanovich, acted for their respective armies.

General Joffre made it clear he wanted to centralise the conduct of the war and make simultaneous offensives on the Western Front. The problem was the armies were all in different states of readiness. Although the British pledged to support the French, the conference determined nothing definite. All they agreed was each army would participate.

New Weapons and New Tactics
Infantry tactics changed in the summer of 1915 due to the introduction of new weapons. British infantry had so far relied on the water cooled Vickers machine gun to give covering fire and each battalion and cavalry regiment had four guns. Although the weapon could fire up to 500 rounds a minute from belts of 250 rounds, it required a tripod to give it a stable firing position and two men to carry it. It was the perfect defensive weapon but it was too heavy to drag forward during an offensive.

The first Lewis guns were issued, one per infantry battalion, to six divisions on 14 July 1915. This air cooled machine gun could be carried by one man and fired from the shoulder or the hip.[204] It could fire over 600 rounds a minute from circular magazines of 47 rounds. It was the perfect weapon for both offensive and defensive situations.

The second weapon to reach the battlefield was the Mills hand grenade.[205] The Royal Engineer workshops had been working on hand grenades since trench warfare began in October 1914. Many handmade variations had been made, some successful, some not so successful and some downright dangerous. The first batch of Mills bombs arrived early in July 1915 and extensive testing and factory production meant they were safer than the workshop models and the homemade examples. It also meant supply would be able to keep up with demand for the first time, giving the infantry a better chance in bombing fights.

The third weapon about to appear on the battlefield was the Stokes mortar.[206] Again the Royal Engineer workshops had been busy converting

204 Developed by US Army Colonel Isaac Newton Lewis, based Samuel Maclean's design.
205 Designed by William Mills.
206 Designed by Wilfred Stokes.

inventions into a weapon, sometimes producing a practical item and at other times creating something more dangerous to the operator than the enemy. The Stokes mortar was a simple device which gave the infantry a weapon capable of providing short range indirect fire. In other words it could shoot where the artillery dared not and it was under the infantry's command. The first order for 1,000 Stokes mortars was made in August and it was soon duelling with the German equivalent, the dreaded *Minenwerfer*.

The Second Action of Givenchy, 15 and 16 June
Field Marshal French called an end to the Festubert battle on 25 May but he told Haig to keep on the offensive, to help the French. Foch planned to attack again on 2 June and Haig proposed to do the same. On 30 May he instructed General Rawlinson to prepare to attack between Chapelle St Roch and Rue d'Ouvert and General Monro to advance south of the canal, only they would have to wait until 11 June, when there was enough ammunition.

First Army spent the next three days reorganising, with the Indian Corps and I Corps extending their sectors, so that IV Corps was left with a small two mile sector to advance from. Then Haig heard that the French attack had been delayed on 8 June and four days later he learned it would take place on the 15th. So IV Corps would attack with 7th and 51st Divisions, while the Canadian Division covered the right flank.

First Army was short of large calibre shells and great attention was paid to air observation,so ammunition could be saved for the final barrage. It would start at 6pm on 13 June with the deliberate shelling of chosen targets. Forty-eight hours later a twelve hour bombardment of the wire and trenches would begin. But the Germans' trenches were well built and the dug-outs were deep, in contrast to the British ones. They were also difficult to spot because of a low rise covered in long grass in no man's land.

At 5.58pm a mine was detonated at the Duck's Bill, near the junction of the 7th Division and Canadian Division. The assault troops were spotted squeezing along the narrow communication trenches, alerting the Germans and they could be seen manning the parapets as the bombardment came to an end. They opened fire as soon as they clambered into the open and their artillery increased fire. It later transpired they had been listening into telephone conversations and knew exactly when zero hour was.

A company of the 1/5th Seaforths[207] covered Brigadier General Watts'[208] left flank while the 2nd Wiltshires and 2nd Green Howards carried out the attack. All but one of the Wiltshires' officers were hit and Captain Richardson was the final one to fall. Colonel Brown sent half his reserve company forward in the hope it could make the final rush but enfilade fire

207 152 Brigade, 51st Division.
208 21 Brigade, 7th Division.

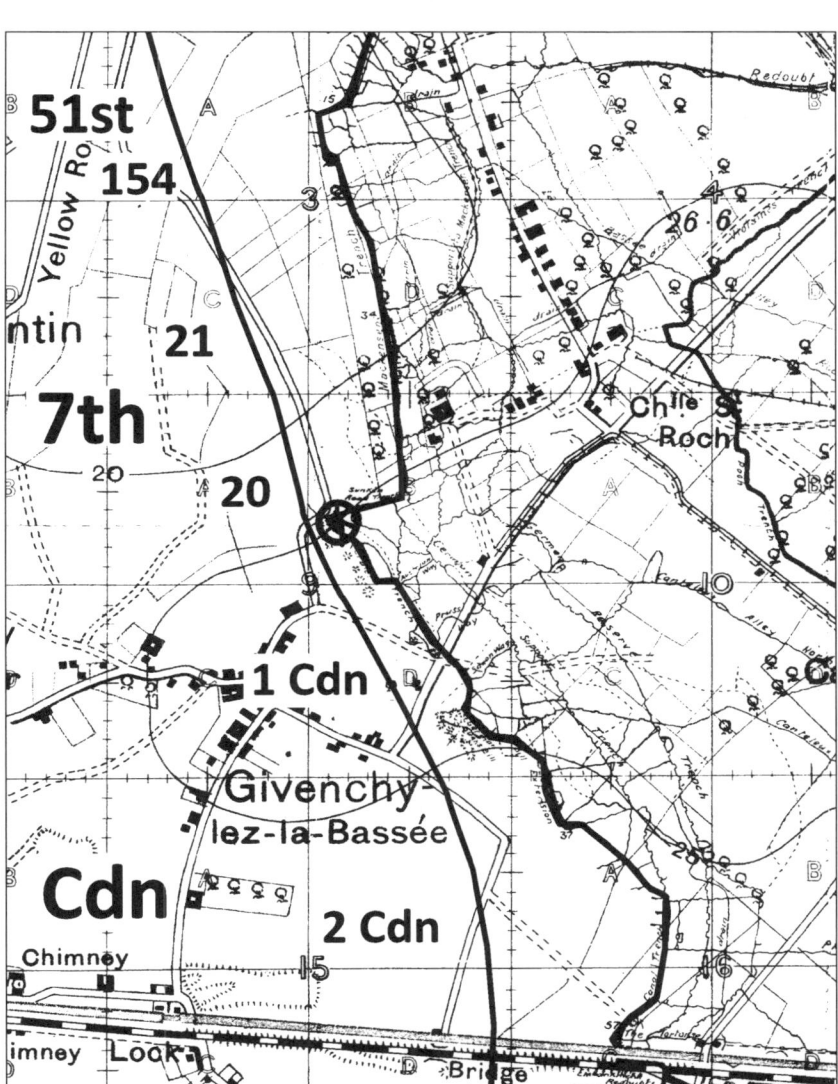

The attack at Givenchy, 15 and 16 June 1915

forced the men to take cover in an abandoned trench in no man's land.

While the plan was to fire Very lights and rockets when trenches were cleared, Captain Nevile had given the 2nd Green Howards' subalterns hunting horns to blow as soon as they entered the German trench. They soon discovered that 'the Germans were able to line their trenches and simply stand up and shoot, for no covering fire could be brought to bear on them.' Captains Nevile and Raley were killed while Captain Blecher was wounded twice. Sergeants Foster and Malpress were shot as they clambered over the German parapet but Second Lieutenant Belcher and Sergeant Whitlock gathered around twenty men in the enemy trench. They held on until it was dark and then withdrew. Only 70 out of 360 Green Howards returned.

The 1st Grenadier Guards[209] were supposed to connect the two attacks but they had to wait until the low ridges on either side had been taken. They had to lie in no man's land to wait for the signal to advance and had lost sixty men by the time they were ordered to withdraw.

The Germans had been shouting 'come along Jocks, we are waiting for you' in between bursts of machine gun fire opposite 51st Division. At 6.45pm Brigadier General Hibbert's men climbed out of the trench into 'just one solid sheet of bullets'. Lieutenant Colonel King was hit at the head of the 1/6th Scottish Rifles and Lieutenant Colonel Hindle was injured leading the 1/4th Loyals forward;[210] both their adjutants were wounded, leaving the company commanders to carry on.

The Loyals captured an advanced trench in three minutes, finding the garrison hiding in their dug-outs. Captains Hibbert, Peak and Whitfield were then hit crossing a water-filled ditch filled with wire. Both battalions then ran into more wire and they fell back to the ditch. The 4th King's Own reinforced the Scottish Rifles but the Germans had infiltrated the Scots line by midnight and Major Nickson decided to withdraw the Loyals from their exposed position.

Howitzers had been tried to cut the wire in front of the 1st Canadian Battalion but the experiment failed. No artillery barrage had been arranged to cover the advance[211] and the few Canadians who entered the German front trench could not capture the strongpoints beyond. Lieutenant Campbell dragged a machine gun across no man's land, propped it on Private Vincent's back and stopped a counter-attack before he was mortally wounded. Vincent fired the last rounds and then dragged the weapon back. Campbell was posthumously awarded the Victoria Cross and Vincent the Distinguished Conduct Medal.

Arrangements were made during the night to renew the attack at 5.30am on 16 June even though there was only enough ammunition for a two hour barrage. The morning mist meant the artillery observers could not see, so Rawlinson postponed operations until 4.45pm. But the German attacks continued and the British found themselves at a disadvantage after their bomb stores were blown up. Cross-fire stopped reinforcements and stores

209 20 Brigade, 7th Division.
210 Both 154 Brigade.
211 1 Canadian Brigade.

moving across no man's land and the rest of the troops had withdrawn by 3pm.

The 2nd Scots Fusiliers could not get through the enemy wire in 7th Division's area while a few 2nd Bedfords[212] sought cover in a crater in no man's land. The 1/6th Scottish Rifles captured nothing but the 1/8th King's[213] secured a lodgement and small groups of men ran across no man's land to reinforce them. Everyone was withdrawn when it grew dark. The 3rd Canadian Battalion[214] was also cut to pieces.

A new attack was postponed to give the artillery extra time to register their targets. The observers then reported the Germans had withdrawn from some of the trenches on the morning of 17 June so Rawlinson decided to occupy them later that night. The troops came under fire as soon as they moved into no man's land because the Germans had returned. Another attack was going to be made on 19 June but General Foch ended the Second Battle of Artois, relieving the British of their obligation to support it. General Robertson[215] informed Haig with instructions for First Army to consolidate its line.

The Loss of Hooge Chateau, 2nd June
The area around Hooge Chateau on the Menin Road was of great tactical importance because it had a great view of the British rear area. Early on 2 June German artillery opened fire on 3rd Cavalry Division's line and the infantry attacked seven hours later. Although the troopers held most of their line, both the chateau and the stables were taken. Two 1st Lincolns companies and one 4th Royal Fusiliers company[216] recaptured the stables on the night of 3/4 June but they were unable to retake the chateau.

The Battle for Bellewaarde, 16 June
Lieutenant General Sir Edmund Allenby wanted to capture Bellewaarde ridge, to limit the German view of the area east of Ypres, so he planned to attack on 16 June to coincide with the Givenchy attack in First Army's sector. No. 6 Squadron RFC were soon spotting for the heavy guns of No 2 Group HAR.[217] Steps were taken to improve communications by laying triplicate telegraph and telephone wires along different routes, so messages had a better chance of getting through. Visual signalling with flags was arranged and carrier pigeons were distributed.

Eight assembly trenches were dug to accommodate the assault troops but German aerial observers spotted them and warned the artillery. No trenches had been dug elsewhere, so it was obvious where the attack was going to be. No man's land was only fifty metres wide in the centre but it

---

212 Both 21 Brigade.
213 Both 154 Brigade.
214 1 Canadian Brigade.
215 Chief of the General Staff.
216 Both 9 Brigade, 3rd Division.
217 Heavy Artillery Reserve composed of batteries of large calibre guns.

widened to 200 metres on the flanks. It ran through a smashed up wood and high explosive shells were fired at the broken tree stumps to break up the wire.

Major General Aylmer Haldane took steps to improve the chances of holding the captured position. Every man carried two extra ammunition bandoliers and extra rations while each battalion was issued with 400 hand grenades and 150 wire cutters. Every soldier carried two empty sandbags ready to build new parapets while two platoons per battalion were equipped with shovels.

A new smoke helmet had been issued to the troops. The canvas bag was soaked in hypo-sulphate of soda to counter the gas; it was pulled over the head and tucked into the tunic collar. The man could only see through the celluloid window until it steamed up and he would soon become hot and short of breath.

The three stage advance would take 3rd Division as far as Bellewaarde Lake. While the artillery would lift from the first objective at zero hour, the second and third lifts would begin when requested. The opening barrage began at 2.30am[218] and the assault troops encountered little resistance when they went over the top at 4.15am. Allenby had set zero hour at dawn, so the Germans machine gun teams struggled to aim in the half-light. The wire had been destroyed, the trenches had been battered and 'what Germans were found alive were too dazed and demoralised by the shell-fire to do anything but hold up their hands and surrender.'

As the 1/10th King's[219] and 1st Lincolns[220] moved forward, the 2nd Irish Rifles and the Honourable Artillery Company[221] advanced without orders. They all moved too fast and ran into their supporting barrage on the second objective. Major Boys led the 1st Lincolns forward to Bellewaarde Lake where Private Breeze captured two machine guns and took twelve prisoners single-handedly. Lieutenant Colonel Boxer was then killed while fetching reinforcements.

Communications again broke down because the observers could not see the flags through the smoke and the wires were still cut. To make matters worse, the 4th Royal Fusiliers, 1st Scots Fusiliers and the 1st Northumberland Fusiliers[222] were annoyed they had been overtaken, so they advanced earlier than planned. By the time Brigadier General Shaw reached the front, no less than nine battalions were mixed up in the overcrowded trenches. German artillery were now aware of the situation and the shell-fire added to the confusion.

The surviving officers kept pushing forward to the German second line and Captains Whigham and Utterson-Kelso took the Scots Fusiliers to the

---

218 There were three short pauses to encourage the Germans to come out of their dug-outs.
219 The Liverpool Scottish.
220 Both 9 Brigade.
221 Both 7 Brigade.
222 All 9 Brigade.

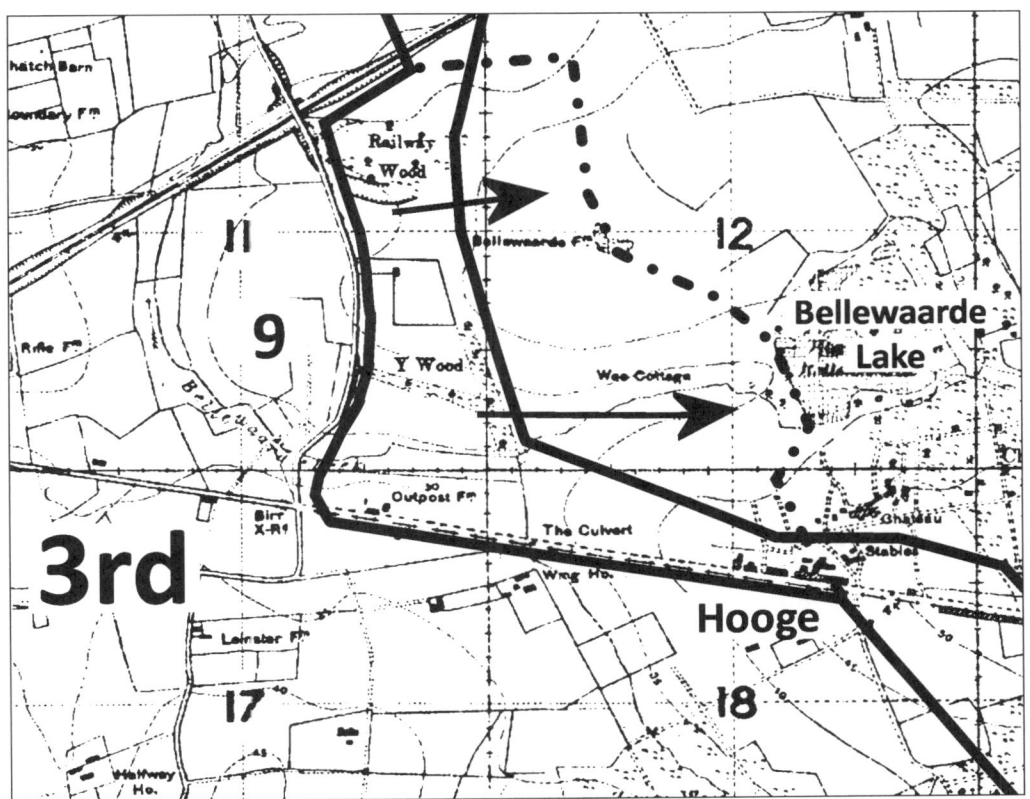

The battle for Bellewaarde on 16 June 1915

final objective. The British observers still could not see the flags so the artillery continued to fire according to the program and their shells soon forced Colonel Stuart to withdraw the Scots Fusiliers. They then had to fight off counter-attacks which lasted well into the night. They eventually withdrew to the German front trenches after they ran low on ammunition. Some of 1/4th South Lancashires held on south of Bellewaarde farm until the early hours but the 1st Wiltshires lost heavily on the right flank and were forced to retire back to the Menin Road after they ran out of bombs.

Brigadier General Markham had been ordered to move his 42 Brigade[223] forward to help secure the position but shell-fire delayed the move forward. Only the 3rd Worcesters and two 2nd Irish Rifles companies[224] were ready when the whistles blew at 3.30pm. The Germans were waiting for the Worcesters and many, including Lieutenant Colonel Stuart, were hit in no

223 14th Division.
224 Both of 7 Brigade, 3rd Division.

man's land. The Irish Rifles could not get far from the east edge of Railway Wood either.

With dusk approaching, the decision was taken to consolidate the captured German trenches with Brigadier General Hoskins' 8 Brigade. It left the Germans in possession of the coveted observation posts on Bellewaarde ridge. The attack had cost 3rd Division over 3,600 casualties, most of them in 9 Brigade.

Actions at Hooge, 19 and 30 July and 9 August
By July the Germans held Hooge chateau while the British held the stables and the few houses along the road. The front trenches were very close together and there was a tunnelling war going on underground. A British mine exploded at 7pm on 19 July, leaving a crater some forty metres across and seven metres deep. The 4th Middlesex[225] were soon consolidating the high lip of earth and its bombers went one way while the 1st Gordons' bombers went the other; they both had to give up their gains.

There were two minor attacks on the evening of 22 July, one near Railway Wood and the other east of the Hooge salient; both failed. The Germans struck back on the morning of the 30th, by which time the 14th (Light) Division was holding the Hooge area with 41 Brigade. Major Cowan and the 175th Tunnelling Company RE had dug a tunnel. They were in the process of placing 1.5 tons of ammonal beneath the chateau stables when the Germans struck first.

Lieutenant Colonel Maclachlan's 8th Rifle Brigade had spent a quiet night in the crater and Lieutenant Colonel Rennie's 7th KRRC were in the trenches across the road to the south. At 3.15am a German mine blew up the stables and then jets of flammable liquid were sprayed over the Rifle Brigade. It was the first use of a *Flammenwerfer*, a portable flame thrower. All manner of trench mortars and artillery shells hit the Riflemen and they fell back to their support line as a thick black cloud spread over the area. The flamethrower crew were shot down as they carried their weapon forward but the bombers continued to drive the KRRC from their trenches until the 1/8th Sherwood Foresters stopped them. Two companies of the 6th DCLI[226] reinforced the line and they all shouted 'let's avenge the old major' after Major Paddison was killed. When others fell back, Sergeant Silver's machine gunners threatened to shoot them if they did not return to the front line.

Major General Victor Couper arranged a counter-attack with two battalions the following afternoon. The artillery opened fire at 2pm and the infantry advanced forty-five minutes later. The 6th DCLI[227] were shot down

225 8 Brigade, 3rd Division.
226 43 Brigade.
227 43 Brigade attached to 41 Brigade.

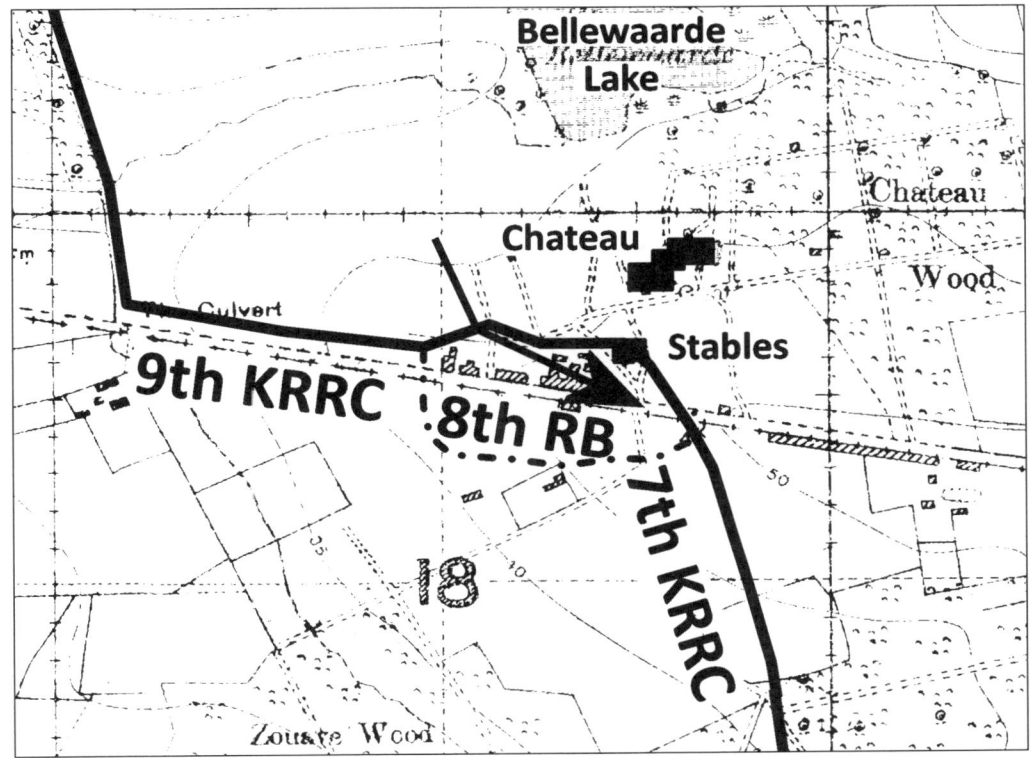

The Loos of Hooge on 9 August 1915

in no man's land and Lieutenant Colonel Chaplin was killed as the 9th KRRC[228] recaptured a few lost trenches. Another *flammenwerfer* attack during the night failed to dislodge them.

Hooge, 9 August

The next attack in the area was to be made by 6th Division, north of 14th Division's sector, and VI Corps took steps to deceive the Germans all along its front. Divisions dug assembly trenches, made fake attacks and simulated other preparations to draw the enemy's attention away from the danger zone. The artillery fired short and long barrages at varied times every morning for a week, to get the Germans used to hiding in their dug-outs from what become known as the 'morning hate' bombardment.

Major General Walter Congreve instructed the infantry to deploy as

---

228 42 Brigade.

close as they dared to the artillery barrage before zero hour, believing it was better to risk casualties from 'shorts', than allow the German machine guns time to get into action. More importantly, there was no limit on artillery ammunition expenditure for the first time.

The assault troops had thirty minutes to file out into no man's land early on 9 August where no man's land varied from 75 on the left to 500 metres on the right. Great efforts were made to deploy the companies in a line parallel to the enemy trench, so they all entered it at the same time.

Lieutenant Colonel Clemson's 2nd York and Lancaster and the 1st Shropshires[229] moved north-east as Lieutenant Colonel Goring-Jones' 2nd Durhams[230] moved towards the crater. The planning paid off and 700 metres of front trench were taken along with the crater. Around 130 prisoners and eleven machine guns were taken while the dozens of bodies bore testament to the effectiveness of the artillery barrage.

The attack set the standard for others to copy but not everything went to plan. Division and brigade headquarters had been issued with portable wireless sets that did not work; they were barely portable either. The first batch of steel helmets were tried as well but some mistook the wearers for Germans in the gloom and shot at them.

Planning for Loos

Planning for an autumn campaign began before the Battle of Artois had ended and General Joffre's strategy involved attacking two points in the German line. One attack would be made in the Artois region and the other in the Champagne region. The plan was to make converging advances which would threaten the salient between the rivers Somme and Aisne. Joffre wanted British support and Field Marshal Sir John French received his proposals at the beginning of June. The British were expected to take over the line north of the River Somme so the French could build up a reserve. Joffre also wanted the British to attack the German line south of the La Bassée canal, on the French left flank.

Although French agreed to cooperate, General Haig was against attacking the chosen area because it was flat and dotted with fortified villages. He wanted First Army to attack the Aubers Ridge again, north of the canal.

The French and British general staffs held a conference at Boulogne at the end of June and they agreed the spring offensives had been too narrow. They needed to attack on a broad front, up to fifteen miles wide, if they were going to break the German line. But the British Army would not have enough infantry, artillery or ammunition for such a large scale attack until

---

229 Both 16 Brigade.
230 18 Brigade.

the spring of 1916. Although the conference advised waiting to make the big push, General Joffre persisted.

Joffre announced his intention to attack as soon as the British had taken over the Somme front at the St Omer conference on 11 July. While he was looking for a commitment from the British, Field Marshal French was only prepared to cooperate once the German line south of Lens had been broken. Joffre asked for support again at the Frévent conference three weeks later but French refused to be bullied into anything. General Joffre eventually went above the head of the British commander when Lord Kitchener visited his headquarters on 16 August. The two made a deal and Kitchener instructed Field Marshal French to 'take the offensive and act vigorously' three days later.

Kitchener had agreed to commit the BEF before it was ready but he was conscious of the string of allied setbacks in the summer of 1915. Firstly, Russia had been driven back hundreds of miles on the Eastern Front. Secondly, Italy had failed to break through the Austro-Hungarian line at Isonzo in June. Finally, the British effort to knock Turkey out of the war was bogged down on the Gallipoli peninsula.

Although GHQ did not want to make the attack, the allies needed a positive result on the Western Front. In Kitchener's words, 'We must act with all energy and do our utmost to help France in their offensive, even though by doing so we may suffer heavy losses.' It was not what Haig wanted to hear.

The main issue was that First Army did not have enough heavy artillery to cover its front. But plans were afoot to use gas to create panic in the German trenches. GHQ had noted the problems caused in the Ypres Salient in April and they intended to do the same. British scientists had spent the summer testing chlorine gas while volunteers were being trained to use it.

The offensive was going to be the biggest carried out by the BEF so far and Kitchener's New Army divisions would be engaged for the first time. Throughout August the roads and railways around Bethune were crammed with troops while new trenches were dug along the chosen front. Meanwhile Haig was considering how First Army's plan was dependent on the weather.

If the wind was favourable, the gas would help the six divisions of I Corps and IV Corps break the German line in front of Auchy, Hulluch and Loos. The three infantry divisions of IX Corps would then push through the gap. Four cavalry divisions were waiting in reserve to deliver the final blow. The Indian Corps and III Corps would make subsidiary attacks north of the La Bassée canal and Second Army would attack in Flanders.

Haig would attack with only two divisions and without the gas if the

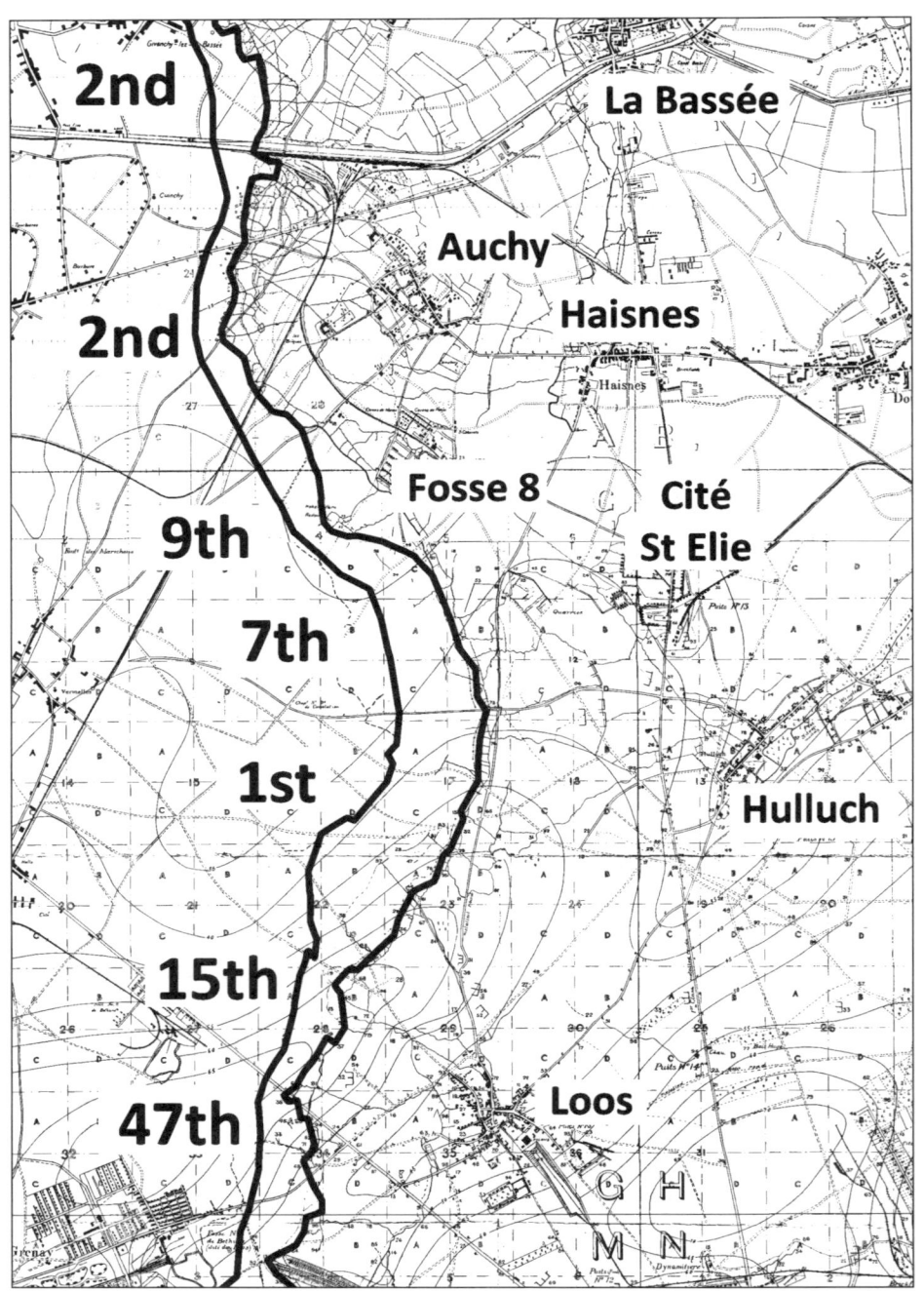

First Army's deployment for the battle of Loos on 25 September 1915

wind was blowing the wrong way on the first day. The 9th (Scottish) Division would capture Hohenzollern Redoubt and Fosse 8 colliery on I Corps' front as 15th (Scottish) Division captured Loos Road and Lens Road Redoubts on IV Corps front. The rest of First Army would join the attack if the wind became favourable over the next forty-eight hours.

First Army faced an undulating countryside scarred by the coal industry. Collieries, known as Fosses, were surrounded by pithead buildings, slag heaps and housing estates while farmers worked the surrounding fields. General Gough's I Corps crossed the La Bassée canal east of Givenchy and skirted Auchy and Fosse 8 before turning south across the Vermelles–Hulluch road. On the left, 2nd Division would form a flank facing La Bassée while the 9th (Scottish) and 7th Divisions advanced through Haisnes and Cité St Elie. Meanwhile, General Rawlinson's IV Corps held the west slope, the Grenay Ridge. As 1st Division headed for Hulluch, 15th (Scottish) Division would push through Loos and 47th (London) Division would cover their flank.

First Army had three divisions of IX Corps and a cavalry division in reserve. The plan was for the two New Army divisions, 21st and 24th, to advance through the gap in the German Second Line and into open country. The recently formed Guards Division was the last reserve and the Cavalry Corps was twenty miles behind the front, waiting to deliver the final blow.

No man's land had been up to half a mile wide in places, but several lines of battle trenches were excavated in no man's land to accommodate the assault troops before the assault.[231] Although the new trenches sometimes halved the width of no man's land, it was still up to 400 metres wide in places. What was once farm land had been left to become scrub, and the wild crops hid the barbed wire and listening posts.

Gas Operations

Although the Allies condemned the use of chlorine gas by the Germans against the Ypres Salient on 22 April 1915, the War Office in London and GHQ in France noted the opportunity it created. Secretary of State Lord Kitchener immediately appointed Royal Engineer officer Colonel Lois Jackson to conduct a feasibility study. Scientists at the Imperial College of Science proved that pressurised cylinders could be used with a soda-siphon system forcing the chlorine through a copper or iron pipe. It would form a yellow-white gas in front of the trench. A gentle wind would then push the gas cloud across no man's land.

The first cylinders were tested in front of a War Office representative at the Castner-Keller factory in Runcorn, Lancashire, in early June 1915.

---

231 Trenches dug especially for a battle. They were later called assembly trenches.

Factory employees stood at intervals along the test site; they raised a flag when the gas reached them and dropped it when they had to put on their mask. More tests proved that captured German gas masks provided thirty minutes of protection.

The War Office had the information it required but there was a problem. Britain's chemical industry could not make enough chlorine gas for the width of front desired by GHQ. The answer was to use smoke candles to supplement the gas and they would be released one after the other to create the illusion of a continuous cloud of chlorine lasting forty minutes, ten minutes longer than the gas masks worked.

The Special Brigade was formed under Lieutenant Colonel Charles Foulkes as a part of the Royal Engineers. The War Office drafted chemistry students who had already enlisted in the Army and contacted chemistry students in universities, asking them to enlist for a special task. They were all taken to Helfaut depot, near St Omer, where the secret project was explained, and although everyone was allowed to leave, the majority remained.

The new recruits were given courses in pistol shooting, navigation and how to predict the strength and direction of the wind. A two-day tour of the front line followed, the only time the men would enter the trenches before the battle began. Meanwhile Foulkes was busy driving back and forth, collecting equipment. He also attended conferences to explain the purpose of his new brigade and he encountered a mixture of interest, pessimism and suspicion from the generals.

Trains delivered the gas cylinders behind First Army's front, lorries then carried them to dumps close to the front line and they were then carried into the trenches by hand. Each one weighed 160lbs and it took four men to manhandle them through the communication trenches to the gas trench.

Although the cylinders were code named 'Accessory Number One', there was no secret what they were and the cylinders were universally hated. But 3,000 cylinders were placed without incident as were nearly 7,500 smoke candles.

An extra trench was added in front of the assembly trenches which had dozens of chambers dug under the parapet to hold the hundreds of gas cylinders in batteries of fifteen cylinders each. Pipes were pointed into no man's land and a wooden platform was built over the top to support the sandbags forming the parapet. The Special Brigade deployed one section per division and each one controlled about a dozen batteries, each manned by a chemical specialist and an assistant. They would open the cylinders and light smoke candles according to the schedule.

First Army headquarters relied on meteorological stations in London, Paris and across northern France to provide hourly weather reports. The gas officers at the front also reported the local conditions. Captain Ernest Gold was First Army's meteorological officer responsible for collating and assessing the results and he briefed General Haig at 6pm on 24 September. His favourable assessment said 'wind southerly, changing to south-west or west, probably increasing to twenty miles an hour.'

The weather forecast looked promising, so Haig gave the order to prepare for the attack. London sent its final assessment at 1am and two hours later Haig heard Captain Gold's prediction for a favourable wind at sunrise. First Army headquarters telegraphed orders confirming the gas release at 4.40am.

The gas engineers put on a red, white and green armband, marking them out as members of the Special Brigade so they could move about freely. They then began opening the cylinders at 5.50am:

Zero Start the gas and run six cylinders one after the other at full blast until they are exhausted.

0.12 Start the smoke and run it concurrently with the gas if the gas is not exhausted.

0.20 Start the gas again and run six cylinders one after the other until they are all exhausted.

0.32 Start the smoke again and run concurrently with the gas if the gas is not exhausted.

0.38 Turn all the gas off punctually. Thicken up smoke with triple candles. Prepare for assault.

0.40 ASSAULT

Despite giving the order, General Haig was still not convinced. He could not feel any breeze as he stood on the top of his observation tower at his Hinges chateau headquarters. At 5am he watched as the smoke from Major Fletcher's cigarette drifted to the north-east but he was still unsure. Fifteen minutes later he messaged I Corps headquarters asking if there was time to cancel but Lieutenant-General Hubert Gough said it was too late. The artillery began the final phase of the barrage at 5.50am as Foulkes' men began opening gas cylinders all along the front and a cloud of smoke and gas began filling the horizon. Forty minutes later, thousands of men began the long walk across no man's land.

As Haig mulled over the decision to release the gas, three diversionary attacks were underway to the north.

Diversionary Attacks on 25 September
VI Corps, North of Bellewaarde Lake
Two mines exploded at 4.19am to alert everyone and a minute later two more detonated, signalling the start of the attack. On 14th Division's front, the 5th Shropshires cleared the German trenches in the centre of 42 Brigade's front, but the 5th Ox and Bucks and 9th Rifle Brigade were pinned down in no man's land. Captains Clarke, Mould and Hunt were killed and Major Delmé-Murray and Captain Fort were injured, leaving few officers left standing to organise the Shropshires' defence and a counter-attack soon pushed the Shropshires back.

V Corps, South of Bellewaarde Lake
On 3rd Division's front, two 2nd Irish Rifles companies entered the trenches and then a third went forward without orders during a counter-attack; few made it across no man's land. It was noted that German snipers were looking for men carrying buckets because they knew they were carrying grenades. The 2nd South Lancashires reached the German line twice, only to be driven out each time. The 1st Gordons advanced early and, finding the wire uncut, side-stepped into the path of the South Lancashires and suffered the same fate.

The 1/4th Gordons found the Germans had abandoned their trenches and they were engaged in a hand-to-hand fight in the open. Although Captain Hopkinson and Lieutenant Henderson reached their objective, heavy shelling and machine-gun fire stopped their men digging in. A midday counter-attack drove the Gordons back onto on the 2nd Royal Scots but many were cut off and captured.

III Corps, south-east of Bois Grenier
The front line on 8th Division's front formed a re-entrant between Bridoux Salient and Well Farm Salient. Wind meant that the smoke screens planned for the flanks could not be used while shallow mines in front of the two salients failed to make craters.

Field guns dug into the front line blasted holes in the German parapet as the men crept forward and then all three battalions charged. An accident meant there were no smoke shells to screen the flank of the attack but it did not stop Lieutenant Colonel Cox's two 2nd Lincolns companies clearing Bridoux Fort where they were reinforced by the 1st Royal Irish Rifles. Only part of the 2nd Berkshires entered the German trenches but Sergeant Johnson cleared the Lozenge. Captain the Hon. Brand led the 2nd Rifle Brigade into Corner Fort on the right flank and Captain Riley took over the advance when Captain Jenkins was killed.

The bombers had twelve different types of bombs and some men forget how to use them all, throwing them unlit; others would not light in the rain. Extra bombers were sent forward but they were still not enough. The Lincolns had lost Bridoux Fort by the afternoon and Lieutenant Colonel Hunt ordered the Berkshires to withdraw. The Rifle Brigade had no option but to follow, despite reinforcements from the 1/8th Middlesex.

Indian Corps, 7th (Meerut) Division at Pietre
The 7th (Meerut) Division had the Bareilly Brigade on the left and Dehra Dunn Brigade on the right. The plan was for a four day bombardment and then gas cloud released from 1,100 cylinders at zero hour while smoke screens covered the flanks. On the second day of the bombardment a Chinese attack was made with the troops showing dummy heads, waving bayonets and shouting before the artillery showered the German trenches, hoping to catch them in the open.

Lieutenant Kent was told he only had 160 cylinders so he placed them all in the Duck's Bill salient. Just before zero a German shell smashed several cylinders and several men had been gassed before they could be covered in earth. When zero hour finally arrived, the gas drifted back across the British trenches, so the Gas Brigade officer turned off the cylinders. Meanwhile, field guns, which were dug into in the British parapet, tore great gaps in the German parapet.

A mine detonated two minutes before zero in front of the 2nd Black Watch on the left flank. Major Wauchope's men had been smothered in gas but Captain Wilson led the survivors towards Moulin du Pietre. Major Bingham led the 69th Punjabis alongside but Major Stansfeld was one of the many officers hit, targeted by German snipers lurking in dug-outs. Captains Couper and Moodie simultaneously led the 4th Black Watch across the German front line and Captains Campbell and Walker joined the advance towards Moulin de Pietre; Major Graham's company of 33rd Punjabis followed in support.

A sizeable breakthrough had been made but the left flank was open, despite Captains Park and Denison of the 2nd Black Watch attempts to secure it. The 58th Rifles also went forward, despite orders to stay put, and suffered many casualties from Germans overlooked during the advance. Subadar Tika Khan also tried to cover the gap on the left flank but he was unable to stop the counter-attack. Colonel Walker was killed going forward to organise the defence and Subadar Muhammad Khan and Lieutenant Gulland of the 69th Punjabis fought on as the rest of the Bareilly Brigade fell back in disarray.

Captain Buckland led the 2/8th Gurkhas through the wire on the Dehra Dunn Brigade's front and Second Lieutenant Meldrum and Subadar Ransur Rana joined the Black Watch. Colonel Morris was killed going forward but Buckland returned with reinforcements. Meldrum was killed as the Germans closed in and while Buckland gave the order to withdraw, many could not escape. Subadar Ransur Rana and a group of Gurkhas fought on until the following day before they were overrun.

The wire had not been cut opposite the 2/3rd Gurkhas so Lieutenants Bagot-Chester and Wood led their men north into the path of Captain Wilson's company of 2nd Leicesters. They were all cut down as soon as they emerged from the smoke. Meanwhile, Lieutenant Colonel Brakespear and Lieutenant Tyson led the rest of the 2/3rd Gurkhas into the uncut wire. Unfortunately, false reports about signal flags seen in the German trench were given so Subadar Bhim Singh's were sent forward. They were shot to pieces in front of the wire. A later attack by parts of the 39th Garhwalis and 2/2nd Gurkhas was also shot down.

A wounded Rifleman Kulbir Thapa squeezed through the wire and into the German trench where he found a wounded Leicesters man. He stayed with him all day and night, dragging him and three other men through the mist to safety the following day. Rifleman Thapa was awarded the Victoria Cross.

The La Bassée Canal sector from the air, with the Brickstacks, and its crater field at the bottom.

Troops head to the front, some on foot and some on buses.

The soldiers dug deep to get maximum protection, unless a high water table prevented them; then they had to rely on sandbag breastworks.

The Germans learned to strengthen their parapets, dig extra trenches and build strongpoints following the battle of Neuve Chapelle.

The weathervane says the wind is favourable for gas, so the mask is donned and the alarm is checked.

One of the artillery's dilemmas of 1915 was how to effectively demolish the wire entanglements in no man's land.

A ground level view of the Brickstacks where every pile hid a machine gun.

A battered German trench following a prolonged bombardment.

The twin pitheads of Loos colliery were known as Tower Bridge while the adjacent slag heap was called the Grandstand.

Many battalions became embroiled in the street fighting in Loos, compromising the situation east of the village.

Medics and orderlies wait to attend to the walking wounded hobbling back from the battlefield.

The British bombers usually found themselves outclassed by their better armed German opponents.

The gas cloud which accompanied 46th (North Midland) Division's disastrous attack on the Hohenzollern Redoubt.

The crowds turn out to see the Germans guns captured during the Battle of Loos.

The 1st Northumberland Fusiliers show off the trophies they took during the fight for the St Eloi craters.

While soldiers did not welcome the extra weight on their heads, the introduction of the helmet saved many lives.

An aerial photograph of Fosse 8, with the colliery top left, the Dump top right and the Hohenzollern craters at the bottom.

Chapter 10

The Biggest Balls Up Ever Known
I Corps Attack at Loos

2nd Division Astride the La Bassée Canal, 25 September

Brigadier General Corkran's 5 Brigade was on 2nd Division's left, north of the La Bassée canal, and it would attack in two parts. Three of his battalions would advance at 6.00am, after only ten minutes of gas and thirty minutes before the rest of the division. They were expected to capture the trenches between Chapelle St Roch and Canteleux, east of Givenchy, securing the division's left flank.

The wind was very light and the gas moved slowly across no man's land; too slowly. It also warned the Germans something was afoot and some lit fires in the second line trenches, hoping the warm air would disperse the gas. A mine detonated under the enemy front trench opposite the brigade left two minutes before zero, warning the Germans an attack was imminent. The mine was detonated in front of the 2nd Ox and Bucks but many of Captain Southey's men had been incapacitated by the gas. Only Lieutenant Pierce Newton-King's group passed through the wire and they were shot down by machine gun fire. Meanwhile the right company pressed on to the support line.

Captain Brook's and Major Bunbury's 1st Queen's companies rushed the German front trench and Bunbury was one of the few casualties. The 2nd Highland Light Infantry were equally successful next to the canal and the two battalions advanced in the open while the bombers cleared the communication trenches. But the success was deceiving because the Germans had withdrawn from their front trench as soon as the mine detonated. They were soon emerging from their dug-outs along the communication trenches and setting up their machine guns.

The cross-fire caught 5 Brigade in the open and the survivors fell back to the German front trench. The 1/7th King's started digging a trench across no man's land to the Duck's Bill and Lieutenant Drew led two 1st Queen's platoons across to reinforce the foothold. But they were too few to change the situation and the able-bodied men ran back after running out of bombs, leaving dozens of wounded behind.

Meanwhile, the 9th Highland Light Infantry waited in their trenches next to the canal bank for 6.30am. But a cloud of gas moved slowly across the

2nd Division's attack astride the La Bassée Canal on 25 September

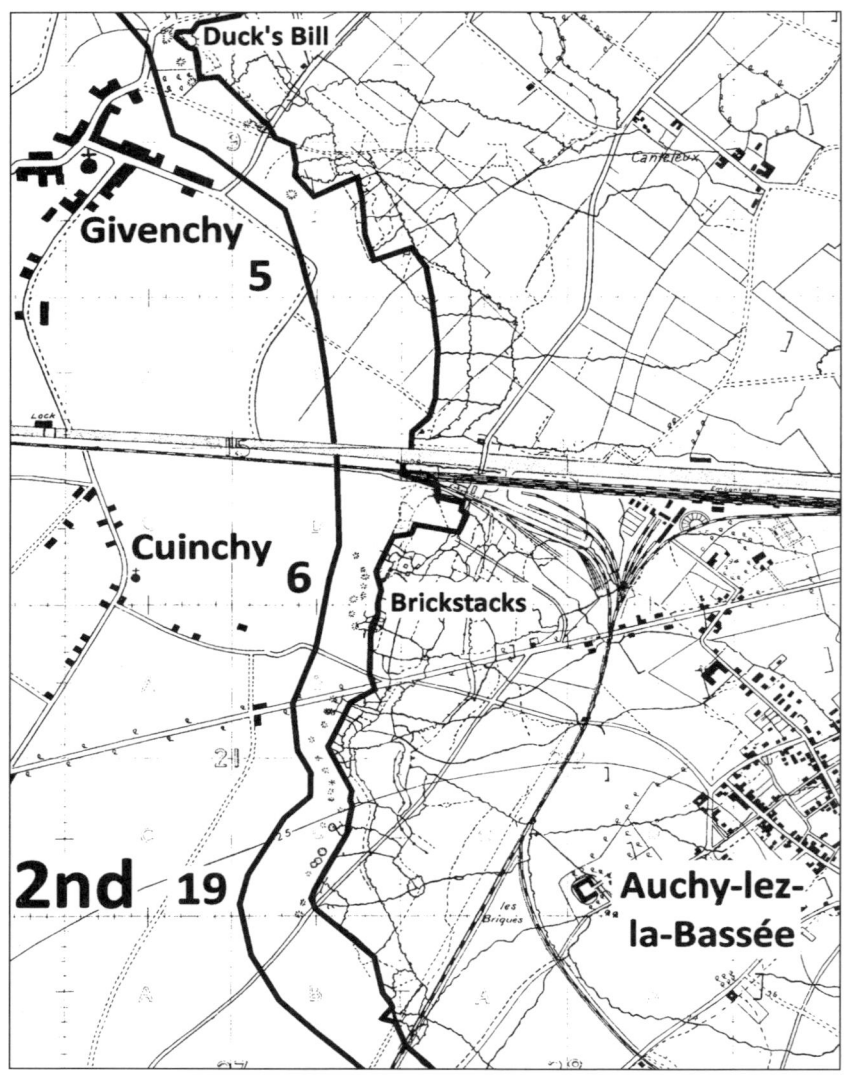

canal and engulfed their trenches; only sixteen men of the two leading platoons were left standing by zero hour. Lieutenant Colonel Murray ordered the support platoons to replace them and they left the trench ten minutes after zero. The machine guns in Tortoise Redoubt[232] cut them to pieces and only one man returned. Murray wisely called off the attack.

Brigadier General Daly's 6 Brigade held the trenches south of the La Bassée canal and the gas officer, Lieutenant White, said the wind would blow the gas along their trenches. The gas released by 19 Brigade was already drifting along their front line, so Daly decided to see which way it would go. It covered 6 Brigade's trenches and crossed the canal to settle on 5 Brigade's position. While the noxious clouds swirled around the canal banks, fires could be seen burning on the German parapets.[233]

Captain Arthur Kilby led his company of 2nd South Staffords along the canal towpath and railway line under crossfire from Embankment Redoubt and Tortoise Redoubt across the canal. Many were hit as they cut through the wire and the company had to withdraw, leaving a seriously injured Kilby behind; he was posthumously awarded the Victoria Cross.

The rest of the Staffords faced the line of craters in the Brickstacks sector but many had been asphyxiated by the time two small mines exploded under the enemy front line. They had little effect because the Germans had withdrawn as soon as they saw the gas. They returned to their trench after the explosions and stopped the Staffords crossing the crater field.

Many of the 1st King's were shot down as they cut through the wire astride the La Bassée road. Captain James Ryan ran back to report the bad news and Lieutenant Colonel Potter suspended further attacks until he had heard further news. None came because Ryan was never seen again.

Mounds of earth surrounding the craters had stopped the artillery cutting the wire in front 19 Brigade. Lieutenant Colonel Rowley had reported it was largely undamaged and over twenty metres wide in front of the 1st Middlesex. No man's land was so narrow that the gas cylinders were placed in the brigade's front trench and the infantry had to start their advance from the support trench, fifty metres behind. Although Brigadier General Robertson's plan was for four waves of infantry to climb out of their trenches and advance simultaneously, not everyone was confident the attack would succeed. A friend of the author Frank Richards[234] said 'If this attack does come off on this particular part of the front it's going to be the biggest balls-up ever known. Unless JC is very kind to us, the majority of the Brigade will be skinned alive.'

As zero hour approached, the gas officer, Captain Percy-Smith, reported 'Dead calm, impossible to discharge accessory.' He was overruled and the

---

232 A mound of spoil on the canal bank.
233 The warm air was supposed to push the gas over the trench.
234 His real name was Francis Woodruff and he wrote a memoir called *Old Soldiers Never Die*, one of the few to be written by someone from the ranks.

gas and smoke drifted obliquely across no man's land for next forty minutes. The attack north of the canal had sent the Germans facing 19 Brigade hurrying to the rear, fearing their trench had been mined. They were right; two mines detonated beneath their front line two minutes before zero hour. But they were soon back in their trench and helmets and rifles could be seen at the parapet before zero hour.

There were so many craters that the 2nd Argylls had to squeeze through a single sixty-metre-wide gap. Lieutenants Bullough's and Gillespie's platoons were shot down but Sergeant Angus McClure led ten men into the German trench. The second company started so far back that no one reached no man's land. Around 300 Argylls were killed or injured in the crater field while McClure was killed and his men were captured after a brief fight.

The 1st Middlesex also faced a line of craters and Lieutenant Colonel Rowley's first three companies scrambled for cover behind the crater lips to escape the murderous fire. Rowley sent three platoons from his reserve company forward, hoping they would rally the survivors. 'All we heard back there was a distant cheer, confused crackle of rifle fire, yells, heavy shelling on our front line, more shells and yells and a continuous rattle of machine guns.' Over 450 Middlesex men lay dead or injured across the narrow strip of ground and German soldiers could be seen standing on their parapet, looking to get a better view of their targets.

Rowley asked the 2nd Welsh Fusiliers to send two companies forward but it took them thirty minutes to squeeze past the crowds of wounded men heading for the rear. Some platoons lost their way in the trenches and they heard the rattle of machine gun fire as their comrades clambered over the parapet. One officer told Robert Graves[235] what happened:

'It had been agreed to advance by platoon rushes with supporting fire. When his platoon had run about twenty metres he signalled them to lie down and open covering fire. The din was tremendous. He saw the platoon on the left flopping down too, so he whistled the advance again. Nobody seemed to hear. He jumped up from his shell-hole and waved and signalled "Forward". Nobody stirred. He shouted "You bloody cowards, are you leaving me to go alone?" His platoon sergeant, groaning with a broken shoulder, gasped out: "Not cowards Sir. Willing enough but they are all f...... dead."'

Another 200 men had been killed or injured. Lieutenant Hill and Second Lieutenant Choate sent back messages from no man's land asking for reinforcements but Rowley had no more to send. All he could do was make sure the battalion bombers and machine gun teams occupied a crater on the right flank, where their fire helped many men escape no man's land.

---

235 Robert Graves' autobiography is called *Goodbye to All That*.

Major General Horne called for another thirty minute barrage south of the canal when he heard of the failure, ready for a new infantry assault at 9.00am. But all the battalion commanders protested it would be suicide to make another attempt, so he called off the attack.

9th (Scottish) Division at Fosse 8

A few days earlier I Corps had extended 2nd Division's sector at the expense of Major General Thesiger's 9th Division. It left 28 Brigade with a single communication trench which the reinforcements and the wounded would have to share.[236] Brigadier General Scrase-Dickens had also neglected to send any night patrols out to check on the wire cutting, so the artillery was firing blind.

The German artillery opened fire on the assembly trenches as soon as the gas cloud began, causing casualties, including the 6th KOSB's commanding officer, Lieutenant Colonel MacLean. The shrapnel also punctured a few cylinders, filling the trenches with gas and many, including Lieutenant Colonel Grahame of the 10th Highland Light Infantry, were asphyxiated. The gas then started to drift back over 28 Brigade's trenches.

The 10th HLI faced Madagascar Trench, and machine guns in Railway Redoubt and Mad Point, on the flanks, caused hundreds of casualties. When Lieutenant Colonel Northey, commander of the 9th Scottish Rifles, went forward to check the situation he found a shell had hit the battalion headquarters dugout and 'there was considerable confusion everywhere and a strong smell of gas… From this moment it became increasingly difficult to obtain any information as to what was happening.' Grahame was incoherent but his orderly told Northey that the Highlanders had captured the first three lines of German trenches. Although the information was false, it would be reported to Brigadier Scrase-Dickens, influencing his decisions for some time.

Meanwhile, the 6th KOSBs faced Mad Point and the Strongpoint at the ends of Little Willie Trench. The swirling gas engulfed the KOSBs so the officers instructed their men to lie down in the open, hoping the gas might clear enough to let them get their bearings. Unfortunately, the support companies did not know about the delay and began moving through the first wave. Confusion followed as the whole battalion advanced together and machine gun fire from Mad Point and Strongpoint scythed through the crowd. Lieutenant Colonel MacLean was already down and the injured Major Horley directed operations from the front trench until he died. Pipe-Major Robert Mackenzie was mortally wounded piping the men forward; he was the oldest casualty at Loos, aged 59.

---

236 Reinforcements normally used 'Up Trenches' while the wounded used 'Down Trenches' to avoid them meeting each other, which was bad for morale.

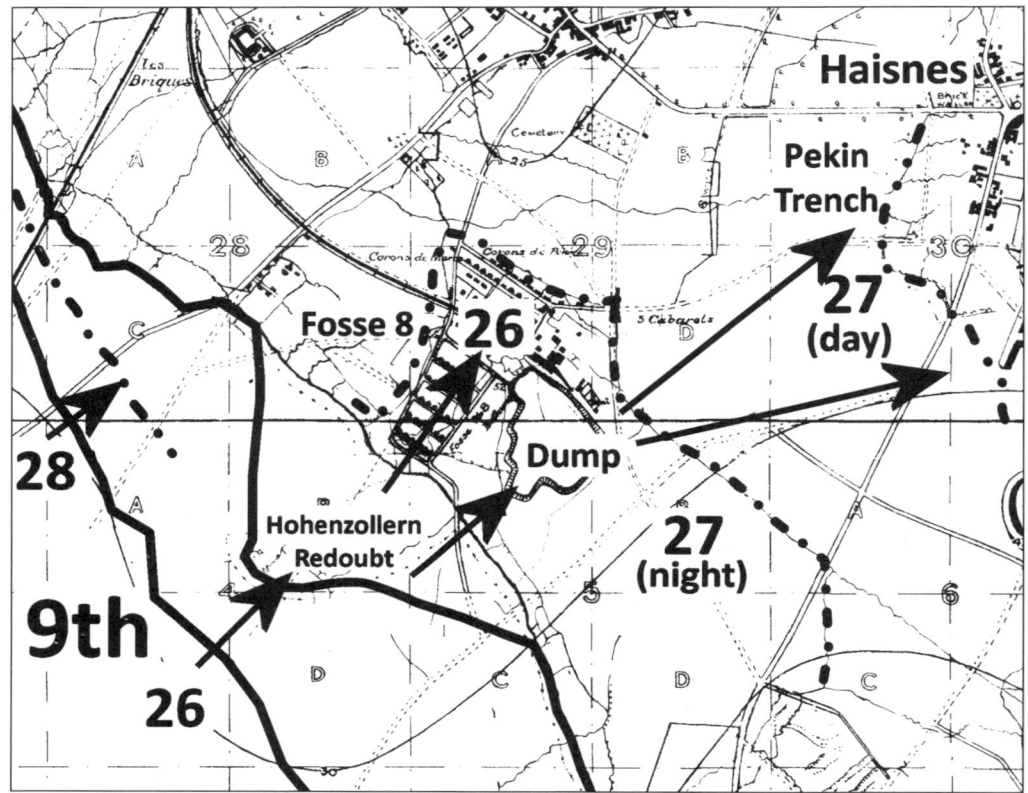

9th (Scottish) Division's capture of Hohenzollern Redoubt and Fosse 8 on 25 September

The KOSB's doubled towards Little Willie Trench only to run into a ditch filled with barbed wire and covered with netting which supported a layer of turf: 'In a matter of minutes the battalion was destroyed, all but one officer and over 600 men were killed or wounded in the death trap.' Lieutenant Watson was the last officer standing and he did his best to form the survivors into a firing line.

The two battalions had been destroyed but General Scrase-Dickins had ordered the rest of the brigade forward because he thought the attack was going to plan. But it took the Scottish Rifles over an hour to get ready and one company fell back retired after meeting a panicking officer running down Reid's Alley trench.

At 8am Lieutenant Colonel Northey received a message from Major Stewart detailing the Highlanders' disaster. He in turn notified brigade headquarters and then went to the front trench to see what was happening for himself. It was indeed a disaster: 'In my opinion there was not a man of the attacking battalion in front of our parapet except the dead and wounded.' Even so Scrase-Dickins instructed two Scottish Rifles companies to support the 10th HLI at 9.30am. Northey ignored the order and sent a message back to brigade, explaining it would be suicide to send any more men forward.

The 11th HLI were struggling along the communication trench when Lieutenant Colonel Fergusson received a message stating the Borderers would have to withdraw unless they got reinforcements. Lieutenant Colonel Fergusson immediately ordered Major Andrews to advance with two companies but they were cut to pieces by Mad Point and Strongpoint. Thirty minutes later a message from brigade headquarters ordered Fergusson to send two companies forward. He ignored it, having seen his two companies shot down and notified brigade of the situation. He heard nothing else, either from no man's land or brigade headquarters, for over two hours.

On the division's right, 26 Brigade faced the Hohenzollern Redoubt, a complex of trenches on a small rise. It then had to clear Fosse 8 colliery which had pithead buildings, cottages and a large slag heap called the Dump.[237] The Scots had been unable to dig assembly trenches because they were too close to the redoubt and they had dug shallow tunnels into no man's land instead.[238] They were opened up the night before the attack so a shallow assembly trench could be dug.

Extra steps were taken to blind the Germans in Hohenzollern Redoubt. Phosphorous grenades were thrown, smoke candles were lit and Stokes mortars fired a barrage of smoke shells. But the 5th Camerons became disorientated as they advanced through the thick cloud towards Little Willie Trench, north of the redoubt. Lieutenant Colonel Cameron of Lochiel and his officers lost contact with their men and few knew the direction of German trenches. The gas helmets made it impossible to recognise anyone and many men collapsed from asphyxiation as they staggered around in the thick cloud.

The 7th Seaforths kept going through the smoke. Their bombers cleared West Face before moving through the Redoubt's trenches while the infantry advanced over the top towards Dump Trench and Fosse 8. They were under machine gun fire from Madagascar and Lane Farm to the west but their main problem was from machine guns in Big Willie Trench to the east. The trench was not being attacked due to the divergent attacks of 9th and 7th Divisions.[239]

Lieutenant Colonel Walter Gaisford's Seaforths pushed on through Fosse 8 pithead, clearing the miners' cottages the Camerons had supposed to

---

237 Brigadier General Ritchie had deployed his battalions according to their glengarries, with the dark patterns to the left and the diced patterns to the right.
238 They were called Russian saps.
239 9th Division was advancing north and 7th Division was moving east, creating a gap between them.

capture. By 7.30am they had reached a flooded Corons Trench on the north edge of Fosse 8 and they then waited for the support battalion to take over. The Seaforths had advanced a mile in one hour but they had suffered fifty per cent casualties and they were way ahead of the rest of the division.

The 5th Camerons reached Little Willie Trench ten minutes later and then came under enfilade fire from Mad Point as they headed for Fosse Trench. The first two lines of men were shot down but the rest pushed on to Corons Trench,[240] cheered on by the wounded Camerons. Colonels Lord Lochiel and Gaisford set up their headquarters in the mine manager's house while their two battalions dug in and looked for 28 Brigade to appear on their left. The 8th Black Watch followed the 5th Camerons through the Corons, under fire from Madagascar and Mad Point. Only 250 reached the forward position, bringing the number of men defending the line around Fosse 8 to around 700.

The 8th Gordons followed the Seaforths across Hohenzollern Redoubt but Lieutenant Colonel Wright halted his men in Dump Trench to await instructions. An hour later he learnt the rest of 26 Brigade was moving through Fosse 8, so he led his men across the summit of the slag heap to Fosse Alley. A company of Black Watch and some Seaforth's advanced alongside the Gordon's, weakening Lord Lochiel's position around Fosse 8. They all kept advancing across the open fields north-east of Fosse 8, heading for Haisnes.

By 9am 9th Division's attack was in disarray. The leading battalions of 28 Brigade were finished in no man's land while the supports were waiting for further instructions. Although 26 Brigade had broken through, it too had suffered severe casualties and only a few hundred Scots were holding on around Fosse 8. Meanwhile the 8th Gordons were pushing on alone towards Haisnes.

The division's reserve, 27 Brigade, had instructions to advance through Haisnes to the Haute Deûle Canal. Brigadier General Bruce ordered three of his battalions to advance when he heard Fosse 8 had been taken but only the 12th Royal Scots could get through the crowded trenches. Lieutenant Colonel Loch led his men past the Dump and across the fields towards Haisnes using Douvrin church tower as a bearing. He found the 8th Gordons waiting in Pekin Trench but the two battalions were pinned down by heavy fire from Haisnes and Cité St Elie when they tried to advance further.

The 11th Royal Scots was supposed to follow 28 Brigade but Lieutenant Colonel Dundas was unaware it had been shot to pieces in no man's land. He could not get past the scores of wounded and gassed men so he made a detour and reached no man's land around 9.30am, an hour late. The officer

---

240 The Corons were the rows of miners' houses.

leading the first two companies mistakenly used Haisnes church as his aiming point and advanced further to the north than expected. Machine gunfire from Auchy cemetery made the Royal Scots deviate to their right, putting them back on track and they were cutting through the wire in front of Haisnes as German reinforcements entered Pekin Trench. They too were left pinned down in front of the village. The rest of the battalion had an uneventful advance to Pekin Trench, where they joined their sister battalion before midday. Meanwhile, the 10th Argylls deployed in support in Fosse Alley because Lieutenant Colonel Mackenzie had heard the position in front of Douvrin was strongly held.

General Bruce's brigade had broken into the German position but the Germans held Haisnes and Cité St Elie. Around 1.30pm the Argylls sent a company forward in response to a call for reinforcements but few made it to Pekin Trench. General Scrase-Dickens knew 28 Brigade had been unable to enter the German trenches west of Fosse 8 but he did not know the details.

General Thesiger wanted Scrase-Dickens to make another attempt a midday but the congested trenches meant the orders did not reach his two battalions for some time. Lieutenant Colonel Northey had, so far, convinced Scrase-Dickens not to send the 9th Scottish Rifles against Madagascar Trench again. The 11th Highland Light Infantry had already had two companies shot down in front of Little Willie Trench. But Thesiger insisted and the first order reached Northey at 11.53am, giving him only seven minutes to prepare. Scrase-Dickens sent a second order at 11.57am delaying the attack to 12.15pm but it never reached Northey and two companies clambered into no man's land at 12.05pm. They were cut to pieces by the Railway Work and Madagascar Trench and Northey stopped any more men going forward to be slaughtered.

The Highland Light Infantry received the first order to advance at 12.03pm, three minutes too late. A few minutes later the message postponing zero hour to 12.15pm arrived but Mad Point and Strongpoint had already stopped the six platoons sent over the top. All Lieutenant Colonel Fergusson could do was recall the survivors and man the parapet in case the Germans counter-attacked.

7th Division's Advance on Hulluch

Major General Thomson Capper's division held the sector north of the Hulluch road. Brigadier General Steele's 22 Brigade was on the left and machine guns in Big Willie Trench had prevented the 2nd Warwicks from completing their assembly trenches, leaving Lieutenant Colonel Lefroy's men in an awkward re-entrant. The 1st South Staffords had no such problems and their assembly trenches[241] had been dug in the centre of no man's land. Even so, they still had 400 metres of open ground to cross to get to Quarry Trench. Long grass hid the German wire from the artillery observers, making it difficult to see if the guns were damaging it, while Spurn Head outpost had stopped General Steele's night patrols investigating the entanglements.

For once, the wind carried the gas and smoke across no man's land but the German machine gunners fired blindly into the cloud. Lieutenant Colonel Lefroy and his adjutant, Captain Duke, were two of the first Warwicks to fall while the machine guns in the Pope's Nose Redoubt badly mauled the 1st South Staffords. The wind only carried the smoke to the wire, leaving Steele's men at the mercy of the Germans in Quarry Trench. The Warwicks and the Staffords then had to lie in the open while men armed with wire-cutters cut gaps under sniper fire.

A large defensive position in the support trench, called the Slit, began firing into the Staffords' right flank and they began to waver. Lieutenant Burke was wounded steadying the men after Captain Henry de Trafford and Lieutenant William Cooper were killed, but they held on. The 1st Welsh Fusiliers moved through the smoke in support and they joined the Warwicks in the long grass.

Private Arthur Vickers of the Warwicks would be awarded the Victoria Cross for opening two gaps for the men to advance through. Two Welsh Fusilier officers, Captains Cartwright and O'Connor, then encouraged the down men to move forward into Quarry Trench where the machine gunners fired until the last minute.

The Germans fled down St Elie Avenue and Second Lieutenant Dibden followed with a group of bombers while the rest of the officers led the rest of the men beyond the German support trench and towards Hulluch Quarries. But the Staffords had failed to silence the Pope's Nose and the Slit so they came under fire from the rear. Fortunately, 20 Brigade's support battalion, the 2nd Borders, had reached Gun Trench to the right and Lieutenant Colonel Thorpe sent Captain Sutcliffe and the battalion bombers to help. They attacked the Pope's Nose in the flank and rear, capturing seventy men. Thorpe also sent Captain Ostle and two platoons to the Slit where they captured 120 prisoners.

The 2nd Queens moved through the Staffords and while Captain Philpot went to the east side of the Quarries, Second Lieutenant Chapman's men found forty prisoners hiding in dugouts. The rest of Lieutenant Colonel Heath's men faced a tough fight in Quarry Trench. Lieutenant Taylor-Jones took command of the bombers after Captain Brocklehurst was wounded

---

241 Called battle trenches in 1915.

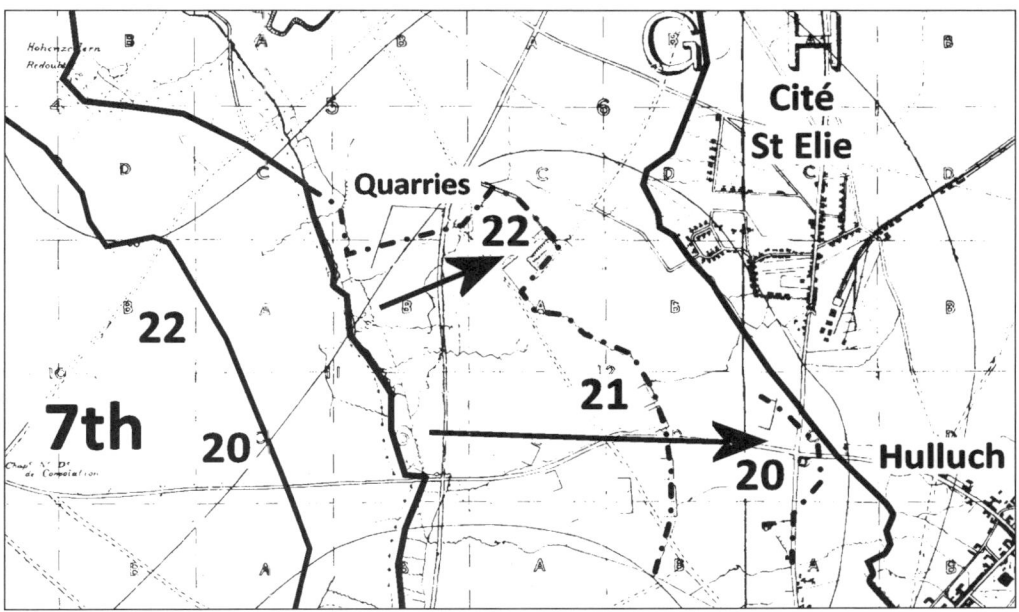

7th Division's advance towards Cité St Elie and Hulluch on 25 September

and they would eventually contact the Scots in Big Willie Trench, closing the gap between 9th and 7th Divisions.

A disrupted 22 Brigade was closing in on Cité St Elie colliery and officers urged everyone forward, expecting reinforcements to join them. The 2nd Queen's captured sixty prisoners in Cité Trench, west of the village, but Colonel Heath decided to wait for fresh troops before advancing into the village because he only had 300 able-bodied men.

The Staffords had cleared Alley 1 Trench and Lieutenant Colonel Ovens could see Germans running from Cité St Elie so he decided to rush Puits Trench in front of the houses. But the mixed group of Staffords and Welch Fusiliers came under fire from the Germans holding the pit village and they had to withdraw to the Quarries.

Brigadier General the Hon. Trefusis had placed the 8th and 9th Devons[242] on the front line, north of the Hulluch road and they assembled in the battle trenches in the middle of no man's land. Again long grass had prevented the artillery observers from directing artillery fire onto the wire in front of 20 Brigade, while an outpost in Silesia Sap had stopped night patrols assessing the damage.

242 The two New Army battalions had replaced two Guards battalions which had joined the new Guards Division.

The Germans in Breslau Trench fired wildly into the gas cloud as it moved slowly across no man's land. Many of Trefusis' men felt suffocated in their gas helmets and some pulled them off, only to fall choking from the gas. The 8th Devons' support companies moved too fast and Lieutenant Colonel Grant's men were silhouetted as they emerged from the cloud. Casualties increased as they crowded together to get through the gaps in the wire.

The Germans in Breslau Trench and Fritz Redoubt kept firing until the last moment and over 700 Devons were hit. Colonel Grant and Captain Kekewich were dead, Major Carden and all but three officers lay wounded, but Captain Gwynn and Second Lieutenant Trott led the survivors into Breslau Trench as the Germans fled along the communication trenches.

The Special Brigade engineers struggled to open the cylinders on Lieutenant Colonel Stansfield's front and the gas was released late; it was still pouring into no man's land as the 2nd Gordons clambered out of their trench. Some men collapsed but the rest walked through the cloud to the sounds of Piper Munro's bagpipes. Machine guns in Fritz Redoubt and Hussey Redoubt traversed backwards and forwards as the Gordons threaded their way through the torn up wire and casualties were again high; Colonel Stansfield was mortally wounded, Captain James Boyd was killed and Captain MacTavish was wounded. But the Gordons cleared Breslau Trench while the bombers overwhelmed Hussey Redoubt on the Hulluch road.

The Devons and Gordons advanced up the slope towards Gun Trench, where a gun battery fired until Sergeant Northam charged and captured the crews. The two battalions each claimed two guns; chalking their Regimental names on their trophies. Captain Thomas Finlay then gathered around one hundred Gordons, all he could find, and they advanced in a single line to Estaminet Corner on the main Lens–La Bassée road. Finlay spotted a column of infantry marching into Cité St Elie to the north, so his men spread out and opened fire, scattering the surprised Germans into the village.

Finlay had dealt with the immediate threat but he had no idea where the rest of the brigade was. The 9th Devons had been shot to pieces in front of Gun Trench and were in no position to help while part of the 2nd Borders were clearing strongpoints near the German front line with the Staffords. Colonel Thorpe was reluctant to send the rest of his battalion forward until 22 Brigade had caught up on his left, so he waited in Gun Trench, with the 1/6th Gordons.

It was 10am before Major Ross and two 1/6th Gordons companies joined their sister battalion at Estaminet Corner, leaving the German reinforcements enough time to deploy in front of 7th Division. Ross instructed Captain Finlay to advance with fifty men but they soon came under fire. Finlay was killed and his men returned to report that Germans were holding the trench beyond the Lens–La Bassée road. Second Lieutenant McPherson led fifteen bombers along a communication trench to deal with them but they too came under fire. Ross decided he could not tackle the trench alone and sent a message asking for help while the Gordons dug in.

By midday all movement had stopped on 7th Division's front. Part of the 2nd Queen's were holding Puits Trench as Colonel Owens held Hulluch Quarries with the rest of 22 Brigade. The survivors of 20 Brigade either faced Hulluch or were pinned down in Gun Trench.

Brigadier General Watts' 21 Brigade had given up moving along the blocked communication trenches but it still took his battalions six hours to reach the old front line. General Capper mistakenly believed 22 Brigade was stuck in no man's land on the left of the division so Watts had instructions to follow 20 Brigade and head for Hulluch. But when Capper heard 22 Brigade was approaching Cité St Elie, he told Watts to send half his command to help 22 Brigade and the other half to join 20 Brigade.

The 2nd Green Howards and 1/4th Camerons were passing the Quarries around midday, heading for Puits Trench, when they came under fire from Cité St Elie. The Green Howards regrouped in Stone Alley and they were joined by the Camerons; they would not go any further. Meanwhile, the 2nd Wiltshires and 2nd Bedfords came under fire from Puits Trench north of the Hulluch road. Around 500 had been hit by the time the officers spotted the thick belt of wire protecting *Stützpunkt* (strongpoint) II between Cité St Elie and Hulluch, so they ordered everyone to take cover in Gun Trench. All four of 21 Brigade's battalions had been committed and they had made no difference. It left 7th Division with no more reserves.

Around 2pm the Queen's saw the Germans were evacuating Cité St Elie so Lieutenant Colonel Heath and Captain Philpot led their men towards the village. But British artillery observers spotted the movement and they thought the Queen's were advancing German infantry. A short bombardment forced most of the Queen's to withdraw to the Quarries but Heath and a few men stayed in Cité Trench until nightfall.

Lieutenant Colonel Owens sent two patrols forward from the Quarries to assess the German positions and they reported that Cité St Elie was strongly held. On hearing the news, General Capper ordered the artillery to shell the village ahead of an attack at 4pm. But the observers did not know about Puits Trench and directed the gunners to fire at the obvious target: the village. Lieutenant Colonel Leatham, of the Wiltshires, appealed against making the attack so it was cancelled. Instead 7th Division consolidated Stone Alley and Gun Trench while Capper made his plans for the morning.

Chapter 11

They Died with Faces to the Enemy
IV Corps, 25 September

1st Division Crosses the Grenay Ridge

Major General Holland's division held the line south of the Vermelles–Hulluch Road. The German artillery shelled 1 Brigade when the cloud began to form and a few cylinders were hit by shrapnel, spraying Brigadier General Reddie's men with gas. A machine gun hidden in Bois Carré hit the 8th Berkshires[243] as they crossed no man's land but most of the casualties occurred when the gas blew back as they cut through the wire. The survivors found the German trench deserted, apart from a couple of machine gun teams, so they pushed on towards the crest of the ridge.

It was a similar story for the 10th Gloucesters. They were shot down by a machine gun hidden in La Haie copse and 'the officers fell as the position of their bodies showed, leading their men... The bodies of our dead indicated how they died, with faces to the enemy.' The battalion strayed to the right in the gas cloud while the wire entanglement proved to be 'a considerable obstacle'. Again the front trench had been abandoned but the Gloucesters had a tough fight for the support and reserve German trenches.

The two New Army battalions had been decimated and the 1st Camerons took the lead, capturing three field guns in Gun Trench before moving over the crest of Grenay ridge. Lieutenant Colonel Graeme called a halt on the Lens Road, so the 1st Black Watch could catch up, and sent patrols forward to investigate the wire protecting Hulluch. Graeme also sent an over-optimistic message, timed at 9.10am, to 1 Brigade headquarters, leaving General Reddie believing Hulluch had been captured. The reality was that most of his brigade was waiting for reinforcements on the Lens road and only thirty men had entered the village.

The wind changed direction during the gas release in 2 Brigade's sector and the cloud covered the assembly trenches. The leading companies of the

---

243 The 8th Berkshires and the 10th Gloucesters joined when two Guard battalions went to the Guards Division in August. They were both New Army battalions.

1st Loyals and the 2nd KRRC were asphyxiated so the support companies moved forward to take their place. But the gas was so thick many climbed out of the trenches and lay behind the parados.[244] Brigadier General Pollard allowed a five-minute delay but it was not enough time to reorganise the men.

At 6.20am it appeared the wind had changed again so the gas officers opened the final cylinders. But the cloud was not as thick as planned because the two Stokes mortars detailed to create a smoke screen had been disabled by misfires. A machine gun dug-in next to a smashed tree trunk called Lone Tree hit the Loyals while another at the end of Northern Sap hit the Riflemen. The waves of infantry became mixed up in the cloud and they then stumbled into a low belt of wire which was hidden in the long grass.

The Loyals left was soon falling back and Colonel Sanderson and Captain Dever were injured rallying their men. As the gas dispersed, Captain Faulkner and Lieutenants Levesey, Wharton and Healey were killed as they tried to form a firing line close to the German wire. Lieutenant Warborough was killed and Lieutenant Gardner was gassed as they carried machine guns forward to even up the fire-fight. Over 500 Loyals would be killed or injured around Lone Tree. Many did what they could to help the wounded; Private Henry Kenny rescued six men before he was injured – he would be awarded the Victoria Cross.

The Rifle Corps were also pinned down in front of the wire as the cloud dispersed, leaving them at the mercy of the German machine guns. 18-year-old Private George Peachment was killed while dragging his wounded company commander, Captain Dubs, to safety; he was also awarded the Victoria Cross. As soon as the 2nd Sussex officers saw the Kings Royal Rifle Corps in difficulties, they decided to help them. Three companies went forward and they were shot down in front of the wire, one after another. Sergeant Harry Wells took command of his platoon after his officer fell, but he was killed after leading men to the wire three times; he was posthumously awarded the Victoria Cross.

General Pollard gave orders for the rest of his brigade to advance when he learnt his men were being shot to pieces. But it took nearly an hour to assemble the final company of the Sussex and two 1st Northants companies, by which time the gas and smoke had cleared. They stood no chance and Captain Anketell Read of the Northants established a firing line around Lone Tree with around sixty survivors. He then moved back and forth along the line directing fire and encouraging the men until he was shot by a sniper. Read was posthumously awarded the Victoria Cross. By 8.30am General

---

244 Snipers aimed at the silhouettes of heads above the parapet, so this mound of earth was built to mask the outline and remove the danger.

Pollard's brigade was broken and his men were dead, dying or pinned down close to the German wire.

Major General Holland had six battalions in reserve around Le Rutoire Farm and two, under Lieutenant Colonel Green, were supposed to fill a widening gap between 1 and 2 Brigades, as they advanced over the Grenay Ridge. General Holland knew 1 Brigade was advancing on Hulluch but the first message from 2 Brigade said the Sussex was fighting in the German trenches, giving the impression it had also broken through. So he instructed General Pollard to 'push on with all speed' and ordered Colonel Green to reinforce 2 Brigade with the 1/9th King's and the 1/14th London Scottish. Green's battalions moved in the open because the trenches were full of gassed and wounded men. 'Their casualties were heavy, but they advanced as if on parade, the Black Watch cheering as we passed.' Lieutenant Colonel Ramsey was particularly conspicuous at the head of the 1/9th Kings, carrying a wand.

1st Division's battle around Lone Tree on 25 September

General Holland sent an order to Colonel Green when he heard about 2 Brigade's plight, telling him to advance, in the hope they would take General Pollard's men forward. But Green was in a better position to assess the situation around Lone Tree. His men were taking cover behind the parados at the British front line; anyone could see the carnage in no man's land if they dared to look up.

By 9.00am Major General Holland knew he had a problem. Captain Ritter and around 600 German soldiers faced Lone Tree and they were re-occupying the trenches about Bois Carré, threatening to cut off 1 Brigade. General Reddie had instructed Lieutenant Colonel Hamilton of the 1st Black Watch to stop them but only thirty of the first company reached their objective. Hamilton decided against sending the rest of his battalion forward but the few who made it were enough to thwart the Germans' plans.

At 10am Brigadier General Davies was ordered to move his 3 Brigade forward to help 1 Brigade: 'Munsters have been ordered to advance north of Bois Carré, and when through German trenches to wheel half right and attack in support of 1st Brigade. Welch follow in support, with orders to push through southern end of Hulluch. South Wales Borderers will be ready to support Welch.'

Major Gorham was moving the 2nd Munsters[245] over the top towards Bois Carré when Major Considine decided to help the hundreds of men pinned down around Lone Tree. He ordered Second Lieutenant Conran to move his company towards 2 Brigade; 'It was not his allotted task, and his orders were clear. A smaller man would have carried out his instructions to a letter. But not so Major Considine. He saw that if the enemy held this sector it would endanger the flanks of our successful attacks in the neighbouring sectors.' Lieutenant Gethin led the rest of the Munsters forward by platoon rushes and the wounded cheered them on, but Considine was shot dead and Company Sergeant Major Leahy was killed rushing to his aid. The Munsters had been unable to break the deadlock and they too ended up pinned down around Lone Tree.

Meanwhile, Green's Force was waiting for instructions but General Holland's three messengers had all been killed. It was after 11am before Colonel Green received his orders and midday before the 1/14th London Regiment[246] and the 1/9th King's (Liverpool) were ready to move off. Major Lindsay wanted to follow 3 Brigade past Bois Carré but Colonel Green overruled him and two companies of each battalion moved forward over the open in short rushes. Some reached the German wire near Lone Tree only to be shot down trying to cut through the wire.

General Holland finally admitted defeat and after over six hours of

---

245 Only 250 men.
246 The London Scottish.

deadlock he sent orders forward for 2 Brigade to outflank the Lone Tree position from the south: 'Collect all available men of your brigade, leaving only sufficient to hold the line. Move them down to the Vermelles–Loos Road and across the German trenches at the Loos Road Redoubt. Then wheel up to your left and attack along line North Loos Avenue and Loos–La Bassée road, so as to get behind the Germans holding up your brigade.'

The withdrawal was going to be difficult and costly but help came from an unexpected quarter before it began. Lieutenant Colonel Prothero's 2nd Welch had left Le Rutoire farm at 12.30pm and had followed the rest of 1 Brigade past Bois Carré. The Welch came under heavy fire from Hulluch as they advanced over the crest of the ridge and they found shelter in Gun Trench. Colonel Prothero could see no sign of the Munsters ahead so he wheeled his battalion to the right, so he could bypass Hulluch.

The change in direction brought the Welch behind Captain Ritter's men. It meant they were going to be surrounded, their ammunition was running out and there was no sign of any help. So 'suddenly the fire from our right slackened and it at last stopped altogether and a German bearing a white flag came towards us. He was sent by the Germans holding out to arrange their surrender. We then captured 160 men and five officers.' Captain Ritter and another 400 men surrendered soon afterwards and Stuart Dolden[247] described the moment of surrender: 'At one moment there was an intense and nerve shattering struggle with death screaming through the air. Then, as if with the wave of a magic wand, all was changed; all over No Man's Land troops came out of their trenches, or rose from the ground where they had been lying. Prisoners were everywhere.'

It was well after 3pm by the time Pollard and Green assembled the survivors around Lone Tree and they left the ghastly scene and moved over the Grenay ridge. The sky was dark and rain clouds were gathering as 2 Brigade established a line north of Bois Hugo, making contact with Scottish troops of 15th Division in Chalet Wood. Green's force assembled in support in and around the Chalk Pit.

The three battalions of 1 Brigade waited all morning in front of Hulluch and although advanced parties of the 7th Division came up on the left, they were too few to warrant resuming the advance. The 2nd Munsters arrived around noon but Major Gorham had too few men to make a difference. For five hours there had been a large breach in the German line and First Army had been unable to exploit it.

After midday 1 Brigade found itself on the defensive when a battalion of German infantry marched into Hulluch and drove the Camerons' scouts back. They spread out through the ruins and manned the trench outside the

---

247 Dolden's autobiography is called *Cannon Fodder*.

village while their officers assessed the situation. Three hours later they attacked from the village, only to be driven back by the Camerons and Munsters. The 2nd Welsh and the 1st South Wales Borderers[248] arrived soon after, but dusk was approaching so General Reddie instructed his men to dig in along Alley 4 trench, west of the road.

Around midnight the Germans made another attempt to dislodge 1 Brigade and while they overran the 8th Berkshires' front line, the support line held on. Some Germans approached the South Wales Borderers shouting 'Don't shoot, we are the Welsh', but their accents sounded foreign so Lieutenant Colonel Gwynn's men waited before opening fire at point blank range. The following morning every man possessed a German helmet.

No one had been covering the gap of 1,200 metres between 1 Brigade in front of Hulluch and 2 Brigade near Bois Hugo all afternoon and evening. It was after midnight before scouts from the two brigades made contact but General Holland still had no one to fill the space with. All he could do was wait for First Army's reserves to arrive on the battlefield.

15th (Scottish) Division's Advance through Loos

Major General Frederick McCracken's division held the front opposite Loos village, but his men had to take the trenches on Grenay Ridge first. Engineers had dug Russian saps into no man's land and they were opened into trenches and connected together the night before the battle. The gas and smoke settled on the trench and the Scots found 'going over the top' was 'a physical as well as moral effort. Half smothered in their smoke helmets they had to scramble out of the 250 metres of fire trench in which they crowded, get through the gaps cut in the wire, and spread out to something over 400 metres of frontage – and this, heavily laden and with rifles with fixed bayonets... As can be imagined, things did not go to clockwork. Men were affected by gas. It was Hobson's choice – to be half choked for want of air, or wholly choked in the attempt to get it.'

It was thought the Germans had machine guns in Northern and Southern Saps and Captain Torrance led two companies of the 12th HLI towards them. Many Highlanders collapsed, asphyxiated, but the rest found that Southern Sap was nothing more than a shallow ditch. The battalion machine gun officer led his four gun teams forward under fire and they used their weapons to hold the position. Second Lieutenant Watson then crossed no man's land with the 6th Camerons' bombers and bombed north until they contacted 1st Division near Lone Tree around noon.

The rest of Brigadier General Matheson's 46 Brigade was smothered in gas as they waited in their trenches. Second Lieutenant Martin Young

---

248 Both 3 Brigade.

shouted at Piper Daniel Laidlaw 'for God's sake, pipe 'em together'; so Laidlaw pulled back his smoke helmet, clamped his lips around his bagpipes and played 'Blue Bonnets'. The tune rallied the 7th KOSBs and they advanced as two machine guns in the Loos Road redoubt traversed left and right, hitting many men. Laidlaw was hit by shrapnel but limped forward, playing 'The Standard on the Braes o' Mar' until a second shell brought him to his knees and mortally wounded Lieutenant Young. But the KOSBs kept going and cleared the redoubt. Laidlaw would survive and he was awarded the Victoria Cross.

The machine guns in Jew's Nose Trench fired on the 10th Scottish Rifles, killing nine officers and hitting many others before they reached the smashed wire. But the survivors were able to clear the trench beyond and they headed over the crest of Grenay Ridge followed by the 12th HLI and the 8th KOSBs. There was a little smoke and mist in the Loos valley but there was no gas, so the soldiers rolled their smoke helmets up on their heads or discarded them so they could breathe the clean air.

Major Glenny led the KOSBs across the valley and up the far slope, using Puits 14's chimney on the horizon as a guide, reaching the colliery around 9.15am. But he could see no sign of 1st Division to the north or the Scottish Rifles to the south as his men deployed along the Lens highway. He did not know 1st Division was pinned down at Lone Tree while the Scottish Rifles had been drawn into the chaotic battle for Loos. Glenny waited anxiously until the 12th HLI and 8th KOSBs joined him sometime later.

On 15th Division's right, Brigadier General Wilkinson's 44 Brigade faced the south end of the Grenay Ridge, astride the Lens Road. Most of the Germans fled at the first sign of the gas but the machine gun teams fought on. The cloud spread over 8th Seaforths trenches and it took them time to deploy in no man's land. Captain Alec Ravenhill knelt on the parapet, pulling his heavily laden men out of the trench until he was shot dead. The Seaforths quickly cleared the Jew's Nose trench but losses had been high; Lieutenant Colonel Thomson, his adjutant and all four company commanders had been hit in no man's land.

The 9th Black Watch were also affected by the gas blowing back but they climbed out of their trench, assembled beyond their wire and advanced. 'It seemed impossible to realise that these lines of disciplined soldiers had been, twelve short months before, almost all civilians... There was no shouting or hurry; the men moved in quick time, picking up their dressing as if on ceremonial parade.' The two machine guns in Lens Road Redoubt shot down many but the survivors captured the trench. Most of the officers

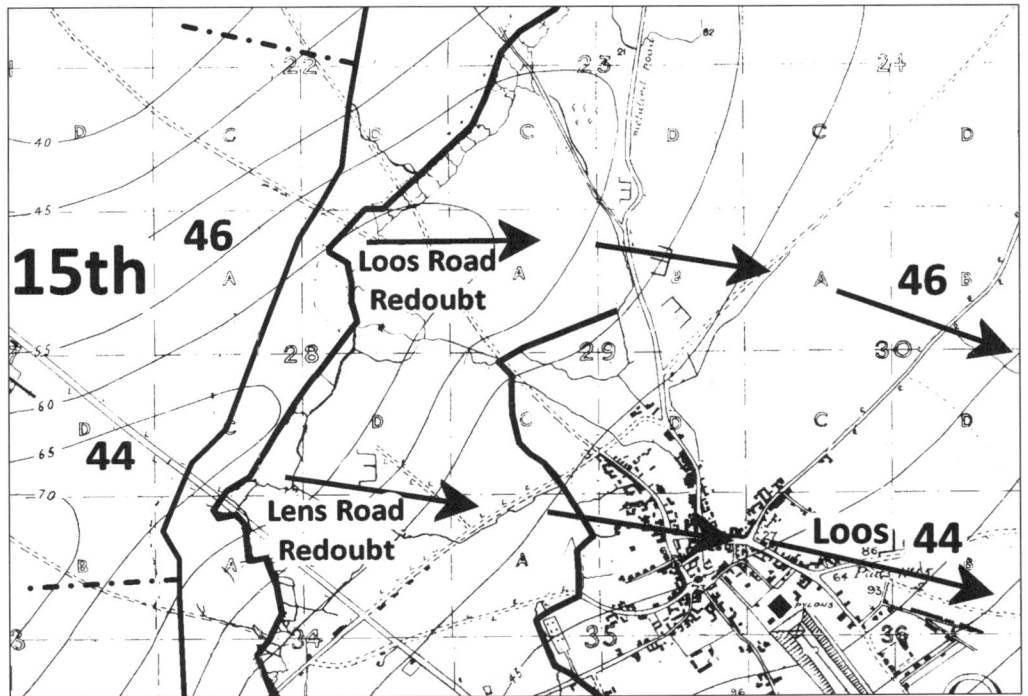

15th (Scottish) Division's advance through Loos on 25 September

were hit and Major Henderson's dying words to his company were 'keep going'.

The two battalions jogged down the steep slope towards Loos village with the 7th Camerons and the 10th Gordons following. The Seaforths came under fire from Fort Glatz emplacement as they cut through the wire covering the village perimeter but the rest of the garrison were still in their billets, unaware the battle had begun. The Scots were moving into the village before many Germans were dressed and ready to fight. But a machine gun hidden in a tomb in the cemetery fired into the Black Watch until the London Irish silenced it. The Scots were then enraged to see Second Lieutenant Sharp shot by a soldier as he accepted the surrender of a German officer.

By 7.00am 44 Brigade was moving along the village streets, dragging aside barricades, breaking down doors and throwing bombs through windows. Most Germans surrendered without a fight and many prisoners and civilians were sent to the rear. 'The speed made by the attack was phenomenal indeed; and the success attained promised to exceed the most sanguine expectations.' The Black Watch cleared the houses along the Grenay Road before taking more prisoners in the shops and houses around the square, where many women and children had been hiding.

By 8.30am many men were assembling on the far side of Loos but others were engrossed in tracking down the Germans hiding in the ruins. The 7th Camerons had left Lieutenant Colonel Sandilands behind so he established his headquarters in the village before trying to find his battalion. He reported 'in Loos itself there were still parties going about bombing and bayoneting Germans running out of houses, and also taking prisoners.'

One group killed a German officer found telephoning instructions from his cellar hiding place. Sergeant Findlay of the 10th Gordons came under machine gun fire from one house so he smashed down the door and took fifty men prisoner. But Second Lieutenant Bruce-Wood, 10th Gordons, rounded up the largest number of prisoners, escorting 275 to the rear before returning with ammunition. Although the Germans had booby-trapped strategic buildings, including the town hall and the church, no one had detonated the explosives in the chaos. Major Blogg and his engineers from the London Division defused the devices before they caused any casualties.

Many Germans remained hidden in the chaos and while some surrendered when they could, others took the opportunity to snipe at the Scots milling around the streets. Captain Bearn had set up the Black Watch aid post in the Moreau family shop on the square and 17-year-old Emilienne Moreau had spent the day tending to the wounded. 'When troops were making efforts to dislodge two German snipers from the next house, who were firing on the stretcher bearers, this young girl seized a revolver from an officer and went into the back of a house and fired two shots at the snipers. She came back saying 'c'est fini'[249] and handed the revolver back to the officer.'[250]

By 9.00am 44 Brigade was assembling on the east side of the village. Morale was high, the battalions were mixed up and there were few officers left to organise them but they climbed up the slope, all 1,500 of them. The garrison of Hill 70 redoubt at the top ran, followed by the mob of cheering Scots; only they were heading south towards Cité St Laurent rather than east towards Cité Auguste, as they should have.

German reserves manning the trench covering Cité St Laurent opened fire on the Scots, pinning them down on the open slope. A second wave of 7th Camerons and 10th Gordons followed over the summit of Hill 70 but they too came under long-range machine gun fire. They returned fire until

---

249 'It is finished'.
250 Emilienne Moreau was awarded the Croix de Guerre and the Military Cross. Loos village school is named after the young school teacher.

Lieutenant Christison warned them to cease fire because they were hitting Scottish troops out in front. He was wrong – it was coming from the Germans in Cité St Laurent. Lieutenant Robertson told his men to dig in the best they could and they began making head cover.

To the north 46 Brigade saw Germans running into Cité Auguste so they cheered and ran after them. But the Germans closed the gaps in the wire behind them, manned a trench and opened fire, pinning the Scots down in front of a belt of wire. They too had to make head cover in the long grass.

By late morning 15th Division's advance was over. Although the Scots had advanced nearly two miles, units had been decimated, the men had no officers and they were scratching for cover. While 46 Brigade was scattered across the east slope of Hill 70, 44 Brigade was in a similar predicament on the south slope. There were only nine hundred men left and they were pinned down in an arc, facing Cité St Auguste and Cité St Laurent. Officers occasionally tried to get their men to advance by short rushes but most were shot as they ran from group to group.

Down in the village below, Lieutenant Colonel Sandilands had led two leaderless companies of the 7th Scots Fusiliers out of the ruins and up the hill. He decided against going beyond the summit and made them dig in on the reverse slope instead. Lieutenant Colonel Lloyd of the 9th Black Watch heard his men had been unable to contact anyone from the 47th (London) Division on Loos Crassier (slag heap) and he went forward to clear up the situation. Both Sandilands and Lloyd could see the lines of Scots pinned down on the open slopes in front and the wire blocking their way.

General McCracken's orders called for his troops to consolidate Hill 70 but the German trenches had to be reversed[251] and the curved redoubt was facing west, which would make it difficult to stop an attack from the east. Sandilands and Lieutenant Colonel Wallace, the 10th Gordons' commanding officer, gathered up all the men they could find, all 400 of them, and put them to work digging in west of the redoubt, using an earth bank as the basis for their new trench.

Although Sandilands was proud to see his battalion flag, a yellow signalling flag with a piece of Cameron tartan sewn to it, flying above the redoubt, he had been hearing worrying reports about the men pinned down in front of his position. Some said they had been practically wiped out while others noted the heavy howitzers were only firing on Cité St Auguste, leaving the Scots in front of Cité St Laurent without artillery support.

The situation was precarious but General Rawlinson thought 15th Division had broken through the German Second Line and while he ordered McCracken to send 45 Brigade though Cité St Auguste, it would take it a

---

251 New fire-steps had to be built and the parapet switched around.

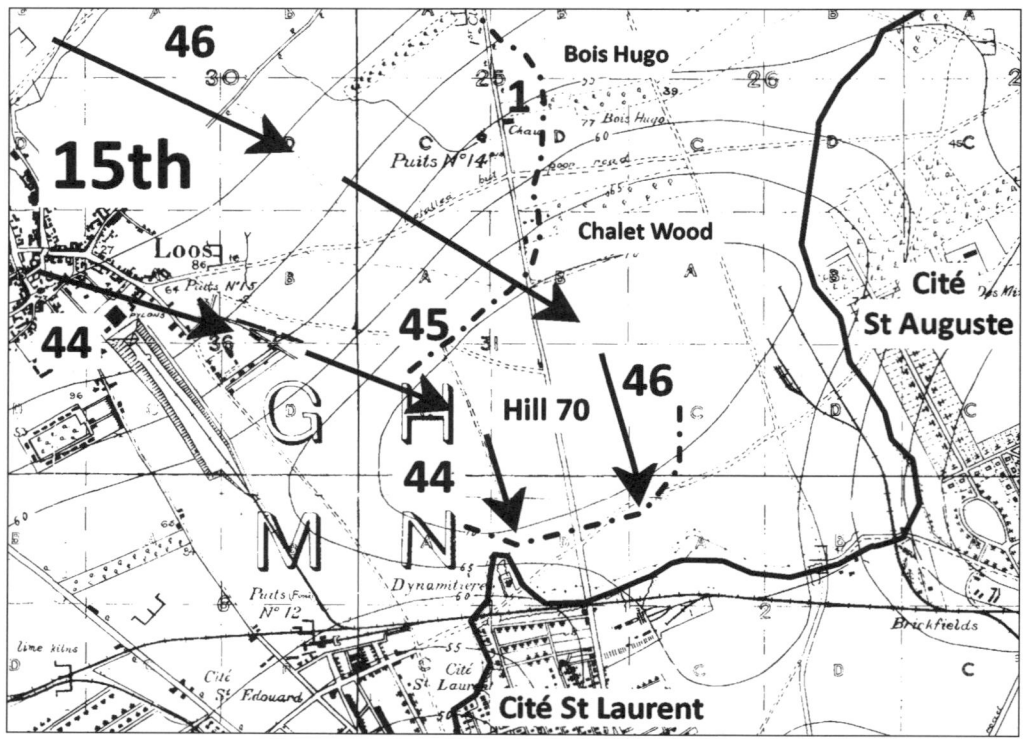

15th (Scottish) Division's advance through Loos

long time to get through Loos. Around midday the first counter-attack hit the Scottish line near Loos Crassier, where Lieutenant Robinson of the 10th Gordons had 600 men from different regiments. Sergeant Aitkin had made it back to the summit of Hill 70 so he could tell Colonel Sandilands about the precarious situation.

Sandilands wanted to recall the Scots to strengthen his hill-top position but a second counter-attack from the Dynamitière, on the northern outskirts of Cité St Laurent, came first. Some Scots opened fire at the advancing infantry but others ran up the hill to where Sergeant Lamb was waving the battalion flag as a rallying point. Those left behind were captured when they ran out of ammunition.

Captain Strang of the 8th Seaforths watched the disaster unfold from the summit of the hill as Lieutenant Johnson rallied the Scots and deployed alongside Sandilands position. They stopped the Germans at the redoubt, with the help of Captain Cardew's engineers of the 73rd Company RE.

Cardew was seriously wounded and Johnson was wounded in the leg before their men fell back to the embankment; Johnson would be awarded the Victoria Cross for stopping the counter-attack.

Although 15th Division had advanced over two miles in four hours its battalions were in a difficult position. The German counter-attacks continued throughout the afternoon but the arrival of 45 Brigade steadied the tired survivors. The 6th Camerons deployed near Chalet Wood, on the left flank, and the 7th Scots Fusiliers reinforced the summit of Hill 70; the 11th Argylls and 13th Royal Scots still had to make their way through Loos. The German artillery soon began to hammer the Scots in their improvised trenches, but the Scots had no artillery support because their field artillery could not move into the Loos valley until Hill 70 had been taken.

47th (London) Division on the Right Flank

Major General Charles Barter had all three brigades in line south-west of Loos, but only two were going to advance. Brigadier General Thwaites' 141 Brigade had to advance across the Lens road towards Loos village. The German artillery opened fire as soon as the cloud of gas was seen but the shrapnel only burst one cylinder. For once the gas moved in the direction it was supposed to and crept down the slopes and over the German trenches.

At zero hour platoon after platoon of London Territorials climbed the ladders, assembled in no man's land and advanced. The 1/18th London Regiment[252] were on the left and one platoon dribbled a football between them, aiming to score a 'goal' in the German trench. Many of the Germans were taken by surprise and the majority fled. Brigadier Thwaites had arranged for six machine guns to conduct indirect fire over the German trenches and it hit many as they ran.

By 7am Major Matthews was able to report that the London Irish had crossed the Lens highway but the smoke screen was thinning out and the few Germans manning the Loos Defence Line in front of Loos cemetery caused many casualties. A machine gun team hidden inside in a stone tomb shot at the London Irish as they cut through the wire but they ran once they were through.

The 1/19th London Regiment[253] were hit in the left flank, where the German trench curved around the flat crest. It could not to be cleared until the Lens Road redoubt had been taken, leaving the two machine gun teams free to shoot at the St Pancras men. Lieutenant Colonel Collinson-Morley was mortally wounded along with his adjutant and many other officers. Captain Hamilton was also seriously wounded but he remained at his post to organise the consolidation of the German trenches.

---

252 The London Irish.
253 The St Pancras battalion.

The St Pancras men then crossed the Lens road around Valley Crossroads and passed through the London Irish. They ripped down the wire netting fence around Loos colliery and secured the base of the huge twin pithead tower known as Tower Bridge. One company skirted around the north side of the huge slag heap, called the Grandstand, and then advanced up the slope of Hill 70 to secure its east end. Despite the success, the St Pancras had no officers and while some advanced up Hill 70 with the 9th Black Watch, the rest became caught up in the fight for Loos.

The 1/20th (Blackheath and Woolwich) London Regiment passed through the London Irish at the Loos Defence Line and Lieutenant Colonel Hubback led his men into an abandoned housing estate called Welwyn Garden City. Some men fortified the houses as Captain Williams led his company up the slope towards Chalk Pit Copse, where they came under fire from the strongpoint called Stützpunkt 69. Although the Londoners captured two field guns in the Chalk Pit, they were unable to knock out two machine

47th Division secures the right flank on 25 September

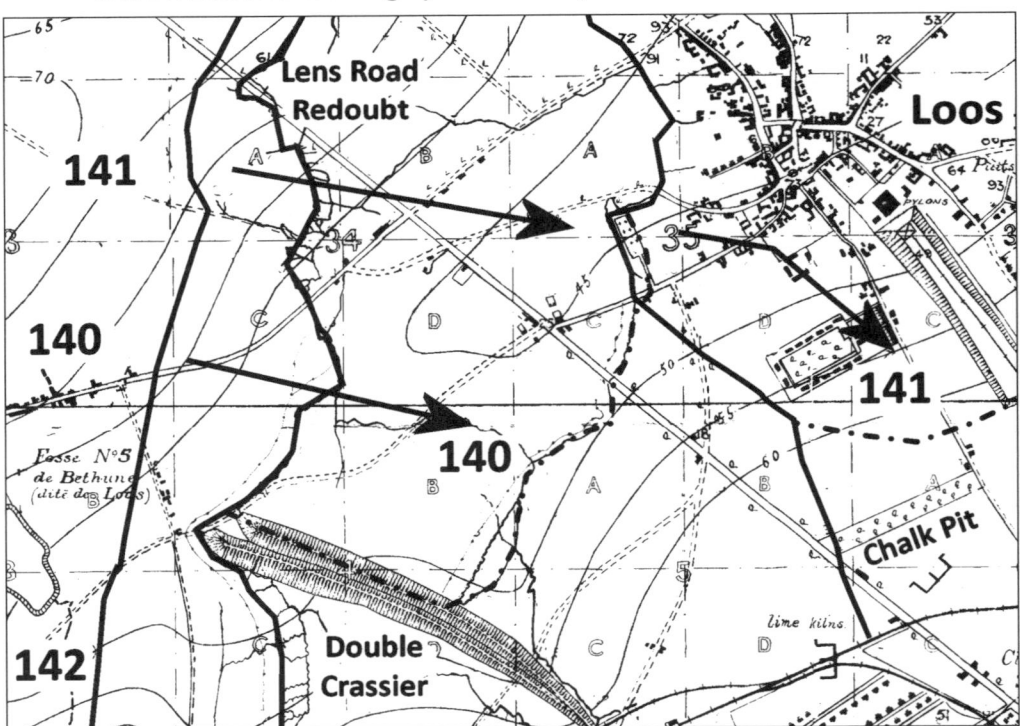

guns and a third field gun in the nearby copse. German reinforcements had soon forced William's men onto the defensive.

By 9.00am 141 Brigade could report it had secured most of its objectives. Lieutenant Colonel Hubback took command of the 1/19th London as well as his own battalion while Major Evans supported the Chalk Pit position with a company of the 1/17th London Regiment.[254]

Brigadier General Cuthbert's 140 Brigade was to secure IV Corps' defensive flank. The 1/6th (Rifles) London Regiment had two companies squeezed into the front trench. The men of the lead company men stood to the left of the ladders, while the second company waited to the right. The Cast Iron Sixth clambered out into the open as the gas clouds moved slowly down the slope into the valley.

The men had to bunch up to get through the smashed wire but most of the Germans ran as the Londoners approached their trench. The bombers followed them down the communication trenches but their damp bombs would not light, so they used cudgels, daggers and captured grenades to round them up instead. Rifleman Challoner led the charge down the slope and captured the few men holding the support line astride the Lens highway. Lieutenant Colonel Faux's men then converted the communication trench into a fire trench and waited to see if there were any counter-attacks from Cité St Pierre.

Lieutenant Colonel Mildren's 1/7th London faced a huge slag heap called the Double-Crassier. The Shiny Seventh lost most of its officers in no man's land but the men ran through the smashed wire and overran the German trenches. The left advanced along the foot of the slag heap and joined up with the 1/6th Battalion as Major Bill Casson's company clambered up Double Crassier's ash slopes and cleared the trench on the summit. German reserves counter-attacked and Company Sergeant Major Hill rallied the survivors and held the trench after Major Casson was killed. General Cuthbert sent two companies from the 1/8th London Regiment[255] forward to help secure the flank as Sergeant Thomas' men carried boxes of grenades to the top of the slag heap.

There was no attack planned for the area south of the Double Crassier but 142 Brigade carried out a Chinese attack to distract the Germans' attention. The divisional carpenters had cut wooden figures and painted them to look like prone men. They were placed in no man's land and strings pulled the figures up at zero hour. The 1/21st and 1/22nd Londoners cheered and raised their bayonets over the parapet at the same time and the dummies were riddled with bullets.

---

254 The Poplar and Stepney Rifles.
255 The Post Office Rifles.

Chapter 12

A Field of Corpses
IX Corps, 26 September

Field Marshal Sir John French and General Sir Douglas Haig had not seen eye to eye over the positioning of First Army reserves for the battle. French had wanted them far back while Haig wanted them further forward, or at least that is what First Army's commander said after the battle. By nightfall on 25 September both I and IV Corps had broken through the first line of German trenches but the assault divisions had suffered high casualties; so high they were incapable of further offensive action. First Army needed 21st and 24th Divisions of IX Corps forward to exploit the break in the German line between Hulluch and Hill 70.

Inexperienced and Unaware
By midday on 25 September, IV Corps front was as follows: General Holland's 1st Division had broken through at Bois Carré but it was still fighting at Lone Tree, 15th Division had advanced through Loos, and 47th Division had secured the corps flank. General Rawlinson was worried about Hill 70 because the Scots were reporting heavy casualties and counterattacks.

General Haig released 62 Brigade, from Major General Claud Jacob's 21st Division, and Brigadier General Wilkinson was instructed to advance to Hill 70 to aid the Scots.[256] But Hill 70 was five miles away and all Wilkinson's battalion commanders were told, 'We do not know what has happened on Hill 70. You must go and find out: if the Germans hold it, attack them; if our people are there, support them; if no one is there, dig in.' So Haig was sending a single brigade of inexperienced troops into the unknown.

Around 3pm the two battalions were moving forward along the Lens road when they were stopped by a military policeman who told them to

---

256 He also released 73 Brigade of 24th Division to reinforce I Corps at the same time.

march in artillery formation because they were entering the 'battle zone'. Experienced officers would have ignored him but the 8th East Yorkshires and the 10th Green Howards knew no different and they lost time deploying to march across the fields rather than continuing along the road. The two battalions eventually reached the old front line, near Lens Road Redoubt, around 4.30pm. Lieutenant Colonels Way and Hadow led their troops forward in columns of fours[257] over the crest of the ridge, unaware German artillery observers across the Loos valley were watching. The men scattered into the ditches as they came under shell fire but the brigade transport could not escape and the road was soon blocked by a tangle of wrecked carts and dead animals.

The Yorkshiremen then spread out and advanced along the Lens road even though they had no maps or guides to lead them. They encountered the 1/20th London Battalion in the German support trench where Lieutenant Colonel Hubback warned them not to go any further. But Colonels Way and Hadow continued up the slope where the East Yorkshires came under machine gun fire from Chalk Pit Copse. They fell back, taking two Green Howards companies with them, and the rest of the Green Howards opened fire because they thought they were under attack. It was some time before the Yorkshiremen stopped shooting each other. Colonel Way eventually led two East Yorkshire companies back up the slope to reinforce the 1/20th London's line while the rest of his battalion joined the house clearing operations in Loos village. Colonel Hadow gathered the shocked Green Howards near the cemetery and tried to work out where Hill 70 was.

The 12th and 13th Northumberland Fusiliers had reached Loos without any incidents and General Wilkinson found General Wallerstein in the square. He learnt 45 Brigade was holding Hill 70 but the Scots were tired and low on ammunition, so two platoons of the 12th Northumberland Fusiliers were sent up the slope to reconnoitre the front line. Unfortunately, the 9th Black Watch and 10th Gordons assumed they were being relieved and they headed down the slope to the village. By midnight, only a single company was holding Hill 70 rather than two battalions.

The 13th Northumberland Fusiliers were ordered to support 46 Brigade around Chalet Wood and the plan was for one Fusilier company to reinforce the Scots while the rest dug in on the slopes of the hill behind. Again the arrival of a single company triggered a relief and it was several hours before the mistake was rectified. Fortunately, the Germans did not discover that only two companies held the line between Chalet Wood and Hill 70 and the reluctant Scots were back in their trenches before dawn.

---

257 They were still carrying their packs because they knew no better.

More Reserves Move Forward

The rest of IX Corps was growing restless as they waited in the rear because the men were both excited and nervous as they experienced the sights and sounds of battle. But the remaining four brigades of 21st and 24th Division had to wait until dusk for their orders. The difficulties experienced by 63 Brigade, 21st Division's leading brigade, demonstrated the problems of deploying the entire reserve so late in the day. The men were hungry because they left camp before their cookers arrived. Pouring rain then soaked them as they marched for three hours along the Lens highway past the lines of gun batteries.

The skyline glowed orange and Second Lieutenant Cragg recalled, 'Right ahead of us was Loos in flames, this was the glare that puzzled us; the twin towers of the mine standing out like great oil towers on a burning oil field.'

21st Division advance onto the battlefield late on on 25 September

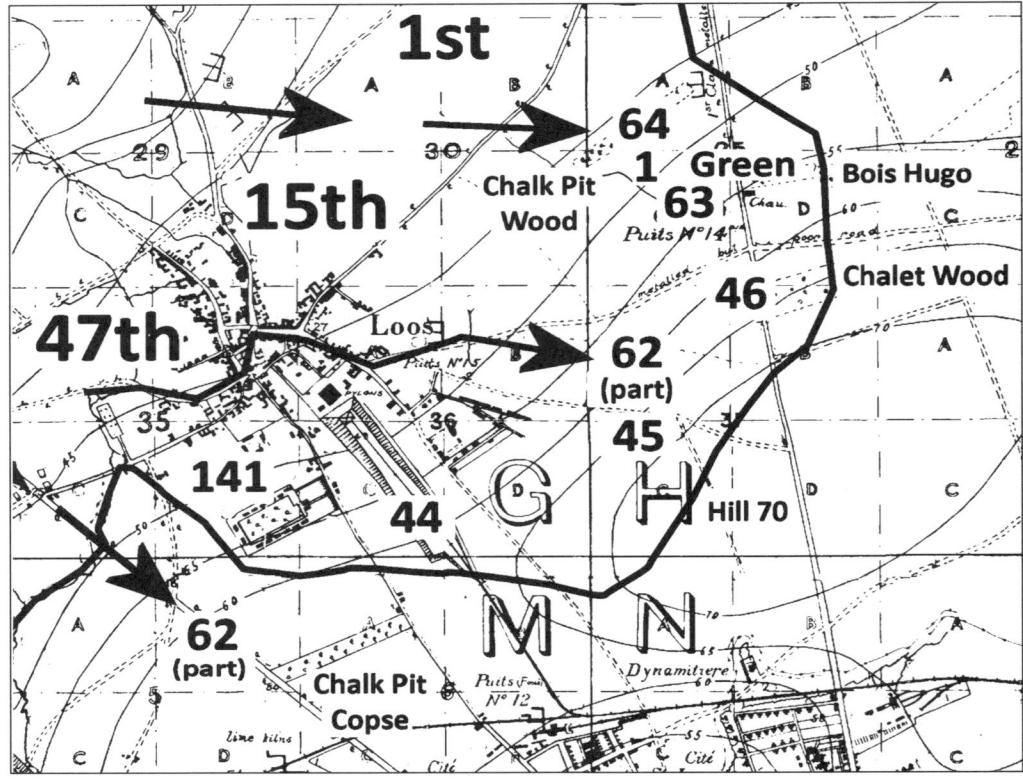

Brigadier General Nickalls followed a compass bearing across the featureless battlefield, and it was after midnight before he found General Mitford on the Grenay Ridge. Meanwhile, his brigade had become split up. The 8th Lincolns and half the 8th Somersets had followed Nickalls but Lieutenant Colonel Denny and the rest of the Somerset companies had gone astray. Meanwhile, the 12th West Yorkshires and 10th York and Lancaster were still marching along the Lens Road.

Nickalls' original instructions were to push on to the German Second Line but First Army changed the plan because it wanted him to attack alongside 24th Division the following morning. But General Nickalls did not get the instruction to halt and he took what was left of his brigade around the north edge of Loos where they came under machine gun fire from Hill 70, where the Scots were fighting for the summit. In the darkness they thought the fire was coming from Chalk Pit Wood which was held by 1st Division's Green's Force:

'Luckily no unfortunate results took place, which might very easily have occurred with new troops advancing to a position at night which was not known to be in our possession. It reflects great credit on the officers concerned, who kept their men so well in hand....The absence of information of what was happening elsewhere was nothing short of disastrous, as no one knew what anyone else was doing.'

Nickalls eventually found General Pollard in the Chalk Pit and while they decided the Lincolns and Somersets[258] would take over Bois Hugo from 2 Brigade, it took until dawn to complete the relief.

Brigadier General Gloster's 64 Brigade had followed 63 Brigade along the Lens Road and then deployed south of the road; 'It took three hours to issue orders; unload machine guns, ammunition, bombs and tools for manhandling; marshal and separate transport; and to form up the Brigade. Any reconnaissance of our line of march was impossible, but it was decided to move on a compass bearing.' They moved slowly across the muddy fields, taking all night to negotiate the abandoned trenches in the dark, and it was nearly daylight when they halted north of Loos. General Gloster correctly assumed 63 Brigade was in front of him and he ordered his men to take cover in nearby trenches.

A combination of poor planning, no staff work and a change of plan had spread First Army's reserves across the battlefield. After a miserable night marching in the rain divisional headquarters did not know where their brigades were, brigades did not know where other brigades were, and few knew where the Germans were.

---

258 Both 63 Brigade.

I Corps, 26 September

General Gough's I Corps had faced an uneasy night. On the left, 2nd Division was still in its original trenches and it had sent three battalions under Lieutenant Colonel Carter south to reinforce 7th Division. In the centre 9th Division had 28 Brigade in its trenches, 26 Brigade holding Fosse 8 and 27 Brigade isolated in Pekin Trench. Meanwhile, 7th Division had 22 Brigade around Hulluch Quarries, 20 Brigade was along the Lens– La Bassée road and 21 Brigade was in support in Stone Alley and Gun Trench.

Brigadier General Bruce had sent two companies of 6th Scots Fusiliers to help 27 Brigade hold Pekin Trench but they were too little too late: 'Darkness was setting in and the situation was critical. Our bombs, being soaked with rain, were useless, and the men's rifles were clogged with mud.' The officers decided to withdraw and the sight of dozens of men moving through the darkness towards 10th Argylls in Fosse Alley led to tense moments before they recognised each other. It then took all night to reorganise along Fosse Alley.

73 Brigade at Fosse 8

General Haig had allocated 73Brigade, 24th Division, to I Corps on 25 September.[259] Brigadier General Oswald's men had just completed three long night marches when General Gough ordered them to secure Fosse 8. It was the first time they had been in the trenches and 'It is regretted that before being launched into such a desperate action steps had not been taken to accustom the men to war conditions.'

Darkness had fallen by the time the brigade reached the old front line and they soon became disorientated in the trenches with no one to guide them. Two companies of 12th Royal Fusiliers became lost so Major Compton led the rest of his men out of the trenches to look for them. But they were spotted as soon as the moon came from behind the clouds and they came under artillery fire. Compton was found by 22 Brigade's brigade major and he led his companies to Hulluch Quarries to help 7th Division, away from where they were needed.

The rest of the brigade found their way to Fosse 8 where they established a new perimeter around the colliery by dawn. The 7th Northants were on the west and north side, the 12th Royal Fusiliers were around Three Cabarets road junction and 9th Royal Sussex held Fosse Alley on the right. But the inexperienced men soon learnt the colliery was the perfect target for the German artillery and they started to waver.

General Oswald had lost control of his command so Brigadier General

---

259 24th Division had landed in France four weeks before and had no battle experience.

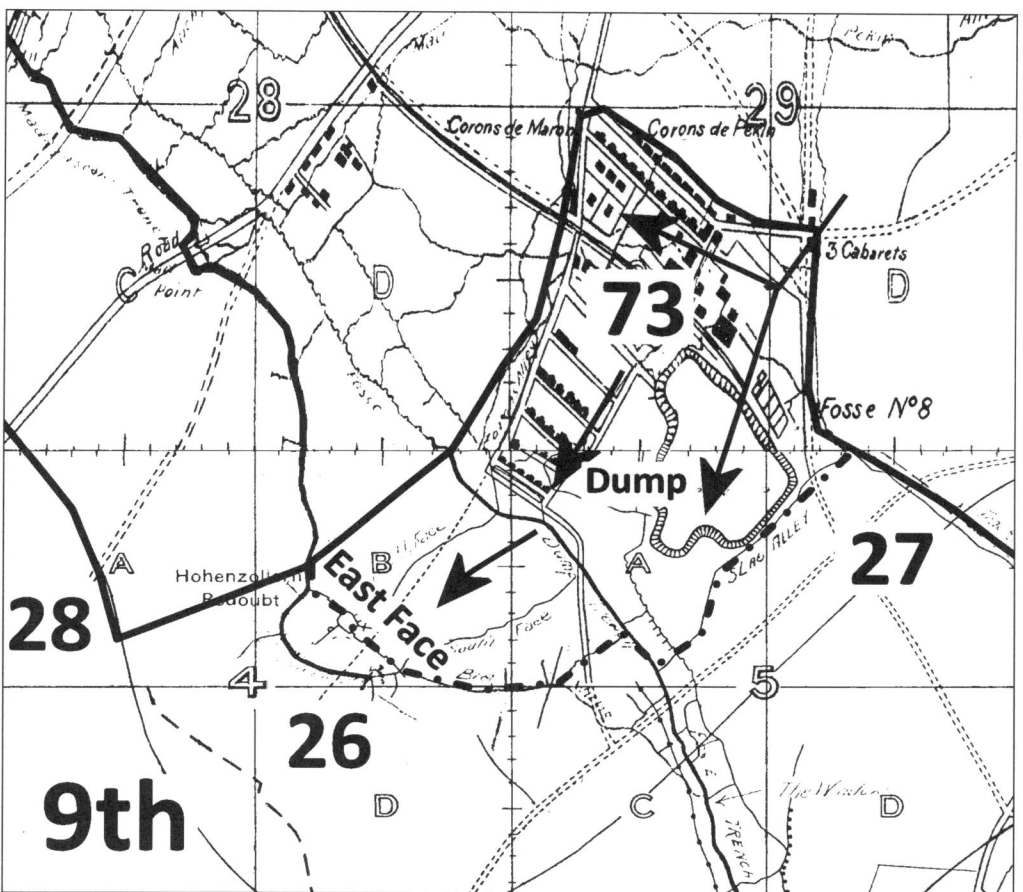

The loss of Fosse 8 on on 26 September

Jelf went to Fosse 8 to take over 73 Brigade and he was shocked by what he found:

'No communication of any kind had been established with my battalions either by wire or orderly, and I attribute this to the fact that all battalions and the brigade staff were quite ignorant of the rudiments of what to do in the trenches; how communications were established, the method of drawing rations, etc., they never having been in trenches in their lives before. I can confidently assert it would have taxed to the uttermost the resources of any Regular battalion, with plenty of experience behind them, to have kept themselves supplied under similar circumstances.'

German infantry had spent the night crawling close to 73 Brigade's perimeter and two red rockets at dawn signalled the start of their attack. One group drove the Northants from Corons Trench and another forced the Sussex from Three Cabarets junction. A third party infiltrated the trenches on the Sussex right flank, allowing bombers to clear the Dump where machine gun teams could fire into 73 Brigade's rear.

As Jelf's men fell back from Fosse 8, Colonel Cameron of Lochiel sent a mixed group of one hundred 8th Black Watch and 5th Camerons to Hohenzollern Redoubt where Captain the Hon. Bowes-Lyon[260] was killed and Lieutenant MacIntosh was mortally injured rallying the stragglers in East Face. General Thesiger was killed by shell burst when they went forward to see the situation for himself.

The Germans were looking to exploit the chaos at Fosse 8 and bombers moved along Little Willie Trench, looking to outflanking East Face Trench. The British bombers again found that the 'German bombers could throw further and were using more powerful bombs.' Corporal James Pollock of the 5th Camerons scrambled into the open and spent an hour throwing grenades into the trench below, stopping the Germans taking East Face; he was awarded the Victoria Cross.

General Haig was at Gough's headquarters when he heard of Thesiger's death and he instructed Major General Edward Bulfin, of 28th Division, to take over 9th Division. But he only had 600 men of 26 Brigade to attack Fosse and Dump Trenches and General Ritchie's troops were unable to get far beyond East Face.

Counter-attacks Against 7th Division

General Capper's plan for the morning of 26 September was to advance east of Hulluch, alongside 1st Division, and 7th Division spent the night reorganising. The 2nd Green Howards and 1/4th Camerons were withdrawn from 22 Brigade's line in the Quarries so they could join the 2nd Royal Scots Fusiliers on the Hulluch road. Colonel Carter's three battalions from 2nd Division assembled alongside.

Unfortunately nobody replaced the Camerons and the Germans had infiltrated the Quarries before midnight. Brigadier General Steele sent a Green Howards company back to fill the gap but a second group of Germans entered the north corner of the Quarries. The 2nd Queen's were preparing to counter-attack when General Bruce was captured in his dug-out and Lieutenant Colonel Heath was killed. Lieutenant Colonels Ovens and Young spotted a German soldier guarding the brigade signals dug-out, so they returned to their men to organise a withdrawal. The 2nd Queen's counter-

---

260 The late Queen Mother's older brother.

attack failed and the 1st South Staffords and 2nd Green Howards had to fall back to the old German front trenches.

German infantry also infiltrated 20 Brigade's wiring parties around midnight and they attacked the Gordons and the Devons in their flanks and rear. Some even reached Gun Trench before they were stopped and General Watts had to spend the rest of the night organising a new line in Gun Trench.

When General Gough reported the Germans had taken the Quarries, First Army sent the 7th Norfolks to retake them at first light; while the battalion was at full strength, it had no battle experience. It approached the quarries at dawn and the lines of men drew fire from every gun in range as they advanced by platoon rushes, just as they had been taught. Over 400 were killed or wounded before the rest went to ground.

The Fight for Bois Hugo and Chalet Wood

Although 63 Brigade was holding the west end of Bois Hugo at dawn on 26 September, its left flank was exposed and German infantry were close to its right flank. At 8am General Gloster received an order to use his 64 Brigade to support 63 Brigade's advance through Bois Hugo and Chalet Wood. Nickalls received the same instructions and Major Storey told the 8th Lincolns that 'all is well' as they waited for zero hour. But some Lincolns opened fire on the Germans withdrawing from Hill 70 to their right, disclosing 63 Brigade's position.

The Germans shelled Chalet Wood and then the infantry drove the exhausted 6th Camerons out of it. Lieutenant Colonel Angus Douglas-Hamilton led his men back into the wood four times until there was hardly anyone left standing. He died of his injuries and was posthumously awarded the Victoria Cross. Two 10th York and Lancaster companies were ordered to reinforce Chalk Pit Wood on the slope below but the whole battalion went forward and advanced beyond it, coming under heavy fire.

General Nickalls was asking for reinforcements so General Gloster instructed 64 Brigade's battalion commanders to meet at the Chalk Pit at 10am. Lieutenant Colonel Leggett was severely injured so the 12th West Yorkshires were late getting their orders. A small attack was stopped at 10.30am but it had successfully located Nickalls' trenches. The Germans then attacked Bois Hugo from both sides, overrunning the West Yorkshires on the left while driving the Lincolns back through the wood. The 10th York and Lancashires were also forced to retire, leaving two companies of Somersets to fight on alone. Lieutenant Colonel Howard later reported how 'We were all in good spirits and blazed away at the Germans who were coming into full view all the time… Things began to get warm now and we

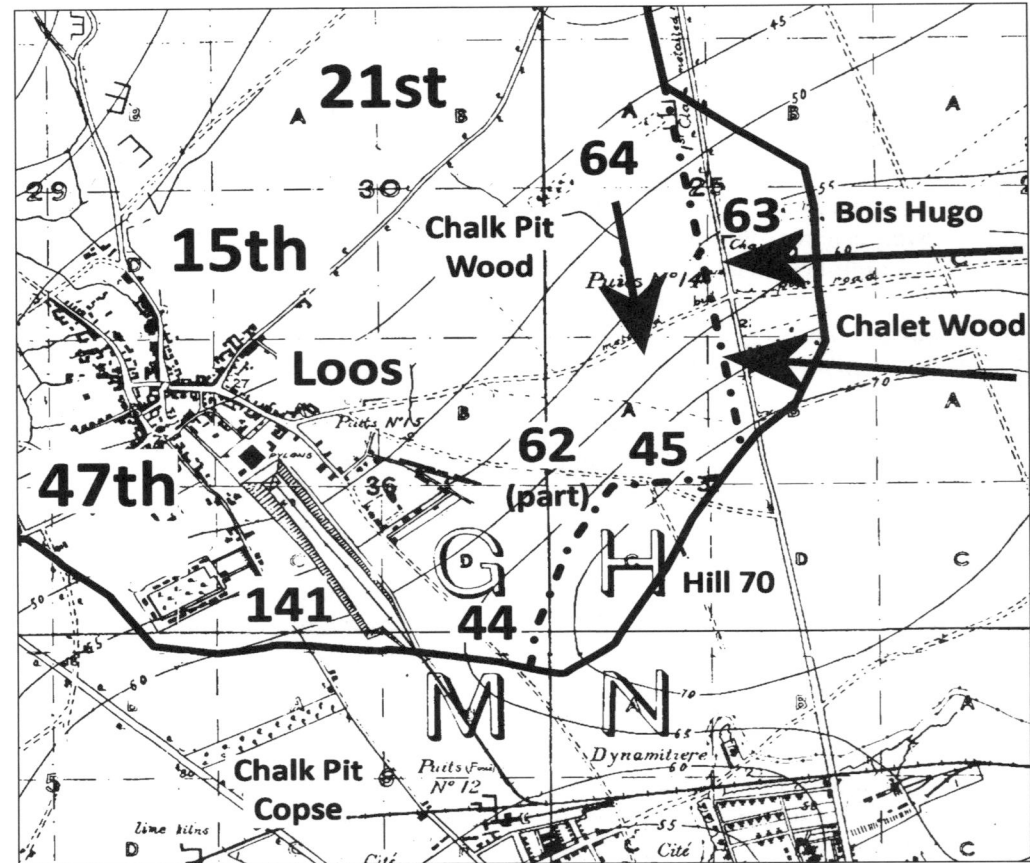

21st Division come under attack east of Loos early on 26 September

all took rifles and shot carefully along the wood wherever the enemy debouched, at ranges varying between 400 and 800 metres. Ammunition ran low so we stripped the dead of theirs and got enough to keep going....'

General Nickalls and his staff captain were killed during the counter-attack and the brigade's lack of experience was apparent as it fell back in disarray; 'officers and NCOs did not give much assistance in trying to rally the men. No attempt was made to carry out the retirement as a military operation, NCOs and men simply retired in any direction and anyhow they liked.' In less than an hour 63 Brigade had ceased to exist.

Nickalls' request for help eventually reached General Gloster. The 14th Durhams were crossing the Lens road when 63 Brigade started falling back and Lieutenant Colonel Hamilton's men 'apparently took them for Germans owing to their wearing long greatcoats.' After realising their mistake, everyone retired down the slope, leaving the woods in German hands.

As the disaster around Bois Hugo and Chalet Wood came to an end, thousands of troops began advancing from the Grenay ridge towards the Lens road. It was 11am and 24th Division's attack was underway. Major Johnson of the 15th Durham Light Infantry watched the sight from the foot of Hill 70:

'We watched through field glasses, as if on manoeuvres, wave upon wave of battalions in extended order moved at right angles across our front about a mile away. Starting near the northern end of Loos we followed their progress intently and critically until we lost sight of them behind the wood [Bois Hugo], or folds in the ground. The scene was fascinating and exciting because we could not see what happened. There was no sign of battle; no noise, no bursting shells, no enemy in sight, just like an Aldershot field-day with troops in wonderful alignment for the most part. Very critically we scanned the long lines, and wondered what their objective could be. It was an imposing sight.'

General Gloster's brigade was supposed to support the main attack and the rallied 14th Durhams and the 15th Durhams were ordered to advance. They did, but rather than moving east towards Bois Hugo, they headed south-east towards the summit of Hill 70, following the angle of the slope. Up ahead were Scots in greatcoats with their gas helmets on their heads and they were mistaken for Germans. But the change in direction took the Durhams past Bois Hugo and Chalet Wood and they came under devastating machine gunfire. Some redeployed to face the threat but many ran back, straight into Brigadier General Mitford's 71 Brigade as it advanced up the slope.

General Gloster had been explaining the situation to Lieutenant Colonels Lynch and Pollock when the 9th KOYLIs 'poured over the top without word of command, like colts at a starting gate that break the tape and get down the course before the starter's flag is down.' The 10th KOYLIs followed and the retreating Durhams passed through the two battalions as they headed for the summit of Hill 70. The KOYLIs were also decimated by enfilade fire from the two woods and they fell back in disorder. It was the end of 64 Brigade and the main attack had not even started.

The Fight for Hill 70
Dawn on 26 September found the Germans holding Hill 70 redoubt and General Wallerstein's 45 Brigade held the west side of the summit. The 13th

Royal Scots' company on the left came under fire from Chalet Wood at first light; their commanding officer, Captain Bruce, was killed. Meanwhile, the 11th Argylls and the 7th Scots Fusiliers held a semi-circle of shallow trenches facing the redoubt.

First Army's plan was to attack the German line between Hulluch and Cité St Auguste at 11am. Rawlinson instructed General McCracken to clear Hill 70 at 9am, so the machine guns in the redoubt could not enfilade the assault. But the heavy artillery were still firing at long range and the field batteries had not had time to register their guns. The Scots then marked their front line with flags but mist obscured the hilltop. They were then supposed to withdraw to a safe distance, but some did not receive the message in time and were shelled out of their trenches by the hour long barrage.

The mist began to clear as zero hour approached and the Scots came under crossfire as they cut through the wire on the summit. Major MacPherson and Captain Robertson of the Royal Scots were hit but some of their men reached the redoubt and the garrison ran. The Scots followed, rather than consolidating the redoubt, and they came under fire on the open slopes beyond; few returned.

The 10th Green Howards and 12th Northumberland Fusiliers[261] had orders to support the attack but they were met by the retiring Scots as they reached the crest. Lieutenant Colonel Hadow shouted 'charge' and the 10th Green Howards ran forward but they did not go far. Hadow, Majors Dent and Noye and Captains Charteris and Lynch were shot down at the head of their men. The Germans then bombed down the perimeter trench to retake the redoubt, leaving many in no man's land trapped until nightfall. Private Robert Dunsire was awarded with the Victoria Cross for rescuing two injured men of the 13th Royal Scots from the summit.

24th Division's Attack on the Second Line

Brigadier General Mitford's 72 Brigade had spent an uneasy night in the German trenches east of Lone Tree. It was the first time the men had been in battle and the experience was overwhelming:

'At times there was fair visibility, for the enemy bombardment of Loos had turned the village into a furnace of flame, with Tower Bridge silhouetted in black outline against the ruddy glow, and the sky was lightened by other burning villages, shellfire and Very lights. From time to time would come a wave of mist, when all was hidden.'

Mitford had sent Major Kay back to the divisional headquarters at dawn but he did not return for five hours and even then he only had vague verbal orders and no details about objectives or the German positions. Mitford

---

261 62 Brigade.

quickly summoned his battalion commanders and told them to prepare to advance at 11am. They ran back to their commands and passed the message on to their company commanders, with minutes to spare. 'We were told that there were plenty more fellows in reserve to go through us, and that the troops on either flank would attack simultaneously with ourselves.'

The 8th Queen's Own and 8th Buffs were leading with the 8th Queens and 9th East Surreys following:

'The attack was carried out at a marching pace in order to save the men's breath for the final charge and bayonet work, and the advance was so steady and formations so regular that it looked more like a field day at Aldershot than part of a great battle. The enemy brought a very heavy rifle fire, machine gun and artillery fire to bear on the attacking lines, and shortened his range to keep pace with the advance with wonderful precision...'

It soon became obvious that 72 Brigade could not cover all the ground between Hulluch and Bois Hugo and the East Surreys were extending their line to the south-east when they saw 63 and 64 Brigades fall back from Bois Hugo. General Mitford also pushed the 8th Buffs, commanded by 64-year-old Colonel Romer, into the widening gap in the brigade centre. German snipers withdrew from the Lens road as the lines of infantry approached and ran back, closing the gaps in the wire before joining their comrades in the trench beyond.

Two field guns in Hulluch fired over open sights as the ranks of men advanced across the Lens road. Half the 2nd Welsh entered the trench covering the village but the Queen's Own faced the belt of wire protecting Stützpunkt III and IV. Lieutenant Colonel Vansittart's men 'dropped to the ground where they were and returned the heavy fire from the enemy's trench. The situation, however, was hopeless. In front was an impenetrable belt of wire, and the line, such as was left of it, raked with rifle and machine gun fire from the front and both flanks, and enfiladed by an equally deadly artillery fire.' They were also under fire from the British artillery because the observers were having trouble identifying targets at such a long range.

The 8th Queens also went to ground, with a belt of wire to their front and open fields behind. The 11th Essex, from 71 Brigade, soon joined them and Lieutenant Colonel Radclyffe reported that 'the bearing of the men was splendid, everyone was as cool as possible. As good as a peace parade, and better. The excitement made it better... We thought we were only moving in support. We never knew where we were. That dreadful lost feeling is one of the worst things to face in war.' The left half of the attack had stalled, leaving over 2,000 men dead or wounded scattered across the fields; another 1,000 men were pinned down.

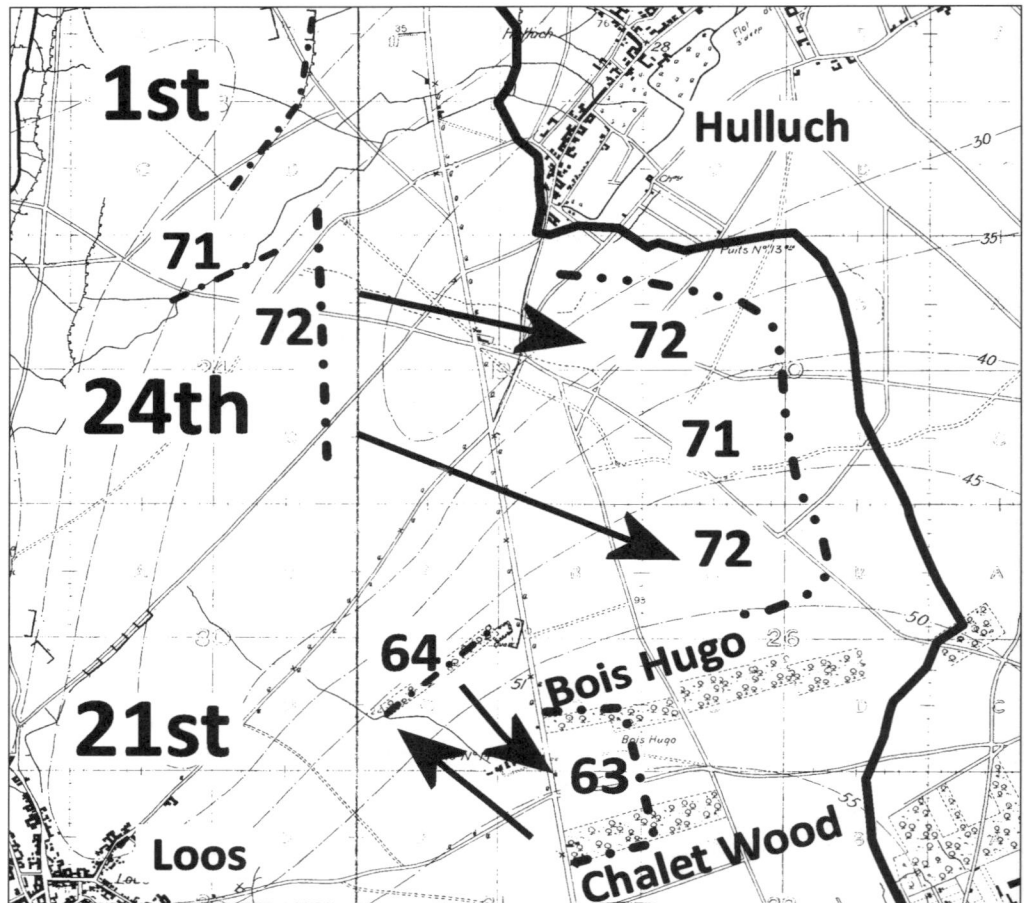

24th Division's attack between Hulluch and Bois Hugo on 25 September

The right half of 72 Brigade had to advance alongside Bois Hugo, unaware Germans were hiding in the trees. Snipers targeted the 9th East Surreys' officers as they crossed the Lens road and Major Welch and Captains Dealtry, Collinson, Barnett and Birt were hit. Machine gunfire from the wood then forced the right hand companies to go to ground while the rest pushed onto the wire. Soon the East Surreys, the 8th Buffs and the 9th Suffolks were pinned down in front of Stützpunkt IV.

By 12:30pm the advance was over and the six battalions had suffered over 2,500 casualties, most of them in the killing zone in front of the

German wire. The Welsh in the trenches near Hulluch were eventually forced to retire but a group of the 11th Essex held on in a sunken road. Dozens of the 8th Queen's Own, 8th Queen's and the rest of the Essex were hit cutting through the wire north of Stützpunkt III.

For more than an hour the Germans shot at anyone who showed themselves in the long grass. Some officers wanted to hold on while the rest wanted to withdraw to a safe distance but the result was inevitable with so few non-commissioned officers left to steady the men. The *Official History* blames the withdrawal on an anonymous individual shouting 'retire' but the sight of walking wounded heading to the rear could have been the catalyst.

Whatever the reason, the retreat began in earnest around 1.30pm. Hundreds crossed the Lens road where they were stopped by Captains Hope and James and the rest of 71 Brigade's staff officers in the old German front line on the Grenay Ridge. The *Official History* states the men 'began to fall back steadily, without panic and at even pace, towards the Lens Road'. The 2nd Welsh saw it differently:

'Suddenly to our amazement and disgust the whole Corps on our right turned round and bolted in a wild panic. The men threw away their rifles and equipment and ran back across the valley and disappeared over the crest of the hill over which they had advanced so magnificently. In this rout they all bunched together and so made a good mark for the German shrapnel and machine guns in Hulluch and consequently lost twice as many as they did advancing.'

When they saw the general retreat, the 9th East Surreys withdrew from Bois Hugo, taking the 9th Suffolks with them. They too fell back over the Grenay Ridge where Brigadier General Shewer and Major Jowett of 71 Brigade stopped them in the British trenches near Lone Tree. Around 500 men, many of them of the 8th Buffs, were left stranded close to Bois Hugo. A badly injured Sergeant Arthur Saunders single-handedly stopped a counter-attack with his Lewis gun, allowing his comrades to escape; he was later awarded the Victoria Cross.

The retreat left the area between Hulluch and Bois Hugo deserted and the Germans soon ceased firing. All that was left to do was to find and care for the injured:

'All our wounded had to be left between the lines. About 2pm the Germans sent out a great many stretcher bearers and medics who worked the whole afternoon binding up our wounded and sending all who could walk or crawl back to us. There were plenty of our shells falling about but although they lost some men these Germans never stopped their work.

Directly it was dark we sent out parties to bring in our wounded and we found several men who had been bound up by the Germans and who had left them telling them that if they were not removed before a certain hour they would be forced to take them prisoners.'

The Germans would call the ground between Hulluch and Bois Hugo the 'Field of Corpses'.

It had been a disastrous day for First Army and a huge lesson in how not to use New Army divisions. Colonel Stewart, 21st Division's chief staff officer, gave the following explanation about the disaster:

'It was that these two divisions would be in reserve in a big operation at Loos on the idea that not having been previously engaged in this way, they would go into action for the first time full of esprit and élan, and being ignorant of the effects of fire and the intensity of it, they would go forward and do great things.'

Chapter 13

They All Seemed to Melt Away
The Battle of Loos Ends

<u>The Guards Division Attack, 27 September</u>
Major General the Earl of Cavan's Guards Division[262] received orders to take over the line north of Loos on the afternoon of the 26th. By midnight 1 and 2 Guards Brigades were on Grenay Ridge while 3 Guards Brigade was south of Vermelles. Lieutenant General Haking wanted the Guardsmen to take Hill 70 and Brigadier General Ponsonby's 2 Guards Brigade would assault the summit while Brigadier General Feilding's 1 Guards Brigade covered its north flank with a smoke screen. But news of the problems on I Corps' front forced General Haig to scale the attack down, so the Guardsmen would secure the La Bassée–Lens road starting at 4pm.

There was a ninety-minute bombardment but orders arrived just before zero and Captains Wynter and Bird led the 2nd Irish Guards, 'keeping their direction and formation perfectly' through the smoke screen. Lieutenant Colonel Butler's Irishmen deployed along the east side of Chalk Pit Wood, with the 1st Coldstream Guards behind. The 1st Scots Guards moved forward at the double, taking some of the Irish Guards with them, as Captain Morrison's two 4th Grenadier Guards companies echeloned behind their right flank.

The smoke screen soon faded away and every gun in range opened up on the advancing Guardsmen.[263] Captain Cuthbert and Second Lieutenant Crabbe reached the Puits with a few Scots Guards and Grenadiers, as did Lieutenant Ayres-Ritchie's platoon of 3rd Grenadier Guards.

The Puits group were soon falling back, and while some took cover in Chalk Pit Wood, the rest kept going, taking many of the Irish Guards with them. At dusk the rest of the Irishmen returned to consolidate Chalk Pit Wood.

Brigadier General Frederick Heyworth had orders to attack Hill 70 with

---

262 The Division had been formed in August by assembling Guards battalions from the Regular Divisions and forming new ones in Great Britain.
263 Second Lieutenant John Kipling of the Irish Guards, son of the author Rudyard Kipling, was killed.

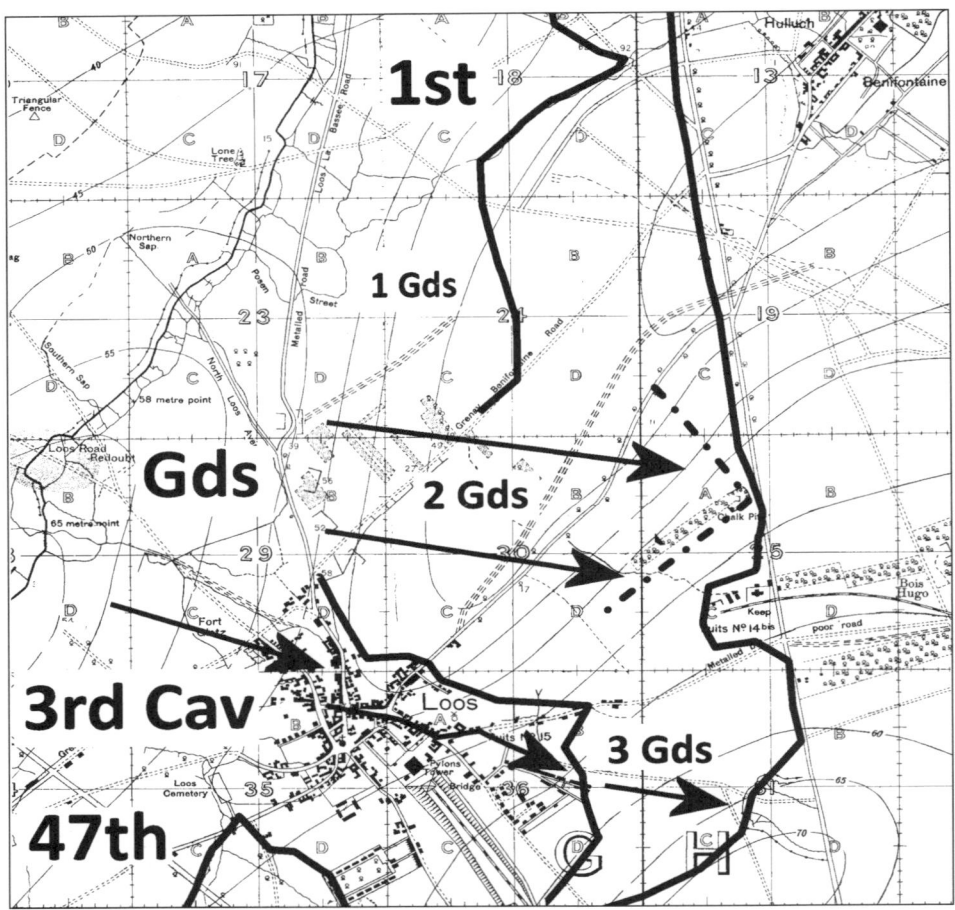

The Guards Division attack Puits 14 and Hill 70 on 27 September

his 3 Guards Brigade at 3pm and the 4th Grenadier Guards and the 1st Welsh Guards deployed into artillery formation near Loos Road redoubt and then advanced into the Loos valley:

'More and more came over the crest by platoons in artillery formation, and the intensity of the shelling increased. Quite quickly the opposite slope took on the appearance of a gigantic moving chessboard as the platoons approached with intervals between them. The steadiness of the march was impressive, and those who thought that Guardsmen were only ornamental soldiers revised their opinions speedily. So inspiring was the sight that scores of the 23rd [London Regiment] men clambered out of their trenches and, under machine gun fire, pulled aside wire entanglements and threw duckboard bridges over the ditches to facilitate the way for the Guards...'

The two battalions were hit by gas shells as they entered Loos and Lieutenant Colonel Murray-Threipland struggled to get the Welsh Guards through the ruins:

'The village was full of wounded British, dead Germans and horses, captured guns and scattered parties of men. Shells were hurtling through the air and houses, some exploding, others falling with a flop in the gardens. The whole place looked as if frenzied gangs of house-breakers had been working over-time. Amongst the flying brickbats, clouds of mortar, and heaps of rubble, squads of men were forming up; men were walking about in a nonchalant manner with no trace of hurry or excitement.'

The loss of Lieutenant Colonel Hamilton was a serious blow to the Grenadier Guards. Two companies struggled through the rubble-strewn streets as Captain Morrison took the rest around the north side of the village where they became involved in 2 Guards Brigade's attack on Puits 14.

Murray-Threipland eventually led his battalion to the top of Hill 70 with a few of the 4th Grenadier Guards. So an attack which been planned to be carried out by two brigades had been reduced to little more than a battalion. Brigadier General Heyworth thought 2 Guards Brigade was holding Puits 14 and it was too late to change his plans when he found out they had fallen back. It was dark by the time the Guardsmen advanced across the summit under a sky lit by star-shells. Only a few of Heyworth's men reached the objective, but they were unable to dig in on the bullet-swept hill top.

Lieutenant Colonel Cator arrived with half the 2nd Scots Guards around 11pm[264] and Colonel Murray-Threipland made them form a rally line below the crest. Even then the Welsh Guards would not retire because 'It was very difficult to get our men back, unless I got personally to them, even then they all wanted to go forward and not back. However, we got as many away as possible...' Two men carried Captain Phillips back while his sergeant used his officer's pistol to fight off the Germans trying to capture him. Captain Thorne stayed with a mortally wounded Major Ponsonby until he could do no more for him and was then killed as he carried a wounded drummer over his shoulder. The rest of the Welshmen faced a long night as they tried to escape the Germans clearing the summit of Hill 70:

'Wounded men were continuously crawling back to this little oasis in the desert of shell-holes. Painfully and slowly, inch by inch, these men would arrive, often sniped at by the enemy. It was such an exposed spot that, beyond helping them into the shallow trench, the men in this party could do little.'

---

264 The rest were lost in Loos.

Two 1st Coldstream Guards companies made a final attempt to take Puits 14 on 28 September but Lieutenants Riley and Style reached the objective with only eight men; only Riley and two men returned. The futile attack ended IX Corps' efforts between Hulluch and Loos and the Guards Division's first battle had not been the success that had been expected.

28th Division Takes Over Hohenzollern Redoubt

General Gough's three assault divisions had suffered badly on the first day of the battle and First Army had only sent five battalions to help I Corps so far. The Germans turned their attentions to Hohenzollern Redoubt after taking Hulluch Quarries and Field Marshal French sent Major General Edward Bulfin's 28th Division to reinforce Gough.

The division was formed at the end of 1914 using Regular Army battalions recalled from overseas stations. It had suffered a huge number of casualties in the attack on the Ypres Salient and battalions had absorbed a mixture of new recruits, reservists and returning wounded men. General Bulfin's men had just finished a tour of the Ypres Salient and they were at Bailleul expecting to rest when news of the emergency at Hohenzollern Redoubt came through. They had to climb back on their trains and head for Bethune.

Brigadier General Pereira's 85 Brigade arrived behind I Corps' front on the morning of 27 September and it received instructions to take over Fosse 8 and the Dump around 1pm. Then news that Fosse 8 had been lost came through and Pereira's new orders were to secure Hohenzollern Redoubt.

The 3rd Royal Fusiliers moved along the trenches but congestion forced half the 2nd Buffs to move over the top towards Big Willie Trench. Both General Pereira and his brigade major, Captain Flower, were injured, so Lieutenant Colonel Roberts of the Royal Fusiliers went ahead to find Brigadier General Jelf. Major Baker spent the night supervising the occupation of the Redoubt while the 2nd East Surreys' bombers attacked both ends of Little Willie Trench. Neither made any progress and Lieutenant Colonel Montague-Bates' men had to consolidate the old German front trench.

General Gough planned a surprise night attack to retake the Dump and the 1st Berkshires were given the task. But it took time to cross the battlefield and German lookouts on the Dump soon spotted them. Very lights illuminated the sky as machine gun fire stopped Major Bird's men scrambling onto the slag heap.

The Berkshires reorganised in Dump Trench as Second Lieutenant Alexander Buller-Turner single-handedly stopped German bombers coming

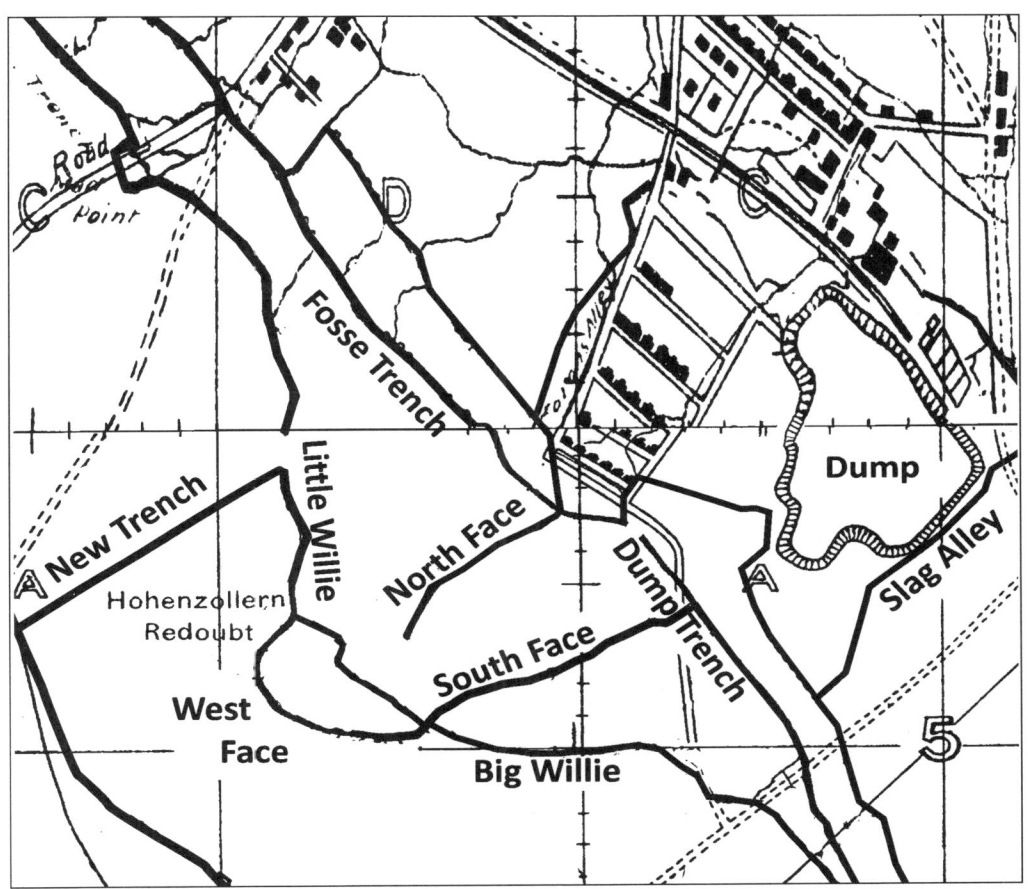

28th Division's struggle for Hohenzollern Redoubt until 30 September

down Slag Alley. He then cleared 150 metres of trench before he was mortally wounded; he was posthumously awarded the Victoria Cross. Lieutenant Colonel Carter still wanted the Berkshire's to take the Dump but they were unable to do so. Major Bird was wounded, his second in command Captain Maurice Radford lay dead, and 300 dead and injured men were left scattered across the Dump.

As 28 September dawned, 85 Brigade only had a precarious hold on the Redoubt, with the Germans in Little Willie Trench to the west and on the Dump to the east. The dawn attack had been postponed by several hours because the reliefs took too long and the Germans watched every move from the Dump. The 2nd Buffs reported 'the congested state of the trenches due to dead, wounded and units waiting to be relieved, admitted very slow progress. One position was in possession of the enemy and these circumstances prevented the companies taking up their positions until after 10am.' The 3rd Middlesex made good progress along South Face but they found themselves trapped in the deep and narrow Dump Trench when they ran out of bombs. Machine guns stopped them escaping over the top and Lieutenant Colonel Neale was killed supervising the costly withdrawal.

The bombardment of the Dump ended at 9.30am but the Buffs were still not in place and they had to advance as soon as they were ready. There was a cheer when they reached the top of the ash slope but the success was short-lived because a combination of German and British artillery fire drove them from the summit.

The Germans then forced their way into Dump Trench, driving a wedge between the two battalions. Lieutenant Williams led the Buffs' defence, losing nearly all his bomb throwers in the appalling conditions. Rain made it difficult to ignite the bombs so the men chain-smoked cigarettes so they could light them. It was impossible to bring rations or water up while the rain covered everything with sticky mud. The following morning the rain became heavier, filling the trenches with water.

The 1st York and Lancasters[265] were supposed to relieve the Buffs during the night of 29 September but the endless line of stretcher bearers stopped them reaching Dump Trench. By 3am Captains Forster and Buckley had still not found their guides, so they went ahead to find the Buffs and it was dawn by the time they returned. The German observers on the Dump spotted the York and Lancasters approaching and they organised a bombing raid to disrupt the relief. They struck when they saw some of the Buffs climbing out of the congested trench and running to the rear.

The Germans had the upper hand until Captain Buckley ordered some York and Lancasters out into the open so they could throw bombs into the trench. Major Robertson and Captain Forster were then about to lead counter-attacks over the top and along the trench.

The Germans had the upper hand until Captain Buckley ordered some of the York and Lancasters out into the open, so they could move along the top of the trench throwing bombs inside, and Major Robertson and Captain Forster eventually restored the situation by leading counter-attacks both in and out of the trench.

A second attack forced the 3rd Middlesex from South Face into West Face. Lieutenant Coles went looking for the Middlesex when the York and Lancasters heard the news but he found no one because they had evacuated

---

265 83 Brigade.

Big Willie Trench. Lieutenant Bates was told to move his platoon into the empty trench but German bombers beat them to it. They were also spraying chlorine gas into the trench to keep the British bombers out.

The York and Lancasters held on with the help of Second Lieutenant Bates and the 2nd East Yorkshire's bombers who had come to the rescue with more bombs. A six hour long stalemate followed, as Private Samuel Harvey ran back and forth carrying bombs across the open, because he could not get along the communication trench. He carried 'no less than thirty boxes of bombs before he was wounded in the head'; Harvey was awarded the Victoria Cross.

The 2nd East Surreys were also under attack and Second Lieutenant Jameson's bombers were being driven back until Second Lieutenant Alfred Fleming-Sandes arrived with boxes of bombs. On Hohenzollern Redoubt the 3rd Royal Fusiliers fared no better as the Germans attacked along South Face. The Fusiliers' flank was exposed when the Middlesex evacuated Big Willie Trench and they were driven down West Face. Then there was panic at dusk when dozens of men clambered out of the trench so they could run back from the redoubt. Captain Lucas gave the York and Lancasters an order to fix bayonets and although their counter-attack failed to capture the Redoubt, it gave the Royal Fusiliers some breathing space.

The East Surreys wavered when they saw the Fusiliers withdrawing, so Second Lieutenant Fleming-Sandes walked along Little Willie Trench hurling bombs at the Germans below. A rifle bullet shattered his right arm so he continued throwing with his left until he was seriously wounded in the face. Fleming-Sandes' actions inspired the East Surreys to hold Little Willie Trench and he was awarded the Victoria Cross.

By dusk the 3rd Royal Fusiliers had driven the Germans out of Big Willie and West Face but 85 Brigade's hold on the Redoubt was weakening. Time after time Second Lieutenants Frere and Gatrell rallied the 2nd East Yorkshire bombers in Big Willie Trench, but the East Yorkshires' commanding officer was unhappy with the situation: 'Our bombers have suffered severely during the day… The second class bombs sent today have helped largely in producing these casualties. I shall require at least 1,500 first class grenades before moving as my stock has nearly run out. The Germans appear to have an immense reserve and succeed always in producing bombs when our own are finished.' The shelling and bombing continued throughout 30 September but neither side gained any ground. 85 Brigade left the trenches that night, exhausted after three days fighting.

As 85 Brigade fought for its life, Brigadier General Ravenshaw's 83 Brigade had a much easier time to the east of the Dump. The 2nd King's

Own had held Quarry Trench while the 2nd East Yorkshires consolidated the trenches facing the Quarries. On the night of 2 October Ravenshaw handed over an improved sector to the Guards Division.

The Fight for Hohenzollern Redoubt Continues
Some reports said Fosse Trench and Dump Trench were in British hands while others said they had been lost. But the Germans held Little Willie Trench, north of the redoubt and the British controlled West Face and Big Willie Trench. Brigadier General Pearse's 84 Brigade only had two guides to help it take over the Hohenzollern Redoubt and some companies lost their way in the maze of trenches. The 1st Welsh occupied the old front line facing Little Willie Trench on the left and the 2nd Cheshires moved into West Face in the centre. The 2nd Northumberland Fusiliers were late entering Big Willie Trench on the right and the Germans attacked at dawn, after spotting the York and Lancaster's running to the rear.

A bombing squad moved down South Face and some went along Big Willie while the rest followed West Face, splitting the Northumberland Fusiliers in two. Barricades stopped them going far but it took the Fusiliers until nightfall to reunite their front, with help from the Cheshires' bombers. The commanding officer, Major Charles Armstrong and his adjutant, Lieutenant Ivan Gilchrist, were killed while Captain Lamb was severely wounded.

Brigadier General Pearse planned a surprise night attack to take Little Willie Trench and the Redoubt but it took far longer than expected to get everyone into position. The 1st Welsh had to share their trench with the troops they were relieving while the 2nd Cheshires found that West Face, their jumping off trench, was only knee deep.

At midnight the 1st Welsh walked quietly towards Little Willie Trench until the German lookouts spotted them. Although 250 were shot down running the last 100 metres, the rest cleared the trench as Lieutenant Colonel Hoggan shouted, 'Forward 41st – Get at 'em Welsh.' But the two companies had become separated in the darkness, leaving the Germans in their middle and on their flanks. The 6th Welsh spent the rest of the night helping dig a trench to link up with Little Willie. Meanwhile, the 2nd Cheshires had captured the Chord, or at least they thought it was, because it had been levelled by artillery fire.

The following day the Germans shelled the Redoubt and Little Willie with trench mortars:

> 'The enemy then opened with Minenwerfer shell – this is what soldiers call "Sausage Up". The shell, having reached the distance

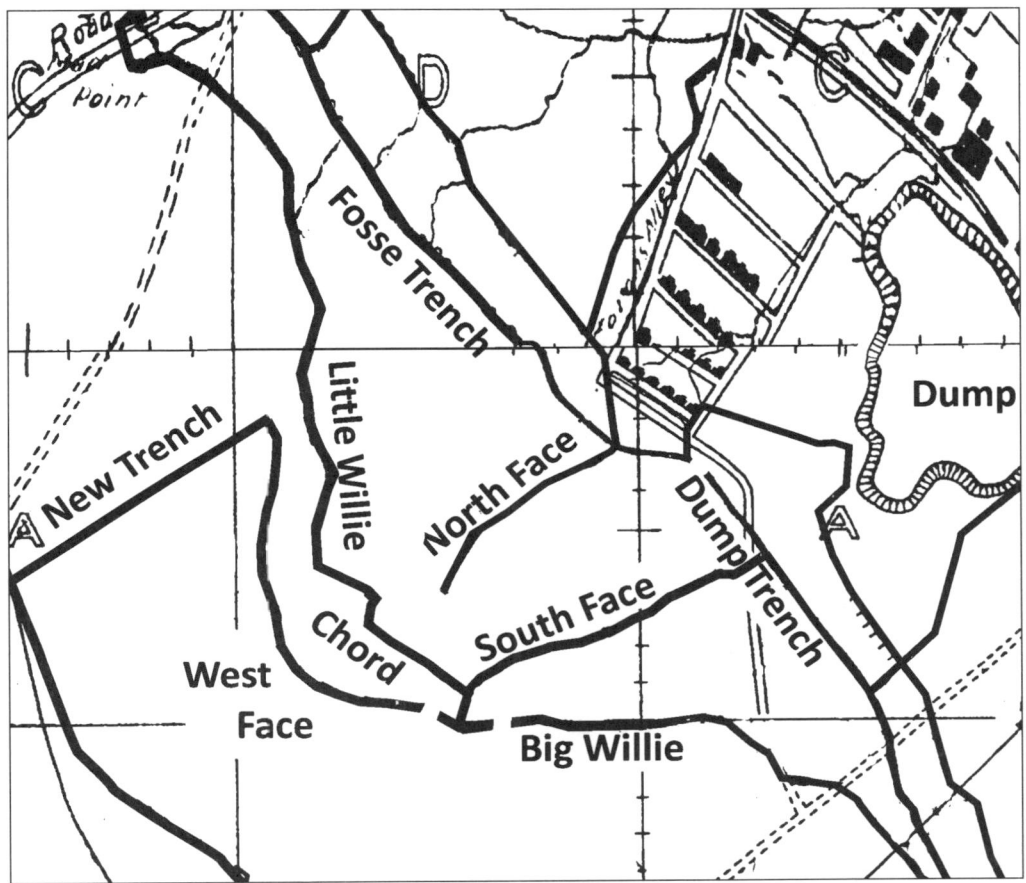

The loss of Hohenzollern Redoubt continues after 1 October

it is regulated for, drops perpendicularly down and can be seen all the way down and can be dodged. The men were now so congested that it was impossible to get out of the way. When one lands in the trench six men in the vicinity disappear.'

By mid-morning the Welsh had run out of bombs and the communication trench was unfinished, so Little Willie Trench had to be evacuated. Major Arthur Hobbs was last seen leading a bayonet charge so the survivors could escape but many wounded were left behind during the chaotic withdrawal. Lieutenant Colonel Lord Crichton-Stuart was killed leading the 6th Welsh's defence of New Trench.

Brigadier General Pearse instructed the 1st Suffolks to retake Little Willie later that evening and they had to move in the open because the trenches were blocked. The attack was delayed until 10.30pm and then to midnight but a final appeal to postpone the attack was refused. Major Sinclair-Thompson deployed his men out, but one company could not be found, another advanced too early and the rest of the battalion went in the wrong direction; the attack failed.

The following morning the Germans drove the Welsh back towards the Redoubt and many were shot down, including Major Arthur Hill and Captain Frank Lloyd, when the 1st Cheshires ran from the Chord and West Face. Captain Freeman's company of Northumberland Fusiliers had to abandon South Face and only twenty-six men escaped. Fortunately, the rest of the Northumberland Fusiliers stopped the Germans at the head of Big Willie Trench.

Most of 28th Division was back in the old British front line and General Bulfin wanted to retake the lost trenches before he handed them over. Brigadier General Ravenshaw's 83 Brigade had just taken over the front when the orders arrived to retake Little Willie Trench and Hohenzollern Redoubt the following morning, leaving no time to reconnoitre the maze of trenches.

The plan was for all four waves of troops to move together and three waves of the 1st KOYLIs and 2nd East Yorkshires lay down in front of their trenches before zero. They came under heavy fire as soon as they stood up and no one reached the German trenches. The 2nd King's Own bombers were supposed to capture the junction of West Face and Big Willie Trench but they advanced in the wrong direction and were stopped by crossfire from South Face and Dump Trench. The Guards Division relieved 28th Division that same evening. Bulfin's Division had suffered over 3,200 casualties and a stressed Bulfin was invalided home a week later.

General Haig was determined to recover Fosse 8 and Hulluch Quarries and Lieutenant-General Haking's IX Corps took over the line on the night of 4 October. The plan was for the Guards Division to take the redoubt while Major General Frederick Wing's 12th (Eastern) Division captured the Quarries. The Guardsmen worked every night to dig assembly trenches and emplacements for 120 gas cylinders but zero hour was still delayed until 9 October. There were complaints from the 1st Coldstream Guards that the British artillery was firing short, so 'next day a score of gunners were put in the front trench and this had a magic effect on the shooting of our guns.'

But the Germans attacked first on 8 October, driving the 3rd Grenadier Guards out of Big Willie Trench. Lieutenant Anson and his bombers were killed and Lieutenant Williams' machine gun team was wiped out. The infantry then pulled back to let Lance-Sergeant Oliver Brooks' bombers through and they retook 200 metres of Big Willie Trench; '…so confident were the bombing party that they were eager to continue operations and invade the German lines…' Brooks was awarded the Victoria Cross. The Germans had been stopped but zero hour had to be postponed to 2pm on 13 October. The Guardsmen continued preparing the front line and the 46th (North Midland) Division was detailed to capture Hohenzollern Redoubt.

46th (North Midland) Division, Hohenzollern Redoubt, 13 October

Major General the Hon Edward Montagu-Stuart-Wortley wanted to bomb across Hohenzollern Redoubt but he was overruled because the Germans had repeatedly proved themselves better bombers. Instead his troops were to have to attack over the top and 138 Brigade would clear the Redoubt and Fosse 8 while 137 Brigade captured the Dump. The infantry would move over the top as bombers cleared the trenches and dug-outs. It was going to be the North Midland men's first battle and there was a serious attempt to familiarise them with the battlefield. The divisional staff built a large-scale model of the redoubt for everyone to study and officers were given a guided tour of the trenches.

Although gas would be used, there were insufficient supplies to incapacitate the Germans. First Army was hoping the mere smell of gas would make the Germans run and it would be released little by little to fill the air with the smell of chlorine. It would finish with a cloud of smoke to hide the assault troops and confuse the Germans.

0 Minutes	*Run two cylinders, then release one cylinder. Finally release two cylinders.*
50 Minutes	*Turn off gas, switch to smoke using mortars, candles and grenades.*
60 Minutes	*Attack.*

There had been insufficient time or space to dig a new gas trench so the infantry had to share their trench with the Special Brigade's cylinders.

The bombardment began at midday on 13 October and the German artillery retaliated, showering the North Midland men with shrapnel. Disaster struck when a shell-burst damaged gas cylinders, spraying 138 Brigade with concentrated chlorine gas. Corporal James Dawson, 187th Company RE (Special Brigade), climbed onto the parapet and directed the infantry away from the damaged cylinders. He then lifted the cylinders into the open, rolled

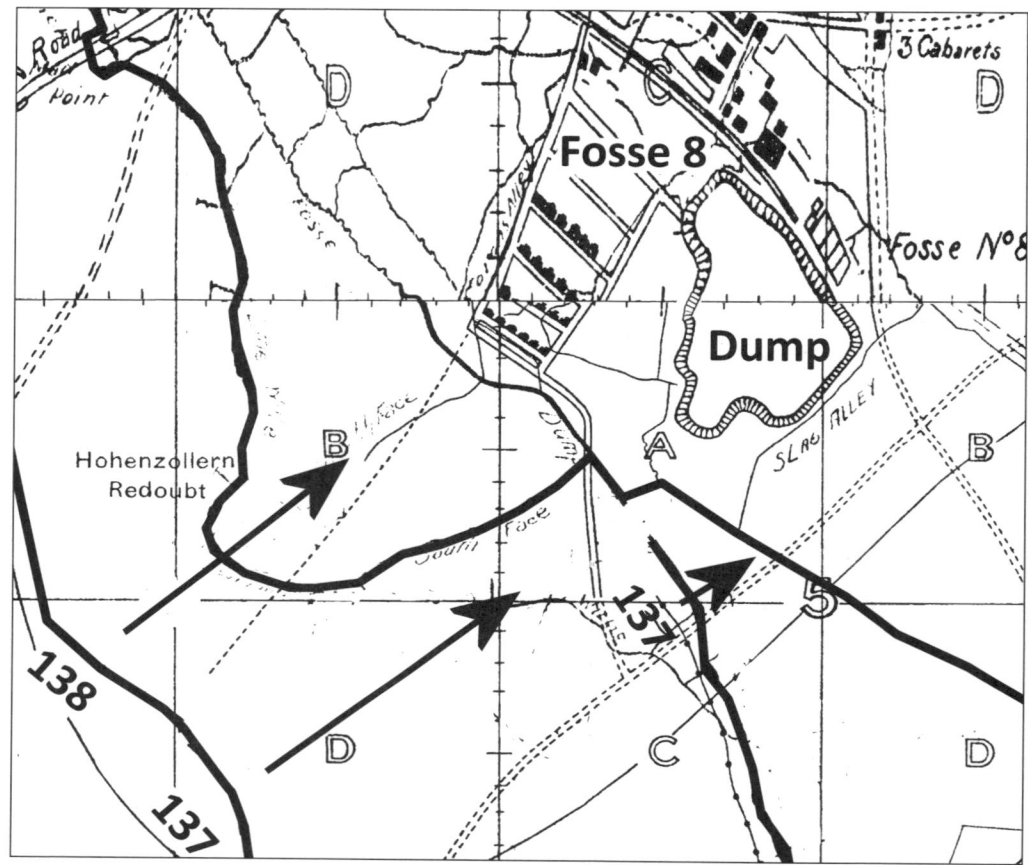

46th Division's attack against Hohenzollern Redoubt and the Dump on 13 October

them away from the trench and fired into them, releasing the gas at a safe distance. It allowed 138 Brigade to return to the jumping off trench in time for zero hour. Corporal Dawson was awarded the Victoria Cross.

Two waves of the 1/5th Lincolns and the 1/4th Leicesters[266] moved through the smoke cloud at 2pm but the third wave was delayed and the smoke was clearing by the time they moved through their wire, allowing Mad Point's machine guns to be fired into their flank. The Lincolns and Leicesters were cut down as they approached Fosse Trench and Captain Madge was the last officer standing as the survivors took cover in shell holes or fell back. One party of 1/4th Lincolns' bombers were wiped out climbing over a blockage in Big Willie Trench and another group was shot

---

266 138 Brigade.

down running towards Little Willie Trench. A wounded Lieutenant Wollaston cleared part of the trench but had to withdraw when his group ran out of bombs. The Germans blocked North and South Face trenches and then fled; Corporal Leadbeater was able to capture a small piece of North Face. The 1/1st Monmouths were supposed to consolidate the Chord, along the north-east edge of the redoubt, but the British artillery had flattened the trench.

The brigade suffered enormous casualties crossing Hohenzollern Redoubt but Brigadier General Kemp decided to send a 1/5th Leicesters company forward. 'Walking along with his pipe in his mouth, Captain Langdale might have been at a field day, as he calmly signalled his right platoon to keep up in line, with "Keep it up Oakham".' A few stragglers joined the advancing company but there were too few to make a difference. All five company officers were hit and the Leicesters found cover where they could after Langdale fell. General Kemp sent another Leicesters company over the top but Captain Paulyn Rawdon-Hastings was killed as he led a bayonet charge into West Trench. The trench was cleared but Second Lieutenant Tomson decided it would be suicidal to go any further, so his men consolidated the trench.

The attack was over by 3.30pm and there were dead and wounded Leicester and Lincoln Territorials all across the redoubt. Sergeant Drewery continued to fire the single working machine gun while Captain Madge pointed out targets and others searched for ammunition. The small group fought on until it was dark; only 110 returned.

At dusk German bombers moved down West Face towards Second Lieutenant Tomson and a group of 1/5th Leicesters. A prolonged bombing battle lasted all night and Tomson later complained that he had to keep smoking so he could light the bomb fuses. The men who brought the morning rum ration heard how he had only had 'two biscuits and over 300 cigarettes' since the attack began.

Brigadier General Feetham had found it difficult to deploy 137 Brigade in front of the Dump. The 1/5th North Staffords had to start from the old front line, 300 metres behind Big Willie Trench; half the 1/5th South Staffords were in the old front line and the rest were in Big Willie Trench. The smoke screen obscured the Staffords as they clambered out of their trenches but machine guns on the Dump traversed back and forth as they deployed.

Lieutenant Colonel Knight led the 1/5th North Staffords forward shouting, 'Forward the Potters' and 'Up the Potters', but the two left companies were decimated and Captain Wood was one of the few to return.

Captain Worthington's company was also cut to pieces and the survivors took cover in an old trench. The support company lost all its officers and the men dived into the same trench. All but two of the bombers were shot down trying to bypass a barricade in the communication trench. None of Knight's men had reached the Dump and 500 of them lay dead or injured. Two 1/6th North Staffords companies followed in support and they too suffered heavily; the men bunched together, making inviting targets. The officers were early casualties. Lieutenant Colonel Ratcliff had no choice but to order the rest of his battalion to stand fast.

Machine guns on the Dump and in South Face opened fire as the two 1/5th South Staffords companies left Big Willie Trench; few made it through their own wire. The third company was shot down as it emerged through the smoke and only seventy-five returned. The final company were carrying sandbags, barbed wire, bombs and ammunition, expecting to consolidate the captured position. Most were hit before the attack was called off.

German bombers counter-attacked the 1/5th South Staffords in Big Willie Trench and Sergeant Beard made sure they held on until Lieutenant Hakes arrived with reinforcements. Another group of Germans then climbed out of South Face only to be shot down running towards Big Willie Trench. Sergeant Beard and Private Barnes then rallied the Staffords to stop a final bomb attack.

Nearly 1,000 Staffordshire men had been killed or injured in front of the Dump, most in the first ten minutes of their first battle. One observer summed up the disastrous attack with the following words:

'It was wonderful seeing the great smoke cloud along the front, and then five minutes before the bombardment stopped, the figures crawling over the parapet and lying down in front, as far as you could see either side. At the moment the guns lifted, all got up and began to run or rather jog. Then they all seemed to melt away...'

The 136 Brigade took over the front line positions in West Face and Little Willie Trench the following morning. The Germans were determined to retake all the lost ground and Captain Warren of the 1/7th Sherwoods fought off numerous attacks on Little Willie Trench during the day. Captain Charles Vickers took over the trench after dusk and played a big part in holding onto the trench as the rest of the brigade settled in; Vickers was awarded the Victoria Cross.

The battle for Hohenzollern Redoubt had been 46th Division's first battle. It had been a bloody one and nearly 3,000 North Midland men had been killed or injured, most of them in the two assault brigades.

12th (Eastern) Division, Hulluch Quarries

The Germans were using Hulluch Quarries as a base to stage attacks against 12th (Eastern) Division, so Major General Arthur Scott planned a three pronged assault to capture them. Two battalions would attack from the west, one battalion would advance from the south and a fourth battalion would capture Gun Trench.

The plan was to advance behind a smoke screen but the men ran out of smoke candles and grenades before zero hour and it was dispersing by the time the attack began. The 7th Suffolks[267] came under fire from the Dump,

12th Division's attack against Hulluch Quarries on 13 October

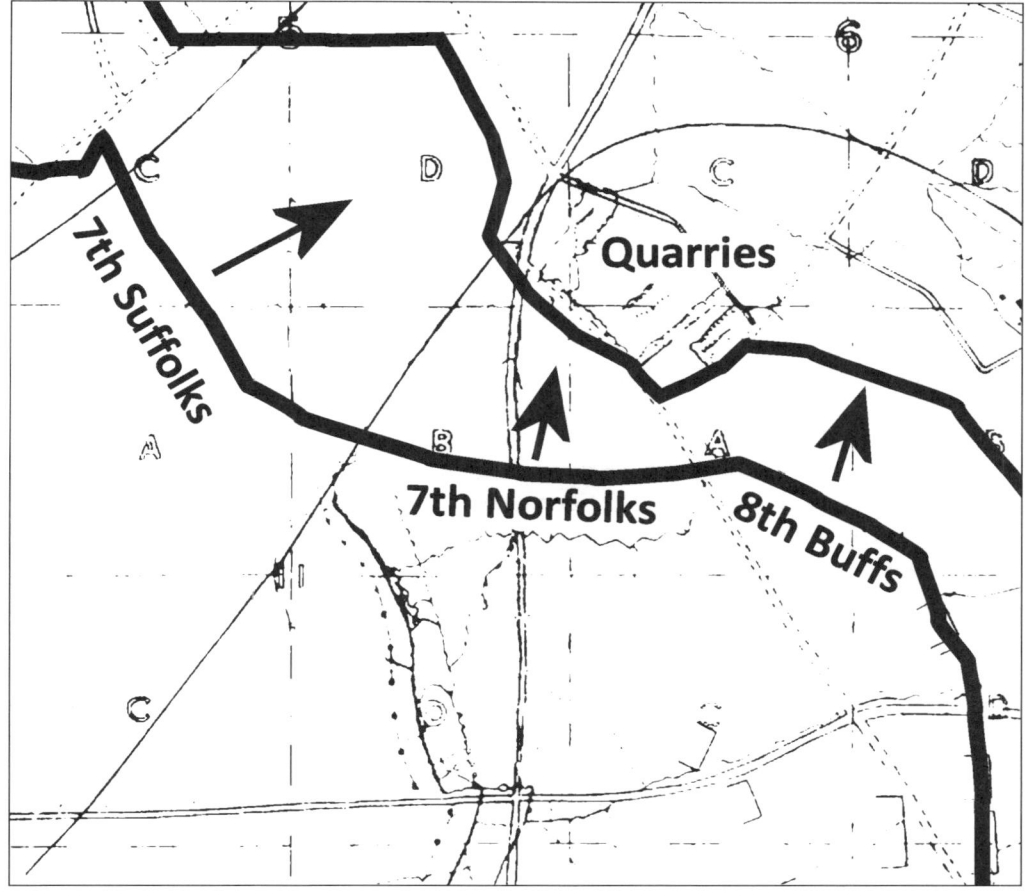

---

267 35 Brigade.

the Quarries and Slag Alley as they advanced towards the north-west corner of the quarries. Major Vere Currey was killed leading his company so his men withdrew and followed the rest of the battalion along a communication trench. Captain Cobbold was killed charging the barrier in the trench on the left but his men reached the Quarries. Captain Sorley[268] was killed and Captain Henry was wounded charging the barricade in their trench on the right so Lieutenant Deighton led the bombers along the communication trench.

The trench mortar barrage supposed to cover the advance towards the south-west corner of the quarries failed to materialise. Lieutenant Franklin's company of 7th Norfolks and Captain Preston's bombers of the 5th Berkshires[269] came under enfilade fire from the quarries and only fifty men reached the Chord. They had reached the trench when Lieutenant Colonel Walter decided to lead the rest of his men over the top to help consolidate it. They were mown down after only a few metres and the Chord had to be abandoned when the bombs ran out. The Norfolks had suffered 430 casualties.

The 8th Buffs[270] had to advance north towards Gun Trench, east of the Quarries, but the Germans had just finished digging a new trench which the artillery observers had not seen and the guns missed it. The wind only carried the smoke part way across no man's land and over 400 Buffs were hit when they emerged from the cloud.

Lieutenant Watts' company 7th East Surreys[271] used 'rush and bomb' tactics to reach Gun Trench but a machine gun shot Captain Tomkins' company to pieces. Lieutenant Findlay's bomb squads also reached Gun Trench but Sergeant Martin felt it was wise to withdraw the survivors to Central Alley. Lieutenant Colonel Baldwin then sent the rest of his battalion forward to consolidate the captured position.

The lack of smoke had left General Scott's men exposed to machine gun fire and he had little to show for the high number of casualties. Hulluch Quarries would continue to be a base for German attacks over the winter.

---

268 Charles Sorley is remembered as one of the war poets.
269 Both 35 Brigade.
270 37 Brigade.
271 37 Brigade.

Chapter 14

Don't Be Downhearted
November 1915 to March 1916

General Haig and Field Marshal French had not seen eye-to-eye over the handling of the reserves during the battle of Loos. Haig told King George VI that French was 'a source of great weakness to the Army, and no one had any confidence in him anymore' during his visit to the front at the end of October 1915. General Robertson agreed and the political fall-out began following the publishing of French's report on the battle. Field Marshal Sir John French handed in his resignation on 6 December and recommended Robertson as his replacement. The resignation came into effect at noon on the 18th but General Sir Douglas Haig was promoted to replace him as commander-in-chief of GHQ.

Meanwhile, the British troops faced a difficult time in most sectors because the Germans had chosen the line they wished to defend. Their trenches were usually on the higher ground and the British were forced to dig in where the ground was muddy and the water table was high. Over the next seven months there were nine small actions along the BEF's front.

Third Army relieved the French between Loos and the Scarpe River[272] only to find itself holding poorly sited trenches. Haig wanted Lieutenant General Sir Edmund Allenby to hold the front with outposts and choose the best line of defence but General Joffre protested because it would have meant abandoning the ground the French had fought hard for.

Instead the Allies would have to improve their positions by pushing the Germans back instead of withdrawing. GHQ wanted to display an 'aggressive spirit', continually raiding to capture prisoners and information while looking for opportunities to capture trenches. It meant little was done to improve the British trenches because they did not expect to be there long. The Germans erected more wire and dug deeper.

The aggressive spirit gave the men battle experience but it did cost lives.

---

272 Facing Lens and Arras.

Often it provoked the Germans to retaliate and the British troops soon learnt their enemy possessed better weapons, including hand grenades, rifle-grenades and trench mortars.

The First Phosgene Gas Attack, 19 December 1915
A German NCO captured in the Ypres Salient during the early hours of 5 December 1915 talked about gas cylinders in the trenches north-east of the town during his interrogation. Another source suggested a gas attack was imminent somewhere in the Ypres area as soon as the winter winds were blowing in the right direction.

General Sir Herbert Plumer's Second Army held the Ypres Salient and Lieutenant General John Keir's VI Corps held the threatened north-east side. Both Major General Edward Perceval of the 49th (1st West Riding) Division and Major General Charles Ross of the 6th Division were warned to take the necessary anti-gas precautions. Officers were posted to monitor the wind direction, with instructions to issue a gas alert if it changed. Patrols were also sent out and while they did not see any cylinders, they heard plenty of hammering in the German trenches. There was also a lot of coughing, a sure sign of leaking gas.

Sentries were posted next to all the alarms, ready to blow a klaxon horn or bang a gong to warn everyone in the open to put on their gas-masks. Additional sentries were posted outside dug-outs, so they could warn the men inside. Sentries were also posted by each signal office, so messages could be relayed as soon as the gas was spotted.

Officers inspected every man's gas helmet and weapon twice a day. The new PH helmet had recently been issued and the two glass eye-pieces were easier to see through and sturdier than the single mica peephole in the old P helmets. The outlet valve also made breathing easier. Despite the improvements, the men still called their helmets 'muzzles' and they still carried their old P helmet as a spare.

The weather changed on 15 December and everyone became extra alert when the wind direction turned. British 4.5-inch howitzers began shelling the enemy front line, hoping to hit some of the gas cylinders but the Germans had buried them deep under their parapet and there was little ammunition to spare.

Before dawn on 19 December sentries saw an unusual parachute flare fired above the German trenches. Red rockets were fired all along the front as it floated down and hissing was heard across no man's land. The time was 5.15am and the sentries woke their officers as the suffocating odour of musty hay drifted in the wind. The Germans were using phosgene gas for

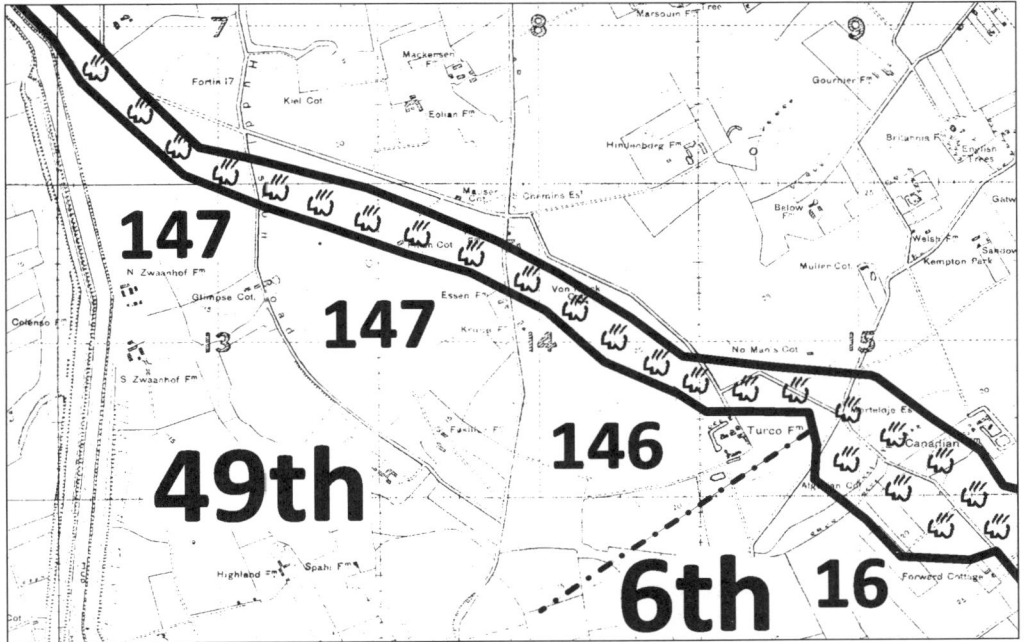

The First Phosgene Gas Attack, 19 December 1915

the first time.[273] Men pulled on their helmets and stood to as 'the sky was one great glare like a vast electric light and the atmosphere was laden with a choking, sickly heaviness.'

Shelling cut all communications with the rear and one company headquarters only heard the single word 'gas' before the line was cut. Gas shells were soon hitting targets behind the line, catching some men unaware. Some men were gassed before they could get their helmets on and 'they lay in agony on the ground, sickly greenish-white in colour; they foamed at the mouth and gasped for breath.' The battalion medical staff were kept busy but there was little they could do to ease their pain.

The German infantry opened fire before the gas started opposite 49th Division, on VI Corps' left. On 6th Division's front the gongs and horns sounded as the garrison manned the fire-step and waited for the attack to begin. For fifteen minutes the gas crept over the British trenches while VI Corps artillery fired on likely targets. Some battalions fired blindly into the cloud but others held their fire until they saw the infantry approaching. But in most areas the Germans refused to leave their trenches and the few who

---

273 Phosgene kills by preventing the absorption of oxygen in the lungs, leading to suffocation.

attempted to cross no man's land were shot down before they had gone far.

Artillery shelled 71 Brigade where it was holding a salient north-west of Wieltje but there was no sign of an infantry attack so everyone was ordered to cease fire and take cover. Meanwhile, high explosive and tear gas shells hit VI Corps' rear but the danger was over. The Germans had cancelled their attack.

The Bluff, 14 and 15 February and 2 March 1916
The Germans were planning a huge offensive at Verdun, starting on 21 February and they spent a month trying to distract Allied attention from the area. Although an attack against the Loos sector was cancelled and plans were made to capture Vimy Ridge, the Ypres Salient was the obvious target. Raids and bombardments began on 8 February and then there was an attack against the Boesinghe sector during the early hours of 12 February. The Germans hit 20th (Light) Division as it relieved the 14th (Light) Division, and the 12th Rifle Brigade lost over 180 men. Two more attempts failed to make any headway while small mines and a bombardment on the afternoon of the 14th were not followed up. More attacks against the Hooge and Sanctuary Wood sectors, where 24th Division held the line, also failed.

An attack was made against the Bluff on the Ypres-Comines canal, two miles south of Ypres, at the same time. The sector was a difficult one for 17th (Northern) Division to hold because of the canal which ran through a cutting flanked by high spoil banks. The high bank on the north side was a useful observation post the British called 'The Bluff', while the Germans called it Kanal Bastion or Grosse Bastion.[274]

No man's land was around 150 metres wide either side of the canal but it narrowed to 50 metres to the north where a German held salient, known as 'The Bean' by the British and 'Der Helm'[275] by the Germans, stuck out into no man's land. There was mining, but the tunnellers struggled to work in the water-logged ground. In places the British front line connected the mine craters with short lengths of trench.

On the afternoon of 14 February, Lieutenant General Hew Fanshawe's V Corps held the area south and east of Ypres. Major General Thomas Pilcher's 17th Division held a 4,500 yard wide sector astride the canal and Brigadier General Fell's 51 Brigade held the area north of the waterway. The 8th South Staffords and 10th Sherwood Foresters were in the front line and the 7th Border Regiment was about to relieve the South Staffords; its bombers and Lewis gunners were already with the South Staffords. The 7th Lincolns were in reserve and two companies had been placed at the Foresters' disposal, ready to retake the Bluff.

---

274 The Big Bastion.
275 The Helmet.

A general military rule was to make one unit responsible for holding a topographical feature rather than using it as a boundary. Brigadier General Surtees' 52 Brigade had been made responsible for the canal and the Bluff but Lieutenant Colonel Wade had a problem. There was only a narrow temporary footbridge across the canal and it was a long way behind New Year Trench. The majority of the 10th Lancashires were on the south bank, leaving Second Lieutenant Walker's platoon on the Bluff isolated from the rest of the battalion.

The canal area was heavily shelled several times on the morning of 14 February and the guns then switched to the area north of the canal and Hooge in the afternoon. General Pilcher requested support from the British heavy artillery when the German trench mortars joined in, while everyone around the canal was put on alert.

The platoon of 10th Lancashire Fusiliers on the Bluff had felt particularly exposed to the shelling so they hid in a tunnel under the embankment. Unfortunately, the Germans detonated a mine at 5.45pm and only three of Second Lieutenant Walker's men escaped. Captain Winser's platoon was sent to replace Walker's but they too were annihilated.

Two more mines detonated under the Foresters' trench, just north of the Bluff, and the German infantry overran their front trench and part of the support trench. They also entered the South Staffords' trenches and the adjacent ravine, driving back the machine gun company sent by Colonel Barker to stop the breakthrough. All along the front line the men were running out of bombs; replacements were sent but they were without detonators. The Borders had to fit them in darkness while under fire but there was only one accident.

The Sherwoods' inexperienced commander wanted permission before using the Lincolns' companies but the wire to brigade headquarters had been cut; the delay allowed the Germans time to reorganise. In the meantime, Major Torrens organised a counter-attack with a mixed group of Lancashire Fusiliers, Sherwood Foresters and 7th York and Lancasters. Although some reached the top of the Bluff, they soon had to withdraw to New Year Trench.

The fighting continued throughout the night and the Germans occupied the British front line from the ravine to the canal; they also had the Bluff. The boundary issue became a problem again when the 6th Dorsets and 7th East Yorkshires[276] were sent to Brigadier General Fell. The Dorsets thought they were being sent forward to reinforce the line rather than recapture the Bluff and it was dark before the confusion had been cleared up.

Bombing parties were organised, each with six bayonet men leading eight bombers while thirty men followed carrying extra bombs. Only the

---

276 Both 50 Brigade, attached to 52 Brigade.

groups were too large for the officers to control and they soon became split up and were stopped. The 7th Borders[277] advanced late, giving machine guns across the canal time to shoot up the right company. A single platoon climbed onto the Bluff and although Captain Mozley reinforced them they eventually had to abandon the position. The fighting around the Bluff had cost 17th Division nearly 1,300 casualties.

The following day the decision was taken to make a plan, rather than continue the ad hoc attacks. General Fanshawe wanted 76 Brigade to get to know the ground, so it entered the trenches that night. Brigadier General Pratt's men faced a moonscape of shell holes and the Bluff was going to be a particularly tough nut to crack. The only approach was the towpath and it could be swept by machine gun fire from the opposite bank. There was plenty of work to be done and Fanshawe set 29 February as a provisional date.

Starting on the evening of 22 February, 52 Brigade began the two-night process of relieving 76 Brigade so it could rest. Daily they practised over a full-scale model of the German trenches, made with the help of aerial photographs. Steel helmets were collected from other units and although there were enough for everyone, some of the assault troops did not like the extra weight on their heads.

New trenches were being dug when a fall of snow on 27 February showed them all up clearly, alerting the Germans. The winter weather meant it would be too cold to let the men stay in the assembly trenches all night and day, meaning extra reliefs. While Brigadier General Pratt[278] wanted a long bombardment, to cover the deployment, V Corps' artillery commander, Brigadier General Uniacke, wanted a surprise attack with no bombardment. After discussing several ideas with General Plumer the decision was taken to start a phoney bombardment at 5pm on 1 March. It would stop forty-five minutes later, to make it look like the assault troops had failed to advance. Brigadier General Pratt would assess the German reaction and report if a real preliminary barrage was needed.

The bombardment on 1 March was supplemented by trench mortars and Stokes mortars and while the trenches on the Bluff were nearly obliterated, little damage was done to the rest. The Germans were even seen erecting new barbed wire in no man's land. An intense barrage followed before nightfall and then the guns returned to the usual slow bombardment, to stop the Germans repairing the damage.

Brigadier General Pratt wanted a surprise attack and all three battalions were in place thirty minutes before zero hour. The assault troops were deploying close to the enemy trench when the sky lit up after a shell

---

277 51 Brigade.
278 51 Brigade.

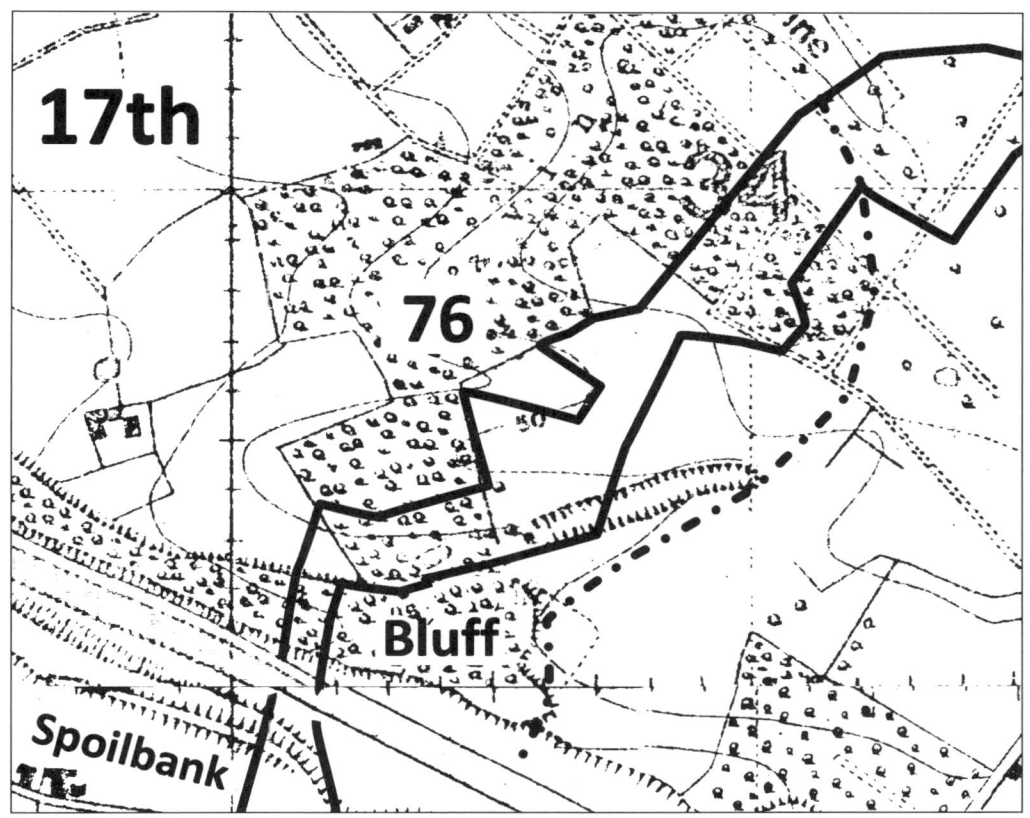

The fight for the Bluff, February and March 1916

detonated the store of flares collected to direct artillery fire. It alerted the
Germans but the final two-minute barrage at 4.30am drove them back
undercover.

A machine gun team shot down the Gordons on the left but Captain
Legard's company of the 7th Lincolns and the 9th Duke's protected the open
flank until Second Lieutenant Sanderson had cleared the enemy trench. The
8th King's Own found no Germans in the first two trenches in the centre
and they occupied a third until the objective had being consolidated. Around
sixty Germans emerged from their dugouts to shoot into the backs of the
King's Own but the 7th Lincolns[279] helped round them up. On the right, the
10th Welch Fusiliers[280] went too far and lost heavily before pulling back.

---

279 51 Brigade.
280 51 Brigade.

The Bluff was a difficult proposition because the sentries would see the infantry forming up. General Uniacke detailed a 60-pounder battery to 'drill the enemy' by firing double salvoes at two minute intervals at irregular times. The idea was the first salvo would send the lookouts under cover where they would wait until the second shells hit. The plan worked perfectly. After the first shells exploded, Captain Ledward was injured as he led the 2nd Suffolks up the Bluff to find the garrison under cover. But they took the Bluff, and New Year Trench and Loop Trench as well.

Over 250 prisoners were taken and Major Crosfield and Second Lieutenant Gardham found nearly fifty Germans hiding in craters in the Suffolks' sector while a similar number were found in tunnels under the Bluff. Unfortunately, men of the 172nd Tunnelling Company were killed by a mine as they searched the tunnels along the canal bank.

The front line had already been thinned out by the time the German artillery retaliated. Bombing attacks were also stopped because the British bombers had plenty of grenades for once. But the captured trenches were a shambles and one became known as International Trench because it contained many bodies of men of three nationalities (British, French and German) who had fallen in the 1914 battles. The weather did not let up and 8 Brigade took over the trenches in a blizzard on the night of 3/4 March. The recapture of the Bluff position had cost over 1,600 casualties.

Hohenzollern Redoubt, 2 to 18 March 1916
Captain Frank Preedy and 170th Tunnelling Company, Royal Engineers, took over the tunnels under the Hohenzollern Redoubt over the winter. His miners were surprised to discover the Germans were already working beneath the British trenches, so they detonated small mines, known as camouflets. The explosions were big enough to destroy the underground workings but they left the surface intact. Preedy then went on the offensive, digging a line of tunnels, spaced twenty metres apart, and a new camouflet was detonated every time they heard the Germans digging. The adjacent tunnels were then pushed forward, converging towards the cleared area. Day after day Preedy's men continued their nerve-wracking work until they were under the redoubt; it had taken three months and fifty mines.

The camouflets were covering up the real danger to the Germans because three deep tunnels were being dug with the aid of drills. By February 1916 they too were under the redoubt. The miners had also dragged over twenty-five tonnes of ammonal explosive into the underground chambers and they were ready to be fired.

Major General Arthur Scott's 12th (Eastern) Division took over the

Hohenzollern Redoubt sector at the end of the month. The plan was for the 8th Royal Fusiliers to capture one old crater and two new craters while the 9th Royal Fusiliers[281] seized the third new crater. They would also secure the Chord, a trench cutting across the redoubt.

The miners detonated the three mines at 5.45pm on 2 March and tons of earth were flung high above the redoubt. Captain Chard, Lieutenant Upward and Company Sergeant Major Sharp captured the three craters on the 8th

The battle for Hohenzollern Redoubt, March 1916

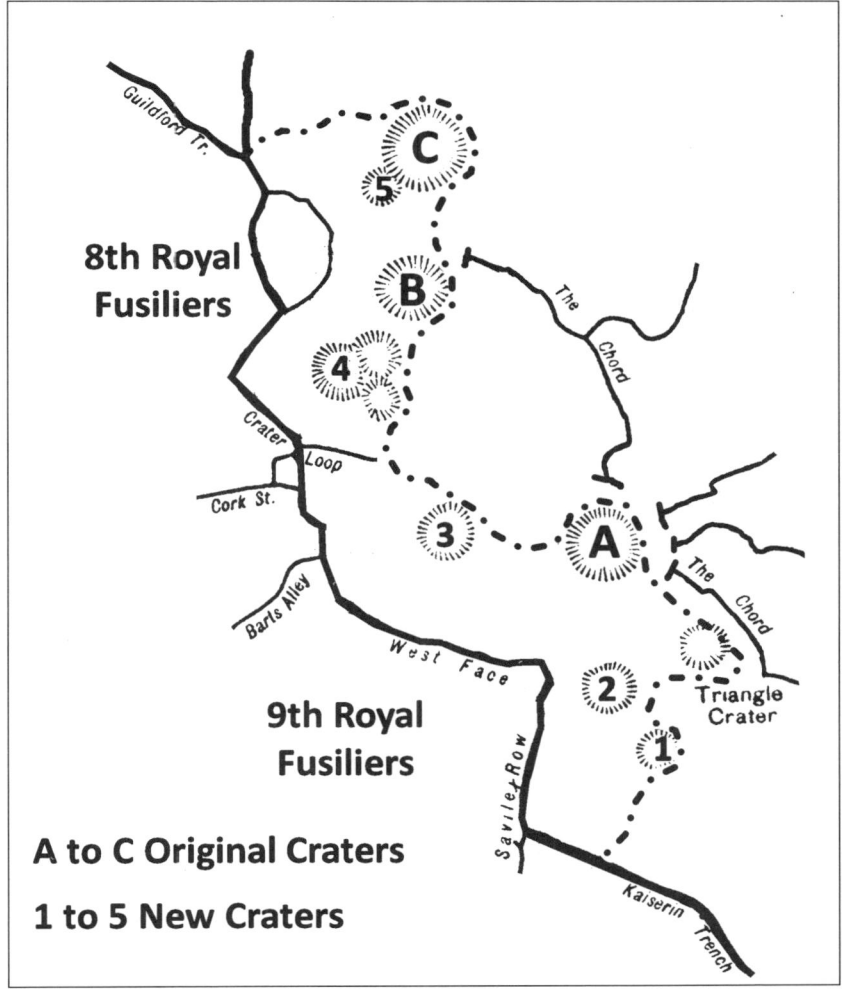

---

281 Both 37 Brigade.

Royal Fusiliers' left but falling debris buried many of the men on the battalion right. The rest came under machine gun fire only to find the Chord had been battered beyond recognition, so Captain Mason withdrew to the craters and Major Cope brought forward the reinforcements to consolidate them.

Half of Captain Phillips' company of 9th Fusiliers was hit by falling debris but the rest secured the right half of the Chord. Captain Cooper's men captured the third new crater along with three old craters and Sergeant Cromyn bombed along Big Willie Trench until his bombs ran out. Captain Preedy's men then moved forward to find the entrance to the German tunnels in Triangle Crater.

The tunnellers were busy exploring and dismantling what they found when the Germans counter-attacked on the afternoon of 4 March, capturing Triangle Crater and the trapped miners. Two days later a company of 6th Buffs tried to retake it, only to become mired in the deep mud. Corporal William Cotter was severely wounded as he withdrew his men to Crater 2 but he remained in command long enough for reinforcements to reach the crater. He died two days later and was posthumously awarded the Victoria Cross.

A few days later 170th Tunnelling Company broke into the German mining system and they laid charges along the tunnels. They withdrew on 12 March and the explosions destroyed the galleries. But the Germans had not given up and they started digging under the redoubt again. Another mine detonated at 5pm on 18 March under Crater C, and the 7th East Surreys inside disappeared in the explosion; only Company Sergeant Major Palmer and three others survived. A second mine killed the 6th Buffs in the three other craters.

The Germans overran the crater field but Captain Scott's counter-attack with the Buffs retook Crater 4. The 6th Queen's Own moved up and established a new line along the near side of the craters, while the Germans dug in on the opposite side looking across a no man's land that no one could cross. After two weeks of intense fighting, 12th Division's battle for Hohenzollern Redoubt had ended, having suffered 3,000 casualties.

The St Eloi Craters, 27 March to 19 April

The village of St Eloi was in V Corps' sector, just over two miles south of Ypres, and the Germans held an area of high ground south of the village called the Mound. The small salient had a good view over the area, which had been turned into a muddy crater field by the firing of over thirty mines. In March 1916, General Plumer wanted V Corps to capture the observation point and 3rd Division would make the assault while the Canadian Corps would hold it.

The 1st Canadian Division had fought in the Ypres Salient and at Festubert by the time the 2nd Canadian Division was rushed to the Western Front in September 1915. The two divisions were deployed side by side in the southern half of the Ypres sector and formed into the Canadian Corps under General Edwin Alderson.

The British artillery opened fire at 4.15am on 27 March and seven mines detonated a few seconds apart, creating large craters around the Mound.[282]

The struggle for the St Eloi Craters, March and April 1916

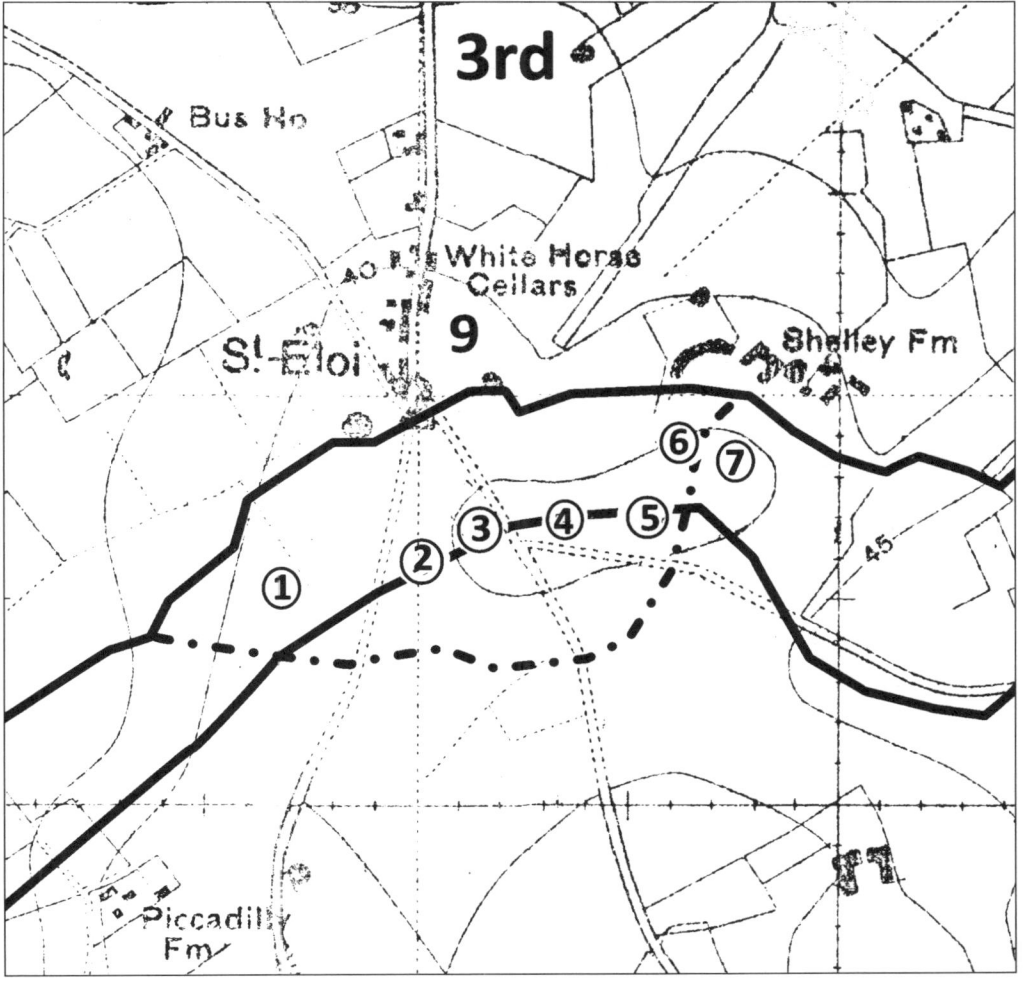

---

282 They were numbered 1 to 7 from west to east.

The 4th Royal Fusiliers[283] waited the prescribed thirty seconds on the left, giving the Germans time to react, and the assault companies were hit by the counter-barrage and machine gun fire as they trudged across the boggy ground. Two platoons reached the craters but they were isolated because the rest were pinned down in no man's land.

The 1st Northumberland Fusiliers did not wait and they were at the wire before the Germans could retaliate. It took time to cut gaps and the second wave joined the final charge. Second Lieutenant Holmes and Lance Corporal Keirsey silenced a machine gun team before it got its range, allowing their comrades to capture the garrison in their dug-outs. A counter-attack struck the Northumberland's right flank but Second Lieutenant Carrick eventually took thirty-five prisoners.

Part of the Mound had been taken but the Germans were not going to give it up without a fight. The area was pounded by shell fire all week and the German infantry captured the craters one by one, with the last one falling into their hands by 3 April. The Canadians were initially going to lend one brigade to the 3rd Division but General Alderson decided to take over the whole sector rather than split the division up.

During the early hours of 4 April, Brigadier General Ketchen's 6 Canadian Brigade began relieving 76 Brigade. The exhausted state of the troops coming out of the line was obvious and when one Canadian soldier shouted 'Cheer up! Don't be downhearted!', the reply came back, 'You'll be downhearted when you see what's up there; I have lost my best chums.'

The relief was difficult because the front line was on an exposed slope and under constant artillery fire. As 31st Battalion faced Craters 6 and 7, 27th Battalion faced Craters 1 through to 5. But the officers soon realised that Craters 2 through to 5 overlapped, forming an impassable water-filled obstacle. It left the Canadians holding a series of unconnected outposts which could only contact each other at night. There were only four machine guns to cover the twelve posts and there was no barbed wire. To sum up, the Canadians only a vague idea where they were and it was 'more of a line on the map than an actual line of defence'.

The Germans knew exactly where they were and the bombardment started at dawn. Lieutenant Colonel Snider had to thin out his front line to reduce casualties, leaving 31st Battalion's platoons out of contact both with each other and with 27th Battalion. Major Daly's platoon still managed to stop a concerted attack by around 150 Germans.

By 6 April there had been 230 casualties from artillery fire and from trench foot, so 29th Battalion started relieving 27th Battalion. There was just a single communication trench and the Germans attacked when they

---

283 9 Brigade, 3rd Division.

realised a relief was underway. They exploited the gap between 31st Battalion and 27th Battalion and three hours later they held Craters 2, 3, 4 and 5. All communications had been cut,and while it was too dangerous to use runners in daylight, they were unable to find anyone in the dark.

After hearing confusing reports, General Richard Turner, commander of the 2nd Division, instructed 27th and 29th Battalions to send their bombers forward at dawn. They were annihilated and thoughts of a raid were dropped. It was impossible to take Crater 2 and 3, so 31st Battalion tried to retake Crater 4 with help from 28th Battalion. The raiding party lost direction as they advanced from Craters 6 and 7 and reported they had captured some small craters north of Crater 4. But with no aerial photography, no trench maps and nothing on the battlefield to guide them, it was impossible to confirm their position.

On 8 April General Turner told Plumer he wanted to pull the Canadians back so they could shell the Germans out of the craters. Either that or Second Army had to attack on a wider front to prevent the German artillery from concentrating their fire on the crater field. On the morning of 10 April, Brigadier General Rennie mistakenly reported his 4 Canadian Brigade had recaptured Crater 3; the raiding party had actually taken some unmarked craters. The confusion continued but as the days passed it was clear the Canadians were not holding what they thought they were, while raiding parties just got lost in the crater field at night.

On the night of 14 April, 24th Battalion relieved 25th Battalion and it immediately had to fight off a bombing attack on Craters 6 and 7. All the runners sent to the rear were hit but a carrier pigeon took a message from 24th Battalion to 5 Canadian Brigade headquarters. The following day Major Ross of the 24th Battalion reported that Craters 2, 3, 4 and 5 were in enemy hands and the news was soon confirmed by aerial photographs. General Alderson immediately cancelled all offensive operations.

On the night of 17 April, 29th Battalion relieved 24th Battalion opposite Craters 6 and 7. Forty-eight hours later a German raiding party attacked Crater 6 where Lieutenant Myers was holding on with only a dozen able-bodied men. Their rifles jammed in the mud and then a shell detonated all their grenades. Eleven escaped; all but one had been wounded. Major Tait ordered a raiding party to retake the lost crater but machine guns in Crater 5 stopped it getting anywhere near. Two 31st Battalion companies were sent forward to make another attack but Tait convinced them it was suicidal to try again. As the battle for the St Eloi craters drew to a close, the Canadians were only left with one crater and they soon abandoned that and withdrew to a safer line to escape the German artillery fire.

Chapter 15

Smiling Over the Parapet
April and May 1916

German Gas Attacks at Hulluch, 27 and 29 April

Six months after the battle of Loos had ended, the front line had hardly moved and no man's land ran close to the La Bassée–Lens road, west of Hulluch and east of Loos. Lieutenant General Charles Kavanagh's I Corps had spent a quiet winter holding the sector but the Germans planned to test the mettle of the division holding the line.

The 16th (Irish) Division had only been in France for a couple of months and it was still learning the art of trench warfare. On the night of 23/24 April a deserter reached the Irish trenches and he said a gas attack was planned. When a horde of rats was seen running across no man's land, it was believed leaking gas cylinders had driven them from the German trenches.

The men were kept busy strengthening their trenches during the day and the wire during the night while blankets were hung from all dug-out doors as protection. There were also momentous events afoot back home as Irish Nationalists took to the streets of Dublin in open rebellion on 24 April. The battle for the city would rage for over a week and while a news blackout would have prevented detailed information reaching the front, rumours would have been circulating in the trenches.

Early on 27 April, a thick cloud of gas crept slowly across no man's land and over the Irish trenches. It forced brigade staff to wear their gas helmets and there were even reports of the smell up to fifteen miles away. Lookouts spotted small groups of Germans armed with pistols and grenades moving through gaps in the wire about thirty minutes later. Then three small mines detonated under I Corps front line at 5.55am. One exploded under the 7th Inniskilling Fusiliers and another under the 8th Irish Fusiliers. The third blew up one of 44 Brigade's trenches in the Quarries area, to the north. The

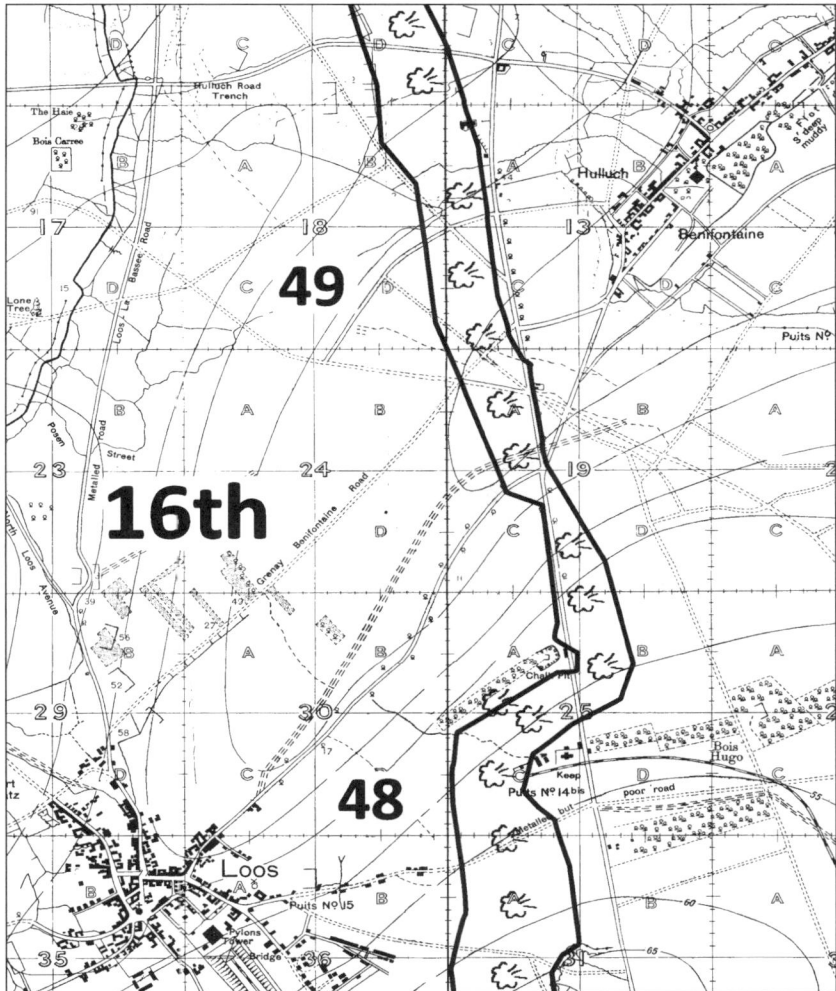

The gas attack at Hulluch, 27 and 29 April 1916

artillery then resumed their bombardment while another batch of gas cylinders sprayed their contents into no man's land.

Again the gas had little effect except for one unfortunate incident in 15th Division's area. After the gas cloud had blown across one company of the 9th Black Watch, Lieutenant Small told his men to dispose of their helmets because they only worked once. He was wrong about this and the wind changed direction and the gas blew back; Small was one of the many men who died.

Several groups of German infantry, around 200 strong, entered no man's land but only three reached the Scottish and Irish trenches. Patrols holding the 9th Black Watch's trenches immediately drove one out. Another captured some of the 7th Inniskilling Fusiliers, including Captain Murray, but they were shot down as they withdrew. Major Ross White came forward to organize the counter-attack which cleared the rest of the Irish trenches. But the cost had been high; over 260 Inniskillings had been asphyxiated and 66 died. The third group entered Chalk Pit Wood but Captain Cooke saw to it that the 8th Irish Fusiliers' drove them out before he was killed.

The gas was causing problems across no man's land as well. Leaking cylinders were filling the trenches with gas and many Germans could be seen running back to their support trenches to escape it. Around 8am another gas cloud began creeping towards the Inniskillings but Lieutenant Mitchell's Lewis gun team shot down all the infantry following it.

Reliefs of the worse affected battalions were organised during the night; the 8th Inniskillings relieved the 7th Inniskillings; the 7th Irish Fusiliers relieved the 8th Irish Fusiliers and a company of the 9th Dublin Fusiliers reinforced the 8th Dublin Fusiliers. The front was quiet but the Germans were planning a second gas attack, only this time at night.

At 3.45am on the 29April a green flare followed by a red flare signalled the start of the attack. As artillery fire hit 16th Division's communication trenches and rear area, chlorine gas was released all the way from Hulluch down to Chalk Pit Wood. Only this time a lot of smoke was released to make up for the lack of gas cylinders. Twenty-five minutes later infantry started crossing no man's land west of Hulluch. The Irish troops were holding their own as the cloud drifted over their trenches but then the wind changed direction, sending the German infantry running back where they were hit by the British barrage.

It was light when the next gas cloud was released and while the Irishmen had plenty of warning, there were far more casualties than expected. To begin with higher command blamed poor gas discipline but it was soon discovered that the helmets were faulty. The anti-gas chemicals had not been applied to the hoods properly and while the production of the new box respirator was speeded up, it was too late to save the 270 Inniskillings who fell victim to the gas. Altogether the casualties from the two attacks on 27 and 29 April were 1,260; 338 died, many of them from gas poisoning.

Gas at Wulverghem, 30 April and 17 June

General Sir Herbert Plumer's Second Army held the Flanders sector and Lieutenant General Hew Fanshawe's V Corps was in the centre facing the Messines Ridge. The whole front was overlooked from St Eloi in the north to the area south of Messines. Major General Aylmer Haldane's 3rd Division had just relieved 50th Division facing Wytschaete while Major General John Capper's 24th Division formed an arc around Messines. Each division had all three brigades up front, each with two battalions in the trenches and two to the rear.

Suspicions were raised when shell fire punctured cylinders near Spanbroekmolen on five occasions around 22 April, each time releasing a small cloud of gas which floated along the German front. So a gas alert was announced when the wind swung round behind the German lines on the 25th. The following day two deserters confirmed that a large number of gas cylinders had been installed in their trenches.

General Plumer's headquarters suspected V Corps' mine shafts could be a target so instructions were given to stop work and camouflage the entrances. General Haldane cancelled work in no man's land on 3rd Division's front because they could not warn the wiring and working parties in the event of a gas attack. Meanwhile, work continued in front of 24th Division's trenches.

On the evening of 29 April, two more deserters were seized near Spanbroekmolen.[284] They said a raid was imminent so a warning was issued and lookouts were posted to watch and listen for the gas. Unfortunately, the message did not reach the rest of V Corps' front and German rifle fire began at 12.35am, to drown out the sounds of the gas release. It had been released at chosen points along a two-mile front, with gaps left where it was not needed. Lookouts soon spotted the clouds billowing from the German trench and gas gongs and horns sounded, as shouts to put on gas helmets echoed along the line.

The wind was fairly strong and no man's land was only around fifty metres wide, so the gas quickly reached the British trenches. Very lights lit up the cloud while a bombardment hit targets across V Corps rear. The gas smothered the 10th Welch Fusiliers,[285] the 8th Queen's, the 1st North Staffords,[286] the 13rd Middlesex and the 2nd Leinsters.[287]

The plan had been for the infantry to follow the shorter intense bursts of gas, while the emissions lasted longer elsewhere, to disguise the extent of the attacks. The high wind was expected to move the gas quickly, so the infantry had been ordered not to wear their gas masks, so they could move faster. But many disagreed and they hung back from the cloud.

---

284 In 76 Brigade's sector on 3rd Division's front.
285 76 Brigade on 3rd Division's right.
286 72 Brigade on 24th Division's left.
287 73 Brigade in 24th Division's centre.

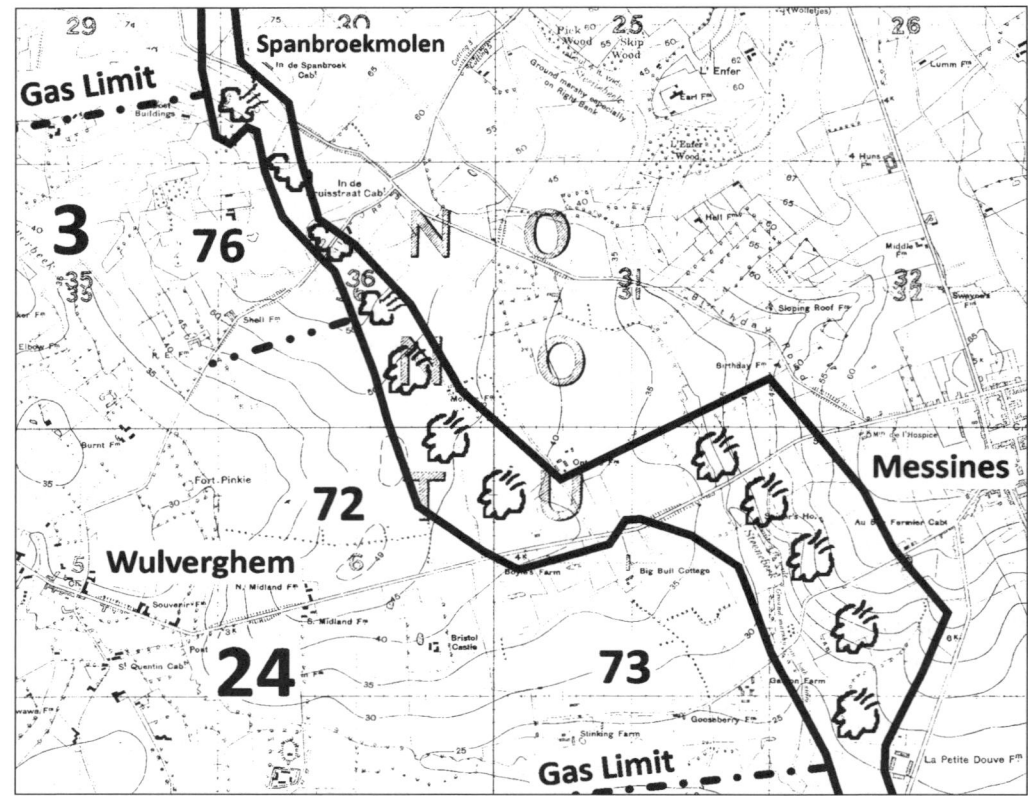

The gas attack from the Messines Ridge towards Wulverghem, 30 April and 17 June 1916

Out in no man's land snipers delayed the men cutting the wire, giving 72 and 76 Brigades time to man their parapet. The snipers then withdrew so the Lewis guns could open fire on the advancing infantry. A few German raiders entered the Leinsters' trench but Captain Murphy's[288] men stopped them lowering explosives into a mine shaft and forced them to retire. By 1.30am the attack was over and the Germans were dragging their casualties back to their trenches.

There were two more raids directed towards a mine shaft, confirming General Fanshawe's suspicions; both were stopped. The Lewis gunners and snipers had been issued with the new box respirators and they reported they gave far better protection than the hood helmets.

The 24th Division was still holding the line west of Messines when a gas alert was ordered on the afternoon of 16 June. The night was bright

---

288 In command of the Leinsters while Lieutenant Colonel Bullen-Smith was covering brigade headquarters.

moonlight so the lookouts could see the German trenches. They smelt gas at 12.20am the following morning. There was plenty of time to put on gas helmets but the concentration was so strong and it lasted for so long that many of the 8th Queen's, 1st North Staffords,[289] 9th Sussex and 7th Northants[290] were incapacitated.

The wind then started to change direction, driving the gas across 17 Brigade's sector to the south-east and eventually back over the German lines. The British artillery opened fire around the same time and the planned infantry attack failed to materialise. While the defensive measures had been a success, reports that the gas helmets had not worked caused alarm at all levels. Production of the new box respirator would have to be stepped up in time to make a difference on the Somme, which was due to start in two weeks.

The Kink, 11 May
The British line curved out south-east of Hohenzollern Redoubt and the ends of the salient were known as the Kink and Hussar Horn. The Kink was a dangerous stretch of trench because the redoubt and Fosse 8 overlooked it. It was also a busy mining sector and while 170th Tunnelling Company had the advantage underground, the German infantry held all but one of the craters above ground.

On 1 May the Germans detonated a small mine in front of Hussar Horn and they exploded a second one four days later. The weather was hot and cloudy on 11 May and the German guns began firing all along 15th Division's line at 4pm. Twenty-five minutes later they concentrated on the 13th Royal Scots holding the Kink and calls were made to the divisional artillery to return fire. But the observers could see nothing through the smoke and dust and then the battalion headquarters dug-out was hit, killing Lieutenant Colonel Raban, Major Wilmer and Captains Ferguson, Jekyll and Yule; the rest of the staff were wounded. Major General McCracken had no communications with the front so all he could do was to send a battalion forward to man a reserve trench.

At 5pm the Germans detonated a mine near the Hohenzollern Redoubt and their artillery switched to the area. Brigadier General Allgood asked for the British artillery to do the same and the bombardment helped the 11th Argylls stop an infantry attack. Forty-five minutes later the Kink was shelled again and over half of the Royal Scots had soon been hit by shrapnel or buried by debris. Before long no one was left standing in the first line.

German infantry crept forward, using the mounds of earth surrounding the craters as cover, and then rushed the Scots front line at 6pm before heading for Anchor Trench. Major Tomlinson withdrew the survivors but

---

289 Both 72 Brigade.
290 Both 73 Brigade.

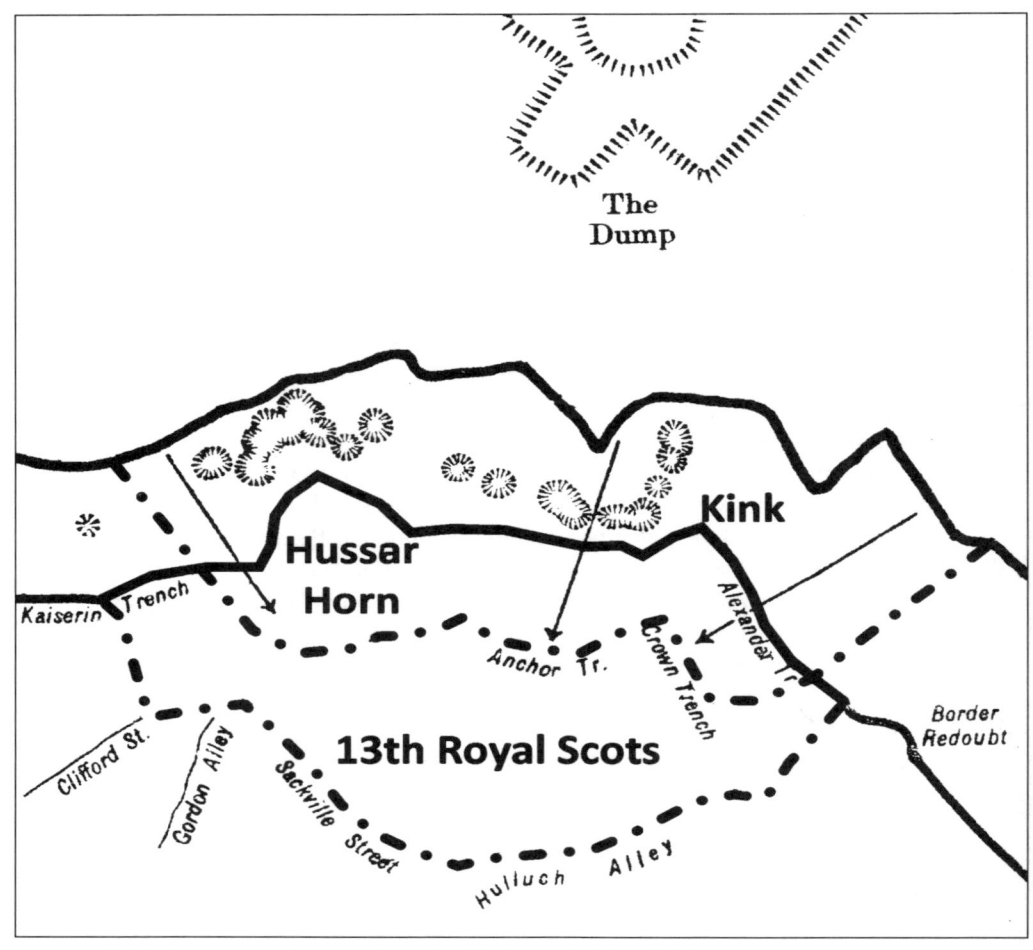

15th Division under attack at the Kink on 11 May 1916

only thirty-five men made it back to Sackville Street, 250 metres behind. Tomlinson was mortally wounded leading a counter-attack so Captain Stevens sent bombing parties forward; they too could not retake Anchor Trench. The British artillery was also unaware the Kink had been lost because communications had been cut, so they continued to shell the craters and the German trenches beyond. The German infantry did not press any further, they had captured what they wanted; all the mine entrances in the Kink. They also found thirty-nine miners trapped underground.

At 6.30pm the officer commanding the 6/7th Royal Scots Fusiliers took over the 13th Royal Scots sector and made plans to recapture the Kink. Machine gun fire stopped the bombing parties getting far, because the communication trenches had been battered in, so General Allgood decided to attack when it was dark. The Fusiliers advanced over the top at 1.30am but machine gun fire stopped them going far and only a few men reached the west end of Hussar Horn.

By the early hours the fighting died down and the Fusiliers set to work re-digging Sackville Street trench. They would have to work under a heavy bombardment. A final attempt to improve the position was made by the 8th KOSBs on the evening of 14 May. They advanced at 6.40pm from Boyau 98 on the right but were unable to reach Boyau 99 some 200 metres away. Further attacks were called off and Major General Frederick McCracken acknowledged that Sackville Street trench was a much safer line to hold than the Kink had been.

Vimy Ridge, May

The British took over another twenty miles from the French at the beginning of March 1916. The new sector started at Loos in the north and ran past Lens and Souchez, across the Vimy Ridge, and then around Arras to Ransart. The area had been quiet compared to other fronts and the French and Germans had been content to leave each other alone.

The 'live and let live' policy ended on 8 February when the Germans captured the hill called the Pimple at the north end of the ridge. Although they had taken a useful tactical position, it was a difficult one to hold; 'the whole ground is a quagmire, practically impossible for attack at present: the front trenches can only be reached by night over the open, and with great difficulty in deep mud.'

Vimy Ridge is a nine-mile long escarpment, stretching from the Souchez stream to the Scarpe River. There is a gentle slope behind the British line which was cut by the Zouave valley. The east slope of the ridge dropped quickly to the plain of Douai, behind the German lines. A narrow no man's land ran along the summit and nothing more than a line of craters separated the British and German trenches in many places.

Although it was easy to dig into the chalk, the trenches and gun emplacements had been smashed by artillery fire. The three British trench lines were 'merely shell holes joined up; hastily organized positions in mine craters; a line of detached posts, accommodated in grouse butts; straight trenches without traverses.' The entire area was strewn with battle debris and while the wire was 'thin and weak, or in bad condition; the positions for machine guns were very poor.'

Meanwhile, the German trenches and dug-outs were dug into the steep escarpment slope, which the British artillery found it difficult to hit. The British were about to discover that the live and let live attitude was just a ruse to make them lower their guard. Although the Germans 'had been smiling over the parapet, they had been pushing on below ground'.

In five weeks 25th Division had suffered 1,250 casualties – a low rate of attrition by Western Front standards – but they had been clinging onto a position they could easily have abandoned for a better one. Instead the infantry huddled in their shell-holes above ground while the tunnellers were kept busy underground. They were difficult days but they were about to get more dangerous.

Major Momber and the 176th Tunnelling Company struck first, detonating a mine on 26 April. British infantry seized the crater and called it New Cut Crater. Three days later a camouflet mine[291] was blown and it detonated a large German mine, resulting in Broadmarsh crater. A third mine was detonated between the two and the 1/6th London suffered eighty casualties securing the crater they named after their commander, Lieutenant Colonel Mildren.

Although the 47th (London) Division had struck the first blow, Major Momber believed that the Germans were digging around a dozen galleries to the south. So the infantry brought timber forward and removed soil from the workings while 176th Tunnelling Company dug as fast as they could. At 4.45pm on 3 May, Momber's miners detonated four mines in the Carency sector. Three created craters and the 1/21st London[292] seized them; they were called Love, Momber and Kennedy after the three commanders involved in the operation. The fourth mine blew black along the tunnel and the explosion barely broke the surface.

All the Germans could do was retaliate with artillery fire, demolishing parts of 25th Division's trenches. Five more British mines were detonated along the Berthonval sector, between Angel Avenue and White Hart Avenue at 8.30pm on 15 May. They destroyed parts of the German outpost line and the 11th Lancashire Fusiliers and 9th Loyals[293] captured all the craters.

So far the Germans had restrained themselves because they were planning a large counter-attack which would capture all the British mine shafts at one go. Slowly but surely, their trench mortars destroyed the British front line while the artillery registered the communication trenches and batteries one by one. The British aerial observers could see no troop concentrations so First Army was instructed to send divisions south to Fourth Army, ready for the Somme offensive. The withdrawals required reliefs and the field artillery in the Berthonval sector were on the move on

291 Camouflets were designed to destroy or disrupt underground workings without damaging the surface.
292 142 Brigade.
293 Both of the 74 Brigade, 25th Division, temporarily commanded by Lieutenant Colonel Crosbie.

the night of 19/20 May. The timing could not have been worse because 25th Division's gunners were pulling out to make room for the 47th Division batteries when the Germans attacked.

General Monro's First Army held the Vimy Ridge sector with Lieutenant General Sir Henry Wilson's IV Corps. On 20 May 47th Division was in the front line while 2nd Division was in reserve, ten miles behind. Major General Charles Barter was on leave, so Brigadier General Cuthbert was commanding the division while Lieutenant Colonel Faux took his place at 140 Brigade. A single 140 Brigade battalion was in the Souchez sector, facing the Pimple, and two 142 Brigade battalions held the Carency sector. Next came 140 Brigade in the Berthonval sector and 141 Brigade in the Carency sector while 142 Brigade was in divisional reserve. Brigadier General Cuthbert also had control of Brigadier General Heathcote's 7 Brigade, attached from 25th Division, and it was holding the P sector to the south.

Lieutenant Colonel Faux's men were in a difficult position in the Berthonval sector. His front line was an exposed outpost line with no dugouts and little wire and his troops could only move when it was dark. The wet ground had hindered work on the support line and the German artillery often destroyed trenches faster than the Londoners could dig them.

The night of 20 May was comparatively quiet but the Berthonval sector was heavily shelled the following morning. Another intensive bombardment hit the sector between Momber and Love Craters along to Royal Avenue starting around 3.40pm; an estimated 70,000 shells hit the area in four hours. They smothered 47th Division with smoke, dust and tear gas and General Cuthbert's artillery fired blind as they tried to give support.

At 7.45pm the German guns extended their range and a mine exploded under Royal Avenue. One minute later the German infantry began jogging across no man's land with Momber Crater on their right (west) and Royal Avenue on their left (east). The leading wave of infantry were half-way across no man's land before they were spotted and they were soon in the Londoners' trench.

The 1/8th and 1/7th London Regiment were quickly overrun on the left and the survivors were captured in their craters and shelters. Captains Portman and Clark of the 8th London and Captain Davis and Lieutenant Brooks of the 7th London were captured. The rest were driven from two support trenches back to a trench half-way down the slope, where the German infantry were stopped by their own barrage. The division's chief engineer, Lieutenant Colonel Crookshank, deployed the engineers in the reserve line at the bottom of Zouave Valley where they rallied any stragglers.

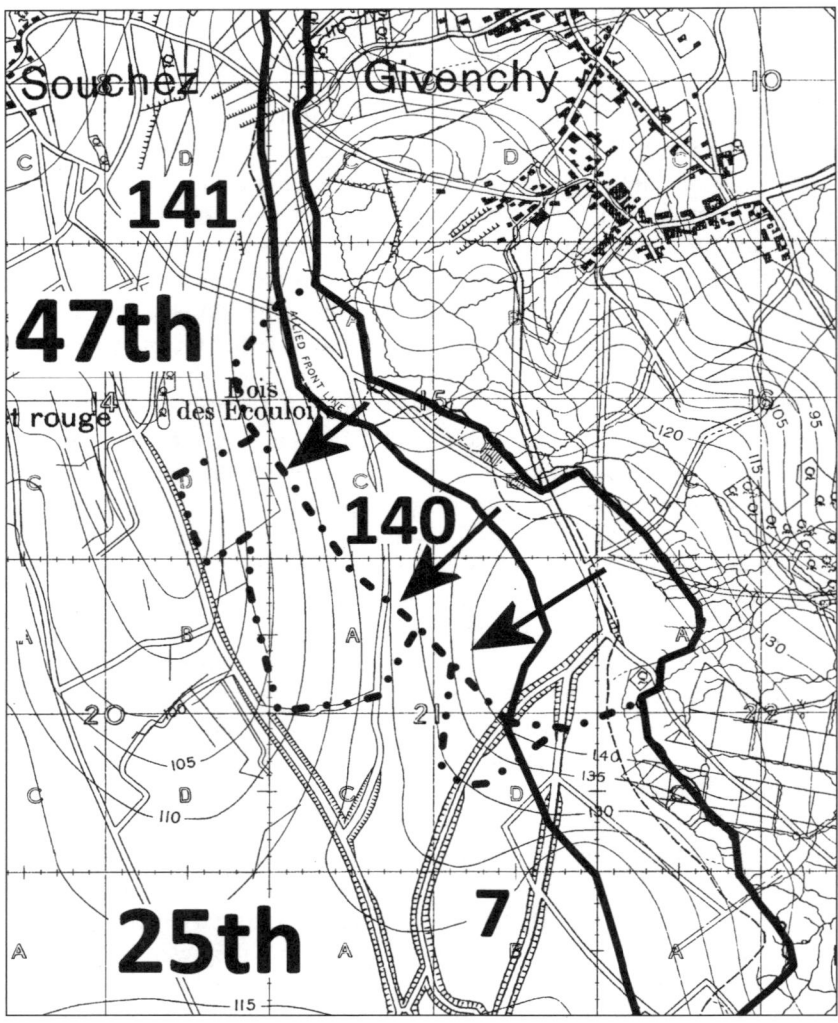

47th Division's fight for Vimy Ridge in May 1916

The 1/20th London[294] and 10th Cheshires[295] were driven from their outpost trench and Broadmarsh Crater on the right. Captain Taylor's men recaptured the crater but Captain Young's men had to withdraw from the support trench as Second Lieutenant Lomas held the Germans at bay with his machine gun; both Taylor and Young were killed. Despite the chaos, Lieutenant Colonel Matthews deployed the survivors in a communication

294 141 Brigade.
295 7 Brigade, 25th Division.

trench and stopped the Germans outflanking his position. Captain Williams' men held the rest of the line until their officer was severely wounded; only seventeen out of 120 returned.

The German infantry had no intention of going any further because they had captured all but one of the British mine shafts, so their artillery created a box barrage[296] around the captured area while their infantry dug in. The London battalion commanders had no idea of the situation until there was a lull in the shelling, and a single counter-attack at around 9pm by Captain Rundell of the 7th London Regiment was stopped along Old Boot Street.

Reinforcements had to wait until it was dark before it was safe to approach the new front line and at 2am the 15th and 18th London went looking for the new German front line. Captain Farquhar went missing at the head of the 15th London Regiment while Lieutenant Colonel of 18th London was injured; it left Lieutenant Colonel Warrender in command of the combined group. They learnt little but Major Whitehead of the 6th London discovered an old French trench which was in a better position and the 6th and 7th London occupied it during the night.

Although 142 Brigade had been moved close to the front and Brigadier General Kellett[297] had continued reporting to 47th Division headquarters, news from the front was still sketchy. General Cuthbert only had a vague idea how far the Germans had penetrated his line until the 1/18th London and 1/15th London attacked at 2am. The only success Cuthbert could report was that the 8th Loyals had retaken 7 Brigade's support trench on the division's right flank.

The following day was quiet and staff officers learnt as much as they could about the German position from the ground as planes from Nos. 10, 18 and 25 Squadrons located trenches from the air. Artillery batteries were moved forward but Generals Wilson and Cuthbert knew ammunition was in short supply because most of it was being sent to the Somme.[298]

Even so, General Wilson told Major General Barter he wanted to recover the lost territory and he planned a night attack by 99, 142 and 7 Brigades.[299] It meant Barter had to organize an attack by three brigades from three divisions at short notice. But when General Haig heard about the counter-attack he made it clear he wanted adequate preparations before the troops went over the top. So General Monro told General Wilson to postpone zero hour until the following evening, to give the artillery all day to register targets and the troops had time to settle in the trenches. But the delay also allowed the German artillery to shell the assault troops as they moved through Zouave Valley; the guns were more accurate than normal because a deserter had betrayed the counter-attack.

---

296 Aiming around the three sides of the captured position, while leaving the nearest face so reinforcements could move up.
297 99 Brigade, 2nd Division.
298 Many shells were defective because of poor quality control in the munitions factories.
299 47th, 2nd and 25th Divisions respectively.

During the afternoon of 23 June Generals Monro and Allenby[300] and GHQ's Artillery Adviser Operations Section officer joined General Wilson at IV Corps headquarters. They heard that Haig wanted to take a position which could be held. Wilson argued they had to strike that evening, before the Germans had strengthened their defences anymore, and Monro and Allenby agreed even though the poor weather had grounded the aerial observers. The guns would begin their bombardment at 7.25pm and the infantry would go over the top an hour later.

The Germans shelled the area all afternoon but the British heavy guns could not reply because they had to save their ammunition for the preliminary bombardment. The German artillery responded when the British barrage started and the guns hit three distinct areas, looking to disrupt the attack. One hit the Talus des Zouaves and the second targeted the communication trenches. The third hit the 1st Berkshires and 22th Royal Fusiliers[301] as they lay in the open on the lower slopes of the Zouave Valley. Over 100 Berkshires were hit and the officer in charge of the assault companies told Major Sharpe it would be nothing short of murder if they went ahead with the attack. Major Sharpe told Brigadier General Kellett at 99 Brigade's headquarters he was unable to attack the German line between Landwehr Avenue and Central Avenue. An officer went to the 22nd Royal Fusiliers with the news and while Major Rostron called his attack off, his runners did not get to one of the assault companies in time and it advanced alone. Although a few men reached the German front trench most were pinned down in nearby shell holes. Two officers went forward to recall the company only to discover it had been all but 'wiped out'.

Meanwhile, the 1/21st and 1/24th London[302] sent bombing teams between Uhlan Avenue and Landwehr Avenue. The 1/21st captured an old trench but Lieutenant Colonel Buxton-Carr's 1/24th London could not make any progress. The only lasting success was on the right where the 3rd Worcesters[303] captured their objective south of Central Avenue.

General Kellett's brigade major and Lieutenant Colonel Barker went forward to discover what 99 Brigade's problem was. They reported they should try again because the German shelling had slackened off, so plans were put in place to attack at 1.30am with the 1st KRRC taking the 1st Berkshires' place. However, General Wilson was concerned the relief could take longer than anticipated and made it clear the attack should be postponed until the following night if the 1st KRRC were not ready when the moon rose at 1am.

General Monro told General Wilson to cancel the attack an hour before it was due to go ahead. The following morning he held a conference and

---

300 Commanding the First and Third Armies respectively.
301 99th Brigade.
302 Both 142 Brigade.
303 7th Brigade.

told everyone that 2nd Division would relieve 47th Division the following night.[304] General Walker then had a week to prepare to attack on 3 June. But that too was cancelled because all the heavy artillery ammunition was being sent to the Somme.

At 2.45pm on 27 May First Army was told no more attacks would be made on Vimy Ridge. The Germans were content with their new position and chose not to occupy the old British support line. Instead they let 2nd Division dig slowly forward until it had formed a new front line, some 300 metres forward of the reserve line. And so the situation remained until the next British offensive in the area opened with the Canadian Corps' capture of Vimy Ridge on 9 April 1917.

---

304 The 47th (London) Division had suffered over 2,100 casualties.

Chapter 16

Inconclusive Sideshows
June and July 1916

Tor Top and Mount Sorrel, 2 to 13 June

General Sir Herbert Plumer's Second Army was holding the salient east and south-east of Ypres in May 1916. Lieutenant General the Hon. Sir Julian Byng's Canadian Corps held a 1,000 yard sector east of the town and the Ypres Ridge, overlooking the German trenches. The low summits were known as Hill 62,[305] Hill 61 and Mount Sorrel. Observatory Ridge ran west from Hill 61 towards Zillebeke and it also provided views over the German line around Klein Zillebeke. The capture of Tor Top and Observatory Ridge would give the Germans great views over the Ypres Salient. It would also 'fetter as strong a force as possible to the Ypres Salient,' reducing the number of divisions available to attack other parts of the German line.

General Byng had Major General Malcolm Mercer's 3rd Canadian Division in line and it had four battalions covering from Hooge to Mount Sorrel. Major General Arthur Currie's 1st Canadian Division was on its right, with two battalions either side of Hill 60. No man's land was less than 150 metres wide along most of its length but the Germans had taken great steps to reduce the wider section. They dug saps across the slopes of Tor Top and then connected them together only 150 metres from the British front line. They also dug saps in other wide areas south of Mount Sorrel.

Air cover was provided by II Brigade, Royal Flying Corps, but low cloud and rain stopped 2nd and 11th Wings flying reconnaissance missions and the planes reported nothing unusual when they eventually flew over the salient on 28 May. Trench mortars began registering the Canadian positions three days later and the artillery started the following day as German planes flew overhead, reporting the fall of shot. Eight observation balloons were also spotted floating high above the German lines.

The bombardment stopped at dusk on 1 June and German infantry

---

305 Also known as Tor Top.

entered no man's land to make gaps in German and Canadian wire. They were back in their trenches by 3am and the artillery resumed firing, putting everyone on alert. The situation around Tor Top and Mount Sorrel was worrying and Major General Mercer and Brigadier General Williams went forward to check if 8 Brigade's two battalions were ready to meet the attack at dawn.

Around 8.30am the firing began increasing until Sanctuary Wood, Tor Top and Mount Sorrel were all being shelled by all calibres. The Canadian and British heavy artillery returned fire around 9.45am but they made no impact on the bombardment. As both 7 and 8 Canadian Brigades alerted their reserve battalions to stand to arms, Lieutenant Colonel Hayter, of 3rd Canadian Division's General Staff, warned 9 Brigade to be ready to reinforce the line. He told the Canadian Corps headquarters and adjacent divisions his situation was serious. He also asked for help from the corps artillery and No 6 and No 5 Squadrons were ordered to spot targets for the batteries.

At around 12.30pm the field and heavy artillery increased their rate of fire as the trench mortars joined in. As one German observer noted: 'The whole enemy position was a cloud of dust and dirt, into which timber, tree trunks, weapons and equipment were continuously hurled up, and occasionally human bodies.' The German spotters had done their homework because the British and Canadian guns were silenced one by one. The rest lost contact with their observers as shrapnel and high-explosive shells cut telephone cables and many were killed or wounded. The two squadrons flying overhead also found it difficult to give the batteries information.

The only safe place from the barrage of shells was the headquarters of the 4th Canadian Mounted Rifles. Lieutenant Colonel Ussher's headquarters were a network of passages and dug-outs under Mount Sorrel called 'The Tunnel'. Stretcher bearers carried wounded inside until shell-bursts caved in the entrances trapping everyone inside; only seventy-six assembled later that evening.

Two early casualties were General Mercer, who was killed, and General William, who was wounded and taken prisoner. It was late afternoon before they were missed and their absence seriously affected how 3rd Canadian Division conducted itself. When General Byng found out, he told the divisional artillery commander, Brigadier General Hoare Nairne, to take command while Lieutenant Colonel Bott of the 2nd Canadian Mounted Rifles took control of 8 Canadian Brigade.

Three mines exploded just short of the Canadian trenches on Mount

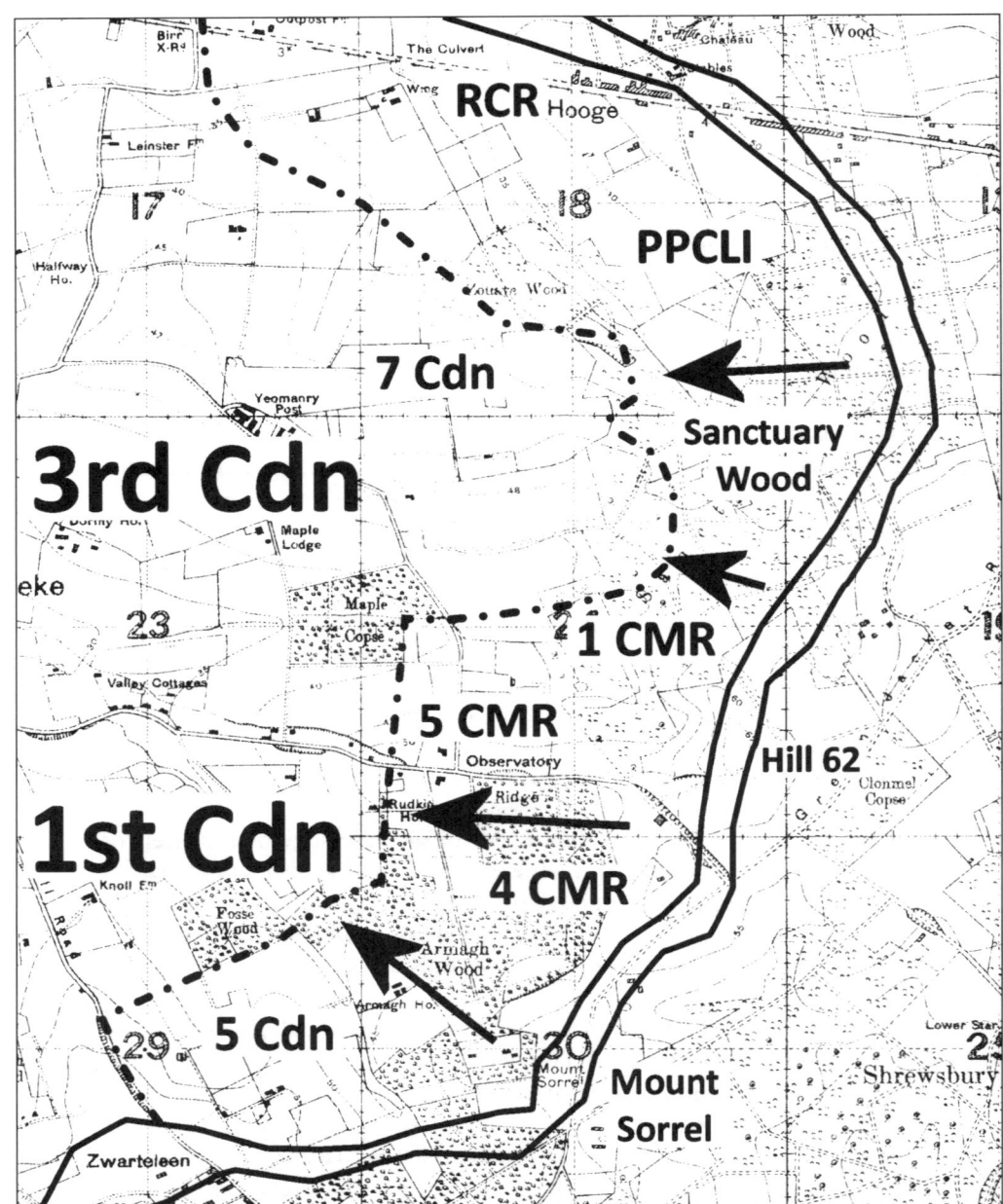

The German capture of Hill 62 and Mount Sorrel on 2 June

Sorrel at 1.07pm and white rockets signalled the start of the attack. Four waves of German infantry advanced towards the Canadians in the bright sunlight and the first wave carried wire cutters to complete what their comrades had started the night before. They were also carrying as many hand grenades as they could, ready to hurl into the Canadian trenches.

Four battalions led the attack, five more were in support and another six were waiting in reserve. The north limit of the assault hit the Princess Patricia's[306] right in Appendix Trench, 500 metres south-east of Hooge. Lieutenant Colonel Buller was killed and every officer of the three companies was hit as they fell back through Sanctuary Wood. The Patricia's rear companies fought a running battle as they withdrew down the communication trenches.

Over 400 Patricia's were killed or injured but they had given the 7th Canadian Battalion time to reinforce the support trench. Although the Germans could have reached the open fields beyond Sanctuary Wood they had orders to capture the high ground. They dug in on their objective even though some officers asked permission to advance further.

The 1st Canadian Mounted Rifles on Hill 62 met the centre of the attack while the 4th Canadian Mounted Rifles were on the right[307] and Mount Sorrel marked the southern limit of the attack. In most places the Canadians were only able to fire their rifles and machine guns for a couple of minutes before the Germans were on top of them and they were quickly overwhelmed. A few groups fought on, isolated from reinforcements and ammunition. It did not take long to surround them and flame-throwing teams were called up to finish them off.

The 5th Canadian Mounted Rifles were in reserve, holding a line of strongpoints across Observatory Ridge. Their interlocking fields of fire broke up the groups of German infantry moving through the smashed up woods. But still they came forward, capturing strongpoints 12 and 13 at the south end of Sanctuary Wood and strongpoint 14 in the centre of Armagh Wood. A forward section of 18-pounders of the 5th Canadian Battery was also overrun on Observatory Ridge.

The only organised resistance came from the flanks. The left flank of the Princess Pat's held onto the Appendix south of Hooge and poured fire into the Germans advancing through Sanctuary Wood. The 5th Canadian Battalion did the same on the opposite side of the breakthrough, shooting at the waves of infantry moving through Armagh Wood. The machine gun teams of the 10th Canadian Battalion and the Motor Machine Gun Brigade were the first reserves to arrive and they established a line of outposts with interlocking fire. stopping groups of Germans looking to advance further.

---

306 7 Canadian Brigade.
307 Both of 8 Canadian Brigade.

By mid-afternoon the Germans held the entire Canadian trench system from Tor Top through to Mount Sorrel. The advance parties kept the Canadian reinforcements under fire while the reserves worked into the night, repairing the battered trenches. They also dug new ones across no man's land, connecting the captured trench system to their old front line along Green Jacket Line. The German outposts withdrew to the new position during the night.

The only place where the attack had failed was south of the Menin road. The Royal Canadian Regiment had not been dislodged from Hooge and the Patricia's left company still held the Appendix. The isolated company stopped three attacks during the night before withdrawing before dawn, carrying as many of the wounded as they could.

About an hour after the attack began, more reserves began reinforcing the isolated strongpoints holding 3rd Canadian Division's line. Zouave Wood was covered by 42nd Battalion,[308] behind the Princess Pat's position. The 5th Canadian Mounted Rifles covered the southern half of Sanctuary Wood as the 2nd Canadian Mounted Rifles formed a line through the west side of Armagh Wood.[309] Lieutenant Colonel Hayter, 3rd Canadian Division's temporary commander, decided it would be foolish to counter-attack so the three battalions created a defensive line around the break-in. He also welcomed 7th Battalion,[310] which deployed in reserve between Zillebeke and Square Wood, behind his right flank. It reinforced the single company of the 2nd Canadian Mounted Rifles manning the support line between Maple Copse and Square Wood.

The rest of the Canadian Corps was sending units forward and General Byng issued orders at 4.25pm to retake the position. He initially wanted 3rd Canadian Division to make the counter-attack the following night but he changed his mind after a tour of the trenches. The division was in no fit state to attack on its own, General Currie's 1st Division would have to help.

Two 1st Division brigades were slated to join the attack and Brigadier Generals Tuxford and Lipsett both put their headquarters in Railway Dugouts, south-west of Zillebeke Lake, to plan the operation. Even so, it was going to be difficult to carry out the attack at such short notice. Only two hours after receiving the order, Brigadier General Hoare Nairne was ready but it was dark before the operation orders were issued. The artillery was supposed to keep shooting as normal, with occasional bursts of rapid fire to drive the Germans into their dug-outs, but there was no time to tell the gunners. Although 7 Canadian Brigade[311] was already in position in the north half of Sanctuary Wood, 3 Canadian Brigade was late getting into position in the south half.

---

308 7 Canadian Brigade.
309 Both 8 Canadian Brigade.
310 2 Canadian Brigade, 1st Canadian Division.
311 With two 9 Canadian Brigade battalions attached.

The 2nd Canadian Mounted Rifles attacked early, securing Rudkin House on the west end of Observatory Ridge at 7pm, which overlooked 3 Canadian Brigade's start line. The Germans counter-attacked Maple Copse and Lieutenant Colonel Baker was mortally wounded organising the 5th Canadian Mounted Rifles' defence. The Canadian attack was supposed to begin at 2am but it was difficult to get everyone into position in the dark and all the battalions were late. The 49th Battalion was in place by 2.10am but the 60th and 52nd Battalions were hit by a German barrage as they formed up. Lieutenant Colonel Hay was wounded while on a reconnaissance ahead of his battalion and he never returned; as a result most of his battalion did not reach the front line in time.

All the problems resulted in zero hour being delayed until 7.10am. The plan was for a thirty minute barrage and then to fire six green rockets from Zillebeke Lake to coordinate the advance. But the rockets would not light in the damp conditions and eight failed to go off, resulting in them being fired at intervals. Some of the front line observers were unsure if they had seen the correct signal while others did not see any rockets.

The result was the 49th Battalion on the left, the 14th and 15th Battalions in the centre, and the 7th Battalion on the right left their trenches at different times. The disjointed advance allowed the German machine gun teams to traverse right and left to concentrate on each advancing company in turn. Only a few parties reached the German trenches and they were all killed or captured. By early afternoon the survivors were all back in their trenches apart from on the left where 49th Battalion was holding onto a few communication trenches.

Lieutenant General Byng's new plan was to use more artillery to smash the German trenches, so he needed less infantry to capture them. Altogether he assembled 218 guns, from the Canadian Corps, Lahore Division and three Heavy Artillery Groups. Although they were all in position on time, bad weather grounded the Flying Corps, making it impossible to register the heavy guns.

All the difficulties delayed the attack and the Germans struck first, east of Hooge, on 6 June, where the 28th Battalion had just taken over the trenches. After four hours of shelling, four mines exploded at 3.05pm demolishing 200 metres of Canadian trenches and killing most of the two companies in them. The rest of the battalion stopped the Germans reaching the support trench but there were insufficient reserves to launch a counter-attack. Another attack near Hill 60 at the same time was stopped by 18th Battalion.

The Germans had achieved what they wanted; a line of observation posts only two miles from Ypres so they could direct their artillery onto virtually any target in the salient. Although General Plumer wanted to retake the high ground, General Haig was concerned a counter-offensive could interfere with the preparations for the battle of the Somme. There were no extra divisions available so Deputy Chief of the General Staff, Major General Butler, told General Plumer to make better use of the artillery he had.

On 7 June the 2nd Cavalry Division sent 2 Cavalry Brigade forward under Brigadier General Campbell. The dismounted troopers were reorganised into three battalions and they deployed ready to counter-attack if the Germans struck again. Two days of good weather allowed No 6 Squadron to photograph the new German positions but the rain soon returned, grounding the planes.

Starting on 9 June, the Canadian Corps artillery carried out intense bombardments at random intervals, each one lasting around thirty minutes. The idea was to disguise the hour of the attack and keep the Germans on their guard. Orders for the recapture of Tor Top and Mount Sorrel were issued at 8am on 11 June and the plan was for 1st Canadian Division to attack at 1.30am on the 13th. Lieutenant Colonel Genet's 58th Battalion had to clear the southern end of Sanctuary Wood on the north flank. Brigadier General Tuxford had two battalions of the 3rd Canadian Brigade astride the Zillebeke road, ready to advance down Observatory Ridge towards Tor Top. Brigadier General Lipsett had one battalion of 2nd Canadian Brigade ready to advance through Armagh Wood to Mount Sorrel on the right.

All the Canadian artillery had been put under the command of Brigadier General Burstall and the guns began a steady bombardment of the German line between Sanctuary Wood and Hill 60 on 12 June. At 8pm another thirty minute intense barrage drove the Germans under cover while the assault battalions moved into the trenches. Then at 12.45am on 13 June the final bombardment began, only this time it lasted for forty-five minutes.

To the north, 20th Division had coordinated its barrages with the Canadian artillery, to make it look as though an attack was planned north of the Menin Road. The infantry went into no man's land to cut lanes in the German wire to add to the deception and four raiding parties captured prisoners. A smoke screen was arranged on the Canadians' left, as 29th and 31st Battalions fired in the direction of Hooge. Stokes mortars also shelled the enemy communication trenches through Sanctuary Wood while bombers raided the north end of the wood. Over 200 smoke bombs were fired at the trenches north of Zwarteleen and Stokes mortars hit the Snout and Hill 60, but a heavy counter-barrage stopped 7th Battalion raiding the trenches.

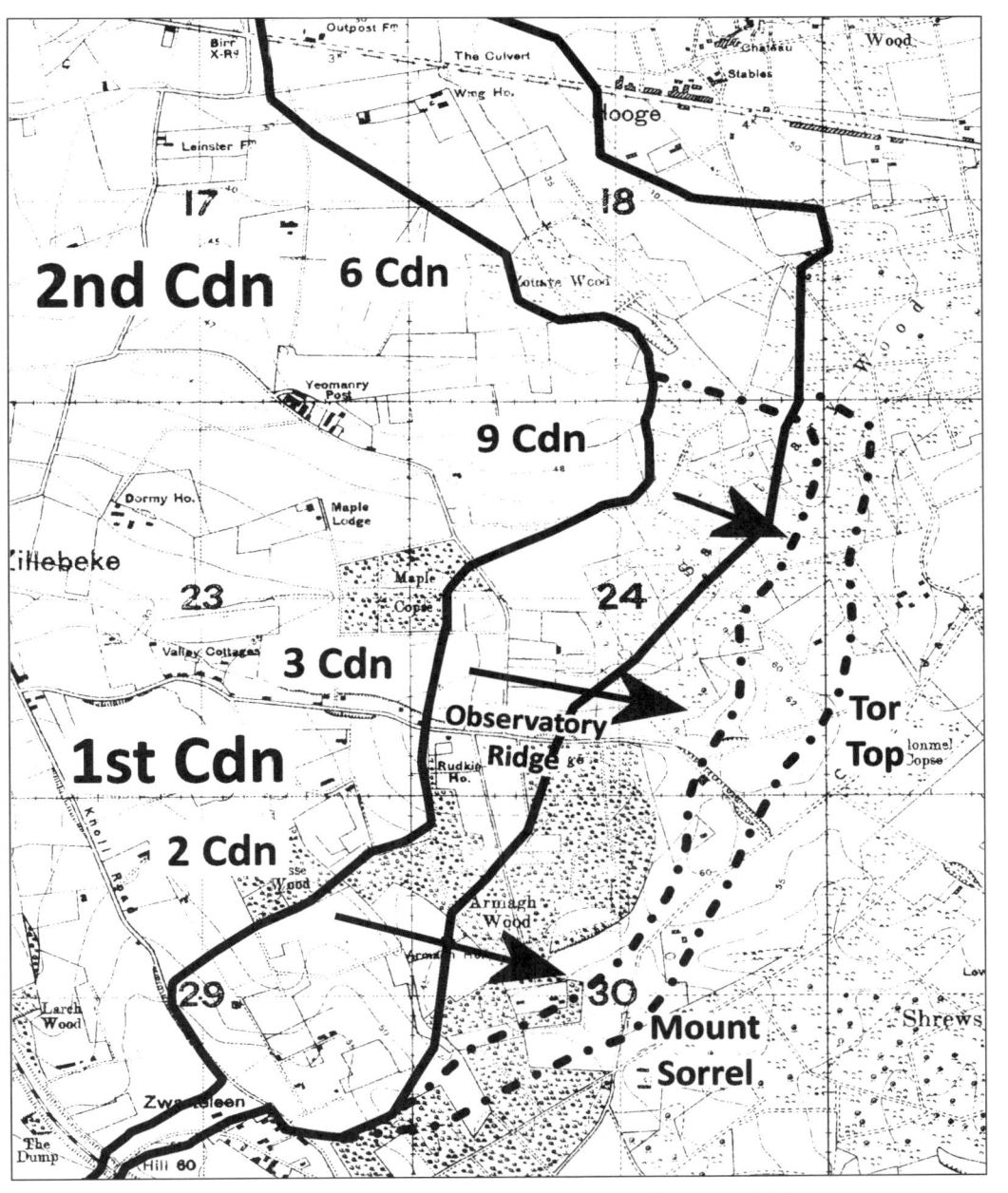

The Canadian Corps' recapture of Hill 62 and Mount Sorrel on 13 June

The Canadian artillery fire kept the German infantry in their dugouts and silenced many German guns. It was so accurate on Observatory Ridge that 16th Battalion was able to send its first two waves into no man's land as the enemy counter-barrage fired overhead. Brigadier General Burstall hoped that the barrage was so successful his infantry could advance 'with slung rifles' and he was nearly right. Four waves of infantry moved through the smashed woods as the rain hammered down. They advanced through the smoke clouds, catching many Germans still hiding from the barrage. On the left 58th Battalion moved through the south side of Sanctuary Wood and recaptured strongpoints 14 and 15. In the centre 13th and 16th Battalions advanced along Observatory Ridge and although they could not take the summit of Tor Top, they stopped the Germans holding it. On the right, 3rd Battalion swept through Armagh Wood and established a new line facing the summit of Mount Sorrel.

Nearly 200 prisoners were taken in the hour, but there was plenty of work to be done as the engineers helped the infantry consolidate their position in the pouring rain. But the Germans knew where they were digging and every gun in range shelled the Canadians well into the following afternoon. The poor weather continued through the night and the artillery took time to arrange map fire targets, knowing the RFC would not be able to help at dawn. Their work paid off because the gunners broke up two counter-attacks in the Mount Sorrel area. The Canadians began establishing a position on the ridge by digging bombing posts in the shell holes along the ridge. They then dug saps back to the support trench, 100 metres down the slope. The Germans did the same on the opposite side of the crest.

The battle of Mount Sorrel had ended in stalemate, with neither side having the advantage of the crest. The German attack and the counter-attack had cost the Canadian Corps nearly 8,500 casualties in under two weeks.

XI Corps Attack at Fromelles, 19 to 20 July

The battle of the Somme opened on 1 July with fourteen divisions[312] advancing at 7.30am astride the River Ancre. It was soon clear that the massive artillery bombardment had failed to silence the German machine guns or artillery and while gains were made to begin with, they were impossible to hold. Fourth Army's left and centre failed to secure anything more than small footholds but the right reached its objective. Casualties had been horrendous: 57,470 of which over one-third were killed, many in the first hour and many in no man's land.

General Charles Monro was still commanding First Army and he was given the task of creating a diversion in the Fromelles area which was held

---

312 Two with Third Army at Gommecourt and the rest under Fourth Army.

by XI Corps. Lieutenant General Richard Haking had Major General Colin Mackenzie's 61st (2nd South Midland) Division[313] and Major General James McKay's 5th Australian Division available to make the attack and neither had experience of making attacks. General Haking issued orders to the two divisional commanders on the morning of 14 July. Movements began at once with I Corps taking over the line south of the La Bassée canal, allowing the 5th Australian and 61st Divisions to shorten their fronts to face their objectives.

The field artillery started wire-cutting immediately while the heavy artillery began registering targets two days later. It was followed by a slow but methodical bombardment which would, according to General Haking 'reduce the defenders to a state of collapse before the assault'. Heavy artillery also started shelling the trenches astride the La Bassée canal, five miles to the south, on 16 July, in the hope the Germans would move guns there to counter them.

The artillery began the final bombardment of the German lines in earnest on 17 July. After four hours of registration and wire cutting the guns would lift their range as the infantry staged a false attack, showing their bayonets and dummy figures above the parapet.[314] It was hoped the Germans would rush out of their dug-outs to man their trenches just as the artillery shortened their range five minutes later. This hoax would be repeated four times and the infantry would advance on the fifth attempt when the guns lifted for the final time at 3pm.

The plan was to release gas to screen the infantry as they crossed no man's land. On the evening of 15 July gas was released from 1,500 cylinders on a wide front south of the attack front, to draw attention away from Fromelles, but it had to be stopped after only fifteen minutes because the wind speed dropped and the cloud drifted back over XI Corps' trenches. General Haking did not want a slight weather change ruining his plans, so every cylinder had to be removed; all 470 of them. General Mackenzie used every spare man and they worked around the clock for the next seventy-two hours, carrying them out of the trenches.

The Germans had not been idle during the bombardment. One raid on Cordonnerie Farm killed and injured nearly one hundred men of the 58th Australian Battalion and another raid captured a Lewis gun post in no man's land. It left General McKay wondering if the battle plan had been compromised. To make matters worse, XI Corps was a poor relation to Fourth Army's offensive on the Somme when it came to guns, ammunition and supplies. By the morning of 16 July several battery positions were still empty and some guns could not fire because they were waiting for shells;

---

313 The division was a second line territorial division formed from Territorials who had originally signed up for Home Service. Its training had suffered because many soldiers had been sent as replacements to the first line division, the 48th (South Midland) Division. But it was still sent to France in May 1916.
314 These false attacks were known as Chinese Attacks.

the dumps behind the front were still woefully short of all kinds of battle stores.

General Haig's Deputy Chief of Staff, Major General Richard Butler, returned to First Army headquarters at Chocques on 16 July. The success on Fourth Army's Somme front on 14 July meant there was no longer an urgent need for the operation. Generals Monro and Haking were told they should only attack if they had the resources for a successful operation. General Haking was confident and General Monro did not object so it was agreed the attack would go ahead as planned.

The plans had been made, the men were ready and the guns and ammunition were being rushed to the front. And then the heavens opened, turning the Fromelles battlefield into a muddy mess, so General Butler returned to First Army headquarters to discuss the weather. General Monro was absent so he told a staff officer that the decision to cancel or postpone the attack was in the general's hands. The artillery plan was already in trouble because haze had interfered with artillery registration and rain on the afternoon of the 16th made it harder to see.

The weather provisionally delayed zero hour to 4am next morning but it was postponed for another four hours after the evening reports had been seen. Monro told GHQ he wanted to cancel the operation if the bad weather continued but GHQ's reply reminded him that First Army had to attack: 'The Commander-in-Chief wishes the special operation to be carried out as soon as possible, weather permitting, provided always that Sir Charles Monro is satisfied that the conditions are favourable and that the resources at his disposal, including ammunition, are adequate both for the preparation and execution of the enterprise.'

Monro reluctantly approved a corps order that evening, setting zero hour sometime after 11am on 19 July, giving the artillery observers time to assess the guns' work. There was more cloud on 18 July but the sky cleared in the late afternoon and No 10 and No 16 Squadrons were able to register the artillery; No 10 Kite Balloon Section could also see for the first time. Later that night, 61st Division's patrols reported everything was quiet but the Australian patrols encountered German wiring parties.

The morning of 19 July was hazy and the weather promised to improve so Haking ordered the artillery to start firing at 11am, while the infantry would advance at 6pm, in full daylight. Unfortunately, the Germans suspected an attack was imminent and their guns returned fire with a vengeance. Communication trenches, dumps along Rue Tilleloy and field batteries were hit and many assault troops were hit as shrapnel and high explosive exploded in the crowded trenches.[315] The feint lifts during the

---

315 The 61st Division battalions were only 550 strong.

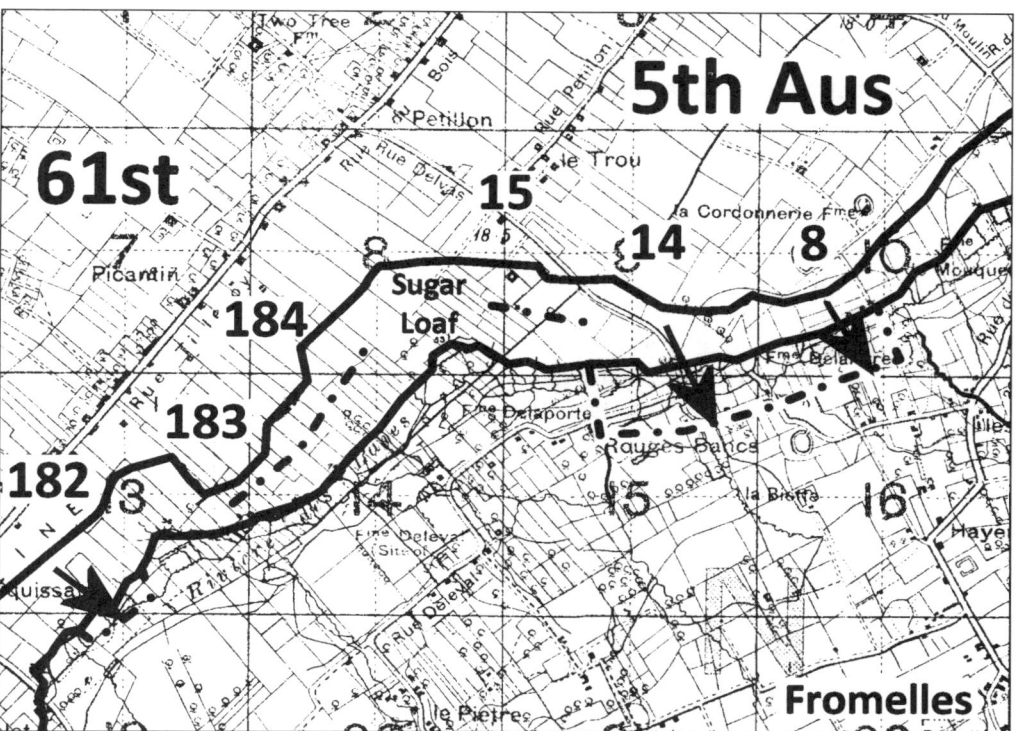

XI Corps attack towards Fromelles, 19 and 20 July 1916

afternoon failed to mislead the Germans and they stayed in their dug-outs right up to zero hour.

The centre of XI Corps' line skirted a salient known as the Sugarloaf and Haking wanted his two divisions to converge on the objective. Once across the front line, the 5th Australian Division and 61st Division would advance side by side. The British trench maps had been compiled from aerial photographs and they showed a network of trenches. Unfortunately, the observers could not see that the support trenches were flooded and had been abandoned in favour of strongpoints hidden in farmhouses. It meant that the barrage would be shelling empty trenches during the later stages of the advance.

5th Australian Division
The Australian troops used ladders and steps cut into their parapet, allowing

them to leave the trenches quickly. No man's land varied in width, so the troops on the right started moving out eight minutes before the left so that everyone deployed parallel to the German parapet at the same time. Promptly at 6pm the guns lifted and the first wave moved forward with each wave following at five minute intervals.

A mine[316] detonated on the left flank but the crater did little to screen 8 Brigade from enfilade fire. Major Higgon was mortally wounded leading the 32nd Battalion while Major Clements and Captain Robertson were injured at the head of the 31st Battalion.[317] After storming the first trench they pressed on only to find no support trench to take cover in while the Germans held Kasten Weg communication trench on the left flank. An attempt to take Delangré Farm failed.[318]

Only now did the Australian officers realise the grid of trenches on their maps were water-filled ditches. Major White and Captain Halkyard, assembled 32nd Battalion in one while Major Hughes was wounded reconnoitring the ground ahead. The 31st Battalion encountered the same problem and Lieutenant Colonel Toll went ahead alone to see if he could find the objective while Major Eckersley chose the best place to start digging.

Toll could not find the objective and returned to find his men under fire by German and British guns so he withdrew his right to the only decent defensive position, the German front line. Captain Mills continued to hold a derelict trench with 32nd Battalion. Meanwhile, 8th Field Company dug a communication trench across no man's land with 30th Battalion's help. Brigadier General Tivey's men then spent a long night in the sodden ditches, facing the occasional surge of water when an exploding shell released dammed-up water.

In 13 Brigade's sector 54th and 53rd Battalions leapt over the German parapet and captured a number of prisoners and two machine guns. They then suffered horrendous casualties crossing the flat fields where they again found no support line, only flooded ditches. Major Harrison, all the company commanders and their second-in-commands, were hit leading 54th Battalion. Lieutenant Colonel Norris and Major Sampson were killed so Captain Arblaster took over the 53rd Battalion. But the survivors kept 'advancing in the long grass as if shooting quail, strolling on and taking a pot-shot every now and again at Germans who were ducking from shell-hole to shell-hole...' Meanwhile, dug-outs behind the front line were being searched and Lieutenant Colonel Cass set up 54th Battalion's headquarters in one which was 'wall-papered, panelled, fitted with two bunks, an armchair, a stove and electric light'. Colonel Pope sent forward two 55th

---

316 Containing 1,200 lbs of ammonal.
317 Lieutenant Colonel Toll of 31st Battalion was injured by the German shelling before zero hour.
318 A message cancelling the attack on the farm never reached the troops.

Battalion companies loaded with stores and tools while 14th Field Company dug a communication trench across no man's land.

In 15 Brigade's sector 60th Battalion could not get through the German wire while machine guns in the Sugarloaf salient pinned down 59th Battalion in no man's land, forcing many to take cover along the Layes stream. Only Captain Liddelow and a few men of the 59th Battalion reached the parapet and they soon had to fall back. Up ahead Germans could be seen peering over their parapet 'looking as if they were wondering what was coming next'. By the time the third and fourth waves entered no man's land, the attack was over. Majors McCrae and Elliot died leading 60th Battalion while most of the company commanders were hit. Although Brigadier General Elliot sent forward a message to dig in, the chosen area was littered with the dead and injured.

The rest of 30th Battalion and part of 29th Battalion carried ammunition across to 8 Brigade as soon as it was dark. The rest of 29th Battalion were sent forward in the early hours in response to reports of counter-attacks because the Germans were also closing in on 14 Brigade's open right flank. But 53rd Battalion's survivors fought on through the night, even after all their officers had fallen. Although 15 Brigade had been asked to cooperate with 61st Division's attack on the Sugarloaf at 9pm, the attack was cancelled. When 58th Battalion went forward it captured nothing, and all of the survivors fell back as soon as it grew dark.

All along the front men tried and failed to build a parapet with sandbags filled with sloppy mud. The initial counter-attacks were stopped but they became better organised and the artillery fire became heavier when the Germans worked out where the Australians were. The biggest attack hit the front and left flank around 3.15am and 32nd Battalion fell back first, followed by 31st Battalion. The lack of officers meant the withdrawal was haphazard and while some were able to fight their way back, others were captured.

Generals Monro and Haking met the divisional commanders at Sailly at 5am ready to discuss renewing the attack. But when they heard 8 Brigade had withdrawn, Monro ordered an end to all offensive action. The artillery fired at targets all around[319] the beleaguered brigade at 5.40am but the senior officer, Lieutenant Colonel Cass, did not receive the order to 'prepare to retire' until two hours later. German machine guns were covering no man's land but many of 14 Brigade's men escaped along the new communication trench. Some groups never received the order and they fought on until they were overrun. The seriously wounded had to be left behind and six Vickers machine guns were also abandoned. Once the firing died down, the

---

319 A box barrage: a three-sided barrage, leaving the open side to withdraw through.

Australians arranged a truce so they could search no man's land for wounded men.[320]

61st Division

At 5.30pm each company filed out of their single gap[321] in the breastwork and deployed beyond the British wire. The move took time to complete and the German machine gun teams were soon concentrating their fire on each opening.

The artillery fire on 184 Brigade's trenches forced the 2/1st Bucks and 2/4th Berkshires to reorganise at the last minute. Sugarloaf salient was beyond the range of the Stokes mortar so the machine guns were free to fire at will at the sally ports, so Lieutenant Colonel Williams made the 2/1st Bucks deploy along Rhondda Sap, a shallow trench stretching into no man's land.[322] Some of the left company reached the north-east side of the Sugarloaf but none returned, and the right company was practically annihilated. The third company got nowhere carrying their tools and materials.

Lieutenant Colonel Beer ordered the Berkshires to climb over the parapet after seeing the slaughter at the sallyports. It made no difference and Beer was killed as he watched his men advance from the parapet. Only a few scattered parties reached the wire before falling back and Brigadier General Carter soon learnt that the wire was still intact.

The enemy barrage had caused many casualties amongst 183 Brigade and it caused many more as the 2/4th and 2/6th Gloucesters ran out of the sally ports. The rest of the men climbed over the parapet but few reached the German wire. The senior officers could do little to change the outcome and Lieutenant Colonel Hamilton was wounded while directing the 2/6th Gloucesters from the front line. Brigadier General Stewart was watching the disaster when he decided to try and help the men pinned in the open. Two pipe-pushers[323] were driven out into no man's land and then detonated. The resulting ditches were then widened into trenches so the wounded could be rescued.

Earth had been dug to build a parapet for 182 Brigade's trenches and the borrow-pit formed a ditch. Underground passages had been built under the sandbags, so troops could leave the trench unseen but they were not used and Brigadier General Gordon's men left via the few sally ports. The 2/6th Warwicks companies came under fire as they deployed on the left and the first two companies ran into the wire protecting the Wick Salient. By the time it was the third company's turn, the German machine guns knew where to aim and they stopped the rest of the Warwicks leaving the trench.

---

320 250 missing bodies were recovered in 2009 and buried in Fromelles (Pheasant Wood) Military Cemetery.
321 Known as sally ports.
322 Major Coulter's 3rd Australian Tunnelling Company had used pipe-pushers to extend the sap by 70 metres.
323 Pipe-pushers were pipes filled with ammonal called Barratt hydraulic forcing jacks.

Two Stokes mortars south of the Trivelet road knocked out the machine guns which could have enfiladed the 2/7th Warwicks so the first two companies deployed and moved through the shattered wire. The guns lifted as they approached the battered breastwork and the men charged the trench, taking prisoners. Many were hit cutting a way through the wire covering the support line and a few reached their objective but the third company could not get any further than the front trench due to enfilade fire. Attempts to expand the foothold to the north were stopped by a counter-attack.

The attack had been a disaster. Early reports told Major General Mackenzie that there were small footholds in the Sugarloaf and in the centre while the 2/7th Warwicks were in the German trenches on the extreme right. He warned his three brigadiers to prepare to make another attack while the artillery shelled the German trenches where the attack had failed. General Haking then told Mackenzie to arrange help for the Australians holding the Sugarloaf. But it soon became clear that the 2/1st Bucks had been driven out of the salient and Haking then cancelled the attack planned for 9pm. Instead there would be a bombardment to cover a complete withdrawal as soon as it was dark.

Later on Haking and Mackenzie discussed the Sugarloaf situation and concluded that 184 Brigade should 'attack the Sugarloaf during the night' after a ten minute bombardment. The plan was cancelled because General Carter reported his troops would not be ready before daylight due to the incessant enemy artillery fire.

The Fromelles offensive cost 61st Division over 1,500 casualties. The prolonged fighting in the Australian sector meant 5th Australian Division lost over 5,500. The battle need not have been fought and the decision to attack in broad daylight had been suicidal. The official Australian historian, Charles Bean, summed up indecisiveness behind the Fromelles attack: 'Suggested first by Haking as a feint-attack; then by Plumer as part of a victorious advance; rejected by Monro in favour of attack elsewhere; put forward again by GHQ as a "purely artillery" demonstration; ordered as a demonstration but with an infantry operation added, according to Haking's plan and through his emphatic advocacy; almost cancelled through weather and the doubts of GHQ and finally reinstated by Haig, apparently as an urgent demonstration…'

Conclusions

The year 1915 began with a realisation by all nations that the war was going to be a long and bloody affair. Everyone had to gear up for total war both by training men and by mobilising industry. Great Britain's lack of national service meant it had to rely on a generation to volunteer and then train them to fight.

The British Regular Army divisions had already been decimated in the 1914 battles and the reservists who had training had already been deployed to France and Flanders. The Territorial Force divisions started entering the trenches in the spring of 1915 and the New Army divisions followed in the autumn. Soldiers from the Empire also played a major role in 1915, particularly those from India and Canada. The Germans, meanwhile, were on the defensive because they were looking for a solution on the Eastern Front.

It left the French dictating strategy on the Western Front and the British considering how to appease their ally while conserving its scant reserves. It also left the Allies with the ongoing challenge: how to break the deadlock of the trenches which were getting more sophisticated by the day. There were so many problems to solve. How to deploy in secret; how to cross no man's land; how to register guns; how to coordinate the infantry advance and the artillery barrage; communications across the battlefield; consolidating captured trenches. The list was endless and it cost thousands of casualties each time the wrong decision was made or the wrong conclusion was drawn.

The battle of Neuve Chapelle in March 1915 was the first set piece offensive planned by the BEF. It began with success, for which the key elements were sufficient trenches for the infantry to assemble in, adequate artillery and ammunition, and the all-important element of surprise. But the plans were tested as soon as contact with the enemy was made and many new problems appeared as First Army tried to capitalise on its accomplishments. The assault troops were moving into unknown territory, while the enemy were falling back across ground they knew. The attacking force had to establish communications across no man's land, causing coordination and reporting issues at every level. Then there were the delays in moving reinforcements across the battlefield while First Army chose to reinforce the failures on the flanks rather than the success in the centre. The battle illustrated that the Germans had reduced the number of troops on their front to an absolute minimum. But they also learnt that a few men in well placed trenches and strongpoints could stop many times their number. They responded by increasing size of the garrisons and strengthening their defences, with the addition of a second line complete with strongpoints.

The gas attack north of Ypres in April came as a complete surprise, even though there had been a couple of warnings. But work on providing gas masks started straight away and a solution, albeit a crude one, was found as soon as possible. The Germans had chosen the site of their attack well and the gas drove the French territorial soldiers and Moroccans from the salient. In fact the gas worked too well because they were not prepared for the success. The Germans could have reached Ypres if they had kept going, cutting off the British in the salient. Instead there was a fight to the death for many units, and the bravery of men who stuck to their positions in later gas attacks is hard to comprehend. The counter-attacks made by the British and French were ill-conceived and rushed affairs. They were hastily organised with little or no reconnaissance while the artillery was badly sited and low on ammunition. They all failed, without getting anywhere near the German trenches.

The Germans also suffered on the offensive as the French, British, Indian and Canadian troops time and again stopped their attacks. There was plenty of proof that a powerful barrage could destroy hastily dug trenches, leaving the infantry to occupy what was left. A thin line of virtually leaderless men with a couple of machine-guns were often able to stop the Germans in their tracks. It was a powerful lesson in the art of defence.

The British had learnt practical lessons from Neuve Chapelle. Strengthened German breastworks had held up, and their machine guns survived the bombardment in their emplacements. The lack of British heavy artillery and the fact that many of the shells proved to be duds had made it impossible to knock out the enemy guns. Meanwhile, the British trench system had not been improved enough to deal with the large number of reinforcements and casualties which had to move through them at the same time. Strict traffic control in the trenches with designated 'Up Trenches' for the reinforcements and 'Down Trenches' for the casualties would become the norm by the time of the Loos battle. There had also been a problem with ranging, resulting in a lot of shells falling short on the British troops. Part of the reason was that many guns were worn out and firing shorter than anticipated. Another factor was that changing atmospheric conditions, particularly air pressure, shortened the range. It was a problem that would soon be recognised and solved.

For the first time thought was put into using the barrage in inventive ways to fool the Germans at Festubert in May. The night attack was a brave attempt to foil the enemy machine gun teams but it failed because their flares and searchlights lit up no man's land. Instructing the Lahore Division to fire at intervals to make it look like the attack was wider just alerted all the Germans in the area. There was also a shortage of guns so the barrage could not be spread wider than the attack, so the Germans knew exactly where to fire when the guns extended their range.

The problem of dud shells and the short firing of guns continued at Festubert. There was also a total lack of coordination between the infantry and artillery; batteries sometimes fired too far in advance, sometimes on the advancing troops, or sometimes even behind them. Keeping the barrage close to the infantry happened more by luck than by design and it took too long to tell the gunners to alter their range. The flat terrain and lack of decent observation points made it difficult to spot new trenches, even in clear weather, leaving the guns firing blind.

The infantry also had real problems moving through the assembly trenches and deploying from the trenches quickly. Once across the deadly space known as no man's land there was the problem of how to get ammunition and supplies forward. The frontage was usually small enough for the enemy machine guns to keep it covered until a new trench had been dug. The same issue applied to getting reinforcements forward; the Germans always reached the front quicker because they did not have to cross no man's land. They knew their own trenches, whereas the British troops were entering new territory. A large breakthrough was needed.

While setting the original zero hour prompted discussions, the setting of later attacks was a serious problem. Senior commanders did not appreciate how long it took to get messages to the front and then organise the troops. As a result the artillery had often fired its barrage before the infantry was ready; a recipe for disaster.

The spring battles had highlighted the need for accurate trench maps because the creation of so many trenches tested everyone's navigation skills. Trenches had been acquiring names since the start of the year but every trench, farm, wood and road feature soon had a name. Some trenches were named after the unit which had dug it while others were named after a street from a home town. Some of the Flemish names were anglicised while others were just given appropriate wartime names, for example: Hellfire Corner, Shrapnel Corner and Sanctuary Wood.[324] The Geographical Section of the

---

324 The Shell Trap Farm was considered unlucky so the name was changed to Mousetrap Farm.

General Staff had begun producing trench maps at the beginning of 1915 but it took time for the names of farms and trenches to be included on the trench maps. It also took time for the Royal Engineer's 1st Ranging Section to map everywhere with the help of Ordnance Survey surveyors. While all the British trenches had to be surveyed under fire, the enemy trenches had to be mapped from aerial photographs, an art which was still in its infancy. The confusion between a trench which could be used to consolidate a position, and a water-filled ditch which would hinder progress was often an issue, particularly at Fromelles in July 1916.

At Givenchy in June 1915, the British troops discovered the deadly consequences of poor telephone security, because the Germans had listened in to find out zero hour. At Bellewaarde they learnt the importance of a controlled advance because an uncontrolled one resulted in confusion when the assault battalions became intermingled with the enemy trenches. At Hooge, at the end of July, the Germans introduced another terror weapon, the flame-thrower. Yet again the British looked to produce their own but rather than making a man-pack version, they focused on producing a ton model which was built in the trenches. While they were effective at clearing local trenches, they were too unwieldy to be really useful.

By the summer of 1915 the BEF had enough divisions to attack on a wide frontage but it was still short of artillery. The battle of Loos was forced on the British by the French and Kitchener agreed to cooperate because of the global situation. First Army would have to fight where it did not want to and before it was ready. The plan was to use chlorine gas to make up for the shortage of heavy artillery and ammunition but there was a lack of that too. So smoke was used to fool the Germans into thinking they were facing a huge gas cloud. General Haig was hesitant about using the gas right up until the last minute and he would have stopped it, if he could. In the event the gas caused more problems than it solved due to the weak and unpredictable wind. Damp air around the La Bassée canal caused problems as did the slope of the ground, because chlorine gas is heavier than air and it wanted to move downhill, which was often towards the British trenches. Sometimes the smoke and gas helped the assault companies move unseen but more often than not it only went part way across no man's land. The men were then silhouetted against the chemical cloud as they negotiated the enemy wire. Many got lost in the cloud, and many became asphyxiated. The gas was as much a terror weapon to the attacking troops as the defending troops and it was not used on the first day of the next big offensive, the battle of the Somme on 1 July 1916.

The artillery at Loos managed to damage the first line of German trenches but enough machine guns survived to wreak havoc in the advancing battalions. British guns struggled to destroy the wire in the long grass in no man's land and the German second line of trenches was too far away to hit. It took too long to redeploy the artillery to help the attacks on the second and third days and they suffered as a consequence.

It was noted that there was a tendency for Regular Army battalions to go to ground as soon as they came under fire. Meanwhile, the New Army battalions would keep going, even if the situation was hopeless; they would achieve more but at much higher cost. The biggest problem was the ability of a single German machine gun team to decimate advancing companies in a matter of moments. There were never enough survivors to secure the objective and the men became unpredictable without officers.

The inexperienced reserves at Loos were mishandled and too much was expected of them. They were held too far back and then sent forward with the vaguest of orders, knowing they would be crossing the battlefield in the dark. They had no meaningful artillery support during the attack on the German second line and it ended in a massacre. After that it was a case of fighting to hold what they had and, as usual, the Germans proved themselves to be better at defending than the British were at attacking. The prolonged battle for Hohenzollern Redoubt was a perfect illustration of trench fighting. The Germans always held the upper hand in a bombing fight and they had the advantage of fighting from their own trenches while the British were always short of trenches to move around in.

The formation of the Guards Division in August is often a subject of discussion. Some say it was a good idea to create an elite formation which would inspire others to lift their standards. Others say the guard battalions should have stayed with their original divisions, so they could spread their experience. Either way few original Guardsmen had survived the 1914 battles and even fewer made it through 1915 unscathed.

The decision to spread experience across the Army was made following the poor showing of the New Army divisions at the battle of Loos. Many New Army divisions exchanged a brigade with a Regular Army division and battalions were then distributed in the hope the Regulars would set the example.

The end of the year saw the introduction of a new gas, phosgene, which attacked the lungs and caused suffocation. Although the Germans tried several large gas attacks in the spring, they never repeated their success at the Ypres Salient back in April 1915. The introduction of new gas masks, which was accelerated due to faults with the old gas helmet, reduced the problems. Gas as an offensive weapon became a thing of the past and instead it was used to discomfort or unsettle troops. Artillery crews were often bombarded with gas shells to disrupt their work.

During the small but bloody battles in the spring of 1916 the Stokes light mortar and the Mills bomb gave the infantry a greater control over tactical firepower; but flexible infantry tactics would be overruled when Fourth Army attacked on the Somme on 1 July. At last the British Army had sufficient artillery and the quantity of ammunition it needed for a prolonged barrage to smash a huge hole in the German line, but the Germans were able to hide their machine guns deep in dugouts in the chalk where they were safe.

The final attack at Fromelles in July 1916 demonstrates some of the worst issues of command on the Western Front. It was an attack that no one really wanted, it was carried out for no apparent purpose, and it was supplied with insufficient guns and ammunition to suppress the enemy. As a result thousands of men were needlessly killed and injured.

This battle brings to an end eighteen months of experimentation; the open warfare battles at the end of 1914 were never going to return. Industry was dictating the course of warfare; new weapons and bigger guns were making their appearance on the battlefield. It was clear to everyone that battles of manoeuvre were over and they had been replaced by a new sort of battle: battles of attrition in which the objective was to wear down the enemy's army.

Index

Army Units and Formations

Places and People